America on the Brink

AMERICA ON THE BRINK: HOW THE POLITICAL STRUGGLE OVER THE WAR OF 1812 ALMOST DESTROYED THE YOUNG REPUBLIC

BY RICHARD BUEL JR.

AMERICA ON THE BRINK

First published 2005 by
PALGRAVE MACMILLAN™
175 Fifth Avenue, New York, N.Y. 10010 and
Houndmills, Basingstoke, Hampshire, England RG21 6XS
Companies and representatives throughout the world.

PALGRAVE MACMILLAN is the global academic imprint of the Palgrave Macmillan division of St. Martin's Press, LLC and of Palgrave Macmillan Ltd. Macmillan® is a registered trademark in the United States, United Kingdom and other countries. Palgrave is a registered trademark in the European Union and other countries.

ISBN 1–4039–6238–3 hardback

Library of Congress Cataloging-in-Publication Data
Buel, Richard, 1933–
    America on the brink: how the political struggle over the war of 1812 almost destroyed the young republic / by Richard Buel, Jr.
        p. cm.
    Includes bibliographical references and index.
    ISBN 1–4039–6238–3 (alk. paper)
        1. United States—Politics and government—1789–1815. 2. Federal Party (U.S.)
    I. Title.

E310.B83 2005
320.973'09'034—dc22   2004052428

A catalogue record for this book is available from the British Library.

Design by Newgen Imaging Systems (P) Ltd., Chennai, India.

First edition: January 2005
10 9 8 7 6 5 4 3 2 1

Printed in the United States of America.

Also by Richard Buel Jr.

In Irons: Britain's Naval Supremacy and the American Revolutionary Economy
(1998)
The Way of Duty: A Woman and her Family in Revolutionary America
(with Joy D. Buel, 1984)
Dear Liberty: Connecticut's Mobilization for the Revolutionary War
(1980)
Securing the Revolution: Ideology and American Politics, 1789–1815
(1972)

For Margaret and Liz

Contents

LIST OF ILLUSTRATIONS

ACKNOWLEDGMENTS

This book was begun during 1999–2000 while I was Ray Allen Billington visiting professor of United States History at Occidental College and the Huntington Library. I am grateful to David Axeen, then the chief academic officer of Occidental College, and Roy C. Ritchie, director of research at the Huntington Library, for arranging a most rewarding year. The staff of the Huntington Library, under David Zeidberg's direction, assisted me at every turn, and my colleagues at Occidental College and the Huntington Library offered me collegial support and stimulation. Crucial portions of the book's argument were developed for lectures at both institutions.

Since that productive year, I have incurred many other debts to libraries and librarians in the East. They include the staffs of the Library of Congress, the National Archives, the New York Public Library, the New York Historical Society, the Connecticut Historical Society, Yale University Library, the American Antiquarian Society, the Massachusetts Historical Society, and the Boston Public Library. I am particularly obliged to Peter Drummey of the Massachusetts Historical Society and Judith Schiff in the manuscripts division of the Yale Library. But my greatest debt is to Wesleyan University's Olin Memorial Library and staff which have supported my work throughout my career. The Olin Library's extraordinary collection in early Americana, thanks to the generosity of the Dietrich Foundation, has placed many of the basic sources for the early Republic within fifty yards of my office. Wesleyan University has also generously assisted my work since my retirement from teaching with an office, technological support, and research funds.

I have been fortunate in having James A. Banner Jr., Kirk Swinehart, and Max Edling read the entire manuscript and John B. Rhinelander read a portion of it. I have benefited from their comments and from the guidance of my agent, Elizabeth Frost Knappman, and my editors at Palgrave Macmillan, Brendan O'Malley, Amanda Fernández, Sonia Wilson, and Norma McLemore.

Finally, I wish to acknowledge my wife, Marilyn Ellman Buel, who in addition to reading and commenting on everything I write, has created an environment supportive of my work despite a very busy schedule of her own. That is a rich gift for which I am profoundly grateful, and next to our two daughters, to whom the book is dedicated, is the greatest blessing of my life.

INTRODUCTION

Could the world's preeminent superpower face dissolution? Today this does not seem possible. But during the first eighty years of our Republic this threat was very real. *America on the Brink* tells the story of the first serious challenge to the nationhood of the United States. The threat arose from the struggle between the Federalist and Republican parties during the two decades after 1795. The nation's survival hung in the balance awaiting the resolution of this conflict.

Though competition between Democrats and Republicans is the hallmark of our political culture today, neither the Federalists nor the Republicans of the early republican period resembled our modern parties. Today's party organizations reach into every corner of the nation and are run by professional politicians who promote a wide range of policies. The first parties formed around regionally centered coalitions of like-minded gentry. By "gentry" I mean men of sufficient prominence to shape public opinion more than they were shaped by it.[1] They brought few agendas to national politics besides securing the achievements of the Revolution they had led. The Federalist gentry acquired their name from their successful sponsorship of the new federal Constitution of 1787. They counted among their ranks many of the nation's revolutionary leaders including George Washington, John Adams, Alexander Hamilton, and John Jay. Even James Madison, an influential member of the Constitutional Convention, was initially a Federalist. But Madison and Thomas Jefferson soon broke with Hamilton, whom Washington named as the first secretary of the treasury. They objected to the size of the revolutionary debt Hamilton proposed to fund. They believed a large debt was incompatible with republican government because the people would not pay it willingly and either would have to be coerced into doing so or would lapse into anarchy resisting taxation. Madison and Jefferson eventually accepted Hamilton's funding plan in exchange for the permanent citing of the nation's capital on the Potomac; before the advent of modern communications, physical proximity to the seat of power was far more important than it is today. But they and their followers, who took the name of Republicans, opposed Hamilton's subsequent management of the nation's fiscal affairs. Hamilton's success in converting the revolutionary debt from a public burden into an asset by paying the going rate of interest on its nominal sum, however, rendered their opposition futile. Though holders of the debt gained the most, the broader public also benefited from reduced taxes and the economic stimulus provided by the creation of $65 million in new capital.

National politics, such as it was, changed abruptly after 1793 when a general European war erupted as a consequence of the radical turn taken by the French Revolution. This war arrayed a coalition of monarchies led by Britain against a newly republican France. Maintaining peace with Britain now became the highest priority for Washington and Hamilton, while Jefferson and Madison thought that preserving the wartime alliance with France should come first. Thereafter "Federalist" came to refer to those who favored an accommodation with Britain at the expense of good relations with France, while "Republican" referred to those who favored friendship with France at the expense of good relations with Britain. This was the central disagreement dividing the two gentry coalitions that dominated national politics until 1815. Though no region's gentry was entirely homogeneous in its political orientation, those enjoying hegemony in the Northeast assumed the leadership of the Federalists while the gentry exercising hegemony in the South and West led the Republicans.

America on the Brink addresses a key enigma of the early republican period: Why did the Federalist gentry, which claimed credit for promoting the nation's consolidation in the 1780s and 1790s, go to such lengths to subvert the national government after 1800? I am referring here not just to the repeated Federalist threats to dissolve the Union, since these never came to fruition, but more particularly to their efforts to sabotage the policies of successive Republican administrations. The Federalists' greatest triumph was to force repeal of the embargo of 1807–1809, which had sought to pressure the European belligerents into respecting the nation's neutral rights by denying them the benefit of American commerce. But the Federalists did not stop there. They also undermined the ban on commercial intercourse with Britain and France, which replaced the embargo, and in the diplomatic struggle leading up to the War of 1812 they consistently took the part of Britain against their own government.

I shall argue that Federalist behavior, rather than British actions, was the *critical* factor propelling the Republicans to declare a war in 1812 that the Federalists opposed. The Federalists then did everything in their power to impede the war's effective prosecution, from obstructing the national government's procurement of men and money to sponsoring the Hartford Convention of 1814. New England's Federalist leaders used this gathering, which took place at a particularly difficult moment in the conflict, to threaten the Madison administration with a separate peace if their Republican opponents refused to accept constitutional amendments designed to enhance Federalist influence over the national government. Their contemporaries never forgave them for this attempt at blackmail, and thereafter New England ceased to exercise the influence it had formerly enjoyed in national politics, though it continued to play a vital role in shaping the nation's economic and cultural life.[2]

Readers may be surprised by so critical a view of the Federalists, since so much of the scholarly literature has portrayed them as a creative minority exercising a positive influence on national development. Twentieth-century historians have accepted the Federalists as they wished to be viewed rather than as their contemporaries saw them because the United States subsequently evolved in ways that seem to correspond to the Federalist vision for America.[3] Most of the relevant literature dates from thirty to fifty years ago when researchers were preoccupied with nation building as a dimension of modernization. They assumed that national political parties were a necessary dimension of the emergence of the modern democratic state.[4] These historians focused on the Federalist commitment to national institutions such as the Bank of the United States, a strong navy, and federally sponsored internal improvements. At the state level they celebrated the emergence of party organizations that could stimulate popular participation in politics while restraining disorders among the populace.[5] More recently the Federalists' hatred of slavery, their greater respect for the American Indian, and claims that they favored the empowerment of women have recommended them to the academy.[6] The only post–World War II examination of New England Federalism to acknowledge the destructive character of Federalist behavior nonetheless put a positive spin on it, arguing that the party moderated the conduct of the Republicans as well as the more extreme rank-and-file Federalists.[7]

America on the Brink attempts no such apology. Instead it portrays Federalist leaders as orchestrating the extremism they pretended to restrain. It also rejects the distinction that recent historians, following the lead of the Federalists themselves, have made between "Federalists of the Old School"—by which is meant the framers, adopters, and implementers of the federal Constitution—and their successors after 1800.[8] This distinction has obscured the problem I seek to address because it suggests that Jefferson's election in 1800 created an entirely different breed of Federalist. However, the distinction works only for the period before Madison's and Jefferson's split with Hamilton in the early 1790s. After 1793 there was far more continuity in Federalist ranks than has been appreciated. Thus the "generational" distinction sheds little light on the behavior of men such as Timothy Pickering, Caleb Strong, Harrison Gray Otis, and James Hillhouse, who before 1800 vigorously promoted the policies of the federal government, but after 1800 did everything they could to oppose them.

In what follows I adopt more of a Republican perspective than has recently been customary, though one that I think that is fully justified by the record.

While it is not my intention to absolve the Republicans from all responsibility for what happened between 1808 and 1815, sensitivity to their concerns has two advantages. First, it enables us to appreciate how the majority of Americans viewed the Federalists at the time, thereby providing a context for understanding Federalist behavior that has largely vanished from recent historical writing. Second, as I argue below, the Republicans were more in touch with the realities of the world they inhabited, despite their involvement with slavery and their sponsorship of expansion, than were the Federalist. This last point constitutes the centerpiece of a hypothesis proposed in the postscript to explain the behavior of the Federalists in the early nineteenth century. The bulk of my text, however, is devoted to describing the politics of the period. Since I do this in a way that diverges from other treatments of the subject, a brief explanation of the course followed below is in order.

I take it as a given that national politics in the early Republic was a gentry preserve dominated by men schooled in factional instead of party politics. Though their provincial experience had acculturated them to jockeying among themselves for public and personal advantage, in national politics they found themselves on one side or the other of a widening gulf over how to manage the Republic's foreign relations.[9] Individuals continued to cross that divide, but the more prominent they became, the harder it was to do so. That left those who sought to guide the destiny of the new nation appealing to a broader public in their quest for political ascendancy. The best studies of the politics of the early Republic to date have focused on the interactions among the elite.[10] The literature has paid less attention to how gentry leaders succeeded in commanding the substantial followings they did. Instead it has assumed that most people then were disposed to defer to their superiors because of habit or patronage. However, the notion of deference has recently been challenged by scholars and as a consequence is now too contested to be useful.[11] Instead we need to examine other features of the early republican era that distinguish it from present-day America.

The most important of these was the revolutionary nature of American culture. The United States had only recently emerged from a revolution as a continental Republic. No American, regardless of race, class, or sex, in the early nineteenth century could escape the legacy of the revolutionary experience, which had touched everyone in the society, many in traumatic ways. Under such circumstances all regarded the nation's republican institutions as experimental. The growth of the population and the extension of European settlement into the West, made possible by unprecedented economic development after 1790, accentuated the contingent nature of national development. Though the extraordinary expansion of the Republic reassured Americans about their future prospects, it also increased their sense of the untested nature of their republican enterprise. That insecurity expressed itself in a predominantly ideological idiom. At the dawn of the nineteenth century Americans were acutely conscious of the role they had played in igniting the revolutionary ferment that had spread from North America to other parts of the European world.[12] Though they disagreed among themselves about how to evaluate that ferment, all possessed revolutionary identities. In ways far removed from our sensibility at the beginning of the twenty-first century, everyone participated in the ideological dialogue that the Revolution had created.

Almost as fundamental in setting this earlier period off from our own was the pervasive localism of American society. A simple statistical comparison suggests the profound nature of the difference. In 1800, the nation's 5.3 million people occupied an area of 864,746 square miles for a population density of roughly 6.1 per square mile. By contrast, the population density of the United States in April 2000 was 79.6 per square mile.[13] In 1800 barely more than 7 percent of the nation lived in settlements of more than twenty-five hundred persons. The remainder resided in widely dispersed communities that had only limited contact with one another. A few cities had emerged along the coastline to promote the exchange of the continent's agricultural staples for foreign imports. They dominated their respective regional economies. In 1800 the four largest were Philadelphia with 81,009 inhabitants, New York with 60,515, Baltimore with 26,514, and Boston with 24,937.[14] In addition, forty smaller population centers in the interior and along the coast contributed to the movement of goods through the leading gateway ports. Some of them, particularly New Orleans and Charleston, performed the same function for their hinterlands as the larger gateway ports did for theirs. But none of the regions was fully integrated with the others in a national economic network. Nor did the peculiar relationships that sprang up between localities and their commercial centers do much to alter the overwhelmingly local character of American society.

An important consequence of this human geography was that early-nineteenth-century Americans inhabited a world in which local institutions usually commanded more power than their state counterparts, and certainly more power than all national institutions except the army and navy. A survey of the national government's bureaucracy during Jefferson's administrations is revealing in this connection. In 1808 the total staff of all the executive departments of the United States came to 126, four fewer than in 1801. The only branch of the federal government to expand during Jefferson's presidency was the post office. But though the number of post offices doubled, each postmaster, usually the lone representative of the national government in his community, hardly constituted an imposing presence. Next to the post office the customs service employed the largest complement of officers both inside and outside the capital.

Though the collectors of the principal ports handled considerable sums of money, their staffs were usually dwarfed by state and local officials who also enjoyed an authority derived from tradition and face-to-face familiarity that federal officials lacked. If conflicts arose between them, local and state authorities enjoyed an advantage over federal ones that belied the formal supremacy of the central government.[15]

The Olmstead affair provides a good illustration of the tenuousness of federal authority in confrontations with the states and localities. In 1778 Gideon Olmstead, a prisoner on board the British armed sloop *Active,* had led fellow prisoners in seizing the vessel just before it was intercepted by a brigantine in Pennsylvania's navy. Instead of the full share of the condemned prize Olmstead and his followers claimed, a Pennsylvania admiralty court awarded them only a quarter share. Olmstead appealed to Congress and won a judgment for the prize's full value. But Pennsylvania resisted honoring this ruling for more than twenty years. It could do so because the federal government had other more pressing matters to attend to and lacked both the resources and will to challenge the state's recalcitrance. When in response to Olmstead's repeated pleas a federal district court finally ordered Pennsylvania to comply in 1803, the Pennsylvania legislature responded with a law requiring the governor to resist the order's execution. Olmstead subsequently applied to the Supreme Court to get the district court's order executed, and Chief Justice John Marshall eventually issued the requested mandamus in February 1809. But the Republican governor of Pennsylvania then called out the state militia to resist the order, while the legislature passed resolutions denying that the federal courts had jurisdiction in the matter. Governor Snyder expected Madison to avoid a direct clash between the federal government and a powerful state that had just helped to elect him president. But when Madison refused to budge on the supremacy of federal laws, the state authorities submitted and honored Olmstead's claim. In return Madison pardoned those who were convicted of resisting federal authority. The resolution of the controversy owed as much to the simultaneous opposition of several New England states to the authority of the federal government—the subject of much of what follows—in a manner Pennsylvania could not condone, as it did to Madison's quiet determination.[16]

Although local authorities were usually more than a physical match for those of the central government, the more significant point is that the farther one was from a locality, the more one had to rely on persuasion rather than coercion to get anything done. In the absence of a rich web of national institutions together with precedents governing their behavior, ideological appeals to the citizenry often proved to be the only way to accomplish national objectives. That is why political leaders expended so much energy trying to form public opinion and why the party institutions of the period failed to develop much beyond the legislative caucus and ad hoc committees. It is also why the key to understanding the rivalry between Republicans and Federalists after 1800 lies in the rhetoric used by each in appealing to the public. Intrigues or conspiracies among factional leaders, while always part of the process, counted for far less than the political rhetoric used by public bodies and prominent individuals in shaping public opinion.[17] Today we approach what politicians say skeptically, expecting much of it to be "spin." During the early Republican era rhetoric was far more highly esteemed, especially in national politics, and often proved determinative.[18]

The central role played by political eloquence in the early Republic has been obscured because that era also saw wild, apparently irresponsible, charges of French and British influence, of Jacobin and monarchical proclivities, which strike the modern ear as lacking any relation to reality. Following the lead of two influential articles published in 1958 and 1967, scholars have taken the passionate nature of the period's political language as its most important characteristic, thereby diminishing the significance of its substance.[19] The rhetoric's shrill tone has invited dismissal as reflecting little more than the fragility of the nation's republican institutions.[20] This interpretation is unfortunate because those participating in the politics of the early Republic attached considerable significance to its rhetoric. Taking it seriously on its own terms provides us with our best access to understanding their experience.

Studies of the early Republican era have also failed to appreciate the challenge America's pervasive localism posed to the early-nineteenth-century gentry who sought to guide the Republic by shaping public opinion. Though the countryside remained dependent upon the commercial centers for its integration into the larger Atlantic and world economies, the power of these cities over their hinterlands was at best tenuous. Most of the state constitutions privileged territory over population in allocating representation in their legislatures with the result that the urban centers were usually at the political mercy of the countryside. The emerging cities, of course, had ways of counteracting this vulnerability, since rural areas remained dependent on them for credit and information. But other circumstances ensured that in shaping public opinion, outlying localities would play vital supporting roles with the commercial centers.

Since early republican America was a literate society, print culture was the dominant influence shaping public opinion and newspapers the principal agents in forming it. They, more than any other medium, possessed the power to mold the sentiments of a widely dispersed people into something approaching a coherent unity. But publishing technology made it difficult for any newspaper to print more than two thousand impressions of a single issue without substantially increasing its overhead. The average newspaper run was closer to five hundred.[21] The limitations of the hand-powered press encouraged the flowering of many different publications instead of the expanded circulation of papers in the larger population centers. In 1810, for instance, a city like New York, whose population was still less than a hundred thousand, supported eight dailies, seven biweeklies, and five weeklies.[22]

The range of an urban newspaper's influence far exceeded the extent of its local circulation thanks to low postal rates that allowed distant subscribers regular, cheap access to its contents. The postal system thus provided inland towns with a constant flow of material from the commercial centers.[23] But this had the effect of encouraging the proliferation of newspapers wherever local market conditions reached the minimal threshold required for sustaining such an enterprise. In 1776 the United States had embarked on nationhood with thirty-seven newspapers, mostly weeklies. By 1810 the total number had risen to 364, though very few of the original lot had survived the intervening thirty-four years.[24] As late as 1790 almost half the papers of the nation were printed in the larger cities. A decade later only 29 percent originated in the commercial centers, a proportion that remained constant until around 1830.[25] Though local papers continued to depend on distant towns and cities for much of their content, they could chose what they received from the commercial centers as well as print original material of their own. Because most publishers found printing a paper consumed the bulk of their energy and resources, and existing copyright laws did not stop them, they took much of their material from other sources.[26] As a result the regular reader of a local paper could be far better informed about distant events then than would be likely today, given the division of labor that currently exists between local and national newspapers.[27]

Public opinion in the early Republic, then, emerged from countless, dispersed, and therefore varied sources. Those seeking to shape public opinion in this decentralized arena naturally sought to have their messages spring from sites that conferred authority. The organs of government, the pulpits, and institutions that had some tradition behind them, such as the Ancient and Honorable Artillery Company of Boston, seemed most eligible in that rough order. Tammany societies together with the Democratic and Republican societies of the 1790s and the Washington Benevolent Societies, which sprang up after 1808, provided another platform for sponsoring opinions, though these groups risked dismissal because they were "self-created" in a way the national and state legislatures and even grand juries were not. One did not even have to be literate, though most adult white males were, to contribute to the political dialogues of the era. The organizers of July 4 celebrations sought passive endorsement of the sentiments contained in their orations and toasts by having their gatherings embrace as many people as possible. This opened up such occasions to women and disenfranchised minorities who sanctioned the proceedings simply by attending them.[28] Though all public venues continued to privilege the gentry over the common people, the pervasive localism threatened to produce little more than a cacophony of voices, each neutralizing the other. Public opinion remained as decentralized in its sources as the republic's political system, enhancing the difficulties that leaders experienced in building support for their policies beyond the local level.

They nonetheless managed to do so, however tenuously, because all opinions were not equal. Here the national government took precedence over state and local governments, at least in matters of national concern, as did large states over smaller ones. Many people speaking with one voice also trumped all but the most exalted individual voices like the president or the state governors and the more articulate members of Congress.[29] Jefferson and Madison had reservations about the monarchical implications of using presidential addresses to shape public opinion. They preferred to leave the task to Congress proposing, debating, and then endorsing resolutions by the largest majorities possible. State governments, conscious of the dependence of the federal government on public opinion, often passed legislative resolutions supportive of its policies. But the same technique could be turned against the national government, and nothing prevented a dissident majority in a state legislature from adopting critical resolutions or memorials. Many state governments retained the custom of having the branches of their legislatures frame formal replies to the addresses of their executives, as the Houses of Parliament replied to the annual address from the throne, to enhance the influence of the sentiments they shared in common. The legal supremacy of the federal Constitution did not extend to forming public opinion, so attempts by a large state government to compete with the president and Congress in shaping it did not seem as quixotic as they would now.

These circumstances made for a less stable national politics than that we are currently accustomed to. But attributing this instability, as some have, either to deficiencies in the gentry's worldview or to personal insecurities reflected in their adherence to a code of honor runs the risk of missing a more important point.[30] Admittedly, the postrevolutionary gentry were human and therefore burdened with the limitations that beset all mortals. That said, American leaders, with the notable exception of a Federalist minority after 1800, addressed the task of preserving the infant republic in the revolutionary world that the United States had helped to create as well as could be expected. Not only did they cope with objective hazards of imposing magnitude, but the political system they created was more stable than has been appreciated, though that stability owed a great deal to the external forces pressing on the Republic.

The place foreign relations occupied in national politics contributed an unwelcome constancy to the emergence of the first political parties similar to the effect the Cold War had on international relations during its heyday. The young nation's vulnerability to the great powers overshadowed all competing concerns because the legacy of the Revolutionary war, which had required the intervention of "friendly" European powers for victory, heightened the anxiety of Americans about the untested capabilities of their Republic. The scale and ferocity of early nineteenth-century European warfare, dwarfing anything Americans had experienced during their Revolution, added to their apprehensions. Napoleonic battles could involve the deployment of ten times as many combatants as the largest engagements of the revolutionary war, and could in a single day slaughter more men than the United States had been able to muster at any point during its struggle for independence. The unprecedented casualty rates resulted from the new mobility of field artillery, which increased firepower on the battlefield, and from Napoleon's genius in concentrating his otherwise dispersed forces. While the New World would be spared this kind of warfare until the Civil War, there was no shortage of "experts" from overseas prepared to argue Europe's military superiority.[31]

Though the European conflict engendered a deep anxiety in all, its character as a struggle between republicanism and monarchy provided the gentry with a ready, ideological means for commanding a following. The Republicans benefited the most from this ideological dichotomy before 1800. After that point France's evolution into a military dictatorship played into the hands of the Federalists. Republican ideas about diplomacy helped the Federalists make the most of their new asset. During the 1790s, when they had been excluded from the executive power, the Republicans argued that foreign relations should be subject to the inspection of the people in a government resting on the consent of the governed. After 1800 Republican administrations used diplomatic exchanges not only to communicate between governments but also to shape domestic public opinion. Aspiring gentry leaders like James Madison and James Monroe established their claim to national leadership with masterful state papers about the nation's foreign relations. The Federalists initially opposed releasing diplomatic correspondence, though during the Franco-American crisis of 1797–1798 they eventually did so to manipulate public opinion. After they lost control of the presidency in 1800, they used the Republicans' commitment to open diplomacy to turn the process to their own ends.

The consequence was that diplomatic dispatches, to which all now expected to have access, became the focal point of national politics. So closely were they scrutinized that almost as much significance came to be attached to what was not there as to what was. Not surprisingly the Republicans waffled on their commitment to transparency when they realized the effect it could have on both politics and diplomacy and were sometimes caught out in the process. But despite the hazards and inconveniences of allowing European governments to shape domestic rivalries, the single-minded focus on foreign policy reinforced the gentry's claim to lead. And their pronouncements issued in and through the organs of the federal and state governments about foreign relations came to constitute the skeletal structure around which the public opinion of the era formed, providing a coherent thread amidst the jumble of voices that sought to shape the Republic's destiny. Individuals continued to speak out, but if they were not prominent and wished their voices to be heeded, they had to complement the pronouncements of prominent elected officials. This is not the way things work today because of the modern media. But one of the fascinations of the past is to explore how it differs from the present. Following the pronouncements of leading men speaking in and through public bodies helps bring the politics of the early republican period into greater focus and yields a clearer picture of the jeopardy in which the Republic found itself in than has prevailed in the recent literature.

1

THE COMBUSTIBLES

Thomas Jefferson and his supporters hailed his election in 1800 as a second American Revolution. They claimed it had secured the triumph of Republicanism over monarchy. Today these assertions seem overwrought. Jefferson's opponents had no intention of reestablishing a monarchy. Instead we admire the peaceful transfer of power between bitter political rivals that took place in this election.[1] To the participants in the drama, however, the rhetoric surrounding Jefferson's victory seemed anything but extravagant. All agreed that something fundamental had happened, marking a decisive turning point in the history of the American republic.

Jefferson and his allies saw the election of 1800 as confirming the loyalty of the nation's political majority to its new republican institutions. The disproportionate influence that slaveholders exerted over the electoral college through the three-fifths clause of the Constitution and the efforts of gentry leaders to narrow the choices the average voter could make failed to compromise their view. Most of the presidential electors in 1800 had either been directly selected by the state legislatures or elected in ways strongly influenced by them. Virginia's general ticket law, for instance, provided that only ballots listing twenty-two different candidates residing in as many separate districts would be counted. The law forced voters to rely on printed forms if they wished to have their preferences recorded. It also excluded the minority—in this case the Federalists—from claiming a portion of the state's electors. Instead, the law ensured that all of Virginia's twenty-two electoral votes went to Jefferson.[2]

The Jeffersonians instead derived their Republican identity from opposition to the Alien Act, which allowed the president to order the deportation of aliens he considered enemies of the United States, and the Sedition Act. Though the former measure was never enforced, the latter had been used since its passage in July 1798 to curb criticism of John Adams's presidency. In granting federal courts jurisdiction over seditious libels, the Adams administration acquired a weapon with which to mount a coordinated campaign against opposition newspapers throughout the length and breadth of the land.[3] Relying on common-law actions in the states would not have yielded the same result since even at the height of Federalist power the Republicans retained firm control over states like Virginia and Kentucky. Federalists claimed the statute penalized only falsehoods because a defendant was allowed to plead truth as a defense. But partisan administration of the law confirmed Republican objections that the Federalists wished to deny voters the ability to call elected officials to account.[4] In challenging the basic premise of Republicanism the Sedition Law became an ideological embarrassment to the Federalists while it helped the Republicans organize political support when and where they needed it.[5] And an unsuccessful Federalist attempt to extend the life of the Sedition Law beyond March 1801, provided the Republican coalition with a rallying point beyond Jefferson's initial electoral triumph.[6]

However, public opinion, which provided the necessary precondition for the Republican victory in the election of 1800, had been shaped as much by events in Europe as by the Sedition Law or the Alien Law. The Federalists had won control of all branches of the federal government in the late 1790s after a rupture between France and the United States over the Jay Treaty with Britain. The European war that exploded in 1793 in the wake of Louis XVI's execution had pitted the revolutionary republic of France against a coalition of monarchies led by Britain, known as the First Coalition. The ideological character of this conflict affected the American public in powerful ways. The majority of the people sympathized with France, because she had aided the United States during the revolutionary war and because she now seemed to be upholding the banner of Republicanism against the rest of Europe. Some Americans feared that if the First Coalition was victorious, it would then turn against the United States as the source of republican revolution.[7] Americans' undisguised sympathy for France, together with the 1778 Franco-American treaty of alliance, led the British government to write off the United States as a French ally. This shaped Britain's approach to the second Washington administration and led her to attempt blocking U.S. commerce with France's West Indian colonies as well as with France herself.[8]

The ensuing crisis brought the Republic to the brink of war with the former mother country. In the spring of 1794 Washington appointed the veteran diplomat John Jay—at the time chief justice of the Supreme Court—as special envoy to Britain to head off hostilities. Washington assumed that Jay was more likely to keep the peace with Britain than was any other prominent American because he held the Anglo-American commercial relationship in high esteem. Jay came home with a treaty, which addressed most of the outstanding problems between the United States and Britain, but at the cost of abandoning the claim that America's neutral flag would protect French property that was not contraband, though British property was protected from French seizure under Franco-American treaties. Thus the Jay Treaty seemed at odds with the Franco-American alliance. Washington reluctantly accepted it instead of risking war with Britain and pushed for its implementation despite intense popular opposition. Much of the resistance was based on fear that a betrayal of France would precipitate war with her. If America's revolutionary experience was any guide, war with one of Europe's two great powers meant military and economic dependence on the other. And what was to stop such dependence from pushing the United States back into Britain's arms, undoing all that had been won in the Revolution?[9]

The souring of the Franco-American relationship over the next few years confirmed the Republican opposition's worst fears. Washington had appointed James Monroe ambassador to France in 1794 to reconcile the French government to a rapprochement between the United States and Britain. Monroe, however, took the part of France against the administration that had appointed him. At the same time the French ambassador to the United States, Pierre Adet, announced that France would equalize its treaty relationship with the United States by seizing American ships and cargoes as the Jay Treaty authorized the Royal Navy to. Adet subsequently tried to influence the election of 1796 in Jefferson's favor by announcing that France would sever diplomatic relations with the United States if Adams was elected.[10] Adet's clumsy threat had no measurable effect on the Electoral College. But French hostility toward the United States increased after Adams became president. France started seizing vessels sailing under the American flag as Adet had threatened. And when Charles C. Pinckney, dispatched to Paris as Monroe's replacement, tried to present his credentials, the French Directory, which then governed France, refused to receive him. Instead French officials threatened to treat him as a common criminal so long as he remained in the country.

Adams responded to this rebuff by reappointing Pinckney to an expanded commission, which also included John Marshall and Elbridge Gerry, and fully empowering them to negotiate a settlement to America's differences with France. During the remainder of 1797 the Directory treated the three American diplomats in an even more humiliating fashion than it had previously treated Pinckney. Through intermediaries, Talleyrand, the French foreign secretary, demanded a formal apology for statements made by President Adams about the Directory. Talleyrand also insisted on money in the form of bribes and loans as the price of peace. But in doing so, he seriously overplayed his hand. The release of the diplomatic dispatches documenting the efforts of Talleyrand's agents, designated as X, Y, and Z, to humiliate the commissioners and extort money from them led to a popular outcry in the United States. It also tipped the balance of power in the Fifth Congress, heretofore evenly divided, in the Federalists' favor. They used the political windfall to lead the nation into a limited naval war against France between 1798 and 1800 in informal alliance with Britain, subsequently known as the "Quasi-War."[11] Conflict with France allowed the Federalists to build up both branches of the armed forces. The government commissioned many new men-of- war, including several frigates built by private subscription.[12] In addition, Washington agreed to assume nominal command of an expanded army that included volunteers as well as regulars, but only on condition that Hamilton exercise actual command. Enlarging the armed services gave the administration a new fund of patronage that rivaled the federal government's civil service. The Quasi-War also led Congress to pass security measures like the Alien and Sedition laws. Finally the conflict influenced the election of the Sixth Congress, which began during the autumn of 1798 and conferred decisive control of both branches of the national legislature on the Federalists.

As leaders of the Republican opposition, Jefferson and Madison turned in desperation to the few states still under Republican control. They drafted resolutions challenging the constitutionality of the Alien and Sedition laws, and the legislatures of Virginia and Kentucky adopted the resolutions. Jefferson's Kentucky Resolutions pronounced the Alien and Sedition laws "altogether void and of no effect," thus laying the cornerstone for a doctrine of nullification that would become central in the defense of slavery. Madison was more judicious in wording the Virginia Resolutions so that the legislature appeared to state an opinion rather than make a legislative determination of whether the law had any force within the state. This, at least, was the gloss Madison subsequently put on his handiwork in a carefully argued report that replied to the eight critical responses the Virginia Resolutions elicited from other states.[13] By the time Madison's defense appeared in 1800, however, events had moved in a direction that made the Republicans feel less desperate and made the Virginia and Kentucky resolutions recede as an object of concern to the Federalists.

Just when it looked as though the Federalists had bested their Republican adversaries, President Adams decided to renew negotiations with France. Adams's decision alarmed those of his domestic allies who felt the United States had every reason to distrust France. They were especially loath to surrender the political advantage they were reaping from the Quasi-War, hoping that the longer hostilities lasted the more Americans would be purged of their affection for their former ally. Subsequent investigators have criticized Adams's behavior while approving the results of his peace initiative.[14] Efforts by members of his own cabinet to portray the president's actions as inconsistent—together with Adams's preference for keeping his own counsel—enveloped this, the most important decision of his presidency, in a cloud of controversy. Stanley Elkins and Eric McKitrick's monumental *The Age of Federalism* paints a picture of an otherwise indecisive president resolving to take the initiative in ending the

Quasi-War in response to his cabinet's objections to his doing so. Adams's fear that Hamilton might attempt a coup, combined with the growing unpopularity of the army that he commanded, eventually led Adams to order the new commissioners to France despite uncertainties about how they would be received.[15]

There is another, more flattering way to understand Adams's behavior. Though in October 1798 the president had been willing to consider declaring war against France, he quickly realized that such a course risked national disintegration. All that was needed to ignite a civil war on American soil was the arrival in the Chesapeake of a small expeditionary force led by one of the military adventurers the French Revolution was producing. Once there, the Virginia gentry that dreaded dependence on Britain would be more likely to join them than resist them. Relying on Britain's navy to deny a French squadron access to North America was unrealistic, since it had twice failed to do so during the revolutionary war and, more recently, had permitted Napoleon to reach Egypt by sea.

Adams's peace initiative was complicated by the political confusion into which the French were falling at the time. Meaningful negotiations made sense only with a stable government, and in the summer of 1799 the Directory appeared to be crumbling. But experience had shown that France's most likely response to domestic instability was foreign adventures. Hamilton's army, top-heavy with officers though otherwise undermanned, would be no match for a French expeditionary force in league with the Virginians. Adams's decision to press negotiations with an untested government rather than chance stumbling into a war that had the potential for destroying the nation involved risks, but was hardly perverse. In retrospect the success of this diplomatic initiative in producing an accommodation with France even made it seem wise.

The news of the Franco-American Convention of 1800 arrived in the United States just before the Electoral College met to choose the next president. But instead of politically benefiting the administration, the diplomatic initiative worked to Jefferson's advantage. Cabinet opposition to his peace initiative had finally led Adams to dismiss Timothy Pickering, his secretary of state, and James McHenry, his secretary of war. The purge created a rift in the ranks of the Federalist leadership on the eve of the presidential election. Alexander Hamilton felt the cabinet dismissals were aimed at him and wrote a bitter personal attack against Adams during the autumn. Hamilton circulated his pamphlet among fellow Federalist leaders, hoping it would influence Federalist electors to substitute Charles C. Pinckney for Adams when the Electoral College voted. But Hamilton's pamphlet also found its way into the hands of a Republican editor who gleefully published it on the eve of the election.[16] It is unlikely that Hamilton's indiscretion would by itself have led to the election of either Jefferson or Burr, the two Republican candidates, had the nation remained at war—however limited—with France, given Jefferson's public identification with the French cause. The Republicans had benefited from the diminished tempo of hostilities between the United States and France during 1800, but only the Franco-American Convention of 1800 assured the American public and the presidential electors that the two nations were no longer enemies.[17]

The election of 1800 proved to be decisive. Though the Federalists had divided in the late 1790s over prolonging the war against France, they remained united in their desire to avoid war with Britain. Losing control of the federal government's executive branch meant losing most of the power they had formerly enjoyed in shaping the nation's foreign policy. As their adversaries grasped the executive reins, Federalist options for opposing Republican initiatives narrowed to Congress and the state governments. The Republican triumph of 1800, then, deprived the Federalists of the principal advantage they had relied on to compensate for the unpopularity of their preference for Britain. At the same time it conferred on the Jeffersonians an advantage, which they hardly needed because most Americans were pro-French. Federalist leaders saw an ominous potential in the new situation. They feared the Republicans would be tempted to provoke Great Britain whenever they lost popular favor because bad relations with the former mother country guaranteed popularity. And would not such a tendency eventually lead to war, since the Republicans did not share the Federalists' understanding of the world and consequently were bound to mismanage the Republic's affairs? War with Britain became the Federalists' nightmare because they were convinced it would force the nation into another alliance with France, as had been the case during the Revolution, and "Frenchify" the United States.[18]

The Federalists had another reason for despair relating to the international situation, though this one had domestic roots. From 1787 through 1789 they had presided over the formation, ratification, and implementation of the federal Constitution in the expectation that the new government would be insulated from popular pressures that were obstructing the solution of postwar problems. The most pressing of these was funding the revolutionary debt. Congress's lack of revenue at the end of the war had allowed speculators to buy up that debt at bargain prices, thus complicating the establishment of public credit by polarizing a minority of public creditors against a majority of public debtors. In 1786, Shays's Rebellion, ignited by a Massachusetts attempt at heroic taxation, had led many of the Revolution's gentry leadership to conclude that the only chance for establishing public credit lay in creating a national government less vulnerable to popular pressures than the state governments were.[19] They counted on the enhanced revenues that a uniform tax on imports, known as an "impost," was likely to produce, even though this tax was unlikely to be properly collected unless the national government also assumed the outstanding debts of the states. Otherwise, state creditors would be deprived of an interest in seeing that the impost was paid. Hamilton did manage to reconcile the interests of the two categories of creditors by assuming most of the state debts, but at the cost of alienating Madison and most of Virginia's leadership. Though the Whiskey Rebellion of 1794 seemed to confirm Republican anxieties about the consequences of oppressive taxation, rising yields from the impost soon afterward vindicated the wisdom of Hamilton's policy. The establishment of public credit in turn validated the political structure created by the Constitution and made preserving the antipopulist character of national politics seem all the more desirable to the Federalists.

The controversy over the Jay Treaty, however, quickly dispelled the notion that the national government could remain insulated from public opinion. Supporters of the Jay Treaty relied on Washington's prestige to neutralize the influence of pro-French sentiment to which the Republican opposition appealed. But as public ire rose, first in response to the terms of the treaty and then over its ratification and implementation, the Federalists had reluctantly mobilized counter pressures outside the government. From the very beginning some Federalists objected to invoking public opinion in foreign policy disputes. Not only did their adversaries have a more spontaneous rapport with the people, but the price of success would be further public involvement in national politics. Appealing to the public, then, undercut the benefits the Federalists had hoped to win by insulating the national leadership from the misguided inclinations of the populace.[20] During 1795–1796, only necessity brought them to resort to so unappealing an expedient.

In 1798 necessity again forced the Federalists to mobilize the people. Releasing the XYZ dispatches created such a public outrage that several Republican congressmen went home while others yielded to what for the moment appeared to be the popular will. These developments had allowed the Federalists to embark on the limited war against France. But they hesitated to take responsibility for a full-scale war for fear of losing the public's support if they appeared to court the conflict instead of having it thrust upon them. While some hoped France would respond to naval hostilities with a formal declaration of war, since this would have made her as unpopular as Britain was, the Federalists had to settle for the Sedition Act, which would allow them to control public opinion if France failed to oblige. When it became clear that full-scale war would elude them and the Sedition Act proved counterproductive, many New England Federalists who held national offices, including Harrison Gray Otis, Timothy Pickering, Samuel Dexter, Chauncey Goodrich, and Oliver Wolcott, preferred to retire from the federal government, at least for the moment. Quite apart from the visible damage that sedition prosecutions were inflicting upon their cause, many had grown tired of bucking the popular tide. Others could not face having to serve in such a culturally primitive, unhealthy town as Washington, to which the government moved in the autumn of 1800.[21] None relished serving as the opposition. It did not help the Federalist cause that Hamilton had publicly quarreled with Adams on the eve of an election whose loss the various factions of the divided coalition blamed on one another.[22]

The Jeffersonian Ascendancy

Adjusting to the new Republican order initially proved less difficult than many Federalists had feared. The tie vote between Jefferson and Burr in the Electoral College gave the Federalists, who still controlled the House of Representatives, the power to choose between the two Republican candidates. Though they were unable to extract meaningful concessions from either candidate, they at least chose their own poison when they selected Jefferson. Other developments made moot their worst anxieties about Republican foreign policy. During 1801 the Truce of Amiens brought European hostilities to a halt. While the great powers were at peace, the pressures they had previously exerted on the United States relaxed. No longer did the nation have to steer a precarious course between Britain and France.

The European truce had its economic downside. The war had created a buoyant market for American staples during the 1790s and had made vessels of United States registry the principal carriers of the world's seaborne trade. Both had contributed to a rapid rise in the federal revenue.[23] The European peace diminished the demand for American staples and negated any advantage American vessels had enjoyed as neutral carriers during wartime. But some areas of opportunity remained, particularly in the East Indies. Six years of flush times had also alleviated the capital shortages that had plagued the American economy since independence. The prosperity of the mid-1790s produced effects apparent to all. Urban dwellers rebuilt their cities, until then left in partial ruins in the wake of the British occupations they had all—with the exception of Baltimore— experienced. The nation, which had possessed four incorporated banks in 1790, boasted twenty-eight by 1800. The new capital resources of the country led to the building of bridges, turnpikes, and the first canals. The national government's fortunes paralleled those of the country at large. Despite occasional dips in tax revenues, the treasury experienced no difficulty in paying interest on the funded debt and even retired some of its principal. While profits from the carrying trade shrank, the export of cotton began to grow in response to the expanding demand of Europe's textile industry.[24]

Federalist leaders neither expected nor welcomed these economic developments. They had been more interested in using the debt for state than capital formation. Perhaps they feared that an expanding economy would benefit their adversaries more than it would them. Though many New Englanders among their ranks would become industrial innovators, the Federalists thought of themselves as merchants engaged in commerce and referred to those of their opponents, who were not southern slaveholding aristocrats, as manufacturers. They had little interest in the expansion of European settlement in the West, which the prosperity of the East was underwriting, except as land speculators and as a siphon for relieving the more settled areas of malcontents. Instead, the inner core of New England's Federalists leaders seemed principally interested in having their ideological anxieties confirmed by Republican behavior. They longed for political vindication. But their only chance for it lay in the Republicans' demonstrating their incompetence, and Jefferson refused to oblige.[25]

The closest the new president initially came to confirming Federalists fears was to support repeal of the Judiciary Act of 1801, under which Adams had appointed many judges to federal office in the closing hours of his administration, thus depriving these officials of their jobs. Jefferson also refused to appoint Federalists to vacant federal offices. Only in the case of the collector of the port of New Haven did this give rise to serious public protest. Over time the removals and Republican replacements of Federalists who died or retired increased. So too did Federalist grousing. But the federal government was still so diminutive and the civil offices at its disposal so few that their disposal excited little controversy.[26] With Jefferson committed to limited government at home and peace abroad, there was little to oppose. New England's Federalists continued to carp at their adversaries, behaving vindictively toward Republicans when they could. But such behavior was a sign of weakness rather than of strength.[27]

The only development that corresponded to Federalist trepidations was the transformation of the French republic into a military dictatorship disguised as a monarchy. In 1800 Napoleon assumed the office of first consul of the "republic." Two years later he arranged for a plebiscite that proclaimed him first consul for life, and in 1804 he crowned himself emperor. The Federalists should have derived reassurance from such a transformation since France under an upstart monarch was far less able to manipulate the American people than she was as a republic. But Federalist leaders took little comfort in what had happened because they construed France's history since 1793 as the trajectory *all* republics were inclined to follow. France's transformation into a military dictatorship in turn shaped their responses to a wide range of issues beginning in 1803.

The most important of these was the Louisiana Purchase. The Philadelphia convention in 1787 had failed to address the possibility that the United States

might expand beyond the borders defined by the peace of 1783, and the
Constitution made no provision for the incorporation of new territories into
the nation. Jefferson was doubly sensitive to the constitutional dilemma that
Louisiana posed. Not only did he wish to reconcile honest opponents to
Republican rule, but Federalist actions in the late 1790s had shown how
important constitutional safeguards were to the preservation of public liberty.
When faced with a choice between acquiring France's title to western lands or
strictly construing the Constitution, however, Jefferson waived his constitutional scruples. By doing so, he eliminated France's last claims to the North
American continent.

This should have reassured the Federalists who felt France was subverting the
governments of her European neighbors. Instead, Federalist leaders construed
the Louisiana Purchase as a violation of the compact between the original thirteen
states. Much of their opposition derived from the assumption that the West
would be Republican and thereby secure their opponents' power in perpetuity.[28]
But the Federalists also accused the Republicans of sponsoring a Napoleonic
expansion that would lead to military despotism. When Jefferson requested congressional authorization to appoint General James Wilkinson interim governor
of the newly acquired territory, Federalists thought their worst fears had come
true.[29] They also objected to the purchase because it contributed to the financing
of Napoleon's military ambitions in Europe. But so long as the renewed European
war remained a distant threat to the United States, Federalists were more concerned with the domestic than the international implications of the purchase.

The Republican-sponsored Twelfth Amendment came up at the time
Congress was debating the treaty that consummated the Louisiana Purchase.
This amendment, proposed by several state legislatures after the 1801 deadlock
in the Electoral College, was designed to prevent another tie by separating the
electoral votes for president from those for vice president. The Republicans
secured the required two-thirds majority in both houses of Congress as well as
the consent of three-quarters of the states before the presidential election of
1804. Diehard Federalists pounced on Republican sponsorship of the Twelfth
Amendment as demonstrating a disregard for constitutional restrictions that
paralleled France's evolution into a military dictatorship. Though surely there
was a difference between amending a constitution in conformity with established procedures and violating it wantonly, many Federalists refused to make
it.[30] Instead they opposed the Twelfth Amendment on the grounds that it would
diminish the role the Constitution gave to the smaller states in selecting
the president. This was a coded way of saying that the alteration would deprive
the virtuous minority, an identity the Federalists reserved for themselves, of the

power to check the behavior of a vicious, corrupt majority—an identity they projected on their adversaries.[31]

Federalist paranoia about the Republicans and the Constitution grew when the Eighth Congress impeached a Federalist district judge in New Hampshire, John Pickering, who was clearly insane, and Justice Samuel Chase of the Supreme Court for anti-Republican sentiments contained in a charge to a federal grand jury. Nor were the Federalists cheered by the declaration of John Randolph, a Republican leader in the House, that tenure on "good behavior" only protected judges from executive removals. Randolph argued that a majority of both houses of Congress could remove offensive judges, and the Senate seemed to agree when it voted to dismiss Pickering from the bench in March 1804. This, together with the pressure that Pennsylvania Republicans were applying against their state's judiciary, fed the Federalists' darkest suspicions about Republican attitudes toward constitutional restraints.[32] Disappointments in the election of the Seventh Congress in 1802 made matters worse. The dark political future the Federalists seemed to face led them to value constitutional barriers to the abuse of power all the more. If these failed, what other remedies to tyranny would remain besides revolution or secession? By 1804, the Federalist leaders, whose base had shrunk to Massachusetts and Connecticut, aided only by tiny Delaware, confronted the very real prospect of their permanent eclipse as a political force in the nation.

Thinking like this lay behind the secessionist conspiracy of 1803–04. At the end of 1803 some Federalists explored the possibility of separating from the southern states and forming their own confederation. Timothy Pickering, at the time the junior senator from Massachusetts, was the most aggressive advocate for pursuing such a course. He fantasized about the northern states joining lower Canada (Quebec) and the Maritimes in a separate nation allied with Britain. Most participants in the exploration—it can hardly be called a plot since it never took concrete form—focused on the domestic obstacles to consummating their fantasy. These included lack of popular support for such a scheme in the region. For the plan to succeed, its sponsors needed to unite New England and then secure the cooperation of New York, New Jersey, and Pennsylvania. They saw fast- growing New York as essential to the plan's success, but Aaron Burr's desire to become that state's next governor complicated the situation. Many New England Federalists followed Hamilton in dismissing Burr as untrustworthy. Hamilton also poured cold water on the scheme of establishing a northern confederation.[33] The secessionist movement of 1804 was more a confession of despair about the future than a realistic proposal for action.

The presidential election of 1804, coming as it did on the heels of Hamilton's death after a duel with Burr, blessed Jefferson with an overwhelming majority in the Electoral College while doing little to reassure those Federalists inclined to despair. Only the electors from Connecticut and Delaware cast their ballots for the Federalist candidate, Charles C. Pinckney, dramatizing the erosion of Federalist power since 1801. Though pockets of Federalism persisted, particularly in the seaports along the Atlantic coastline, the election of the Eighth Congress confirmed Federalism's precipitate political decline. This fed the secessionist impulse while at the same time undermining its viability. George Cabot, who was critical of secession's practicality, concluded that it could work only if the Republicans "by their folly and baseness involved us in a war with Great Britain."[34]

Federalism seemed to be weakening even within New England. Rhode Island and Vermont, always mavericks, were in process of becoming Republican states, and New Hampshire oscillated between Republican and Federalist control. Even in its southern New England strongholds, Federalism found itself on the defensive. Despite the limited nature of federal patronage, the Republican victory in 1800 had bestowed on Jefferson the power to cultivate influential allies within Federalist states. Connecticut stemmed the Republican tide by amending its electoral laws to ensure that the Republican opposition remained a permanent minority in its legislative assembly. The state, small and fully settled, also encouraged dissidents to migrate elsewhere.[35] But Massachusetts Federalists were not so blessed.

Massachusetts's expanding frontier in modern Maine, which did not achieve statehood until 1820, proved to be a breeding ground for challengers to the state's Federalist gentry. Many of the increasing number of Republican congressmen that Massachusetts sent to Washington after 1800 came from this less settled region, which provided the base for a growing opposition to the Federalists.[36] The Massachusetts Federalists were not even secure in their own backyard. In 1804 the Republicans captured control of the state's second-largest town, Salem, in the heart of Essex County, which the so-called "Essex Junto"—a group of Federalist leaders from the North Shore—regarded as their bailiwick.[37] Republicans also scored significant victories in the North Shore towns of Marblehead and Lynn. Federalists continued to control the Massachusetts legislature through 1804, but they proved unable to translate that advantage into effective support for Pinckney's presidential candidacy. This happened despite the passage of a general ticket law for the selection of the state's electors. Like Virginia's general ticket law in 1800, it was intended to force voters to rely on guidance from the majority party—in this case the Federalist's—in selecting electors and to suppress the voice of the minority. But the Republicans proved more adept at supplying the electorate with ballots and as a result walked away with the state's entire delegation of presidential electors.[38]

Massachusetts Federalists Dig In

The separatist movement of 1804 mushroomed from Federalist concern about their declining national influence. But despite numerous setbacks, Massachusetts Federalists remained confident about their ability to control the state's political system because of a feature in the Constitution of 1780. Under its provisions every town in the commonwealth possessed of one hundred and fifty "polls," in effect adult males, was entitled to send one representative to the Massachusetts House of Representatives. Towns with more than one hundred and fifty polls could send an additional representative for every 225 additional polls. Thus the oldest settlements near the coast, home to one-third of the state's population, could counteract the power of the more numerous towns in the interior and Maine by expanding their delegations in the lower house of the legislature. Before 1805, few towns had pursued this option: the costs of supporting their representatives acted as a deterrent, as did the desire to keep the House from becoming unwieldy. Even Boston, absolved from most of the burden of supporting its representatives because the legislature met there, had declined making much of this feature of the constitution. From 1780 to 1804, it had limited its delegation to seven representatives, content with other advantages it enjoyed from being the seat of the state's government.[39] Boston's delegation could be relied upon to attend legislative sessions faithfully and vote as the town desired. The outlying towns suffered from the disadvantage that their representatives were less likely to attend or to be in the right place when needed. Moreover, their behavior was not subject to the same sharp scrutiny as Boston's representatives or the representatives from other nearby towns. The composition of the Massachusetts Senate also contributed to the casual approach Boston took to the size of its delegation in the House of Representatives. The upper branch of the legislature represented property rather than population, and Boston experienced little difficulty in selecting the four senators allotted to Suffolk County.

Only in 1806 did Boston begin expanding its delegation in the Massachusetts House in response to the growing surge of representatives from the state's Republican towns. In that year and 1807 the town voted to elect twenty-seven delegates and in 1808 expanded its delegation to thirty-one, though only twenty-nine actually attended.[40] The Federalists claimed they were still acting with restraint, since their polls would have authorized a delegation of forty-six representatives.[41] But there was no disguising the dramatic shift in the town's approach to its legislative delegation and the determination of Boston's Federalists leaders to extract as much leverage as possible from the town's constitutional entitlement. Boston played this game better than its nearby rivals. Salem only managed to increase its delegation from six to nine representatives in 1808.[42] Boston's behavior after 1805—along with Federalist Newburyport, Plymouth, and Gloucester—suggest that the state's Federalist leaders acted in concert to check the growing power of their Republican adversaries, confident of their local advantages even as they lost national influence.

One such advantage was wealth, though by early-nineteenth-century American standards Boston was neither especially large nor wealthy. After the middle of the eighteenth century the city had been supplanted by Philadelphia as the major gateway port for British North America's overseas trade.[43] The revolutionary war contributed little to Boston's recovery of its former position, though the city became the privateering capital of the revolutionary confederation and the continent's preferred port of entry between 1780 and 1782. By 1800 even Baltimore had surpassed Boston in population. Yet the region over which Boston presided had continued to grow after the Revolution. The combined populations of Boston and its neighboring ports, including Plymouth to the south and Salem, Beverly, Gloucester, Marblehead, and Newburyport to the north, far exceeded that of Baltimore. And the commonwealth's registered tonnage was greater than New York's even as that city replaced Philadelphia as the leading gateway in the early nineteenth century.[44] Massachusetts Bay also made substantial investments in infrastructure. Parson William Bentley's diary details a turnpike and bridge boom, financed by the returns the region's commerce brought in from around the world. Commercial prosperity spread its mantle into the interior as well as along the seacoast, creating a market for lumber and livestock and providing the basis for the social and cultural flowering of rural communities.[45] Boston seized upon the occasion to beautify itself under the architectural guidance of Charles Bulfinch, an endeavor that brought a flood of artisans into the metropolis. Some of them came from as far away as Connecticut and all were dependent on their Federalist patrons.[46] The Federalists had no exclusive claim to wealth, since there were Republicans, like the Crowninshields and the Grays of Salem, who were just as wealthy as the Derbys and the Pickmans, prominent Salem Federalists.[47] But the Federalists held more of the wealth in the other large towns of the state—and deployed it lavishly for political ends.

New England's Congregational establishment constituted an even more significant asset for the Federalist elite. Between them Connecticut and Massachusetts possessed six hundred Congregational churches.[48] Connecticut's laws providing for public support of Congregational ministers and compelling church attendance of all inhabitants dated from the 1680s.[49] Massachusetts's Congregational establishment emerged a decade later. Since the 1690s the vast majority of Massachusetts's Congregational clergymen had relied for their support on the town tax collectors. Though their legal privileges came under increasing pressure as the religious homogeneity of Massachusetts fractured, first in the Great Awakening (1740–1750) and subsequently in the social upheaval generated by the Revolution, the Congregational clergy managed to solidify its relationship with the state in the Constitution of 1780.[50] Article 3 of the state's Bill of Rights declared that "the people of this Commonwealth have a right to invest their legislature with power to authorize and require" the towns to support "public worship" and to maintain "public protestant teachers."[51] While this wording did not preclude religious freedom, the acts of the legislature did, by requiring all who were not members of an incorporated church to pay taxes to support the local Congregational church.

However, their political victory in 1780 failed to protect either the clergy or Congregationalism from the shocks the Revolution inflicted on the religious life of all Americans. Among these, the effect of wartime inflation upon the salaries of ministers was probably the least important. Far more troubling was the progressive loss of moral tone resulting from the protracted, inconclusive nature of the war. The military experience of young men removed from the constraints of family and community, schooled in the techniques of violence, and returned to a society where their economic prospects were bleak, led to a rise in crime. The depreciation of the currencies resulted in widespread oppression in the domestic marketplace and increased the incentives for trading with the enemy.[52] Finally, the prolonged nature of the struggle proved an embarrassment to the clerical leadership that had so enthusiastically backed the Revolution on the grounds that a righteous God could not permit the British to win the struggle without repudiating the moral order of His creation. Though everyone was relieved when peace finally came in 1783, no one could deny that the morals of Americans had dramatically declined from what they had been in 1775.[53]

For Congregationalists, one measure of that decline was the persistent expansion of the dissenting Protestant sects, especially the Baptists and Methodists. They continued to gather converts despite the disorders of the Revolution.[54] The Second Great Awakening that began around 1800 sped up the process of religious differentiation, though religious unity would have declined independently of the revival because dissent was the twin of economic expansion. The established churches experienced difficulty in retaining the loyalty of those infected with enthusiasm when resources were available to support new sects. The linkage between economic expansion and dissent in turn meant the eastern portions of Massachusetts felt its effects as much as did the newer settlements of the west. All the sects outside the establishment, with the exception of the Episcopalians, used camp meetings to gather converts.[55] Disorders came with these meetings and, together with the public spectacle of baptism by immersion, made the activities of the new faiths seem all the more undesirable to the orthodox.[56]

The Congregational clergy could have responded by closing ranks, as they had done during the Revolution. But the Congregational leadership was dividing at the beginning of the nineteenth century between orthodox and liberals. In 1804–1805 the struggle over the Hollis Professorship of Divinity at Harvard had dramatized the rift. After the Revolution, liberal parishioners in Boston who were Federalist in sympathy had sponsored the recruitment of sympathetic clerics for the city's churches. The prospect of better livings and the superior cultural amenities of the city led to a concentration of liberal preachers in and around Boston.[57] This in turn altered the balance of power between them and the conservatives in Harvard's Corporation and Board of Overseers. After electing Henry Ware to the Hollis Professorship, the liberals went on to gain full control of Harvard College.[58] The victory emboldened the Unitarian movement, which placed as much emphasis on cultural as religious life, to come out of the closet. The less educated and less affluent, who resented the Boston churches for violating the expectation that once a minister was settled he would remain at his post for life, reacted to Unitarianism with horror. A shared sense of injury acted as a powerful unifier among the orthodox. The vast majority of the conservative leaders had graduated from Yale College, which since its inception had been resisting Harvard's heresies.[59] The orthodox founded the *Panoplist* to counter the influence of the liberal *Monthly Anthology* and in 1808 established Andover Theological Seminary to counterbalance Harvard's role in training the clergy. The two factions struggled with each other over the ensuing two decades, destroying the last semblance of Congregational unity well before the legislature disestablished the church in 1833.[60]

This rift did not make Congregationalism look like a promising ally for a political movement. But while the orthodox and the liberals struggled over theological matters, other developments drew them into a common political alliance. One was the deism of Thomas Jefferson, which tarnished the religious credentials of the Republican Party. This made it possible for the clergy of both camps to portray the rise of Republicanism in New England as a result of the decline in revelation-based Christianity. The second was the threat the conservative Congregational clergy saw in the popular religious disorders around them. The Federalist leadership of New England, sensing a congruity between their problem in parrying the challenge of Republicanism and that of most Congregationalists in resisting religious dissent, emphasized the common ground they shared. Current evils could be traced to French atheism and immorality as well as to Napoleon's military despotism. Nor did Federalist leaders experience much trouble in first identifying and then celebrating the practical piety and foreign missions of early-nineteenth-century British Protestantism that paralleled similar developments in America.[61]

Many Congregational clergy and lay leaders in Massachusetts and Connecticut found the allure of Federalism irresistible. Some of the clergy had begun preaching political sermons in the late 1790s, though not always with the approval of their congregations. Both the number and ideological extremism of the politicized clergy increased in the first years of the nineteenth century as leaders grew more confident that their flocks were receptive.[62] A common political identification with Federalism helped bridge the chasm between the liberal Brahmins and their orthodox counterparts. After 1800 the religious advantage enjoyed by the Federalists blossomed as their most enduring asset, since it throve on suspicion of change and was committed to resisting the many innovations that were taking place throughout New England.

Massachusetts Federalists also sought to capitalize on their control over the state's judiciary. They used this advantage to harass leading Republicans through libel prosecutions of newspaper publishers, reversals of local civil decisions on appeal, and in the administration of criminal justice.[63] The most controversial such exercise of their power occurred in 1806 in connection with the murder of the son of Benjamin Austin Jr. The victim's father was a Boston Republican who had authored several pamphlets and newspaper pieces criticizing the legal profession. A notice published by a young Federalist lawyer, Thomas Selfridge, that Austin was "unworthy of credit" led to a public encounter between Selfridge and Austin's son that ended with Selfridge fatally shooting him. Federalist magistrates first sheltered Selfridge from jail pending a grand jury investigation; next, following Chief Justice Theophilus Parsons's charge, the grand jury indicted him for manslaughter instead of murder; and eventually a Federalist petit jury acquitted him entirely.[64]

In defending Selfridge, the Federalists had demonstrated the political muscle they could exert through the courts. However, the hangings of Selfridge's and Parsons's effigies on Boston Common suggested their achievement was at best a qualified one. It certainly failed to address the Federalists' larger political problem of their weakening influence over the state's government. Instead it is tempting to see the Selfridge affair as contributing to the Republicans' success in capturing control of all branches of the state legislature and electing a governor in the following spring. In the long term, though, the fortunes of Federalism in New England would depend as much on developments in the wider world as on their ability to dominate strongholds like Massachusetts.

Europe in Flames

In May 1803 the truce between Britain and France had collapsed, leading to a resumption of the European war. The development was not entirely unwelcome to Americans who hoped for a revival of the neutral carrying trade, one of the principal driving forces behind the boom of the 1790s.[65] As champions of commerce, the Federalists rejoiced since economic stagnation threatened their power base. In 1805, however, the European war took a more ominous turn when Britain formed the Third Coalition with Austria, Russia, and Sweden against France, which had allied with Spain and was in the process of absorbing the petty German principalities. The expansion of hostilities to involve so much of the continent of Europe led Britain to outlaw much of the neutral carrying trade the United States had been conducting between France's West Indian colonies and the European homeland. Until then Britain had allowed American vessels to carry cargoes from the French islands provided that in doing so they entered an American port and unloaded before reloading and clearing for Europe. In the *Essex* decision the High Court of Admiralty ruled that this manner of circumventing Britain's Rule of 1756, which denied to neutrals in wartime a trade not open to them in peacetime, would no longer be tolerated.[66] Shortly thereafter, on October 21, Britain won a decisive victory over the combined fleets of France and Spain off Trafalgar, establishing her undisputed supremacy at sea for the remainder of the Napoleonic Wars. The victory strengthened the Royal Navy's hand in enforcing the new legal doctrine against American carriers, thus liquidating the last vestiges of the informal alliance that had existed between the United States and Britain since the Quasi-War against France in the late 1790s. As a consequence, the number of American vessels seized by the British expanded dramatically at the end of 1805.[67]

The seizures inspired a spate of protests, referred to at the time as memorials, against the new restrictions from the merchants of the nation's principal ports—New York, Philadelphia, Baltimore, and Boston—reinforced by those from secondary ports like Salem, New Haven, and Norfolk. All expressed concern that Britain intended to use the Rule of 1756 to assert arbitrary control over America's commerce and complained of the sudden, unexpected change in British policy as a violation of the nation's neutral rights. They urged the national government to secure a revocation of the restrictions, and most pledged their support for any measures the national government pursued as a remedy.[68] The Boston Memorial was the one exception. While it asserted that acquiescing in Britain's claims would constitute "an abandonment of rights openly recognized, and a dereliction of the most important commercial interests of our country," it recommended that the federal government send a special mission to Britain. The Boston Memorial expressed confidence that Britain's "sense of her own interests, and respect for the rights of others" would lead to an accommodation.[69]

James Madison, the secretary of state, had been drafting a lengthy statement titled *An Examination of the British Doctrine which subjects to capture a neutral trade, not open in time of peace* while the merchants were putting together their memorials. Madison's brief appeared as a pamphlet in January 1806,[70] followed by a short report to Congress detailing the ways in which both great powers were infringing on the rights of neutrals.[71] Representative Andrew Gregg from Pennsylvania responded by calling for a blanket prohibition on the importation of all British goods.[72] Since roughly 40 percent of the government's revenue derived from British imports—some of which, such as textiles, were manufactured from American-grown cotton—Joseph Nicholson of Maryland proposed being more selective about what was banned.[73] Meanwhile twenty-eight senators, including both Connecticut senators and Timothy Pickering from Massachusetts, endorsed resolutions condemning Britain's violations of the nation's neutral rights as "unprovoked aggressions" and requesting the president "to demand and insist upon the restoration of the property of their citizens."[74] The Senate and House could not agree until mid-April on which British items should be excluded or when the prohibition should begin. Even then, the non-importation measure would not take effect until the end of the year.[75] Meanwhile Jefferson had commissioned William Pinkney, the author of Baltimore's recent memorial, to join James Monroe, now U.S. ambassador to the Court of St. James, in attempting to resolve the outstanding differences between the two countries.

Their instructions called not only for the relaxation of the Rule of 1756 and indemnity for seizures arising from Britain's enforcement of it, but also addressed the impressment of seamen off vessels of American registry. Though the British had been seizing Americans they claimed were Britons since the mid-1790s, the tempo of these incidents increased after 1805. Britain's attempt to expand its blockade of Napoleonic Europe stretched the Royal Navy's manpower to the limit and made every additional hand valuable. Some impressments even took place in American waters, occasionally leading to violence and in one case the death of an American seaman.[76]

Monroe and Pinkney sent home a treaty, much as Jay had eleven years before, but without any indemnity for past impressments and only informal concessions from the British about prospective ones.[77] The British were prepared to be more generous about the re-export trade, but Jefferson did not bother sending the treaty to the Senate for ratification because these concessions were accompanied by an objectionable caveat that left Britain free to take them back if the United States failed to defend her neutral rights against the French. On November 21, 1806, France had responded to Britain's May blockade of the European coast from the Seine to Ostend with the Berlin Decree. It proclaimed a French blockade of the entire British Isles. Since France had only a few warships at sea, this amounted to even more of a paper blockade than Britain's claim to have closed access to roughly two hundred miles of the French and Belgian coasts.

Americans initially assumed that the Franco-American Convention of 1800, which embraced a broad definition of the commercial rights of neutrals, would exempt them from the Berlin Decree. In any case her paper blockade of Britain posed less of a threat to American shipping because of France's diminished naval power.[78]

Jefferson wanted to continue negotiating with both belligerents, but the situation in Europe was not auspicious. Each, having achieved supremacy in one domain of the conflict but not the other, looked for ways to strike at its adversary through third parties. America's neutral commerce provided an inviting means. In early January 1807, shortly after signing the Monroe-Pinkney treaty, Britain had retaliated against the Berlin Decree with an order issued by the Privy Council that banned neutral shipping from the coastal trade of France and her allies. Napoleon responded in kind by excluding all British products as well as ships from entering the portions of the continent that he controlled. And in July 1807 the Treaty of Tilsit added Prussia and Russia to Napoleon's "continental system." With her trade increasingly in jeopardy, Britain enforced her restrictions on American commerce with greater energy.[79]

While both powers were escalating their pressure on the commerce of neutrals, Britain precipitated a crisis with the United States by attacking an American frigate. The Royal Navy had deployed part of its naval force in the western Atlantic to deny French vessels refuge in American harbors. They also enforced the Rule of 1756 as well as their blockade of parts of continental Europe by stopping American vessels as they left or entered home ports instead of when they approached or cleared the European coast. British naval vessels patrolling the American coast often put into American harbors for provisions. Despite the controversial nature of their mission, they could count on local suppliers eager to take their money. However, in relying on American sources of provisions Royal naval commanders ran an increased risk of their crews deserting.[80]

In June 1807, HMS *Leopard*, a two decker of fifty guns, got wind that the American frigate USS *Chesapeake* of thirty-eight guns was about to sail for the Mediterranean with four men who had recently deserted from Royal Naval vessels. As the *Chesapeake* departed Cape Henry, the *Leopard* intercepted her and ordered her to come to so she could be searched. When the *Chesapeake*'s captain rightly ignored the order, the *Leopard* fired several broadsides into the *Chesapeake*, killing three and wounding eighteen of the crew before the American frigate struck her colors. The British then boarded the *Chesapeake* and removed the alleged deserters. Three of the four sailors, all of whom claimed to be Americans, were of African descent. Soon afterward the British hung one of the men in Halifax for desertion.[81]

The British government disavowed the actions of the captain and commodore responsible for the incident, but it failed to discipline them properly.

Britain also demanded, as a precondition to rendering satisfaction for the outrage, that the United States first revoke an order Jefferson had issued after the incident banning all British warships from American waters. This provided the background for Jefferson summoning the Tenth Congress in October 1807, more than a month earlier than usual. At the time the president favored war. He had instructed Madison to send tough instructions to Monroe in England demanding not only reparations for the *Chesapeake* incident, but a blanket pledge from Britain that she would stop impressing seamen from American vessels.[82] However, Jefferson's cabinet succeeded in dampening the tone of the president's message to Congress. While his address recommended warlike preparations, it urged patience until the outcome of Monroe's negotiation in London was known. In the middle of December patience became irrelevant after news arrived of Monroe's failure to secure satisfaction for the *Chesapeake* incident. Instead of agreeing to abandon impressments, the king had issued a proclamation commanding the Royal Navy to seize "his subjects" from neutral vessels. Unofficial intelligence that Britain would impose sweeping new restrictions on neutral commerce accompanied the text of this royal order. At the same time word came from France that it no longer regarded the Franco-American Convention of 1800 as exempting United States vessels and their cargoes from the Berlin Decree. Both European powers seemed to be pursuing a path that could lead to war.[83]

This was an alarming prospect for all who recalled that the nation, allied with France, had barely survived the revolutionary war against Britain. Additionally the nation's merchant marine, scattered as it was across the broad expanse of the world's oceans, remained helpless hostage to the depredations of potential adversaries. Menaced simultaneously by both great powers, the Republican leadership hastily decided to withdraw the nation's shipping from hazard with an embargo.[84] It took only two days for the administration to prepare its proposal, which Jefferson made formal on December 18. The Senate acted immediately, suspending its normal rules. The House consumed three days deliberating the measure before passing it. Jefferson signed the embargo into law on December 22.[85] By confining American vessels to their home ports, the government hoped to reduce the Republic's vulnerability on the high seas. If war proved unavoidable, the nation would still retain some discretion as to when and which of its possible enemies it would confront. Congress's primary concern was to secure the nation's floating property. Some also hoped that the denial of the benefits of American commerce might persuade the belligerents to respect the nation's neutral rights.

The first embargo law attached only minor penalties to violations of its provisions. Because the Republican leadership felt it was acting to protect the national interest, they expected voluntary compliance. The abrupt departure of several

American ships from Philadelphia, New York, and Boston in the four days that separated the introduction of the measure from its becoming law did little to change this expectation.[86] Many more merchants had already responded to the threatening behavior of the belligerent powers by voluntarily abandoning prospective voyages, and the onset of winter would persuade most of the remainder, at least until the beginning of March. By that time everyone expected the situation to change. Though Monroe had failed to win satisfaction for the *Chesapeake* incident, George Canning, the new British foreign secretary, had dispatched a fully empowered ambassador, George H. Rose, to Washington to settle the matter. At the same time John Armstrong, U.S. ambassador to France, would have a chance to press the French government on how it reconciled its Berlin Decree with the Franco-American Convention of 1800. If Jefferson could not win diplomatic satisfaction from both powers, he might still succeed with one. In the meantime the nation could prepare itself for whatever the future might bring.

2

MASSACHUSETTS ABLAZE

During the winter of 1808 the prospect of achieving a diplomatic resolution to the nation's problems with Britain dimmed. Though Ambassador George H. Rose arrived in the United States in mid-December, formal negotiations over the *Chesapeake* incident did not begin until February. By then the administration had become impatient to have the matter settled and sought to separate the issue of impressment from this particular manifestation of it, as the British government had initially requested. The American government now hoped to bargain the lifting of Jefferson's ban against British warships in American waters for substantial reparations. But the British foreign secretary, George Canning, had instructed Rose to demand that the United States first disavow all attempts by its naval officers to encourage British seamen to desert, apparently responding to complaints from Royal naval personnel on the North American station. They alleged that the *Chesapeake*'s captain, James Barron, had acted provocatively by sheltering British deserters and had refused to return them when requested by the senior officer of the British squadron at Lynnhaven Bay, Virginia. Accusations to this effect had appeared in Federalist newspapers the previous August. Federalist commentators did not go so far as to argue that public ships of the United States should be subject to searches by the warships of Great Britain. But they did object to attempts to protect deserters who were not American citizens under the nation's flag. And they feared the Republicans intended to use the incident to provoke a war with Britain.[1]

Capitulating to Rose's demand would amount to the United States acknowledging complicity in precipitating the incident. In the judgment of the leading diplomatic historian of the period, Canning intended the demand as a delaying tactic.[2] If so, it succeeded. After a substantial but unsuccessful effort to find a way around the roadblock, the Jefferson administration requested Rose's recall.[3] That halted Anglo-American diplomacy at the beginning of March 1808, fueling Federalist suspicions that the administration intended to quarrel with Great Britain. While the Rose negotiation was coming to naught, the nation got a clearer idea of the challenge it faced from overseas. At the end of January, a text of the British Order-in-Council of November 11, 1807 finally arrived. It required all American vessels en route to continental ports from which the British flag was excluded to enter a British port and pay British duties on any goods not of U.S. origin. A month later Americans learned that Napoleon had retaliated with a decree issued at Milan on December 17 that made any vessels submitting to British regulations liable to confiscation. This was followed in April by the Bayonne Decree, which sequestered all American vessels entering French ports under the pretense that, in view of the embargo, they were really British vessels in disguise. By the advent of spring most of the nation's commerce was subject to seizure by one or the other great power.

Prospects for a quick resolution to the crisis in the nation's foreign relations vanished just as winter—until then nature's enforcer of the embargo—ended. The situation in Europe, together with diplomatic failure at home and the passage of the seasons, compelled the administration to abandon the idea that the embargo was a precautionary expedient. Since the nation remained unprepared for armed conflict with either of the European powers, let alone both, the embargo acquired a new, coercive rationale. The assumption that European nations were vulnerable to American economic pressure had Jefferson's and Madison's sanction. It had lain behind Madison's proposals during the early 1790s for imposing discriminatory duties against nations not having commercial treaties with the United States, as had been the case with Britain until the Jay Treaty of 1795–96. Both men hoped the growing dependence of Europe on America for the necessities of life could be used to pressure the belligerents into respecting the rights of neutrals. Though Americans might have to forgo access to European manufactures, this would have the desirable effect of encouraging domestic industry. Both men shared the vision of a new Republican world order in which the imposition of commercial sanctions replaced military operations—long favored by the state-building monarchies of Europe—as the principal means for resolving international conflicts.[4]

Most Americans today find such notions as visionary as the Federalists at the time insisted they were. But many Americans at the beginning of the nineteenth century, including the majority of the Republican leadership, found them compelling for several reasons specific to their era. First, commercial coercion possessed an impeccable revolutionary pedigree. Non-importation had forced limited concessions from Britain in 1766 and 1770, and the Continental Association had been the Continental Congress's first line of defense against her in 1774–1775 before hostilities erupted. Revolutionary experience demonstrated that commercial boycotts were hard to construct because their effectiveness depended upon their being seamless. They were also easy to subvert because the first to abandon them would reap enormous rewards at the expense of those still observing them. But Americans had compelling reasons for preferring commercial restrictions to warfare. Most had vivid memories of the economic and social disruptions that had accompanied the revolutionary conflict and prized highly any strategy for dealing with the great powers that promised to absolve them from the horrors currently being endured by Europe. The domestic price of restricting the nation's commerce might eventually outweigh the benefits of avoiding hostilities, but while peace lasted the Republic retained the option of choosing its adversary and the occasion on which to go to war. In the meantime it could develop domestic manufactures and grow stronger while avoiding the humiliation of outright submission. The pain that commercial restrictions inflicted upon most Americans was also tempered by their limited integration into the Atlantic economy. Though overseas trade brought undeniable advantages to everyone participating in it, few had become so dependent on its benefits as to be unable to do without them, at least temporarily, especially given the domestic alternatives that the prosperity of 1795 to 1807 had begun to provide.[5]

Turning the embargo into a weapon of commercial coercion, however, required additional legislation. The original act had applied to American shipping, though foreign vessels departing or "clearing" American ports could only export the domestic produce they had on board when notified of the law. In early January Congress passed a supplemental act that forbade the export of specie and American produce in foreign vessels and subjected the owners as well as the masters of American vessels that cleared for foreign ports to heavy penalties. At the same time, this act exempted the coastal trade and the fisheries once bonds to observe the law had been posted. In March, Congress made it unlawful to export American produce by land as well as by water, but gave the president discretion in issuing licenses to merchants so they could recover their property in foreign ports. Congress acted more forcefully at the end of April in response to recommendations from the secretary of the treasury, Albert Gallatin, about strengthening the embargo. The new law required complete manifests of cargoes for all vessels clearing the United States, subject to the forfeiture of both cargo and vessel and the fining of the principals involved. It also authorized public armed vessels and revenue cutters to enforce the embargo and gave collectors broad discretionary powers to detain vessels and "unusual deposits" of goods in ports adjacent to foreign territories. Vessels clearing such ports now required the president's special permission.[6]

The Federalist Response

Because the *Chesapeake* incident had raised the specter of a war with Great Britain, many Federalists had secretly greeted the embargo with a sigh of relief.

Yet the Federalist newspapers in the nation's major ports immediately branded it as a "French" measure.[7] By this they meant not just that it favored France over Britain, which indeed was the case since Britain depended more on its seaborne commerce than did its adversary, but also that France had ordered its enactment. There was no concrete evidence supporting such an accusation, but Federalist suspicions were aroused by the failure of the administration to publish a note from the French foreign minister, Jean Baptiste de Champagny, to the U.S. ambassador, John Armstrong. Congress had begun deliberating about the embargo just after the arrival of dispatches from France. Mistrustful Federalists surmised that they included a note from Champagny to Armstrong transmitting a secret order from Napoleon to impose the embargo. Some even alleged that the haste with which the administration had laid the embargo could be attributed to Napoleon's desire that Britain's commerce be simultaneously excluded from both the European and American continents.[8]

Federalist newspaper publishers felt entitled to take so strong a stand on so little evidence because they believed their party had been lied out of national office by the opposition press in 1800. Since the Sedition Law of 1798 penalized only false statements made with malicious intent, Federalist writers concluded that Republican opposition to the measure proceeded from a determination to construe the freedom of the press as license to prevaricate.[9] Republican behavior, once they had won control of the national government, reinforced Federalist suspicions. Jefferson's supporters initiated several common-law prosecutions for seditious libel in the state courts where truth would not serve as a defense.[10] In Connecticut the Republicans also resorted to common-law prosecutions against seditious libels in the federal district court. In doing so, Federalist editors claimed the Republicans were grasping for far more power over the press than Federalist leaders had ever claimed.[11] On January 2, 1807, Samuel W. Dana, a representative from Connecticut, drew Congress's attention to the prosecutions in his state by proposing that a congressional committee investigate "whether it would not be proper . . . to allow the parties prosecuted the liberty of giving truth in evidence."[12] Dana's proposal was intended only to embarrass the Republicans. Federalist experience with the Sedition Law had convinced them that nothing was more likely to confer authority on a libel, true or false, than a prosecution. Thinking in this vein put a premium on pushing the boundaries between truth and half-truth to the limits. Any scruples about making heroic inferences supported by only the most circumstantial evidence were quieted by the alleged pervasiveness of French influence and the disadvantage the Federalists labored under by being tainted with Britain's unpopularity. The Federalist belief that only Great Britain stood between them and the military tyranny of Napoleon made license in attacking their opponents seem appropriate because the stakes were so high.[13]

The tone of the Federalist press aroused the concern of the recently elected Republican governor of Massachusetts, James Sullivan. Heretofore Sullivan had been careful to eschew identification with the political extremes of either party.[14] Originally from Maine, he had moved to Massachusetts proper early in his career. A chronic lameness resulting from a youthful accident with an axe precluded his aspiring to the military eminence his brother John achieved as major general in the Continental Army. James instead distinguished himself by serving on the province's committee of safety, in the state House of Representatives, and eventually on its Superior Court. The war made him a nationalist, and in its aftermath he favored revising the Articles of Confederation. In 1787–1788, Sullivan wrote a series of influential letters, under the pen name of "Cassius," advocating the ratification of the federal Constitution. Though he grew critical of the French Revolution's betrayal of its liberal promises in the early 1790s, he nonetheless identified with the emerging Republican minority in Massachusetts. At the same time, as one of Massachusetts's leading jurists, he remained acceptable to the Federalists, who helped elect him as the state's attorney general for seventeen consecutive years. Sullivan initially agreed to become the Republican gubernatorial candidate in 1805 and suffered two defeats before winning election in 1807. Socially, Sullivan copied the ways of his Federalist counterparts far more than did most other Massachusetts Republicans. Though he lacked a Harvard education, he entertained lavishly and fitted his servants out in a distinctive livery.[15] A likeness of him rendered late in life represented him as a majestic Republican patriarch.

Sullivan hoped to quiet the political storm he sensed was brewing in Massachusetts at the beginning of 1808. Though he had personal misgivings about the embargo, he endorsed it in his January 8 address to the state legislature as an appropriate response to attempts by both great powers "to controul and direct the affairs of other nations against their consent." He then turned to the growing Federalist abuse of the press. In a pamphlet attacking the Sedition Act in 1801, Sullivan had argued that freedom of the press was subject to limitations.[16] In January 1808, he cited sponsoring sedition against the authority of the laws and "wicked men" inviting "foreign powers to the invasion and conquest of our country" as specific examples of those limitations. In his inaugural address the previous June, Sullivan had declared that the nation's best hope in defending itself against the great powers was to remain united.[17] He now recommended uniform support for the embargo as the most likely way for the nation to win redress for the wrongs inflicted upon it. His comments concluded with an expression of amazement that some "should assume the designation of friends to their country while they are endeavoring to destroy the national union," a reference to the continued willingness of prominent Massachusetts Federalists to talk about secession.[18]

Both Republican-controlled branches of the legislature dutifully reiterated Sullivan's sentiments, though the House of Representatives underscored a different dimension of the developing controversy over the embargo. Reacting to reports in the English press, it lamented that Europeans had "already . . . calculated upon our internal weakness and measured its extent by the opposition of our councils."[19] The two branches of the state legislature then joined several other state legislatures in passing resolutions declaring their support for the course the national government was pursuing.[20] Internally the combined declarations of the state's governor and the two branches of the legislature spoke with greater authority than the anonymous, sometimes inconsistent, messages issuing from the Federalist press opposing the embargo. In one breath Federalist scribblers complained it favored British interests by eliminating American competition on the high seas; in the next that it was part of a Napoleonic plot to bring Britain to her knees.[21]

Nor did the Federalists seem initially to make much headway in exploiting the commercial distress of the ports. Parson William Bentley noted in his diary that a "procession of Mariners & persons without employment from the Embargo" had been parading "the streets of Boston with a flag at half mast, to excite alarm." A petition signed by 110 mariners claiming to be unable to support their families had been presented to the selectmen of Boston who in turn passed it on to the House of Representatives. But when the House invited twenty-five of the signers to meet with a specially appointed committee, only six showed up, joined by three who were non-signers. Further inquiry revealed that only one of the nine had a family. Bentley attributed these shenanigans to "our internal enemies," adding prophetically, "We must expect much more."[22]

Bentley's powers of divination had not led him to expect the dramatic intervention of Timothy Pickering, Massachusetts's junior senator in Washington, into the state's politics. Overcoming an initial hesitancy about committing himself to violent revolution in 1775, Pickering had gone on to serve as quartermaster general of the Continental Army, succeeding Nathaniel Greene in that post. In the 1790s Washington had appointed him secretary of state during his second administration, after Edmund Randolph had resigned in disgrace. Pickering retained the office for most of John Adams's administration, emerging as an intemperate champion of Britain and an advocate of hostilities with France until July 1800, when he had been dismissed. Upon retiring from state, Pickering moved to the Pennsylvania frontier for financial reasons. But his Massachusetts friends succeeded in luring him back by purchasing his stake on the frontier for a price that freed him from his debts and enabled him to buy a small farm in Essex County. They then saw to his selection by the Massachusetts legislature as U.S. senator. Though in 1804 he had been deeply involved in the conspiracy to have the northern states form an independent confederation, the precise nature of the plan as well as Pickering's role in it would not be positively confirmed until many years later.[23] A contemporary described him as "a large-framed, muscular man, with a prominent Roman face."[24] Parson Bentley, who knew him personally and disliked him intensely, characterized Pickering as possessing "[a]n obstinate temper, an irresistable pride of judgment, an oppressive envy, & a haughty demeanor," and noted that "incessant enmities [had] given this man his character."[25] The likeness of Pickering taken from a portrait by Gilbert Stuart conveys the impression of a man fully as resolute as James Sullivan but more wily and irascible.

During February 1808 Pickering drafted a letter to Governor Sullivan that he asked his Massachusetts friends to publish in early March on the eve of the gubernatorial election.[26] It appeared in Boston as *A Letter from the Hon. Timothy Pickering, a senator of the United States from the state of Massachusetts, exhibiting to his Constituents, a view of the imminent danger of an unnecessary and ruinous war*. The notoriety of its author guaranteed that the work would attract considerable attention independently of the alarm conveyed in its title. Pickering began by accusing Jefferson of suppressing a key letter from the French foreign minister, Champagny, to the American ambassador in Paris, John Armstrong. This conferred authority on the allegation because senators, who had a constitutional role in the conduct of foreign affairs, could be presumed to have inside knowledge about such matters.[27] Pickering also made much of the speed with which the embargo had been rushed through the Senate, contrasting it with the administration's inability to get timely satisfaction for the *Chesapeake* incident. He argued that the combined effect of Britain's wartime restrictions still left U.S. vessels more freedom to navigate the seas than they were accustomed to enjoying when Europe was at peace. Turning to the impressment of American seamen, he noted that the commercial states had forborne complaining about a practice that Britain considered her indispensable right. Rather than condemning Britain for threatening American interests, Pickering celebrated her for alone "withstanding the power that menaces the liberties of the world." Britain was doing the United States "no essential injury" in retaliating France's decrees with her Orders-in-Council. Pickering asserted that the missing French dispatch alone accounted for the course being pursued by the administration: "In this concealment must be wrapt up the real cause of the Embargo. On any other supposition it is inexplicable." He concluded by warning that if the embargo led to war with Britain, the nation would be "causelessly, and . . . blindly . . . plunged into a state of dreadful anxiety and suffering." He also claimed that Jefferson was unwilling to reveal Napoleon's orders because it would be "*dishonorable*" to do so.[28]

Other prominent Federalists were convinced that Jefferson had cravenly submitted to French pressure in calling for an embargo and that his cowardice precluded him from ever coming to an understanding with Britain.[29] But Pickering had another objective besides heading off a war with Britain by getting the embargo repealed. This was evident from the request contained in his *Letter* that Governor Sullivan transmit it to the Massachusetts legislature. The request was calculated to embarrass Sullivan. If Sullivan complied, he would implicitly lend credence to its contents. If he refused, he would appear to confirm Pickering's charge that the Republicans were suppressing incriminating information. In fact some insiders suspected Pickering had coordinated the released of his *Letter* with Ambassador Rose so as to take the Massachusetts Republicans by surprise. So long as the negotiations continued in Washington, the administration would be hobbled in releasing documents that might expose the falsity of Pickering's allegations. Pickering, on the other hand, began penning his *Letter* once Rose had concluded the talks were leading nowhere.[30] That left Sullivan having to deal with Pickering's *Letter* on his own, which he did by declining to forward it to the legislature. Proper procedure, Sullivan maintained, required Pickering to address both the Senate and House directly, the one through its president, the other through its Speaker.[31] Pickering, in turn, used Sullivan's reply as justification for republishing his *Letter*. His correspondence with Sullivan also appeared in a separate pamphlet, which went through three editions.[32]

Pickering's original *Letter* remained the principal weapon with which Massachusetts Federalists hoped to unseat Governor Sullivan. In addition to being widely reprinted in a variety of newspapers—the Federalist *Boston Gazette* reported that forty thousand newspaper copies had been put into circulation—it also appeared in sixteen separate pamphlet editions, allegedly totaling thirty thousand copies throughout the United States.[33] Though Federalists in six other states sponsored editions of Pickering's *Letter*, and the recalled British envoy, George Rose, carried it back to Britain where it went through ten additional printings with ministerial support,[34] a total of seven printings took place in New England. Such an intense effort in the Bay State and its environs suggests the Federalists hoped to secure the election of a majority of the Massachusetts legislature in addition to replacing Sullivan. They attached preeminent importance to the approaching state elections because control over Massachusetts seemed to hold the key to Federalism's future both in the region and the nation.

For precisely the same reason, Pickering's *Letter* did not go unchallenged. The state's other senator, John Quincy Adams, quickly issued a rebuttal that appeared in the Republican newspapers and as a pamphlet titled *A letter . . . on the present state of our national affairs: with remarks upon Mr. Pickering's letter to the governor of the commonwealth.* As the eldest son of a leading revolutionary ideologue, politician, and diplomat who had succeeded Washington as second president of the United States, the younger Adams was uniquely bred to public service. After filling several diplomatic posts in Europe during the 1790s, he had returned to Massachusetts in the wake of his father's defeat in 1800. In 1803 the Federalist-controlled state legislature appointed him United States senator. But Adams maintained his political independence from his sponsors, supporting the Louisiana Purchase in 1803 and subsequently endorsing a resolution adopted by the Republican congressional caucus that protested the attack on the *Chesapeake* in 1807. His reply to Pickering's *Letter* in 1808, which he addressed to Harrison Gray Otis—president of the state's Senate—to underscore the impropriety of the course Pickering had pursued, signaled Adams's decisive break with the state's Federalist leadership.

After questioning the propriety of Pickering's appeal to a state legislature against the actions of the federal government, Adams charged him with trying to imprint "the public mind with impressions contrary to the rights and interests of the nation" by omitting all reference to the British Order-in-Council of November 11, 1807. Though official notification of this order did not arrive in North America until after the embargo had been laid, the administration had received numerous reports from overseas warning of its sweeping prohibitions. Adams described it as an "all-devouring instrument of rapine" that had already led to the detention of many American vessels and would have led to a great many more had it not been for the embargo. British encroachments on neutral rights going back to their invocation of the Rule of 1756 in the Essex decision and the blockade of 1806 rather than secret influence and fear of Napoleon accounted for the embargo. Adams also attacked Pickering's attempt to justify Britain's policy of impressment and accused Pickering of advocating unconditional submission to Britain's attempts to control American commerce. In Adams's estimate Pickering advocated substituting colonial subordination to a foreign power for full independence.[35] This was strong language that betrayed the lingering enmity between Pickering and the Adams family. But it was also backed with references to circumstances Pickering had chosen to ignore. Adams's *Letter* went through nineteen separate printings, more than Pickering's *Letter* did, ten of which appeared in Massachusetts, and played a role in Sullivan's surviving the ensuing election.[36]

However, Adams and the Massachusetts Republicans failed to counter the Federalist bid to recover control of the state's legislature. Elections for the almost evenly divided Senate took place concurrently with that for the governor; elections for the House, in which the Republicans until now enjoyed a more comfortable margin, a month later. The zeal with which Federalists denounced Adams and circulated Pickering's *Letter* contributed to an outcome that conferred control of both branches of the legislature on the Federalists.[37] But the disarray of the Republicans resulting from the governor's handling of patronage may also have influenced the outcome. Sullivan refused to respond to the political assault of the Federalists by replacing Federalists indiscriminately with Republicans, and in the process had alienated many Republicans including those who dominated the state's executive council, with whom the governor shared the power of appointment.[38] Finally the Federalists derived benefit from the increasing economic distress the embargo was causing.[39]

During the first third of the year the state's merchants had abstained from purchasing from local farmers and mechanics the countless supplies and services they customarily ordered to fit out their spring voyages for the West Indies, Europe, and beyond.[40] In addition, some sailors and port workers lost their jobs because the embargo had curtailed the export of fish. The Republicans argued that the sufferings related to the embargo were far less than those they would have experienced from a war and urged patience under the lesser affliction.[41] They believed the Federalists were exaggerating the economic hardships. The embargo had been in effect for less than five months, and the seamen and other casual laborers most affected by it had plenty of employment alternatives. But Pickering's *Letter*, dissatisfaction with Sullivan's leadership, and the increasing economic pressure persuaded already Federalist towns to expand their representative delegations to the maximum while discouraging Republican towns from doing likewise. In retrospect, few Republicans felt the people had risen unambiguously to repudiate them in Massachusetts. Instead, a Federalist minority had orchestrated their victory through astute manipulation while the Republicans were napping.[42]

The Massachusetts Legislature as Political Theater

The commencement of the legislative session in late May 1808 signaled the beginning of an unprecedented political drama, which riveted the attention of the state's political public. Custom provided for the governor to address the legislature and for each branch to reply before proceeding to the business of the session. The adoption of the federal Constitution had confined these exchanges largely to state matters as befitted a government whose sphere of action was local. Indeed, in 1799, the Massachusetts legislature had responded to the Virginia Resolutions of 1798 challenging the constitutionality of the Alien and

Sedition laws by denying "the right of the state legislatures to denounce the administration of [the] government to which the people themselves, by a solemn compact, have exclusively committed their national concerns."[43] On this occasion, however, Sullivan and his Federalist adversaries wasted few words on local concerns. The newly constituted Federalist majority in the House of Representatives bore the principal responsibility for the shift in focus. It did so by passing a set of resolves, introduced by Laban Wheaton, before Sullivan was ready to address the legislature. These resolves repudiated the endorsement the previous, Republican-controlled House had given the embargo in January.[44] The Senate quickly concurred with the House's action.

The Wheaton Resolves purported to reflect the public's response to the "National Government" interdicting the people of Massachusetts "from the use of the ocean." The preamble complained that "the surplus produce of their fields and the fisheries" were "perishing . . . for want of a market" and warned of "the ruinous consequences which must ensue from the continuance of the present system of measures." The resolves then condemned the "unprecedented extent" and "unlimited duration" of the embargo. They questioned whether it did not lay the foundation for "oppressive monopolies and exclusive privileges," as well as prepare "the country for the habitual surrender of the LEGISLATIVE POWER into a single hand," a reference to Jefferson's delegation to Sullivan of the power to issue licenses for conducting the coastal trade. The resolves also questioned the constitutionality of an embargo designed to "coerce foreign nations," describing it as "a novel and dangerous experiment . . . pregnant with disastrous consequences to our own" nation. They concluded by distinguishing between government and administration. The "latter can only be entitled to the confidence of the people, when by a fair and frequent display of their purposes and policy, they [the administration] rescue themselves from the imputation of partiality and prejudice, and undue fear or affection in the conduct of foreign and domestic concerns."[45]

Republican members of the House objected that the Wheaton Resolves promoted opposition to the policies of the national government.[46] But the opinions of individual legislators—Laban Wheaton at the time was known only as a lawyer from Bristol County—would certainly have counted for little, at least before they were endorsed by the legislature, compared to the opinions of the governor of the state. Sullivan was fully aware of the political challenge that the Federalists were posing and of the potential significance of his remarks in view of the growing political ferment that was taking place in Massachusetts. But during the spring of 1808 he had become afflicted with a debilitating ailment, described at the time as an "organic disease of the heart" complicated by epilepsy, which had prevented him from addressing the legislature before the Federalists had introduced the Wheaton Resolves. Privately Sullivan regarded Pickering's *Letter* and the Federalist campaign to recapture control of Massachusetts's government as a personal betrayal and warned Jefferson darkly that the "Essex Junto" was bent on separating from the rest of the nation and allying with Britain.[47] Jefferson in turn construed Sullivan's alarm as evidence that the governor was "entirely distempered," it being an open secret both inside and outside the commonwealth that Sullivan was losing ground mentally as well as physically.[48] The Federalist sponsors of the Wheaton Resolves gambled that Sullivan would be loath to respond forcefully to their challenge, preferring instead to preserve his reputation as a moderate.

What followed revealed how fully the Federalist stratagem had succeeded. Sullivan's speech focused on the nation's foreign relations rather than attacking the manipulative strategies his adversaries were pursuing. Sullivan ignored the Wheaton Resolves and instead delivered a lecture on the importance of unity in maintaining the nation's independence in the face of pressures from abroad. The closest he came to responding directly to the Federalists was to warn that "an opposition of one or more of the States to the authority of the national government . . . [could lead to] . . . *a national anarchy.*" Sullivan noted: "This [would be] a more dangerous and distressing evil than the anarchy resulting . . . from the commotion of subjects rising against civil government; because the opposition in this case would . . . be organized at the commencement of its insurrection." He also reiterated the previous House's warning that "[t]he political speculators in *France* and *England*, calculate their success against us without disguise, on our own factions and divisions." But Sullivan's confidence that upon "the nearer approach of public danger, the great body of the people will be again united" diminished the force of what little criticism he had directed against his domestic opponents. His only recommendation was that the national government continue to exercise the powers delegated to it while "the State Governments" observe "those lines of power which were designated when the federal government was carved out."[49]

Henry Dearborn, Jefferson's secretary of war from Massachusetts, expressed disappointment with Sullivan's speech, but was thankful that it had not been worse.[50] Given the sanction the Wheaton Resolves had already received from both branches of the legislature, Republican leaders had no expectation that either the Senate or House would make amends. The Senate did concur with Sullivan's plea for national unity, but at the same time reiterated most of the themes contained in the Wheaton Resolves. Nonetheless the tone of the Senate's reply was moderate compared with that of the House. The thin Federalist majority in the Senate made them cautious lest they provoke the minority into issuing a protest, which would have the effect of neutralizing the impact of their statement.[51]

The House of Representatives adopted a far more aggressive tone. Its reply acknowledged that the state legislatures should approach with caution the discussion of national issues, but pleaded "your Excellency's example to sanction the propriety of making . . . [the embargo] the subject of Legislative consideration." It then picked up on Sullivan's reference to " 'an opposition of one or more of the States to the authority of the National Government' " to elaborate on the distinction between administration and government in justifying its continued opposition. In times of crisis the legislature would be derelict in its duty if it failed to represent the sentiments of the people to the executive authorities. Otherwise an enraged populace might "burst out in violent and perhaps uncontrollable [*sic*] expressions of distress." That provided on opening for a sustained assault on the embargo. Though peace might be preferable to war, the national government should "never . . . abandon the all-important interests of commerce." The House majority trumpeted the distress that the embargo had spread through all classes of society, but declined to join Sullivan in ameliorating any of that suffering. Instead it argued that the national government should let "our merchants and mariners . . . pursue their accustomed business, leaving those most immediately affected to judge of the hazard."[52]

In taking such sharp issue with Sullivan's address, the House invited a protest by the minority that the Senate majority had avoided. The Massachusetts legislature followed the parliamentary practice in which peers who dissented from the majority in the House of Lords, were accorded the privilege of recording the reasons for their dissent, either individually or collectively, in the journal of their proceedings. The House of Commons had discouraged such protests on the grounds that the people's representatives had to speak with one voice if they were to counterbalance the influence of the Crown.[53] Though such a precedent had less relevance in a republic, the Republicans in the Massachusetts House had misgivings about appearing to violate an expectation associated with the promotion of liberty. But since they accounted for more than a third of the elected members in the House, they felt compelled to speak out against the Federalist majority.[54] To remain silent under the circumstances would deprive their constituents of the influence to which they were entitled, especially when it looked as though Sullivan was losing control of the situation.

In their protest the House Republicans accused the Federalists of trying "to paralyze . . . the operation of the National Administration in a measure calculated . . . for the Public Good." They also opposed the Federalist majority's objective of getting the embargo rescinded. The minority warned this would have one of two effects. Either it would "prostrat[e] our sovereignty and substantially recoloniz[e] us in relation to Great Britain" by involving the United States in a war with France or it would provoke a war with Britain by depriving

Congress of any other alternative. The minority condemned the encouragement the majority were giving to evaders of the embargo at home and "to the belligerents abroad" by conveying the impression that Americans were a divided people. Finally in a reference to the approaching presidential election the minority accused the Federalists of trying, "by altering the general sentiment," to pave the way "for a radical change in the substance of our social institutions."[55]

Massachusetts had recently learned that the Republican congressional caucus had nominated James Madison to be Jefferson's successor. Since Madison supported the embargo, the Federalists could hope that his presidential ambitions would shipwreck with the measure. And their Massachusetts leaders, still smarting from their failure to control the state's electoral votes in 1804, were determined to name a Federalist delegation of presidential electors in 1808. While Sullivan remained in the governor's chair, however, attempts to do so by legislative appointment rather than some form of election by the people, as had—with the sole exception of the election of 1800—previously been the custom, faced an executive veto. Fortunately for them, Sullivan's declining health made it seem likely that he would weaken with time. Postponing a decision until legislative appointment was the only way in which the state could cast its electoral votes looked like a promising strategy, since it was a fair bet that neither a sickly Sullivan nor his lieutenant governor would be willing to assume responsibility for denying the state its voice in the selection of the next president. The Federalist majority accordingly asked Sullivan to adjourn the legislature until the second Thursday in November.

Sullivan was reluctant to agree because he realized exactly what the majority was up to and said so. But his illness made him even more reluctant to wrestle with them over the issue, especially as many legislators had already departed. On June 9 Sullivan acquiesced in the postponement the Federalists requested, only noting that "the way will be fairly open for any objections which I shall . . . feel myself obliged to make" at the future meeting of the legislature. He backed away from pledging a veto for two reasons. His heart was no longer in any struggle that was not absolutely necessary, and by November the rest of the country might have made Massachusetts' electoral votes irrelevant in selecting the next president.[56]

Capitalizing on Developments at Home and Abroad

The adjournment of the legislature threatened to deprive Massachusetts Federalists of their principal means for sustaining the political momentum they had built up by the first week of June. But that in no way diminished their determination to turn other developments to account. On July 4 Fisher Ames died in

Dedham after a prolonged illness. Ames had emerged as a leading Federalist orator in promoting the ratification of the federal Constitution. In 1789, after
defeating Samuel Adams in a run-off election for a seat in the First Congress, he
had supported an expanded jurisdiction for the federal judiciary, Hamilton's
proposals for funding and assumption of the revolutionary debt, and the
Washington administration's accommodation with Great Britain. Many credited Ames's rhetoric with being the single most important factor in persuading
the House of Representatives to appropriate the funds required to implement
the Jay Treaty in 1796. In 1797 Ames retired from Congress to Massachusetts
where he spent the rest of his days penning essays for Federalist newspapers like
the *Repertory* and the *New England Palladium*. In 1803 he had helped to found
the latter paper, which sought to enhance its influence by presenting every clergyman in New England with a free subscription.[57] An edition of Ames's *Works*
appearing in 1809 reprinted his later political essays. However, well before its
appearance, the Massachusetts Federalists seized upon his death to orchestrate an
elaborate funeral ceremony reminiscent of the spectacle the Sons of Liberty had
staged in 1770 for those martyred in the Boston Massacre and more recently the
public mourning occasioned by George Washington's death in December 1799.

A procession of more than a thousand marchers followed the corpse flanked
by the high priests of Massachusetts Federalism including Harrison G. Otis,
Theophilus Parsons, Christopher Gore, George Cabot, and Pickering. The
organizers assigned Governor Sullivan and Lieutenant Governor Levi Lincoln
insignificant positions behind the family, neighbors, and the townsmen of the
deceased. Published reports of the funeral suggest they chose not to attend.[58]
John Quincy Adams was pointedly excluded from any formal role, though until
he had resigned his Senate seat in June rather than submit to the instructions of
the Federalist majority in the legislature, which had gone out of its way to
designate his replacement a year before his term expired, protocol would have
entitled him to priority behind the corpse if he were not a pallbearer.[59]

No authoritative copy of the eulogy delivered by Samuel Dexter on that
occasion has survived. However, the *Columbian Centinel* carried a brief sketch of
Ames's character by an author that likened him to Edmund Burke. This writer
speculated that "[i]f health . . . had cooperated with his profound and unexampled genius," Ames might even have excelled Burke. Instead "a feeble and morbid
physical constitution, an unconquerable modesty, and an unfeigned and invincible attachment to domestic enjoyments, restrained the range of a mind which
indulgent nature had rendered almost uncontrollable [*sic*] in its power."[60]

Critics of Federalism were less impressed with Ames's eloquence. John
Quincy Adams objected to Ames's rhetorical fulminations about the inevitable
tendency of republics to degenerate into despotism. In his extended *Review* of

Ames's *Works* the following year, Adams criticized his adoration of all things British, his abhorrence of all things French, and his contempt for all things American.[61] But for the moment the Federalists reveled in being able to mourn the loss of someone of such stature, and Federalist newspapers disseminated reports of the funeral ceremony throughout the length and breadth of the commonwealth.[62]

The Federalists' most important asset, though, remained the embargo. The longer it lasted, the greater the incentives became to violate its provisions as the price of American staples rose in overseas markets. This lent additional credibility to the Federalist claim that if the embargo were removed, the trade open to the United States would be greater than "we should have in profound peace, when every nation monopolizes its own."[63] And several developments during the summer of 1808 enhanced the allure of trading with the British. In late June the *Salem Gazette* published a copy of royal instructions dated April 11, 1808, to the commanders of British ships of war and privateers. They forbade interference with any vessel carrying lumber or provisions from the United States to the West Indies and South America, even if the vessel lacked proper clearance papers. In mid-July it also published an order from the governor of Nova Scotia instructing customs officials to receive neutral vessels as British ones.[64] Such notices could be construed as indications that the embargo was having the desired effect, at least on Britain. Reports of the inflated prices that American provisions currently fetched in the West Indian market and signs of economic distress in Britain exemplified by news of British merchants petitioning Parliament for a relaxation of the Orders-in-Council directed against the neutral American trade contributed to this impression. But the instructions and orders also suggested a design on the part of the British government to subvert the embargo by inviting Americans to violate its restrictions.

News from Spain magnified the effect of British instructions and orders still more. Shortly after the Massachusetts legislature had disbanded, word arrived from Gibraltar that the Spanish people had rebelled against the forced abdication of their monarch, Charles IV, in favor of Joseph Bonaparte.[65] The insurrection gave Britain an opening on the Iberian Peninsula. Command of the sea allowed them to dispatch an expeditionary force there in early July under the future duke of Wellington. The summer season permitted that expeditionary force to live off the land for the moment. In the longer term, though, they would need outside supplies. The British government accordingly modified its Order-in-Council of November 11, 1807, with a new order dated July 6, 1808, lifting the British blockade of the Iberian Peninsula. Though it remained unclear whether the British would treat American vessels making for Spain and Portugal as they had promised to treat them in the western Atlantic, American merchants smelled commercial opportunity. If British officials were prepared to wink at American trade with Canada and the West Indies, they would surely encourage it with Spain and Portugal now that they had armies there. The opportunity seemed especially enticing because this trade would give greater access to the continental market than Napoleon seemed prepared to allow American merchants, assuming he meant someday to restore the American property he had sequestered under the Bayonne Decree. In addition, Americans might benefit from the informal protection of the British navy as they had during the Quasi-War of 1798–1800. This promised to reduce the costs of insurance and increase the profits of the merchants, as well as raise the price of domestic staples that had been depressed by the embargo.[66]

The Federalist leadership of Massachusetts seized upon the Spanish insurrection to mount a new assault against the Jefferson administration and by extension the Republicans of New England. On August 10, the Boston town meeting, citing "great events in Europe, which materially change the aspects of our foreign relations," voted to ask Jefferson to suspend all or a part of the embargo immediately and to call Congress into emergency session to repeal it. Their address claimed that "the existing restraints upon their maritime Commerce" could now be removed "in a mode consistent with the laws & policy by which they were imposed." Though Congress had given Jefferson the authority to lift the embargo during its recess, he was authorized to act only if the belligerents suspended hostilities or changed their "measures affecting neutral commerce" so as "to render that of the United States safe."[67] Boston's petition was based on the fiction that Britain's lifting of its blockade of the Iberian Peninsula had revoked all her offensive Orders-in-Council. Boston's town meeting also instructed the selectmen to forward the town's address to the "Selectmen of the other Towns of the Commonwealth" so that they, in turn, might follow Boston's example. In doing so, Boston tried to cast herself in a role she had played in precipitating the Revolution more than forty years before, when the town's committee of correspondence had begun sending circular letters to the other towns of the province.[68]

Boston Republicans immediately addressed Jefferson, protesting the town meeting's actions as an "improper interference to weaken" the measures adopted "to restore our commerce and protect our injured seamen." In addition, the town's Republican committee sent a circular to the selectmen of the Republican towns in the state asking them to disregard any communications from Boston's selectmen.[69] Several of the nearby towns—including Salem, Marblehead, Charlestown, Hingham, Andover, and Worcester—obliged by rebuffing Boston's invitation to bring its address before their town meetings. Salem's selectmen accused Boston of trying "to embarrass the Government, excite irritations, and promote division," and Charlestown declined "to distract the councils of the nation by intruding opinions which cannot promote the interest of our fellow citizens, or our national honor." The selectmen of other towns questioned whether Boston was not premature in responding to "the great events" to which its petition referred.[70] In distant Berkshire County, Ezekiel Bacon assured Joseph Story in Salem that local Republicans were determined to resist "[t]he *fire ball* which has been thrown out amongst the People by the Boston faction" and if necessary were prepared to "try where the physical force and strong arm of the Nation lies."[71]

Despite Republican opposition, seventy-one Massachusetts towns did petition Jefferson as Boston suggested, and they were joined by a few Federalist towns from the other New England states and New York, including Providence and New Haven.[72] The Republican press in Massachusetts attempted to neutralize the effect of the Federalist petitions in several ways. First, political commentators emphasized that the petitions asked Jefferson to go beyond the authorization that Congress had given him to lift the embargo if one of the belligerents should completely repeal its orders or decrees. They noted additionally that it was physically impossible to call Congress into session earlier than October 20. The Republican press also impugned the authority of the petitioning towns. The *Essex Register* claimed that the petition to which Ipswich had agreed was the act of only fifty of the towns' four hundred freemen at a meeting where Timothy Pickering had presided and was the principal speaker, though he was not a legal resident. Republicans dismissed other petitions from small towns on the grounds they had no direct interest in commerce. The Federalist petition movement led several Republican towns as well as a county convention to pass resolutions supporting the embargo. Finally, many Federalist petitions from the larger towns drew public criticism from the Republican press.[73] All this set the stage for Jefferson to reply to the Federalist petitions and addresses.

Jefferson's answer to Boston's petition was restrained though uncompromising. He observed that each of the belligerents had sought to "admit our commerce with themselves, with the view of associating us in their war against the other." Submitting "our rightful commerce to prohibitions and tributary exactions from others" constituted a "surrender of our independence." Congress had resorted to the embargo both to conserve the nation's resources and to give "the belligerent nations" time "to revise a conduct as contrary to their interest as it is to our rights." Though the measures of the belligerents had yet to change, Jefferson hoped that a European peace, or a repeal of the obnoxious edicts might have authorized him to act as the petitioners desired. But "no change of measures affecting neutral commerce" was "known to have taken place." While the "edicts remain," Jefferson insisted, "the Legislature alone can prescribe the course to be pursued." In an additional public letter to Boston's Republicans, who had dissented from the petition adopted by the town meeting, Jefferson suggested that if it had been understood that the choice was between war or the embargo, the town would have preferred the latter to the former. He also expressed confidence that all Americans would eventually acquiesce in Congress's forthcoming "enunciation of the general will."[74]

Jefferson hoped to draw the nation together as much as possible in his replies to the Federalist sponsored petitions from Massachusetts. But Boston's example of directly addressing and petitioning him had been followed by so many towns that, instead of replying to each individually, he had to resort to a form reply.[75] Of even greater concern was the increasingly public character of the liberties being taken with the embargo. It was an open secret that grain was becoming cheaper in Massachusetts Bay than it was in the grain states, strongly suggesting that the eastern importers were stockpiling it for export.[76] While the Federalist press eschewed reporting violations of the embargo, the Republican press began to publish evidence that, cumulatively, pointed to wholesale evasions. These included accounts about a flow of European dry goods into Halifax and Quebec that was too extensive for the Canadian market; the falling price of provisions in Britain's West Indian islands; and the arrival of American vessels in foreign ports.[77] The most egregious of the reports—that sixty American vessels had arrived in Havana in one week—appeared in late September 1808, concurrently with Jefferson's reply to the Boston petition.[78]

Privately Jefferson blamed the evasions on Sullivan's indiscriminate issuance of certificates exempting coasters from the embargo. Sullivan had been instructed to ensure that eastern Massachusetts, which was dependent on flour imports from the southern states, did not go hungry. Sullivan claimed his actions were necessary to head off the threat of rebellion that would erupt at the first hint of a grain scarcity. Such claims signaled to Jefferson that Sullivan could no longer be relied upon, and the president alerted Henry Dearborn that military intervention might become necessary if Sullivan completely buckled.[79] But that did nothing to counter the Federalist claim that the government could not enforce the embargo and that efforts to do so were hurting Americans more than the belligerents.[80] Such complaints undermined the likelihood that foreign governments would respond to the measure as the Republicans hoped. They also demoralized the populace at large. By mid-September Madison felt that "nothing but some shocking proof [from abroad] of the success of the Embargo can arrest the successful perversion of it by . . . the enemies of their Country."[81] But when the Republican newspapers blamed Federalist opposition for encouraging the violations, Federalist writers invoked the distinction, to which the Massachusetts House of Representatives had previously given currency, between breaking a law and opposing it. While the Federalists made no apologies for opposing the embargo, they refused to admit that their actions might be subverting it. Yet in almost the same breath they warned that one of the principal costs of persisting with the embargo would be public morality.[82]

At the end of the summer a widely republished newspaper series measured the effectiveness of the Federalist campaign against the embargo. "Hampden" argued that the prevalence of violations were an indication of the embargo's unconstitutionality because a constitutional measure would have commanded popular support. From that premise he reasoned that no one was "bound to regard" the embargo as law and warned those charged with enforcing the measure to act temperately if they wished to avoid violence.[83] Others replied to Jefferson's claim that the embargo was an attempt to maintain the nation's independence by arguing that giving up commerce amounted to "surrendering our independence in the most complete and absolute manner."[84] Their alternative remained letting merchants decide for themselves whether the risks of overseas commerce were prohibitive. In light of the developing opportunities in the Iberian Peninsula, Federalists claimed with increasing plausibility that this course would permit the nation to prosper. Left unstated was the possibility that putting the nation's commerce at the service of the British might provoke a war with France.[85]

Some Federalist newspapers in Massachusetts followed the Hampden letters with a series titled "A Separation of the States and its Consequences to New England" by "Falkland." This author reminded his readers of Virginia's original opposition to the Constitution, charging that the state's antifederalism had stemmed from its abhorrence of the principle of "equal rights" and its fear that an independent judiciary would force debtors to pay their creditors. It alleged that Virginia had favored a war with Britain in the 1790s because of its jealousy of New England's commercial success. Its author placed the responsibility for disunion sentiment on the philosophic dreams and domineering spirit of Virginia.[86] "Falkland" spent the remainder of his series contrasting the North with the South to demonstrate that the North, by which he meant New York and New England, needed the South far less than the South needed the North. During the revolutionary war the North had supplied many more men to the army than Virginia had, while currently the northern states accounted for more than half the nation's commerce, raised more than half the revenue of the national government, and was home to three-quarters of its seamen. Though "Falkland" acknowledged that withdrawing from the Union would be "an evil which can never be sufficiently deprecated by every true patriot," he implied that persisting with the embargo constituted a still greater one. His series concluded by warning that the rest of the nation was growing impatient with a policy that not only made the United States the laughingstock of the world but was also fast reducing New England to "imbecility and poverty."[87]

"Falkland" deployed in public a threat that had a longer history in the factional wrangling between Republicans and Federalists than most realized. Secession had first been broached in the 1780s by Massachusetts congressmen concerned about the divergent interests of the North and South. During the 1790s northern congressmen had privately threatened their southern colleagues with a disruption of the Republican experiment to make them more compliant. And at least one New England newspaper had published a series that openly advocated dissolving the union.[88] Two could play that game, though, and Jefferson had deftly touched on a Federalist vulnerability in his reply to the Boston Republicans' address by pointing to the likelihood that war would follow the lifting of the embargo. In early October the Federalist leadership of Essex County resolved to confront this prospect directly. In the wake of the town petition movement initiated by Boston, they assembled sixty-four delegates from twenty-one Essex County towns at Topsfield. The convention then issued a set of resolves in response to the "extreme publick danger . . . [and] general and deep distress" of the moment.

After restating the accusations contained in Timothy Pickering's *Letter to Governor Sullivan* about the administration's uniform "partiality for, and subserviency" to France, the Topsfield resolves declared that the people were authorized by Jefferson's neglect of the town petitions to apply directly to Congress, and that if an appeal to Congress did not yield the desired result, they should "rely for relief on the wisdom and patriotism of our state government." The convention not only called for a lifting of the embargo but also for a guarantee that such a "perpetual" measure would never again be enacted. It saved for last the delicate issue of whether the administration would use the popular dissatisfaction with the embargo "to inflict a still more fatal wound" on the country of war. The Topsfield resolves denied there was any "cause of war with Great-Britain," adding that "such a war would be unjust [and] unnecessary." The convention also challenged the notion "that the removal of the embargo will . . . necessarily involve us in a war," but argued that if it did, "it ought to be a war with France and not with Great-Britain." It claimed the nation's commerce, "unrestrained by self-destroying measures," could prosper "without interfering in any degree with those principles of maritime law, which Great-Britain deems essential to her existence" and which "she will never yield." Nor was it consistent with either "the honor [or] the permanent interests of the United States" to "drive [Britain] . . . to the surrendry [sic] of . . . claims so essential to her in the mighty conflict in which she is at present engaged; a conflict interesting to the morals, to religion, and the last struggle of liberty."[89]

Escalating Political Pressures

By the autumn of 1808 the Federalist leadership had created an unparalleled political ferment within Massachusetts. But their activities had only a limited effect beyond the state's borders. Aside from New Hampshire, whose legislature became more Federalist in hue early in the autumn, and Rhode Island, which now joined Delaware and Connecticut as solidly Federalist states, the rest of the nation showed little interest in following where Massachusetts led. Though Vermont selected three Federalist presidential electors out of the state's quota of four, its state government and its congressional delegation continued to be Republican.

Beyond New England the Federalist leadership could only clutch at straws. Federalists held tenuous control over Maryland's House of Delegates because the state constitution gave its landed elite more representatives than it accorded Republican Baltimore and its fast-growing environs. But New York, beyond the city and one or two rural enclaves, remained under Republican control, as did Pennsylvania and New Jersey.[90] The New Englanders could count on the support of a number of congressmen throughout the South and West, some of whom would become Federalism's most vocal and effective spokesmen. But these Federalists represented enclaves at odds with the gentry hegemonies of their regions. Though they were ready enough to ally with the New Englanders, their Federalism derived from their powerlessness in relation to their immediate Republican surroundings.[91] Finally, the agitation in Massachusetts against the embargo was pushing other state legislatures into aggressively supporting the administration's measures.[92]

If Massachusetts leaders had hoped to recover the vanguard role they had played during the Revolution, they were disappointed. The embargo might strengthen them in some areas. But it failed to deter a clear majority of the states from endorsing the decision the Republican congressional caucus had made the preceding spring when it nominated James Madison and George Clinton to be the next president and vice president of the United States. Well before the Massachusetts legislature met by adjournment in mid-November to determine how its slate of presidential electors would be selected, it had become clear that the embargo, though a major embarrassment for the Republicans, would not lead to their loss of control over the national government. However, this knowledge did not stop certain Massachusetts Federalist towns from instructing their representatives to choose presidential electors in a convention of both legislative houses as a strategy for getting around a possible veto by Sullivan, whose health had briefly revived at the end of the summer.[93]

When the legislature met in mid-November, the House rejected Sullivan's recommendation that the electors be selected by the people voting in districts. Instead it voted to join with the Senate in putting forward a slate of nineteen Federalists electors instructed to vote for Charles C. Pinckney and Rufus King. One hundred and thirty House Republicans conspicuously abstained from these proceedings while the Senate Republicans protested the legality of the legislature's action.[94] Since most assumed that the Federalist candidates did not stand a chance, Governor Sullivan, whose condition by this time had again worsened, forwarded the votes of the Massachusetts electors to Congress accompanied by an explanation of how they had been chosen. The only advantage the Federalists derived from this victory was to signal their control over the state's legislature.

The Federalists put their political muscle to better use when the legislature adopted a series of "patriotic resolves" that drew national attention. The resolves were framed by a committee appointed to consider the expediency of the legislature adopting "measures . . . to procure a repeal" of the embargo. Citing the "extreme and increasing pressure" the embargo had imposed on the people, the committee concluded that its continuance would "soon . . . endanger our domestic peace and the union of these states." The committee accordingly recommended that the Massachusetts legislature instruct its senators and representatives to "procure [the embargo's] repeal."

So far the committee had behaved in a manner appropriate to the legislature's constitutional role, whatever one thought of the wisdom of their position and their veiled reference to disunion. It stepped beyond customary boundaries, though, in considering Jefferson's recent address to Congress. Though Jefferson had avoided referring to the embargo as the only alternative to war, the committee read his message in that fashion and voiced the hope that Congress would find a way "to avoid the necessity of electing between these great public calamities." The committee then asserted that Jefferson's proclamation of July 1807 banning British warships from American waters after the *Chesapeake* incident, rather than impressments and the Orders-in-Council, was the principal obstacle standing in the way of an "amiable adjustment" between Great Britain and the United States. This implied that all that was needed to resolve the disagreement between the two countries was Jefferson's revocation of his proclamation.[95] On November 15, the House and Senate adopted the committee's report with concurring resolves. The House ordered three thousand copies of both the report and resolutions printed at public expense, but declined to present Sullivan with a copy of its handiwork before adjourning until the following January.[96]

The actions of the Massachusetts legislature drew a quick, hostile response from the nine Republican members of the state's seventeen-man delegation in the

United States House of Representatives. "The Reply of the Majority of the Representatives from the State of Massachusetts—in Congress" accused the Federalist majority in the Massachusetts legislature of grounding their resolutions on an "entire misapprehension of those causes, which . . . have inflicted a deep wound on our national prosperity." The reply reviewed why the embargo should not be deemed the "sole 'cause of the public distress' " and repeated the official reasons for the embargo because they "appear either to have been utterly unknown to the [Massachusetts] Legislature, or to have unhappily escaped their recollection." The Republican congressmen then turned to Jefferson's order banning British warships from American waters. Since the United States government had acceded to Britain's request to separate this matter from other subjects of controversy between the two governments, how could it be construed as the key to unlocking the diplomatic impasse to which the Federalists in the Massachusetts legislature alluded? If the alternatives to the embargo were indeed humiliating submission or war, the Republican congressmen concluded that the embargo remained preferable to war because submission was out of the question.

Massachusetts's Republican congressmen had no illusions that the state's Federalist legislators would be swayed their arguments. Instead their audience was the people about whose good sense and patriotism the Federalist legislature had tried to raise doubts. The Republican congressmen dismissed such doubts as being "so disreputable to the known character of the great people of Massachusetts—that we cannot allow them for a moment to prejudice our fellow citizens in their esteem." But that did not stop the Republican congressmen from condemning the evasions of the embargo "which have in some sections of the country been too much countenanced and encouraged." They repeated the warning that the violations were leading "other nations [into] a belief, either that we were unable to sustain ourselves without the benefits of their intercourse, or that we had become too far devoted to our private ease and pursuit of our luxury, to submit to the privations which were called for by the occasion." And they expressed a hope that the recent federal elections would convince foreign powers "that the American people would . . . maintain with constancy, firmness and energy, those laws which their public councils had constitutionally pronounced." The reply also denied there was any "*constitutional* or *peaceable*" way "in which the state legislature could "interpose its voice between the constitutional authorities of the nation and the execution of the national laws." Instead it affirmed confidence in Congress's capacity to maintain the nation's rights and the willingness of the people to follow where the national government led.[97]

Unfortunately the results of the autumn congressional election, which reduced the number of Republican representatives in the Massachusetts delegation to Congress from nine to one, undercut the effect of the reply of her Republican congressmen. Nonetheless the setback had the beneficial effect of bringing Republican complacency about the threat posed by the Federalists to an end. The Republican press had initially decried Pickering's *Letter* of the preceding March as a bad joke laden with deceptions "not a child in the street believes to be true."[98] Some hoped that it would "utterly ruin all Confidence which might heretofore have been reposed in him as a public man."[99] After the Republicans lost control of the Massachusetts legislature in May, they still remained confident about reversing that setback at the next election.[100] The likelihood that Massachusetts's electoral vote would prove irrelevant to the selection of Jefferson's successor helped allay their anxieties about the growing Federalist agitation during the autumn. But the Topsfield convention's resolves, the legislature's endorsement of the idea that persisting with the embargo endangered the union, and the Federalists' success in winning almost total control over the state's next congressional delegation finally wakened the Republicans to their peril.

The Republicans still refused to credit their adversaries as posing a serious danger by themselves. The potency of the Federalists instead derived from British officials working in tandem with them to shape American opinion. The Republicans reached this conclusion long before January 1809 when the *New England Palladium* published a copy of a private letter, one the administration had been reluctant to release, that George Canning had sent to William Pinkney on September 23, 1808. In it, Canning insinuated that the American government had adopted the embargo, as Pickering had charged, out of compliance with Napoleon's wishes.[101] Almost half a year before that a writer in the *Independent Chronicle* speculated that the British consul in Norfolk had rushed reports of the Spanish insurgency supplied him by Admiral Cochrane into the American papers with an eye to influencing the coming election.[102] The *Essex Register* subsequently published correspondence, allegedly between a Briton and his Federalist friend in Massachusetts, in which the Briton congratulated the Federalists on making the embargo unenforceable. The Federalist responded by expressing the hope that Britain's opening of the Iberian trade would contribute to the abandonment of the measure.[103] The Federalist legislature of Massachusetts seemed to signal a further willingness to cooperate with Britain in humiliating Jefferson when it accused his administration of mishandling the negotiation with Ambassador Rose.

Though Massachusetts Republicans were forced on the defensive, they at least faced up to the effectiveness of the relentless, multilayered assault their adversaries were mounting. As Sullivan lay dying, Federalists in Newburyport industriously circulated among the other Essex County towns a memorial to Congress that would be signed by more than thirty-eight hundred people. It reiterated all the objections to the embargo contained in the joint resolutions of the state's legislature.[104] Boston's Republicans reacted with a set of resolves reflecting their alarm. The resolves complained that the Federalists had gone beyond encouraging and excusing the aggressions of a foreign power to attempt "a kind of coercion on the government of their country, to surrender [its] essential rights" by "threatening to break out in acts of violence against the laws" if they did not get their way. However, the attempt of Boston's Republicans to condemn "[m]eetings of individuals," like the Newburyport and Boston town meetings and the Topsfield convention, that published resolves encouraging "a spirit of insubordination," suffered because they resembled Federalist practices in all but the substance of their sentiments. Moreover, the recent congressional elections suggested the Federalist sentiments were finding decidedly more favor in the commonwealth than Republican ones were. Former congressman William Eustis, one of the few Harvard graduates among the Republican leaders in the state, apologized to Jefferson for the feebleness of their effort.[105] Though the leaders of both parties joined to bury Sullivan—who died on December 10— in style, the Federalists knew by the end of 1808 that it was only a matter of time before they would completely control the state.

3

DIVIDING TO CONQUER

Until the end of 1808 the political drama unfolding in Massachusetts had seemed of little consequence to the nation at large. During the autumn Washington's *National Intelligencer*—the national government's semi-official mouthpiece— showed more interest in the guarded endorsement the government of Vermont was willing to give the embargo than in Sullivan's struggle with the Massachusetts legislature.[1] Republican leaders outside New England were aware of the political ferment taking place in the Northeast. And as the autumn progressed they complained about the "factious misrepresentations, incendiary gazettes, and infamous cupidity" that in conjunction "with traitors abroad" were compromising the embargo's effectiveness.[2] In the late summer, Federalist gains in the New Hampshire election had alerted Republicans to the political advantage their adversaries were reaping.[3] The realization, however, did not lead to a repudiation of the course they had taken while the embargo remained the only obvious alternative to war.[4] Nor as Congress assembled did Republican leaders worry that the Federalists would gain control of the national government, however they lamented the direction in which events were moving in New England.[5]

Congressional Strife

Nonetheless all eyes turned to Washington for direction as the Tenth Congress assembled for its second session in November 1808. The rising number of vessels that departed illegally from American ports at this time did so in anticipation that Congress would soon either lift or modify the embargo.[6] Nor was anyone surprised when the congressional session opened with a protracted debate in both houses about the future of the measure. The debate produced little of substance that had not already emerged in the political sparring that had dominated Massachusetts politics for the past seven months. There were, however, some significant changes in emphasis. For one, Massachusetts took less of a leadership role in the congressional debate than her importance in New England entitled her to take. On November 11 Senator James Hillhouse of Connecticut offered a resolution for repealing the embargo followed by several speeches supporting the motion.[7] Allowing Connecticut to assume a leadership role sent a message to the administration that opposition to its policies extended beyond the boundaries of one state.

Hillhouse's credentials were such that few Federalists could object to his assuming the role he did. A graduate of Yale in the class of 1773, he had—after distinguishing himself during the British raid on New Haven in 1779—represented the town in the lower house of the state legislature from 1780 until 1785. Between 1789 and 1791 he served on the state's Council or upper house before taking a seat in Congress as one of the Connecticut's representatives from 1791 to1797. There he became an able defender of Hamilton's fiscal program as well as an advocate for alignment with Britain. When Oliver Ellsworth accepted appointment as the second chief justice of the United States, Hillhouse replaced him in the Senate. During his second term as senator he shared Washington lodgings with Timothy Pickering and won notoriety by proposing a series of amendments to the federal Constitution that called, among other things, for the annual election of the House of Representatives, three-year terms for senators, and one four-year term for the president. Allowing him to speak first against the embargo in the Senate suggested the Federalists were prepared to amend the Constitution rather than accept a recent ruling by a federal district judge in Massachusetts that the measure was constitutional.[8]

On November 26 Republicans in the House of Representatives succeeded in heading off a Federalist attempt to follow Hillhouse's lead when its Foreign Relations Committee proposed three resolves. The first stated that "the United States cannot, without a sacrifice of their rights, honor and independence, submit to the late edicts of Great Britain and France."[9] On November 28 a debate began on this proposition that consumed the better part of two weeks. Forcing Congress to focus on so abstract a statement, which few would care to oppose, was far less advantageous to the Federalists than debating a motion like Hillhouse's, even if it should fail to pass. In the end only two members of the House had the temerity to vote against the Foreign Relations Committee's first resolution.[10] Nonetheless, the debate drew attention to the emergence of a new master orator among the Massachusetts delegation to the House of Representatives who would influence Federalist strategy in Congress until he retired in 1813. This was the relatively youthful Josiah Quincy, who had entered Congress in 1805 at the age of thirty-three.

Quincy was the grandson of Braintree's richest denizen, made suddenly wealthy at the end of King George's War by the lucky capture of a Spanish treasure ship. His father, Josiah Quincy Sr., had taken a prominent role in the early phase of Massachusetts' revolutionary movement only to die in April 1775, just after the outbreak of hostilities with the mother country. Young Quincy, only three at the time, had grown up under the tutelage of two grandfathers, one of whose nephews had recently founded Phillips Andover Academy. Josiah spent eight years there before entering Harvard in 1786. He found Cambridge much more to his liking than boarding school, where unrelenting supervision had stifled his imagination. Harvard's instruction also played to his elocutionary strengths by focusing on daily recitations. Excelling at these exercises, Quincy had been chosen English Orator for the commencement in 1790. He then read law with the prominent Boston attorney William Tudor. Quincy won easy access to the clubs and civic institutions that Boston's aristocracy were founding, such as the Wednesday Evening Club and the Massachusetts Historical Society. But he also relished involvement in the town's public life and accepted an invitation to give the Fourth of July Oration in 1798 as well as nomination as the Federalist candidate to replace Harrison Gray Otis in Congress two years later.[11]

Quincy lost his first election campaign and had to wait half a decade before taking a seat in the Ninth Congress, which assembled in November 1805. By then he had concluded the Federalists' only hope of influencing the national government lay in dividing the Republican majority. Initially he courted a group of dissident Republicans known as the Tertium Quids because they offered an alternative to both the Federalists and the administration, which emerged during Jefferson's second term. John Randolph, a mercurial Virginian, was their leader. Jefferson and Randolph had first parted ways in 1804 over a scheme for compensating northerner purchasers of Georgia's Yazoo lands, who had been defrauded when the Georgia legislature repudiated the grant under which the lands had been sold. Subsequently, in the Eighth Congress, Randolph objected to the creation of a secret fund to promote the acquisition of West Florida from Spain. Such an appropriation offended Randolph's ideological expectations about Republican purity and transparency. Entering into secret intrigues to enlarge the republic would make it indistinguishable from a monarchy.[12] When Jefferson had Randolph removed from the chair of the powerful Ways and Means Committee, Quincy saw an opportunity for alliance with the Quids based on resisting further expansion of the nation once the Yazoo controversy was resolved. But he soon realized that Randolph's personal eccentricities made it unlikely the Quids would ever become a significant splinter group. A disease during adolescence had stunted Randolph's physical development, leaving him with a high treble voice and without a beard. He compensated with elocutionary aggressiveness and a willingness to challenge anyone who reciprocated in kind to a duel.[13] After concluding that courting Randolph's followers was futile, Quincy turned to provoking the Republicans. His recent biographer describes him as embracing a "politics of exasperation."[14] The phrase aptly captures both

Quincy's state of mind and the reactions his behavior elicited from his opponents. However, the change involved little divergence from his initial strategy. Quincy simply adopted different means and in the process became known for the rhetorical extremes he was willing to deploy in testing Republican unity and resolve.

The speech he delivered on the Foreign Relations Committee's first resolution relating to the embargo heralded his emergence as the enfant terrible of the congressional Federalists. In it Quincy turned tables on the committee by insisting that the United States had in fact submitted to foreign dictates by abandoning its overseas commerce with the embargo. The notion had previously appeared in Federalist newspapers, but no one had yet advanced it upon the floor of the United States Congress. Quincy now used it to construe the committee's resolution against submission as the announcement of Congress's intention to repeal the embargo. That line of argument enabled him to support the resolution and in the same breath denounce the embargo, which he remorselessly attacked as unequal in its operation, unenforceable in the commercial states, and unconstitutional. Quincy pressed his challenge by asking where in the Constitution Congress had been granted the power to destroy the nation's trade? If the commercial states had understood that the power to regulate trade would be construed as the power to destroy it, they would have insisted on the same guarantees for their commercial interests that the southern states had obtained for slavery. Quincy painted the Federalists as the true heirs to the revolutionary tradition of resistance to oppression and by implication the real custodians of the nation's honor.[15]

The course Quincy had taken involved more than rhetorical daring. Though few of the nation's leaders felt entirely exempt from the code duello that had taken root in America during the revolutionary war, affairs of honor found more favor among the gentry of the South and West, who were predominantly Republicans, than it did in the Federalist Northeast.[16] When a congressman took offense at what a Federalist said, he was likely to represent that part of the nation where gentlemen were expected to defend their honor at the hazard of their lives. Some northern Federalists were prepared to participate in the culture of honor. Congressman Barent Gardenier of Ulster County, New York, had been seriously wounded in a duel with George W. Campbell of Tennessee the preceding March. In this case, Gardenier had issued the challenge after Campbell insulted him following Gardenier's speech against transforming the embargo from a precautionary into a coercive measure. Standing up to Campbell had conferred on Gardenier a distinction that few of his Federalist colleagues enjoyed, and he was one of two congressmen to vote against the Foreign Relations Committee's first resolve.[17] Some construed Quincy's address on this resolution as a challenge to Campbell, its reputed author, and a rumor circulated afterward that Campbell had killed Quincy in a duel.[18] But Quincy had resolved in advance, as had several other New England congressmen including Pickering, neither to issue nor to accept challenges.[19] They did this at little cost to their reputations back home, though it opened them to a barrage of insults that might not otherwise have come their way from their congressional colleagues.

Quincy's assault on the embargo did nothing to deflect the Republicans in Congress from strengthening the measure. It took the House only two days to agree to the Foreign Relations Committee's second resolution, which called for a general ban against all "vessels belonging to Great Britain or France, or to any other of the belligerent Powers, having in force orders or decrees violating the lawful commerce or neutral rights of the United States." This resolution addressed a loophole in the embargo that still permitted the entry and clearance of foreign vessels to and from American ports. Under existing law these vessels could bring in overseas imports, though the exportation of American produce was forbidden. The resolution also called for a law prohibiting "the importation of any goods, wares, or merchandise, the growth, produce, or manufacture of the dominions of" Britain and France, and underscored the Republican majority's resolve to pursue commercial coercion.[20] But neither resolution addressed the fundamental issue raised by Federalists of how the embargo was to be enforced in the face of the growing opposition it was encountering in the eastern states.

The Senate finally took that matter up on December 8 after decisively defeating Hillhouse's motion for repeal. A committee appointed to consider enforcement at the beginning of the session submitted a report structured around the recommendations of the secretary of the treasury, Albert Gallatin. These included requiring vessels that sailed from United States ports to post much higher bonds so that the penalties for violating the embargo exceeded the profits; limiting the time in which these bonds could be canceled before incurring forfeiture; giving customs officers sweeping authority to detain vessels, to prohibit their loading, to force the unloading of suspicious ones, and to seize suspicious goods; making the unauthorized loading of a vessel grounds for forfeiture of cargo and ship; bestowing on federal enforcement officers immunity from suits in the state courts; defining opposition to the embargo as a federal crime; expanding the number of fast-sailing, shallow draft revenue cutters; and placing the state militias at the service of federal officials charged with enforcing the law. Most of Gallatin's recommendations were incorporated in a bill, which, when it came before the Senate, touched off a debate whose ferocity far exceeded anything heretofore witnessed over the embargo.[21] And the acrimony of the Senate debate quickly spilled over into the House of Representatives.

On December 21, the Republican leader of the Senate, William Branch Giles, delivered a widely publicized speech that set the tone for what followed. Giles began with some of the objections raised against the bill, including the size of the bonds, the powers of the collectors, and the burdens these measures would impose on the fisheries. He then pointed to the wholesale evasions that were taking place in New England, where the authority of the collectors was being routinely defied and seized property had been forcibly rescued.[22] Such activities fully justified a resort to military force to restrain them. But Giles went further by suggesting that circumstances also justified suspending the writ of habeas corpus. Who was to blame for such draconian remedies? Not the administration or its policies, as the Federalists had been arguing, but British influence acting through the agency of "unprincipled Americans." What was "the nature of the offences they have been induced to commit? Is it treason?" Giles asked. "No, . . . but it partakes essentially of its character. If instead of an incipient war, we were in an actual state of war, it would be treason, and treason of the basest sort. . . . It is violating the laws of our country, and co-operating in counteracting their effects upon our enemies for the sake of money." Were such remedies unconstitutional? "If . . . we should be driven by our fears from affording the means of executing the embargo laws," would that not amount to declaring to the world that Congress was "afraid to execute" a law they had just resolved not to repeal?[23]

This speech, with several others Giles had delivered defending the embargo, met with sufficient approval among the Republicans in Washington that they took pains to forward copies of them to their embattled partisans in Massachusetts.[24] To counter Giles's influence the Senate Federalists again turned to Hillhouse. After arguing with some justification that the southern states were violating the embargo as much as the northeastern ones were, he reviewed in detail each provision of the proposed enforcement bill to demonstrate its arbitrary, unconstitutional nature. He reserved his harshest criticism for the provision that authorized the president to deploy the army, navy, and state militias to enforce the law, questioning the wisdom of a policy that required military action to enforce it and bluntly asserting that the measure threatened liberty. That failed to influence the Republican majority, though, and the bill passed the Senate on December 21.[25]

Because of the press of other business the House did not consider the enforcement bill until December 27. The interval of a better part of a week gave Federalists in the House time to prepare a more concerted response than they had mounted in the Senate, employing voices from beyond New England. James Sloan of New Jersey led the Federalist assault. Sloan had previously distinguished himself as the champion of an effort to move the nation's capital from Washington back to either Philadelphia or New York. He now predicted the electorate would repudiate the sponsors of the measure in the same way a previous electorate had turned against the Sixth Congress for the Alien and Sedition acts and the direct tax of 1798.[26] Joshua Masters, a Connecticut native representing New York, expanded on Sloan's opener by declaring that "the contest [is] between liberty and tyranny, between oppression and free government." He admonished, "If you progress in your present system, it will be necessary to have a standing army to protect you against the resentment of the people." Passing the bill would only result in rousing the "spirit of the nation" against its government. Invoking imagery from Milton's "Paradise Lost," Masters predicted the people would "hurl you down into that detestable and abominable place where the worm never dies and the fire is not quenched." Masters then turned Republican ideology against the embargo: "We are waging war against the public opinion. The voice of the nation is against the proceedings of Government, and this system is not the system of the people." He also was the first to argue in Congress that the Union was at stake. "Commercial jealousy is roused and will increase; and without a united interest in commerce . . . a separation of interest will . . . endanger the Union, and shake the Constitution to its centre."[27] A Republican resolution, introduced while the enforcement bill was under consideration, to enlarge the army, which then had only two thousand men, to fifty thousand seemed to lend plausibility to Federalist claims that the nation was threatened with military despotism.[28]

Gardenier now seized on the resolution for expanding the army to play upon ideological anxieties he knew many Republicans entertained. Either the measure's proposers intended "to raise a standing army in time of peace" or the "Government" intended to embark on war. Gardenier for one would not vote for such a measure unless war, no matter how "unnecessary and unjust" had become so imminent "that the interest of the country demanded" it. But he argued that if the embargo was really an alternative to war, raising fifty thousand men was unnecessary. Like Hillhouse, Sloan, and Masters, Gardenier opposed the measure because it was dangerous to liberty. He taunted the Republicans with their opposition to the creation of an army of twelve thousand men in 1798. If they had feared a military despotism when Washington was in command of so small a force, had Gardenier not every reason to fear an army four times that size? Gardenier claimed "the public liberty" was already threatened because "under pretence of enforcing the embargo, an unconstitutional power was proposed to be placed in the hands of the Executive officers" to exercise "arbitrary power . . . properly upon mere suspicion." To put at its service "a strong and overwhelming military force" would seal freedom's doom. He felt it to be his duty to "place himself here, upon the ramparts of the Constitution, and give alarm to the country."[29]

Attempts to turn Republican ideology against the administration provoked an angry response from John W. Eppes of Virginia, Jefferson's son-in-law. Eppes condemned Federalist efforts, both in and out of Congress, to mislead the people of the eastern states. He objected particularly to claims about the embargo's permanence, the trade the nation could look forward to enjoying should it submit to Britain's regulations, and the hostility of the southern states to commerce. He claimed that the edicts of the belligerents had had a far more devastating effect on the nation's economy than the embargo and that the representatives of "the people of the Eastern portion" were keeping "the real situation of the country" from their constituents. He dwelt especially on "the strange union of sentiment between gentlemen in opposition and the British Ministry" about the unenforceable nature of the embargo, accusing the Federalists of encouraging the belief that the Republic was powerless to compel obedience to its own laws. Eppes also felt the Federalists were misleading the British Ministry about the extent of discontent with the embargo and accused the "Essex Junto" of acting in concert with agents of the British government to encourage evasions of the law. Eppes acknowledged that England and France might refuse to withdraw their decrees, but vowed that in that eventuality, "we must fight. . . . We have declared we will not submit and there is no species of effectual resistance but war."[30] In the wake of Eppes's tirade, a decisive majority of the House endorsed expanding the army to fifty thousand men.[31] Shortly afterward the House voted seventy-one to thirty-two to pass the Enforcement Act, which Jefferson signed into law on the January 9, 1809.[32]

Eppes's insistence that the only alternative to the embargo was war drew attention to a fissure that had begun developing within Republican ranks in Congress. While some were ready to risk war should the embargo prove unenforceable, others clung to the embargo precisely because they feared war. The schism had first emerged when the House of Representatives considered Senate amendments to one of its bills designed to get the expanded gunboat navy Jefferson had ordered built in the wake of the *Chesapeake* incident to sea. The original House measure called for enough men to man 171 gunboats together with "ten small vessels of war," all of which were suitable for enforcing the embargo.[33] In the Senate Hillhouse countered with a proposal for fully mobilizing the nation's naval force, including "all the frigates and other armed vessels," most of which had been laid up after the war with Tripoli in 1805. Many Federalists despised Jefferson's infatuation with gunboats and saw an advantage in fully mobilizing the nation's naval resources. Since frigates were unsuited for enforcing the embargo, the principal effect of Hillhouse's proposal would be to increase the cost of the House measure, which might scare economy-minded Republicans away from it entirely. New England's senators unanimously supported Hillhouse's amendment, and enough

Republicans joined them to pass it.[34] The Republican Joseph Story, who had just replaced the recently deceased Jacob Crowninshield as a Massachusetts representative in the House, then took the Senate's action as his cue to recommend full naval mobilization to his colleagues before the Senate's amendment had been officially communicated to them. Story wanted Congress to face up to the prospect of war and to make provision for an "efficient system" of waging it by expanding the naval establishment.[35]

Story hoped to make his fellow Republicans realize that they needed a credible alternative to the embargo, which could not be politically sustained much longer.[36] Instead his comment was construed as impudence and provoked intense objections from among the ranks of his own party. David R. Williams from South Carolina protested that the navies of most other countries had ended up augmenting Britain's navy. "Did the gentleman wish to follow the example of Denmark, and have our towns Copenhagened?" Here Williams alluded to an incident that had occurred during the summer of 1807 when the British blockaded and then attacked Copenhagen after the Danish court rejected an ultimatum that it surrender its fleet. The Danes suffered three days of ferocious bombardment from the land and sea before submitting. Story replied that Britain would have trouble subduing fifty American frigates even with her navy of more than a thousand commissioned ships. But Williams objected to the expense of such an armament.[37] House leader Wilson Cary Nicholas from Virginia then intervened to quiet this squabble among House Republicans. Though he acknowledged the United States could expect to make little headway against Great Britain "on [the] water," and therefore should concentrate on its land forces, he would abide by the majority's determination about how best to defend the nation. The majority Nicholas had in mind was the Republican one in Congress and he expected Story to follow his example.[38]

On January 9, when the House took up the Senate amendments, Nicholas's admonition failed to influence the freshman representative from Massachusetts. Instead Story defended a large, deep-water navy, arguing that every frigate that the United States sent to sea would oblige a hostile nation—there could be no doubt that he had Britain in mind—to match it with two frigates each requiring the support of eight to ten merchantmen in the western Atlantic.[39] Story's line of reasoning elicited a barrage of objections from other House Republicans, some of whom questioned the wisdom of taking Britain on where she was strongest, while others objected to the navy's expense. Republican concerns also touched on ideology. Williams doubted whether an expanded navy could be manned without pressing men into the service, and George Troup of Georgia warned that a large navy would lead to an expansion of the debt, heavy taxes, and corruption. Lemuel Sawyer from North Carolina thought the "absolute despotism exercised by naval commanders" was "incompatible with civil liberty," and he preferred to abandon the nation's commerce if it required a navy.[40] Some Republicans did back Story, but in a manner that promoted further divisions among them. John G. Jackson of Virginia, Madison's brother-in-law, wanted to send "our little pigmy force" to sea "notwithstanding the giant navy of Great Britain." Rather than submit to her superior force, Jackson thought "it would be more honorable to fight, while a single gun could be fired." Sentiments like Jackson's simply inflamed the anxieties that other Republicans entertained about war. These congressmen preferred commercial coercion to war because they feared hostilities might have the same effect on the nation's form of government as it had had on the French republic.[41] In the end the House voted to adhere to most aspects of its original bill, though in conference with the Senate a measure giving the president discretion over what elements of the navy should be mobilized eventually prevailed.[42]

By law the term of the Tenth Congress would end on March 4, 1809. Shortly after Congress had declared its determination to adhere to the embargo, the Republicans realized that as matters then stood it would remain in force—unless one of the great powers lifted its restrictions against neutral trade—until the Eleventh Congress met, which normally would not be until the following November. Few Republicans felt comfortable with such a prospect. One way of coping with their dilemma was to provide by law for the Eleventh Congress to meet at some earlier time to address the problems its predecessor had left unresolved. But when the House took this matter up, a disagreement immediately arose about when the new Congress should assemble. Some favored May, others September. Those who preferred the earlier date generally wished to replace the embargo with hostilities. Those who supported the latter date hoped prolonging the embargo would eventually relieve the nation from the necessity of going to war.[43]

The growing division within Republicans ranks offered the Federalists an opening that Josiah Quincy now exploited. In a speech delivered on January 19, he accused the Republicans of not being serious about hostilities, adding that "no insult, however gross, offered by either France or Great Britain, could force this majority into a declaration of war." Quincy went well beyond the observation that the majority of Republicans preferred peace to war by insinuating that the Republicans were indifferent to questions of honor. This became unmistakably clear in his subsequent assertion that the Republicans "could not be kicked into such a declaration by either nation." Quincy alleged that the Republicans were only talking of war to reconcile the people to a continuance of the embargo.[44]

The idea that one could not respond appropriately to an insult, indeed could not even be "kicked into" that response, was a figure of contempt peculiar to the language of honor. The code of honor assumed that gentlemen adhered to standards of behavior that those lacking gentility would observe only when subjected to degrading forms of coercion. To have this message delivered by Quincy magnified the provocation since everyone knew that he did not feel bound by the standards many Republican members of Congress and their constituents observed. Quincy realized that invoking figures of honor to humiliate the Republicans was risky and quickly added a gloss designed to place his remarks in a less outrageous context, though one that rankled the Republicans no less. Its gist was that thrusting the nation into a war for which it was unprepared, after having first annihilated the nation's commerce and revenue, would inevitably lead their constituents to repudiate the Republicans.[45] However, his calumny about Republican honor remained to inflame the incipient division between the Republicans of the South and West from those of the North and East. While the Southerners and Westerners blustered at the aspersions cast upon them, the Northeasterners could be relied upon to resist a violent resolution to the Republicans' dilemma.

Quincy's remark evoked angry Republican denunciations. Eppes attacked him for trying to deceive the people about the permanence of the embargo; Jackson accused him of treason; Ezekiel Bacon of Massachusetts warned him against trying to dissolve the union.[46] But the most commonly heard protest was that Quincy was playing to the Massachusetts legislature, which was about to reassemble, hoping to spur it toward adopting extreme measures, possibly resulting in a civil war.[47] That accusation measured with precision the growing Republican concern over the political contest that was about to take place in Boston. The intensity of Republican denunciations also provided a reliable indicator of Quincy's success in touching on the weakness of their coalition. This was the tension between those who preferred war to humiliation and those who were not yet prepared to risk hostilities. No Federalist phrase, with the possible exception of Pickering's claim that Britain had done the United States "no essential injury," was more frequently alluded to during the next six years by the Republicans because it was a pointed reminder of the fragility of their coalition as they struggled with challenges both at home and abroad.[48] And it was all the more infuriating because everyone in Congress knew that war with Britain was the last thing Quincy and his fellow Federalists desired.

Quincy must have been pleased when Republican Wilson Cary Nicholas rose in the House on January 24 to propose that the embargo be repealed and the nation "resume, maintain, and defend the navigation of the high seas against any nation or nations having in force edicts, orders, or decrees, violating the lawful commerce and neutral rights of the United States."[49] Replacing the embargo with naval warfare against both the offending powers seemed like an appropriate response to Quincy's taunt. But Nicholas had phrased his proposal in ambiguous language. Did he mean that American vessels would only defend themselves if attacked? Or did he mean, as was usually the case with the issuance of letters of marque, to authorize them to attack the commercial vessels of the powers preying on American shipping? Pressured for clarification, he said a week later that he had meant the latter.[50] This clarification, according to Jefferson, produced a "sudden and unaccountable revolution of opinion" resembling "a kind of panic" that took place "chiefly among the New England and New York members" of the Republican caucus. Jefferson felt it permitted the Federalist minority "to controul . . . [the] legislature and Executive authorities," forcing "them from the measures which" they otherwise would have pursued. The change was inexplicable to Jefferson because he believed "the Essex Junto" had been checked in pursuing a "forcible opposition."[51]

However, the breakup of the Republican majority was less mysterious than Jefferson pretended. The northeastern members were not prepared to support the issuance of letters of marque and reprisal because they believed doing so would immediately provoke a war with Great Britain, which their region would not accept. They were acutely aware that many customs officials in the Northeast were either colluding with violators or resigning their positions in response to armed challenges to the embargo and the widespread refusal of juries to convict violators.[52] A purely defensive arming that gradually escalated into war was the most the region could be expected to tolerate. The majority of the Republican caucus rejected the preference of the New Englanders and New Yorkers because they were convinced Federalist merchants would selectively resist the occasional French privateer but otherwise submit to Britain's commercial regulations in their pursuit of profit. If the embargo was to be abandoned, they wanted war with Britain rather than a reversion to the informal alliance with her that had transpired during the Quasi-War or some other measure that the New Englanders might pervert.[53]

The Struggle for Massachusetts

In reaching their divergent positions, both Republican factions were influenced by political developments taking place simultaneously in New England and particularly in Massachusetts. The Federalist campaign to recapture full control of the Massachusetts government had resumed almost immediately after Governor Sullivan's funeral on December 16. If death had not removed him from the scene, Sullivan's stature among moderates would have done little to protect him from the Federalists' determination to capture control of the state's executive office.[54]

But Levi Lincoln, who as lieutenant governor had succeeded to the chair, provided a much more inviting target. Lincoln resembled Sullivan in some ways, having played almost as prominent a role in the development of the Massachusetts legal system. In 1781, for instance, Lincoln had helped initiate the legal actions that led to the judicial abolition of slavery in the commonwealth. After rising to prominence in the Massachusetts bar, he had accepted appointment as attorney general in Jefferson's first administration. Since the post was largely a sinecure—Jefferson seldom consulted him beyond asking his opinion about the constitutionality of the Louisiana Purchase—Lincoln had taken charge of the distribution of federal patronage in New England as well as defending the administration against Federalist criticism in the newspapers.[55] These services qualified him to be Sullivan's running mate after returning to his native state in 1805, and he had been elected lieutenant governor with Sullivan in 1807. But Lincoln lacked Sullivan's personal charisma and social standing and had too partisan a reputation to appeal to moderate Federalists. Moreover, the tone of his letters to Jefferson, which bordered on the obsequious, suggested he expected to derive more benefit from his access to Federal patronage than he would be able to provide in the way of support for the national administration.[56] Finally he was only a few years younger than Sullivan, and his eyesight was failing.

Several Federalist-controlled town meetings fired the opening salvos in the campaign to oust Lincoln by passing resolves against the Enforcement Act just before the state legislature was scheduled to reassemble. Republican critics alleged that this blitz had been orchestrated during the previous November's legislative session.[57] Republican suspicions fed on the first wave of resolves, some of them from as far away as distant Maine, being framed before definitive news of the Enforcement Act could have reached the towns that adopted them. However, their authors had had access to Gallatin's recommendations together with notices of repeated Federalist failures to water down the proposed legislation. Still, the Republicans were justified in sensing eagerness on the part of the Massachusetts Federalists to capitalize on the Enforcement Act.

On January 13, 1809, the staunchly Federalist *New England Palladium* printed a special supplement in large type under the banner heading "*The CONSTITUTION gone!!*" that provided an abstract of the new law. The *Palladium*'s supplement stuck to generalities because it lacked access to the official text.[58] The paper suggested a more appropriate title for the law might be "An Act to suspend the Rights of the People and to create an absolute Dictator for an indefinite period." It went on to claim that the Enforcement Act "far transcend[ed] the Boston Port-Bill, or any of the arbitrary acts of the British Parliament affecting this country" prior to 1776. The *Palladium* called for public meetings immediately and unanimously to pass resolutions declaring that "all persons who should countenance, support, or assist in the execution of such a tyrannical law . . . be considered hostile to the good people of these States." It expressed confidence that the people of Massachusetts *"never will submit"* to a law like the one Senator Hillhouse had denounced in Congress. The *Palladium's* diatribe concluded that the Enforcement Act posed "the dreadful, horrible alternative of *Civil War*, or *Slavery"* unless "New-England declares firmly, but *temperately*, as one man, that she will not submit." This task the *Palladium* urged the people to entrust to the legislature, which "once more" would "preserve their country . . . from the grasp of arbitrary power."[59]

Subsequent issues of the *Palladium* carried the resolves of several towns denouncing the act and calling on the state government for redress. This flurry of activity served as prelude for a Boston town meeting on January 23 and 24, on the eve of the legislative session. Though the Federalist managers of the meeting were forced to consume most of January 23 defeating alternative resolves proposed by the Republicans, the town eventually voted to petition the General Court against the embargo and the measures espoused by Congress to enforce it. Boston's petition adopted the following day condemned the embargo as an attempt to wage a disguised war contrary to American interests and proclaimed the administration's efforts at *"compelling obedience"* to be unconstitutional. It went on to charge that the only reason why Congress had passed so extraordinary a measure was to make a war with Britain and an alliance with France inevitable. The petitioners then urged the state's legislature to "devise means of relief against the unconstitutional measures of the General Government." Immediately following the adoption of the petition, the town meeting endorsed a set of resolves that declared "we will not voluntarily aid or assist in the execution" of the Enforcement Act. The resolves also condemned all who did so "as enemies to the Constitution of the United States and of this State, and hostile to the Liberties of this People."[60] The proceedings of the Boston town meeting joined the resolves of what by then had become a dozen other Massachusetts towns as well as the resolves of a county convention purporting to represent twenty-three towns expressing similar sentiments.

Neither Lincoln nor anyone witnessing the spectacle unfolding in Massachusetts could have been in doubt about the seriousness of the challenge the Federalists were mounting. The *National Intelligencer* recognized the importance of the confrontation between the governor and the legislature when it republished Lincoln's lengthy address and the replies of both houses in their entirety.[61] Lincoln tried to focus upon what he assumed was his adversaries' principal vulnerability: "The New-England States have been represented, to their injury, and to the injury of the United States, as distracted by divisions, prepared for opposition to the authority of the law, and ripening for a secession from the Union." He would have wished that such apprehensions were "unfounded," but Lincoln confessed that in Massachusetts "existing difficulties and the apparent indications of greater ones, have produced instances of excitement, violence, and indiscretion" that had to be confronted.[62]

Lincoln's reference to future difficulties stemmed from a letter that the secretary of war, Henry Dearborn, had just sent the governors of the New England states asking them to appoint militia officers "of known respect for the laws . . . near to each port of entry" with orders to respond to the requests of collectors for assistance in enforcing the embargo.[63] On January 23 Dearborn issued an additional directive to military personnel in Boston, calling on them to assist the customs officials in preventing unauthorized vessels from leaving the port. When the directive was published a week later in Boston, it caused a sensation.[64] A memorial posted in the various insurance offices of the town for individuals to sign claimed the port was being closed down by military power exactly as the British had closed it in 1774. It also hinted that the U.S. government could expect to meet with the same resistance Boston had directed against Britain if a speedy remedy was not forthcoming. To underscore the claim that Boston was being unjustly singled out for military persecution, the *Palladium* simultaneously published a report that vessels, allowed to clear from New York in ballast for New Orleans, were making for Havana and were fetching astronomical prices there.[65]

In such circumstances, Lincoln's plea to the legislature to forget past dissensions and unite for the common interest of the Union was futile. The governor occupied stronger ground when he appealed to the Constitution, which entrusted "our commercial intercourse and national defense" to the national government. Though "it is not unbecoming any member of the union to add its concurring energies to national measures," or even to "question their justness or policy" while under consideration, there was a point at which "controversy and opposition" were no longer appropriate. Once a measure had been put to the vote and decided upon by a "government . . . capable only of executing the deliberate volitions of a real majority of the citizens," it had to be obeyed "or government loses its existence, and the people are ruined." Lincoln acknowledged that New England's commercial sufferings were severe. But with the rest of the world enmeshed in war, Americans could not expect to be absolved from all afflictions. "If our privations have preserved a portion of our prosperity, our peace, and the opportunity of yet selecting between alliances, [as well as] peace and war, are we certain that the price has been too great?" Congress faced the unenviable task of formulating policies for a public of "diversified sentiments." If it had to wait for unanimity, "our rights would never be defended, and our country would be ruined." Instead the majority had to decide.[66]

Lincoln's address took a less fortunate course when he tried to face down "reports, that the administration, and the southern people, are hostile to commerce, and unfriendly to the eastern states." He denounced these allegations as "calculated" to produce "uneasiness, jealousies, and dissentions." When lawful, constitutional government was opposed by "incendiary and libellous publications," was it a violation of "liberty of speech and the press" for public opinion to support the government and "discountenance its opposers"? Lincoln questioned whether people in the streets or in town meetings, "pressed with deep personal interest, and excited from erroneous conceptions" were equipped to decide whether the acts of the national government were in fact "unnecessary, unconstitutional, oppressive, and tyrannical." He feared that "false views, misstatements, and groundless alarms . . . from the representatives of our own election" were hurrying "well-meaning men into acts pregnant with awful consequences." If Massachusetts succeeded in dictating "measures to Congress, and by opposition, or a convulsed state of things, force[d] their adoption, then would . . . one State have obtained a disastrous triumph over the United States" and "our rights and our strength would be scattered to the winds." Lincoln trusted Americans were not "prepared to proclaim to a suffering and enslaved world" that Republicanism had failed, and urged his fellow citizens "to endure privations a few months longer" so that the embargo could have its intended effect on foreign nations.[67]

Anyone sensitive to the tone of Lincoln's speech—and the first reports of it had reached Washington by January 30—would have recognized that he had accomplished little besides placing himself at the mercy of his enemies. Sensing their advantage, the Massachusetts Senate took a week to draft an answer to the governor's address. Harrison Gray Otis, then president of the Senate, played a major role in drafting this and several other documents the legislature produced during its winter session to ensure Lincoln's downfall. Otis, the son of a wealthy Boston merchant, could claim prominent revolutionary figures like Mercy Otis Warren and James Otis as aunt and uncle. After graduating from Harvard, he had entered the legal profession. But Otis owed his fortune to astute investments in Boston real estate during the town's postwar period of prosperity and expansion. In 1796 Boston had elected him to represent them in the General Court, and in 1797 he had entered Congress at an even younger age than Josiah Quincy would, serving there for two full terms. On returning to Boston in 1801, he acted as U.S. district attorney until Jefferson removed him from office. Undaunted, Otis sought various state offices and was elected to consecutive terms in the House between 1802 and 1805, followed by eight years in the state Senate, over which he presided as president from 1808 to 1811. The reply, which he did so much to shape, was adopted by a margin of only one. But Otis was not prepared to let the narrowness of the Federalist majority temper the "truculent" tone of the document, which took special pains to turn Lincoln's words against him.[68]

The Senate reply began by asserting "that our enemies alone could have represented the New-England states" as on the verge of rebellion, adding that the embargo was solely responsible for rousing the people of the state. It then turned to Lincoln's claim that opposition should cease after the constitutional authorities enacted a law. Surely that could not be the case with the embargo because the speed with which it had passed precluded many members of Congress, not to mention the people at large, from questioning either its wisdom or policy. If objections were now barred, was not a principle being established that "would render our free government a despotism?" The Senate reply went on to vindicate the town meetings against doubts Lincoln had raised about their competency to decide "on great, complicated . . . constitutional questions." Many of the meetings had been attended "by men second to none for their legal and political knowledge. . . . Can such assemblies of the citizens merit censure in a republican government?" The Senate majority declared their confidence in the people's "knowledge of their rights and duties, and their firmness and perseverance in maintaining them." While it cautioned them to act "with delicacy," it rejected Lincoln's plea for patience. Why should the people "be called upon to 'endure privations' any longer" when public sentiment was close to the point "where patience and submission end"? Though the Senate majority remained confident that the people would "rally round the national Constitution," it warned they were not prepared to "sink . . . into the frightful abyss" to the brink of which the national administration had brought them.

The House reply expanded on both the tone and substance of the Senate reply. How could anyone "be weak and wicked enough to construe a disposition to support [the] Constitution and preserve the union, by a temperate and firm opposition to acts which are repugnant to the first principles of both" as improper? The House denied that exposing the unconstitutional tendency of misconceived measures threatened the union. Instead it vowed "never [to] relinquish" the right "of discussing the measures of our general government with freedom and firmness." It was the legislature's duty to question "the policy and capacity of that administration . . . which in a few years, has reduced this great, active and enterprising nation, from an unexampled height of prosperity, to comparative poverty and idleness." The House majority held the Jefferson administration responsible "for a system of measures as . . . imbecile a[nd] weak against foreign nations, as it is oppressive and ruinous to our own." It condemned the Enforcement Act as "arbitrary and oppressive" and contrary to "the first principles of civil liberty, and the fundamental provisions of the constitution." It claimed the Republicans had sacrificed the rights of the eastern states to those in other regions and maintained that "the decision of the majority, to be binding," had to "be constitutional and just."

The House majority reserved its heaviest fire for Lincoln's comments about "individual indiscretions and rashness of sentiment and action" colliding with the actions of the national government. Lincoln's caution applied more aptly to the Whiskey Rebellion, "that period of our federal history, in which an insurrection, fomented by those who assumed to themselves exclusively the designation of republican, and aided by the machinations of French intrigue, had nearly prostrated the national government." New England's way of responding to "the pressure of political calamities" was through town meetings "wherein the general sense of the people might be collected." This was the course pursued during the Revolution, and "[h]ad the British ministry of that day attended to the voice of the people so expressed," they might have avoided the breakup of the empire. "The expression of the public sentiment" was now even more "necessary to counteract the errors and misrepresentations of those who falsely" represented to the national government that "the measures they were pursuing were satisfactory to the people." In the opinion of the House Federalists, the suppression of town meetings would constitute an unacceptable threat to liberty.

As committees drafted these two replies, Federalists in both the House and Senate busied themselves with orchestrating additional measures designed to embarrass the Republicans locally and nationally.[69] The most significant was the report of a joint committee of both houses appointed to decide how the legislature should respond to the town memorials that were flooding the General Court. This report hailed the "numerous representations, made as if by one consent from different parts of the country" as "strong proof of the impolicy and injustice of the measures complained of." Rather than "enumerating the disgusting catalogue of public wrongs, displayed," the report chose to distill the leading subjects of complaint. The first was "[t]he impolitic, unnecessary, and unconstitutional interdiction of commerce" by Congress. The committee recommended that Massachusetts unite "with other States, whose interests and objects are similar to our own, for the support and vindication of their just rights by constitutional and peaceable means." Second in importance was the "apprehension that the nation is to be speedily plunged into a war with Great Britain." The committee lamented that the national administration had given "too much ground" for such anxieties. It chided the Republicans for not standing up to French aggressions against neutral rights "in a manner becoming a great and powerful nation," which would have relieved Britain of the need to retaliate with her Orders-in-Council. Though the people of Massachusetts would support the administration in a "just and necessary" war, the committee was confident that "a sincere disposition to conciliate on our part, would . . . prevent" a conflict with Great Britain. Last, there was the Enforcement Act itself.[70]

The joint committee's report served as preamble to a set of resolutions in which both houses of the legislature concurred. The first resolution followed the report in declaring the Enforcement Act unconstitutional, though it recommended "all parties aggrieved by [its] operation . . . abstain from forcible resistance." The second authorized the Massachusetts legislature to petition Congress for repeal. The third pledged the state legislature's cooperation with other states in procuring amendments to the Constitution to protect commerce and "to give the Commercial States their fair and just consideration in the government of the Union." This resolution also authorized the transmission of the committee's report and resolutions "to the Legislatures of such of our sister States, as manifest a disposition to concur with us in measures to rescue our common country from impending ruin." The draft of a bill titled "AN ACT to secure the people of this commonwealth against unreasonable, arbitrary and unconstitutional searches in their dwelling houses" accompanied the resolutions. The bill, directed more against the embargo than the Enforcement Act per se, invoked the Massachusetts declaration of rights and the federal Constitution as authority for subjecting anyone attempting to enter the house of a citizen without a search warrant to heavy though unspecified penalties in proportion to the "aggravation of said offence."[71] Lincoln promptly vetoed the measure and the Federalists in the Senate lacked the required two-thirds majority to override his negative.[72] But Lincoln could not stop the Senate from printing five hundred copies of the joint committee's report and resolutions that accompanied it together with a text of the bill. On the same day that the Massachusetts Senate ordered these documents distributed throughout the state, copies of the resolutions and the bill to prevent searches of dwelling houses appeared in Washington's *National Intelligencer*.[73]

Capitulating to the Minority

The resolutions of the Massachusetts legislature together with the vetoed bill arrived in the nation's capital just as Congress was about to count the electoral vote. Though the composition of the Electoral College had seemed to make it a foregone conclusion that Madison would be the next president, nervousness about the upcoming transition in the shadow of what appeared to be imminent war had contributed to the failure of executive leadership when, in retrospect, divisions within Republican congressional ranks so urgently called for it.[74] On the same day that Madison's election was confirmed, William B. Giles rose in the

Senate to move for the repeal of the embargo except as it applied "to Great Britain and France, and their dependencies." Giles's proposal called for "prohibiting all commercial intercourse with those nations and their dependencies" and a ban on "the importation of any article into the United States, the growth, produce, or manufacture" of either nation. Additionally, Giles sought to exclude "all foreign armed ships from the waters of the United States."[75] He intended his measure as a compromise to accommodate the Northeast. Though Giles felt the embargo would have worked had its effectiveness not been undermined by the opposition, he was prepared to make this concession in the hope that the majority of New Englanders would soon realize that Britain was the nation's "real enemy" and that an eventual declaration of war against her was inevitable. Giles acknowledged France's behavior was little better, but only Britain had the power to maintain her "monstrous and extravagant claim . . . to the despotism of the ocean." Giles hoped to win Federalist support for his proposal by showing that Britain's objective was monopolizing the world's seaborne commerce. He also attacked the idea that because Britain was seriously threatened by France, it was not in the Republic's interest to resist her invasion of American rights. Giles assumed Britain would eventually win the European war because Napoleon's dictatorship was less politically stable than Britain's monarchy. This meant that Britain's "lawless, unrelenting power" constituted the primary threat to the nation's future. Once the opposition abandoned their "prejudices and jealousies," Giles was confident they would join in the national effort against her, possibly as early as May.[76]

The response of Federalist senators to Giles's motion was not encouraging. On February 14, James Bayard of Delaware construed non-intercourse directed against both powers as, in effect, a measure designed, as Giles had confessed, to lead to war with Britain. If there were to be war, Bayard thought it more to the nation's interest to wage it against France. Senator James Lloyd from Massachusetts elaborated on Bayard's argument, claiming that non-intercourse was simply a disguised way of declaring war against Britain. Since the British would continue capturing American ships evading her orders, a war—for which the United States was totally unprepared—would inevitably erupt between the two nations. Lloyd added that a war against France similar to the Quasi-War of 1798–1800 would lead to a reconciliation with Britain and produce the same "*cornucopia* of wealth to our country" as the Anglo-American rapprochement of 1795–1799 had.[77] Hillhouse reiterated Lloyd's claim that non-intercourse was the equivalent of a declaration of war against Britain, hammering at what had clearly emerged as the weak point of the Republican coalition.[78] Unfortunately, the Republican response to Federalist objections in the Senate has not survived. The record only shows that a decisive majority endorsed Giles's proposal.

In the House, where a motion for modifying the embargo easily trumped Nicholas's attempt to replace the embargo with naval warfare, a record of the debate survives. Quincy greeted non-intercourse as the Federalists in the Senate had, by calling for the abandonment of all efforts at commercial coercion, both because they were useless and because they made reconciliation with Great Britain impossible. "As long as they remained, the people in the portion of country [from] whence he came, would not deem an unsuccessful attempt at negotiation to be a cause for war." Since Quincy was under pressure to state the circumstances in which New Englanders would accept a war he had alleged the Republicans could not be "kicked into," he added that once "an earnest attempt at negotiation . . . unimpeded with these restrictions" failed, the easterners "would join heartily in a war."[79] Nicholas was unimpressed with Quincy's pledge and complained of "thirteen or fourteen States" having to "submit to [the dictates of] one," which was no different than Congress "transfer[ing] its powers to any State Legislature, or to any town."[80] David R. Williams added sarcastically that Quincy seemed to have forgotten part of the Massachusetts "creed," which called for "Unfurl[ing] the banners of the Republic against the imperial standard!" This, he added, in an allusion to Canning's letter to Pinkney of September 23, 1808, which had first appeared in the *New England Palladium* on January 6, was "just such a project as Mr. Canning might dictate."[81]

The "Massachusetts 'creed' " Williams referred to was the report of a committee of the state House of Representatives written by Christopher Gore that had just appeared in the *National Intelligencer*.[82] Though of humble origins, Gore's father had been a loyalist and had fled the country during the Revolution. The son, a Harvard graduate, had remained behind, serving as an officer in the Continental artillery, though his duties had been largely clerical ones. After the war, young Gore became committed to strengthening the federal government. He represented Boston in the Massachusetts ratifying convention of 1787 and was appointed by Washington to serve as the first U.S. attorney for the district of Massachusetts. In 1796 Washington had named him to the claims commission set up under Article Seven of the Jay Treaty. Unlike some Americans, Gore was well received in England and enjoyed his service there until 1804, when the commission disbanded. On returning to Massachusetts, he had entered the state senate in 1806, participated as counsel for the defense in the Selfridge murder trial, and eventually was elected to the state House of Representatives in 1808 after a failed gubernatorial challenge to Sullivan. Everyone expected Gore to be the Federalist candidate for governor again in April 1809 and it was widely understood that he had authored the committee report on Edward A. Crowninshield's resolutions, proposed the previous November to counter the opposition to the embargo articulated in the Wheaton Resolves, with this ambition in mind.[83]

Gore's report, dated January 28, 1809, accused the federal government of being so partial in its release of information about the nation's foreign relations, over which it had exclusive jurisdiction, as to deprive the committee of adequate grounds on which to evaluate the resolutions in question. However, since Crowninshield's resolutions had suggested that both belligerents "had, with equal wantonness" violated the rights of the United States, the committee felt justified in correcting the idea "that the same measure of opposition . . . to both nations, was . . . required." Gore's report reviewed the course pursued by the two belligerents against neutral commerce, omitting—as Pickering had in his *Letter* of the previous year—all reference to the British blockade of May 1806. Doing so was crucial to representing Britain as retaliating French aggressions rather than initiating them. Gore then taxed Jefferson for failing to resist France's Berlin Decree, as he argued the Adams administration had resisted a similar measure in 1798. His report concluded by calling on the federal government to "repeal the Embargo, annul the Convention [of 1800] with *France*[,] forbid all commercial intercourse with the French dominions, arm our public and private ships, and unfurl the republican banner against the imperial standard." After two days of deliberation, the House accepted his report by a large majority.[84]

The pithy conclusion of Gore's report appeared in the *National Intelligencer* in the same issue as the text of the Senate's reply to Lincoln. They followed by less than a week publication of the inflammatory resolves the Massachusetts legislature had adopted accompanying the bill making it a state crime to execute portions of the federal Enforcement Act. The House reply to Lincoln appeared in the next issue.[85] Such a barrage signaled to congressional Republicans that the situation in Massachusetts was completely out of control. If there were any lingering doubts on that score, they were dispelled by yet another legislative report censuring Lincoln for executing the Enforcement Act. It condemned him for bypassing high-ranking Federalist militia officers in readying troops to assist the collectors. This report concluded that there was nothing in either "the Constitution or Laws of the United States [that] authorizes the President, under existing circumstances," to summon "the militia of this State" to assist the civil magistrates. The committee disposed of the objection that the Enforcement Act of January 9, 1809, had done just that by citing a legislative resolve declaring the act unconstitutional. The report argued instead that Lincoln's actions violated the Massachusetts Constitution, the state's Bill of Rights, and Massachusetts law.[86]

By February 15, Congressman David R. Williams had more on his mind than Gore's exhortation to "unfurl the republican banner against the imperial standard." He also had evidence that other states were joining Massachusetts in sponsoring sedition against federal laws. That is why he proposed that instead of non-intercourse, prohibitive duties on all goods imported from Britain and France replace the embargo. He justified breaking with the Republican leadership because he had "just learned that the Governor of the State of Connecticut had refused to execute the injunctions of the President made in pursuance of a law of the United States. If the embargo could not be executed," Williams concluded "that certainly a non-intercourse could not."[87] Williams referred to the answer of Governor Jonathan Trumbull to Secretary of War Dearborn's January 18 letter asking Trumbull to designate militia officers that the collectors in the state's ports might apply to for assistance. On February 4, Trumbull had declined to do so, denying that the president was authorized "under the constitution or laws of the United States" to make such a request."[88] This was tame compared to the response the Federalist press in Massachusetts had given to Dearborn's directive of January 23. But the development shocked Williams and other congressional Republicans because it marked a significant shift in Connecticut's conduct.

The previous autumn the Connecticut legislature had passed a series of resolves condemning the embargo that were nonetheless exemplary when compared to what was transpiring in Massachusetts. The Connecticut General Assembly then disclaimed any "right of immediate interference, in the foreign relations of our Country" and confined its objections to enumerating the "unnecessary and grievous" domestic effects of the embargo.[89] A minority protest that appeared in Hartford's *American Mercury* seemed to overrespond to the legislature's action, denouncing its resolutions for attempting to "*correct, control, counteract or awe* the regular deliberation and action of the constituted authorities of the nation."[90] In fact, though the minority's language described the course of action taken by Federalist towns and county conventions in Massachusetts far better than the behavior of the Connecticut legislature, it accurately registered the influence the larger state could be expected to exercise over its smaller neighbor.

Trumbull's response to Henry Dearborn charted a new course that confirmed the minority's concern when the governor declared it to be "the opinion of the great mass of the citizens of this state, that the late law of congress for the more rigorous enforcement of the embargo, is *unconstitutional* in many of its provisions, interfering with the state sovereignties, and subversive of the guaranteed rights, privileges, and immunities of the citizens of the United States: I have from these considerations, deemed it peculiarly and highly improper for a state executive to contribute his voluntary aid in support of laws bearing such an aspect."[91] Trumbull's claim that the state's citizens were convinced of the Enforcement Act's unconstitutionality rested on the resolves of far fewer towns than had spoken on the matter in Massachusetts.[92] But Williams also knew that Trumbull had summoned his legislature into emergency session in response to the request by these towns that he do so. If the Federalist-dominated legislature of Massachusetts was any guide, no good was likely to issue from this session, especially since it was unlikely the governor of Connecticut would have taken so strong a stand were he not confident that his sentiments would subsequently be endorsed.

Williams's worst fears proved to be justified. When the Connecticut legislature met on February 23, Trumbull declared, "Whenever our National Legislature is led to overleap the prescribed bounds of their Constitutional powers, on the state legislatures, in great emergencies, devolves the arduous task . . . to interpose their protecting shield between the rights and liberties of the people and the assumed power of the General Government."[93] The General Assembly then passed a set of resolutions approving of the governor's actions, pronouncing the embargo and the Enforcement Act "incompatible with the Constitution of the United States," and warning all executive officers in the state that they were "restrained . . . from affording any official aid, or cooperation" in executing them. The General Assembly also pledged collaboration with Massachusetts in seeking such amendments to the Constitution as were "necessary to obtain more effectual protection . . . for Commerce." Finally it framed an inflammatory address asserting that the embargo and Enforcement Act were unconstitutional and provided for its distribution to the people of Connecticut.[94] This time the protests of the Republican minority in Connecticut's General Assembly would ring truer, though they would be equally ineffectual.

The transformation that had occurred in Connecticut also seemed to be spreading to the other New England states. Representative Benjamin Talmadge of Connecticut had drawn Congress's attention to a Vermont grand jury that had presented as a grievance one of Jefferson's proclamations ordering local civil and military officers to interdict the movement of goods into Canada. Congressional Republicans like Williams were also aware that the New Hampshire legislature had recently shifted from grudging acquiescence to outright opposition to the embargo. Then there was the refusal of some Rhode Island militiamen to obey their governor's orders to enforce the law, apparently at the behest of the resolves of a Providence town meeting.[95] The behavior of the smaller New England states could be blamed on the example of Massachusetts, but that failed to neutralize the double benefit the Federalists derived from New England's disaffection. A divided republic could no more expect to wage a successful war than it could expect to sustain a prolonged embargo. War or the embargo under such circumstances was more likely to breed civil war and disunion.

From the congressional Republicans' perspective, dodging the humiliating alternatives of having to deploy force against one's own people or submitting to

the edicts of a foreign power hinged on the people of the Massachusetts repudiating the state's Federalist leadership in the spring elections.[96] The problem
Republican congressmen faced as the winter waned was how to promote such a
change. Giles's proposal for substituting a non-intercourse directed exclusively at
Britain and France in place of the embargo offered Republicans some prospect
for escaping from their dilemma. On February 16, Wilson Cary Nicholas
announced in the House that he would support Giles's proposal despite his conviction that the only honorable alternative to the embargo was war. Nicholas was
prepared to abandon arming American merchantmen in favor of non-intercourse
because he recognized that unity among the Republicans was necessary in
responding to the crisis created by "one of the States of this Union [which was]
about to pass a law, imposing penalties on persons employed in the execution of
[Congress's] laws within that State." Nicholas hoped that Massachusetts would
not enact such a law, and, if it did, that "the people at the spring elections, will
choose men solicitous to heal, by every means within their power, the wounds
inflicted on the Constitution." If "the people of Massachusetts" did not "apply
the proper corrective," then it was an open question whether the other states
would preserve a political connection with those who denied the binding
authority of the general government by punishing "the public officers of the
United States . . . for the faithful performances of their duty." Non-intercourse
recommended itself as a way of abandoning the embargo—which was destroying
the Republicans in New England—without completely surrendering the sovereignty of the nation to a Federalist minority.[97]

Though both Giles in the Senate and Nicholas in the House promoted non-
intercourse as a rallying point for those interested in supporting the authority of
the national government, disillusioned Republicans joined irreconcilable
Federalists in attacking the measure. Thus representative William Milnor of
Pennsylvania, a Federalist, agreed with the Republican David R. Williams that
because the embargo could not be enforced, neither could non-intercourse. Led
by Quincy, the Federalists sought abandonment of all efforts at commercial
coercion.[98] They argued that Britain's dependence on seaborne trade would
justify her in regarding non-intercourse as a provocation. Republican critics, on
the other hand, feared that the measure amounted to submission to Britain since
her naval superiority ensured that British vessels would have access to American
trade through neutral intermediaries, which she could deny to France.[99]
Ambiguity about whether non-intercourse was resistance or capitulation together
with a fear that it would bear disproportionately on the South and West led
Republicans like John Clopton of Virginia to join George Campbell and
Nathaniel Macon, who were cool to war but regarded capitulation as unacceptable, in rallying support among Republicans for the original embargo.[100] But the

growing opposition of New England Republicans as well as the Federalist insistence that the embargo had to go—because it was unenforceable—quickly aborted such efforts.[101] John Randolph's assessment "We are marked, not merely to Europe, but to ourselves, as a divided people, imbecile and distracted" seemed altogether too apt.[102]

The Federalists still could not be sure that a declaration of war would not follow abandonment of the embargo. Efforts continued during the last week of February to amend the non-intercourse bill so as to authorize naval warfare against both great powers or against one whenever the other lifted its decrees or orders.[103] The Massachusetts legislature responded to the threat by framing a memorial to Congress designed to block such a development. The memorial construed non-intercourse against both belligerents to be in reality a measure directed only against Britain, the "natural tendency" of which would lead to war with her that "would necessarily produce a fatal alliance with France." It raised the same objection against arming American merchantmen. The memorial claimed Napoleon's "contemptuous indifference" to "the sacred obligations of our treaty with that Government, and the established principles of the law of Nations" made an accommodation impossible. This the memorial contrasted with Britain's "strong desire to make atonement and compensation for injuries . . . and to adjust the respective rights and claims of the two Nations on such a basis as to prevent future Collisions." Even if France and Britain were considered on a par in respect to their decrees and orders, Congress should consider "the present state of the World" in deciding against which to go to war. Siding with Britain against France would allow the nation "the satisfaction of aiding in that glorious struggle now carried on in Europe against the tyranny of France." But if the United States sided with France, "we should necessarily aid the gigantic strides of her Emperor towards universal Dominion, and assist in annihilating the Independence of Nations, and the Freedom of the World."[104]

The Senate accorded the Massachusetts memorial a warmer welcome than the House, entering it into its journal at James Lloyd's request, which ensured it would be printed at government expense. When Quincy tried to get the House to follow suit, Thomas Newton of Virginia objected that the memorial served only "party purposes." Quincy countered that "the right of a Legislature to comment on the measures of the Government" was secured by the Constitution and argued that because the memorial "articulated the opinion of a large commercial State," it was "entitled . . . to the attention of the House." But James Holland of North Carolina observed that "there was not a new idea contained in the memorial; not one which the gentleman had not favored the House with during the session, and some of them in the very words of the gentleman himself." Objections like this persuaded Quincy to settle for referral to a committee since the House's passage of the Non-Intercourse Act as the session approached termination seemed to preclude a declaration of war against Britain.[105] The fourteenth section of the new measure repealed the embargo as of March 15 except insofar as it affected Britain and France. Non-intercourse was not to take effect until May 20, 1809, so that all parties affected might have ample advance warning. The Senate agreed to the law the following day.[106] Federalist congressmen had enough wit to realize that Britain was unlikely to go to war over non-intercourse, especially after the reverses she had recently suffered in Spain, and that the victory, at least for the moment, was theirs. They had neglected, however, to count the cost.

4

PAYING THE PIPER

An imminent change in national administrations during the winter of 1809 had contributed to the willingness of the Republican majority in Congress to replace the embargo with something less than a declaration of war against one or both of the belligerents. Most agreed that if war were to be declared, it had best be done by the new Congress scheduled to meet at the end of May 1809 rather than having the Tenth Congress bestow such an onerous burden on its successor and a new president. Warnings from New England's Republican congressmen that embarking on a foreign war could lead to a civil war also had their effect, though here the actual danger derived as much from the Republican response to the Federalists as from Federalist threats of resistance and secession. The Republicans of Essex County in Massachusetts resolved to form voluntary associations to enforce the embargo and pledged that five thousand of them would oppose any attempt to sever the Union and link New England with Britain, a sentiment with which the Republicans of distant Hancock County in Maine concurred.[1] The Republicans of Litchfield County, Connecticut, condemned "*the attempt* to *form a combination* of the *legislatures* of *the several states*; for the *avowed purpose* of *controlling* the *measures* of the *General Government*" and pledged their lives in resisting "any *forcible* opposition" to the laws of the United States.[2] These voices were seconded by others outside New England. The Republican Committee of Salem County, New Jersey, vowed "to use every exertion in support of the government of our choice against the wicked machinations of those who are attempting to overthrow it."[3] And the Republican Committee of Talbot County, Maryland, after branding the Federalists as "MEN of expatriate principles, subsidiary to a foreign Power, divesting themselves of, and discarding every Principle of DUTY," promised "at every hazard of our Lives & Fortunes to support the Government of our Choice."[4]

The Federalists did nothing to diffuse the atmosphere of crisis that surrounded Madison's accession to the presidency. Instead of letting nonintercourse stand as a humiliating confirmation that the Republicans could not be "kicked into war," they continued to protest that the measure risked war with Britain. But since Britain had declined to use the embargo as a pretext for retaliating against the United States, either militarily or commercially, she was unlikely to do so in response to non-intercourse. And a bargain between Madison and the British minister in Washington, David Erskine, struck forty-five days after the new president's inauguration, entirely eliminated that risk. In it Erskine pledged that his government would suspend its objectionable Orders-in-Council by June 10 if Madison suspended non-intercourse against Britain. Since Erskine claimed he was fully empowered to offer these terms and confirmation from Britain could not be expected until long after non-intercourse was scheduled to go into effect on May 20, Madison issued a proclamation on April 19 suspending the law insofar as it affected Britain.[5]

With the lifting of the embargo on March 15, hundreds of American merchant vessels that had been held in their home ports, some for more than year, set sail. Under the Erskine Agreement these vessels could make directly for British ports and bring back British goods on their return voyages. Nothing could have been more gratifying to Federalist merchants interested in the British trade. The Republicans had their own reasons for heaving a huge sigh of relief. Instead of having to decide between war and peace, the first session of the Eleventh Congress would only need to make minor adjustments in existing law to implement the Erskine Agreement. Though the bargain failed to address the issue of impressment, the Madison administration was grateful for a respite from the ferocious partisanship that had characterized national politics while the embargo was in effect. Republicans in general felt they had purchased domestic peace with honor, since they could claim that their restrictive commercial system had produced a desired change in British policy. The Federalist press countered by claiming their opposition to all commercial restraints had produced the desired effect. Practically speaking both sides were winners since the Federalists got access to the overseas commerce they desired while the administration could look forward to a restoration of public revenues that had suffered badly as a consequence of the embargo.[6]

Responding to the Repudiation

The general elation vanished quickly. Upon receiving word of what David Erskine had wrought, his government immediately repudiated the agreement on the grounds that Erskine had exceeded his powers. Transatlantic communications were such that the first unambiguous indication that the British government would not stand by its ambassador's pact did not arrive until after the first session of the Eleventh Congress had adjourned, and official word was not received until mid-July.[7] Madison heard of the repudiation while at his Virginia home, Montpellier, after the national government had gone into summer recess. Though Congress had empowered the president to suspend the Non-intercourse Act as it affected any belligerent that revoked its commercial restrictions, the law made no provision for the situation he now faced. This left Madison uncertain as to whether he possessed the legal authority to reimpose non-intercourse. Consultation with his scattered cabinet took another two weeks, so it was not until August 9 that he issued a proclamation reinstating non-intercourse against Great Britain.[8] By then the vast majority of return voyages were already under way, leaving the Republican policy of trying to bring commercial pressure to bear against the belligerents in complete tatters.[9]

The British Ministry also replaced Erskine with Sir Francis Jackson. Jackson had acquired the infamous nickname of "Copenhagen" Jackson for the role he had played in delivering the British ultimatum to Denmark's prince regent demanding the surrender of the Danish fleet. Designating Jackson as Erskine's replacement seemed to send the message that the United States should not expect conciliatory overtures from the British government, especially as Jackson did not come empowered as a minister plenipotentiary.[10] Some Republicans urged Madison to refuse to receive him, but the president had good reason for disregarding this advice.[11] Jackson might still be authorized to make atonement for the repudiation of the Erskine Agreement, perhaps involving satisfaction, however belated, for the *Chesapeake* incident. Moreover, on May 24 the British Ministry had waived the force of its Orders-in-Council, at least until July 20, so far as they affected American vessels that had cleared under the assumption that a suspension had taken place. Republican critics dismissed this as just another British ruse, since the exemption was not officially communicated until July 31 and would not be known in some of the nation's seaports until early August.[12] But together with a new Order-in-Council dated April 26 that liberalized restrictions on the northern European trade even as it proclaimed a blockade of Holland, France, and Italy, the waiver supported Federalist claims that Britain's intentions toward the Republic remained reasonable and honorable.[13]

A copy of Canning's instructions of January 23 to Erskine, which was released to support the foreign minister's contention that Erskine had exceeded his powers, arrived in America at the end of July.[14] The instructions contained three stipulations: (1) that the United States repeal all restrictions on Britain's public as well as private vessels; (2) that it acknowledge the validity of the Rule of 1756 which denied neutrals access to a trade in wartime they had not enjoyed in peacetime; and (3) that it consent to the Royal Navy's enforcement of U.S. commercial restrictions against France. Republican commentators dismissed the instructions as the manifestations of a "proud and insolent government" and clung to Erskine's claim that his actions had been authorized by inferring the existence of additional, secret instructions. The Republican press suspected Canning of plotting to lure the nation's commercial vessels onto the high seas for the purpose of seizing them if they did not choose to make for British ports once the agreement had been repudiated.[15] Republicans also accused the Federalists of inviting the British repudiation by irresponsibly portraying the administration as being under French influence. And they vociferously denied a rumor circulating in the Federalist press that the administration had known Erskine was exceeding his instructions when entering into the agreement.[16]

Federalist commentators countered by excelling their Republican adversaries in making heroic inferences from limited information. The Federalist press asserted that Madison had concluded the agreement in full knowledge that a repudiation would be forthcoming in order to inflame popular sentiment against Britain.[17] A writer in the Baltimore *North American* complained that "[t]he *French faction* in this country are once more calling all hell to their aid to prevent a friendly arrangement with Great Britain and to engage us in a war with that country." This writer went on to suggest that criticism of Britain was being sponsored by Secretary of State Robert Smith's family, which had $400,000 worth of property sequestered in France. The Smiths, with other Americans in a similar situation, had an interest in going to war with Britain because Napoleon was unlikely to release their property unless the United States acceded to the emperor's wishes.[18] While placing responsibility for the collapse of the agreement on the Republicans, the Federalist press denied that the actions of the British government were hostile toward the Republic.

As Jackson began a series of informal meetings with the secretary of state in early October, he could not have been oblivious to the controversy surrounding his mission. It quickly emerged that he had nothing further to offer by way of explanation for his government's repudiation of the Erskine Agreement. He also lacked powers to enter into any arrangement that could lead Great Britain to revoke its Orders-in-Council that did not observe the restrictions contained in the published instructions to Erskine. Once Madison realized what the administration was confronting, he insisted that Smith and Jackson confine themselves to formal, written exchanges. Besides creating an official record, this allowed the president to exercise control over Smith, whom he did not fully trust.

In these written communications Jackson continued to insist that no explanation of the British government's repudiation of the agreement was in order beyond the publication of Canning's instructions of January 23, 1809. He also claimed these instructions had been communicated to Madison prior to the conclusion of the agreement, which implied that Madison had known that

Erskine was acting without authority. Finally Jackson denied Erskine had additional instructions, as the American government assumed, and he rejected Smith's claim that had the United States government known the published instructions were the only instructions, it would have declined entering into the agreement. Structuring his exchanges with Smith in this manner supported the inference current in the Federalist press that the administration had had from the start objectives other than an Anglo-American reconciliation.[19]

Had Jackson's correspondence with Smith remained confidential, such allegations might possibly have been forgiven if not forgotten in the ensuing give and take of negotiation. But everyone knew that whatever Jackson committed to paper would almost certainly one day appear in print. Nor could Jackson have been oblivious to the way the Republicans were likely to react to his stoking the fires that the Federalist press was busy kindling. On November 8, the administration responded to his "gross insinuation" by notifying him that it would receive no further communications from him and would request his recall.[20]

Jackson's dismissal confirmed the Federalists in their assessment of Republican motives, since in their estimate the administration again hazarded a rupture with Great Britain. Risk there may have been, but it remained unlikely that the situation would spiral into a war because Britain's attention was focused on the European conflict; French victories in central Europe—particularly Napoleon's decisive triumph over the Austrians at Wagram on July 5–6—had allowed the emperor to redeploy his forces against the British in Spain and Portugal. Risk also was low because the administration had instructed William Pinkney in London to assure the ministry that the United States would welcome any envoy that could contribute to improving relations between the two countries.[21]

The American public first learned of Jackson's dismissal from a brief notice in the *National Intelligencer* that appeared on November 13. That same day Jackson drafted a circular to the British consuls in the United States informing them of his dismissal. On November 21 the Georgetown *Independent American* published a copy of his circular. In it Jackson justified his behavior by claiming his only offense had been to insist on two points. The first was that Erskine's instructions had been communicated to Madison before the conclusion of the agreement, which he claimed the secretary of state had admitted was the case; and, the other, that these instructions were the only ones Erskine was empowered to act on. Jackson then added disingenuously, "In stating these facts . . . I could not imagine that offence would be taken at it by the American government, as most certainly none could be intended on my part." The secretary of state subsequently described Jackson's circular as an appeal from the British government to the American people.[22]

During the autumn of 1809 Madison was less concerned about the encouragement Jackson gave to the domestic opposition than would have been the case had the incident occurred earlier in his presidency. Britain's repudiation of the agreement spoke far louder than any words that could be mobilized to justify it. In the same letter in which Madison communicated to Pinkney the course that the Smith-Jackson negotiation had taken, he expressed his confidence that "public opinion" was rallying to "the system pursued in our foreign relations." That optimism was based in part on the recent elections in Maryland, where the Republicans had regained a small majority in the House of Delegates, and in Vermont, where the legislature had elected a Republican governor and council. In addition, reports from Massachusetts, New Hampshire, and Rhode Island "prognosticate[d] that the next elections . . . will reverse those which took place during the fever which the Embargo was made to produce." Finally, the public's disappointment with the extent of the trade licensed by the Erskine Agreement, which was "limited to the B[ritish]. dominions," and which Madison described as "but a mouthfull, and not as the people were told it wd. be a bellyfull," was having a beneficial effect. All these considerations made Madison confident that Congress would "in some form . . . keep up a counteraction to the misconduct of both Belligerents."[23]

The eagerness with which the Republican press blamed Jackson's behavior on the Federalists confirmed the president's sense that public sentiment was shifting in the Republicans' favor. "Columbianus," writing in the *Essex Register*, ascribed Jackson's conduct in large part to "the men who pass among the first in our country" and who considered "[t]he cause of Britain . . . their own cause." Another writer in the same paper proclaimed Jackson's "insolent and inflammatory libels on the administration of our government" to be "the diabolical productions of a British faction, nourished and supported within our country by the British government to alienate the affections of the people from the republican form of government." He condemned the Federalists for justifying Britain's policy of "rapine and plunder" as part of a *"grand and philanthropic design"* and for their willingness to accept Americans being "denationalized by the omnipotence of a press-gang" because Britain was contending for the "LIBERTIES OF THE WORLD."[24]

On November 29 the administration released the diplomatic correspondence between Smith and Jackson as Madison addressed the newly assembled second session of the Eleventh Congress.[25] The official record paved the way for a more pointed gloss on Jackson's conduct in a *National Intelligencer* piece in which Madison very likely had a hand. Its author, "Publius" found Jackson's lack of empowerment by his home government as objectionable as his insistence that the United States had known Erskine was violating his instructions. By limiting himself to receiving only such proposals as the American government chose to make for settling outstanding disputes, Jackson had "constitute[d] himself a tribunal for deciding upon the propositions of the American government." Jackson thereby placed himself in a position where he would be under no pressure to accede to an accommodation unless the United States bid high enough for one. "Publius" argued that Jackson would not have dared to behave in such a manner had he not assumed "there . . . is a British party in America." His boasts about Britain's "great system of policy" in relation to neutral commerce, "*deliberately adopted and acted on*" were not geared to Republican sensibilities. He also insinuated that Americans had abandoned "honorable and manly resistance" to Napoleonic despotism, though it was very much alive "in the Sovereign of the British nation and in the hearts of his subjects." Few readers could fail to identify in Jackson's words an echo of Timothy Pickering's claim that Britain alone stood as "a barrier to the entire submission of Europe to the power of the emperor of the French."[26]

Republicans thought that Jackson's provocative behavior would at least help to unite all patriotic Americans. Well before the "Publius" series appeared another writer in the *National Intelligencer* had expressed the hope "that the honorable portion of the federalist party . . . would rally around their government."[27] But the Federalist press unabashedly embraced Jackson's cause as their own. Almost immediately, it protested that Jackson had not given the offense the administration had taken. A writer in the *Connecticut Mirror* responded to the publication of the Jackson-Smith correspondence together with the commentary of "Publius" on it by defying anyone to find in the diplomatic exchange evidence of "*official indecorum.*" Instead Federalist commentators accused the administration of treating Jackson badly and the *National Intelligencer* of trying to incite the public against anyone who claimed the contrary.[28] From there it was but a small step to arguing that the real cause of the government's disgust with Jackson was that he did indeed have full powers to settle all the differences between the two countries. A newspaper essay titled "The Diplomatic Policy of Mr. Madison Unveiled" reasserted the now hackneyed notion that the administration had from the first seen the Erskine Agreement as an opportunity for provoking a crisis with Britain and that Jackson's dismissal without cause showed its continued adherence to this strategy.[29]

Republicans were outraged at Federalist behavior. "Columbianus" accused those who protested that Jackson had been dismissed for insufficient reason of seeking to "dissolve our union." He particularly objected to "British hirelings" insulting "us with the condemnations of our own government." "Marblehead" blamed the insults to which the United States had been repeatedly subject on "a domestic faction" that thought nothing of violating its country's laws and frequently menacing the government "with insurrections and rebellion." After reviewing the course that Britain had pursued toward the United States from the

Peace of 1783 to the treachery of the Erskine Agreement, capped by Jackson's insults, "Timoleon" called "for open WAR."[30]

Though their aversion to war had proven to be the Achilles heel of the Republicans during the second session of the Tenth Congress, the Federalists were cautious about approaching the public at large as they had the nation's legislature lest an enraged public pressure Congress into a conflict the Federalists wanted to avoid. Realizing they were playing with fire, they adopted a more defensive stance, at least for the moment. They tried to assuage the public's anger by warning against allowing a false sense of dignity mixed with a desire for revenge and malice to "disgrace this country." And they reminded Americans that as an appeal to the public against the government, Jackson's behavior came nowhere near what Edmund Genêt had been guilty of in 1793 when he had appealed to the American people against Washington's Neutrality Proclamation.[31] Finally, they drew attention to the increasing pressure France was exerting against American shipping while ignoring that it might stem from the French perception that non-intercourse favored Britain at France's expense.[32]

The respective responses of the partisan press to Jackson's dismissal demonstrated that for the moment, at least, the public would speak in a voice divided along partisan lines. In the absence of a chief executive who was prepared to assume responsibility for shaping public opinion, the best prospect for extracting unity from the collapse of Jackson's mission lay with Congress. Madison declined openly to advise the Eleventh Congress on what course it should follow beyond expressing his hope that whatever it did would command "a unanimity becoming the Occasion, and be supported by every portion of our citizens."[33] On December 5, William B. Giles assumed the initiative with a lengthy resolution that he laid before the Senate. It condemned Jackson's correspondence with Smith for conveying the "highly indecorous and insolent" notion that the U.S. government had entered the late arrangement knowing full well that Erskine lacked "competent powers." It also denounced Jackson's circular to the British consuls as an "aggravated insult and affront to the American people and their Government" that attempted "to excite their resentments and distrust against their own Government." And it concluded with a pledge to support the executive's dismissal of Jackson, promising if necessary "to call into action the whole force of the nation . . . to repel such insults and to assert and maintain the rights, the honor, and the interests of the United States."[34]

The resolution set off a prolonged debate in both houses of Congress that yielded something very different from unanimity. Giles's decision to highlight the belligerent implications of his resolution may have been partially responsible for the ensuing debacle.[35] Though most of his comments focused on Jackson's behavior, Giles also stressed the real possibility that Britain would respond to Jackson's dismissal and the reimposition of non-intercourse by declaring war. Giles assumed that the prospect of war with Britain would silence the opposition, but he added that those who desired peace would be more likely to get their wish by supporting the government. His pleas for unity had some effect on the Senate, which endorsed his resolution in mid-December with only the senators from Connecticut and Massachusetts opposing.[36] But the fate of his resolution in the House, where it had been forwarded, was far less encouraging. The debate there lasted for the better part of three weeks—December 18 to January 5—during which time it encountered fierce opposition. Unlike the Senate debate, the House debate gave rise to as many expressions of opposition as support for the foreign policy of the administration. It also led to an extended discussion of whether the nation was ready or able to wage war against Great Britain as House Federalists seized on Giles's tactical blunder to renew the pressure that had been so effective in dissolving the Republicans' cohesion in the Tenth Congress.

Elisha Potter from Rhode Island outlined a position that blamed Madison and the Republicans for the current state of Anglo-American relations. Though Potter admitted that Jackson's behavior reflected a hardening of British attitudes toward the Republic, he blamed the embargo for it. "It taught her the imbecility of our own Government to carry it into execution: and it taught her . . . that she could do without us, and that our sufferings by the measure were greater than hers."[37] Potter concluded his tirade by protesting that Jackson's dismissal and Giles's resolution unnecessarily risked provoking a conflict the United States was unprepared for.[38] Samuel Dana of Connecticut, added that issuing hollow military challenges would waste the "national character" just as much as adopting unenforceable regulations like the embargo or the ban on British warships in American waters, which had been defied for several months after it was issued.[39] Laban Wheaton of Massachusetts, rewarded with a seat in the Eleventh Congress for sponsoring the Massachusetts resolves bearing his name in the 1808, objected to embarking on a war without first counting the cost. Invoking memories of the Revolution, he predicted widespread poverty and vice would ensue.[40] Thomas Gold of New York added insult to injury by claiming that Madison had taken advantage of Britain in the Erskine Agreement rather than vice versa, and Edward St. Loe Livermore, Essex County, Massachusetts's Federalist mouthpiece in Congress, questioned the resolution's constitutionality.[41]

The Republicans responded to this cacophony of complaints with expressions of exasperated rage. Richard Johnson of Kentucky asked sarcastically whether the Federalists meant to demonstrate by their opposition to constitutional laws made by Congress that they preferred to have Parliament legislate for them. John Ross of Pennsylvania accused the Federalists of trying to bring down the administration. Nathaniel Macon of North Carolina argued that the embargo had produced the agreement and the repeal of the embargo the repudiation of it. Macon feared that war was the only way to win justice from Britain, but he wished to postpone it as long as possible. Other Republicans blamed the Federalists for leaving only submission or war as available options by sabotaging the embargo.[42] The Virginia Republican Thomas Newton expressed most eloquently the rising anger of his colleagues. "The unprincipled violations of the embargo operated to favor the views of Great Britain, by lessening the efficacy of that salutary measure." Newton denounced the "inflammatory publications against the Government of this nation, opposition to laws constitutionally made, and crude and wicked projects, the object of which was to sever the Union." Such activities inspired "[t]he lynx-eyed tyrants of the world" to "demolish the last asylum which benignant Heaven has given to persecuted man. The British Government would not dare to trample on the rights of the nation if union were to dictate the measures that should govern our conduct in all our foreign relations." Americans could not expect redress so long as "the energy of union is wanting" and "in the estimation of our own rights, intellect is so deficient, as to discern in the acts of the British Government neither insults nor injuries." Newton ended his long, impassioned declaration with a call to his fellow citizens to "rise in the majesty of their strength, and communicate to the national arm the power of the nation."[43]

The House finally endorsed the Giles resolution at 5:30 the morning of January 5, 1810, but the vote was far from unanimous: seventy-two to forty-one. Several prominent Republicans, including Nathaniel Macon, voted with the Federalists against the resolution for procedural reasons. That did not help Macon in subsequently piloting a "navigation" bill through the House after assuming leadership of the Foreign Relations Committee. The bill, which Gallatin and Madison had a hand in shaping, came to be known as Macon's Bill #1. It was designed to shift the burden of commercial coercion from Americans to the belligerents by excluding all British and French vessels, whether public or private, from U.S. ports and confining imports from those countries and their colonies to U.S. vessels coming directly from the point of origin. This last provision was inserted to stop the Halifax trade in the Northeast and Amelia Island trade in the South, which had become the principal routes for evading non-intercourse after it was reimposed against Britain. Macon defended the bill as a compromise that avoided both war and submission by an even-handed affirmation of neutral rights. He also touted it as an improvement on the previous efforts at commercial coercion because it would be easier to enforce and therefore would be sustainable.[44]

Though Macon's Bill #1 received a bad press then and subsequently, it possessed several little-appreciated virtues. First it deprived the Federalists of an opportunity to play on the aversion some Republicans had about going to war. The most Macon's measure risked from Britain was retaliation in kind, which would have had the welcome effect of strengthening non-intercourse and encouraging American manufactures. Macon's Bill #1 was also consistent with Madison's signal that the administration was prepared to receive a new minister from Britain. The only objection to it from the Republican perspective was it was too weak either to have a decisive effect on the belligerents or to shape domestic public opinion. Some expressed a preference for sticking with non-intercourse, even though it was now observed largely in the breach.[45] But these reservations did not stop the House Republicans from passing Macon's Bill #1 with a vote of seventy-three to fifty-two.

The victory proved to be a hollow one because the Senate, led by the secretary of state's brother, Samuel Smith, opposed the bill's commercial restrictions. He succeeded in having the Senate amend it so that it did little more than exclude the public vessels of both powers from American waters.[46] Most historians have construed Smith's opposition to Macon's Bill #1 as reflecting a personal hostility to Gallatin. The secretary of the treasury believed eliminating the public debt was still the nation's first priority. Short of being able to pay it down, Gallatin was determined so far as possible to resist its increase. From his perspective war was to be avoided if at all possible since war could lead to unrestrained borrowing. If an expanding debt did not eventuate in the oppression of the people to satisfy the claims of public creditors, it was still likely to spawn a system of corruption similar to the one Britain's executive was thought to use in managing Parliament. The Smiths and their mouthpiece, the Baltimore *Whig*, resented Gallatin's caution. In this they appeared to be joined by Giles and Michael Leib in the Senate and the influential Philadelphia editor of the Republican *Aurora*, William Duane.[47]

Smith was not advocating capitulation. He favored armed convoys, and the Senate continued to show more interest than the House in naval armaments. The Senate's amendments to Macon's Bill #1, however, gave those in the House who attached importance to its commercial provisions reason to complain that what remained was submission.[48] They persuaded the House to reject the Senate's amendments and to send Macon's Bill #1 back to the upper house for reconsideration. In doing so the majority underscored its continued preference for commercial coercion rather than war. But the Senate refused to budge beyond agreeing to a conference. And the conference got nowhere because Macon feared yielding to the Senate would lead to armed convoys, which in his estimate meant war.[49]

Time and patient work might still have led to a compromise acceptable to the Republican majority in both branches of the legislature had it not been for the eccentric Virginian John Randolph. Though Randolph was absent from the House until March 12 recovering from an illness, he had not been silent. In mid-January he began publishing a series of newspaper essays subsequently reissued in pamphlet form under the pseudonym "Mucius." In the opening essay he stressed the depleted condition of the nation's finances and denied that the administration was in a position to defend itself against insults like Jackson's or to pressure the great powers into doing the Republic justice. Such an approach was calculated to alienate the Smiths, but he made doubly sure of the result by designating the Smith brothers—together with Giles and Joseph Varnum of Massachusetts, who while Speaker of the House had denied Randolph important committee assignments—as the leaders of the French faction in America. Randolph argued that all attempts at commercial coercion had to be abandoned because defending commerce was clearly beyond the government's capacities. Though Randolph did not by himself pose enough of a threat to unite the congressional Republicans, he had served notice that he would support the Federalists in trying to divide the Republicans if and when he returned.[50]

On March 22 Randolph made good on this threat by moving, at the conclusion of a lengthy debate on continuing the volunteer army instituted by the previous Congress, for a reduction of the military establishment. Eight days later, just after the House voted to adhere to its version of Macon's Bill #1, he moved for a repeal of all commercial restrictions.[51] Randolph's second motion placed the House in an awkward situation because it allowed him to point to another alternative to Macon's Bill #1 besides war, the threat Macon was using to keep many Republicans in line. Since the Non-Intercourse Law was due to expire at the end of the current session, Congress could simply "sneak out" of non-intercourse by letting the law lapse. In calling Macon's bluff Randolph placed the Republican leadership in a situation that John Taylor, also of Virginia, likened to "floundering in the mud."[52] Faced with the possibility of humiliation, Macon withdrew to his select committee to salvage what he could from the debacle. He emerged a week later with a new proposal, one that was largely the work of Taylor, but to which Macon still lent his name.[53] Macon's Bill #2 strove to command the majority of both houses of Congress by finding their lowest common denominator. The new bill discarded the commercial restrictions of the previous bill, but it tried to avoid total surrender by authorizing the president to reinvoke non-intercourse against either belligerent if the other lifted its commercial restrictions against neutral commerce.[54]

In seeking a majority, Taylor and Macon alienated even further those who had objected to Macon's Bill #1 because it was too weak. Thomas Gholson, of Virginia, protested that Macon's Bill #2 removed "every species of opposition to the belligerent edicts." Gholson wanted to amend Macon's new bill by introducing provisions prohibiting the importation of British and French goods and employing both the army and navy to enforce them. Gholson's suggestion ran counter to a growing concern of some in Congress about the depleted state of the revenue. The embargo and non-intercourse had led to two consecutive Treasury deficits. What was needed was a measure that built up the nation's resources. Richard Johnson, who like Gholson wanted to put some teeth into Macon's Bill #2 and would become a military hero during the War of 1812, proposed that all imports from Britain and France and their respective dependencies bear a duty 50 percent higher than the current rate. Though higher duties would not entirely compensate for the sagging revenue, the proposal carried in the House.[55] To address the remainder of the budgetary shortage, the majority agreed to reductions in the army and navy combined with a hefty rise in internal taxes.

Meanwhile the Senate continued to push for armed convoys and amended Macon's Bill #2 accordingly, but balked at the tax increases voted by the House. Congress only avoided having its session end in a barren deadlock when the Senate agreed to forgo armed convoys in exchange for the House dropping its tax measures. Both then united to pass Macon's Bill #2 into law. But that left the session's principal accomplishment the offer to each of the great powers to ally with it against its adversary once it revoked its commercial restrictions against American commerce. The Republicans in Congress blamed each other as well as the Federalists for failing to provide the people with stronger leadership.[56] Connecticut Federalist Theodore Dwight noted with delight "[t]he 'agonizing spasms' of the old Embargo-gentry, at parting with that last child of the 'Restrictive' family."[57] Nor was Congress's response to the challenge posed by the great powers the only matter on which the second session delivered less than seemed to be called for. It had also failed to make any headway in rechartering the Bank of the United States, whose legal existence would terminate on March 4, 1811. There would be a chance to address these issues again in a third session, scheduled to begin in the late autumn of 1810. However, judging from the current session, little could be expected of it. The only consolation available to disgruntled Republicans was that by the time the Eleventh Congress next met, the people would have spoken with their selection of the Twelfth Congress. But they would have to do so without much guidance from Washington.

Republican Consolations

The repeal of the embargo in March 1809 had failed to save Levi Lincoln from defeat in the ensuing state election. The merciless Federalist onslaught directed at him culminated in a four-thousand-word legislative "Address to the People," in which both Christopher Gore and Harrison Gray Otis undoubtedly had a hand.[58] This address acknowledged that a state legislature's interference in matters delegated to the national government, especially when it involved "negotiations with foreign nations," risked "confusion" that could terminate "in a dissolution of the Union." But it argued that the General Court had no choice but to try stopping "a course of measures to which it is physically as well as morally impossible for the People of this Commonwealth much longer to submit." The petitions flooding the legislature bore witness to "the miseries and grievances of their situation." The address attributed Republican commercial restrictions to a "habitual [but unrealistic] predilection for France." It argued that quarreling "with Great-Britain . . . exposes our country and commerce in every vulnerable point, and affords no hope of honour or indemnity, [while] a war with France would not be very much different from the only state of peace which she is disposed to maintain." It recommended rallying behind the Federalists. The national government would not "willingly drive to extremities a section of the country which they believed to be a united people." But "nothing less than a perfect union . . . among the Eastern States can preserve . . . them." The choice facing the people of Massachusetts was "between . . . [remaining] citizens of a free State . . . or . . . [becoming] a Colony free in name, but in fact enslaved by sister States."

The Federalists did everything in their power to circulate this address as the state elections approached. In addition to having it republished in all the Federalist newspapers, five separate pamphlet editions appeared.[59] The legislature also ordered many of the reports, memorials, and addresses it had produced during its recent winter session collected into a single volume. In addition to its "Address to the People," the volume contained Lincoln's address and the replies of both houses, Gore's report on Crowninshield's resolutions, the report of the joint committee on the town petitions with accompanying resolutions about the unconstitutionality of the Enforcement Act, the report of the House committee on the orders Lincoln had issued the militia, and the memorial of the legislature to Congress. Two thousand copies of *The Patriotick Proceedings of the Legislature of Massachusetts, during their session from Jan. 26 to March 4, 1809* were printed at public expense. Each town in the commonwealth was to receive at least two copies. A preface to the booklet referred to "*the alarming doctines and arbitrary measures of the lieutenant governour*" which had exposed him "*to merited censure.*" It also congratulated the legislature for having "*checked the mad career of a cabinet, which had no guide but its fears and prejudices, and a second time* [for having] *roused our country to a resistance against oppression.*"[60]

The Republicans had little with which to counter this Federalist onslaught aside from the resolves of two county conventions, only one of which was apposite, and a protest signed by eighteen Republican senators against accepting the report on the town petitions.[61] The protest warned that a Federalist-controlled state government might join "[a] partial confederacy of States, against the General Government." The Senate minority pointed to the directive the House and Senate had given their presiding officers to forward the report to "such of our sister States as manifest a disposition to concur with us" as evidence for their claim. They feared partial combinations of the states might "in the progress of excited passions, and the succession of revolutionary events, become *the bloody line of final Separation and* [national]*Dismemberment.*" The Senate minority also challenged the right of a state legislature to pronounce on the constitutionality of a federal law and strongly condemned the Massachusetts legislature for declaring the Enforcement Act "*not legally binding on the citizens of this State.*" Such a resolution had a tendency "to sow the seeds of insubordination, insurrection, disunion, and anarchy" in ways Washington had explicitly warned against in his Farewell Address.

Even had the House minority joined in the protest of the Senate minority, it could hardly have matched the effect of *The Patriotick Proceedings* because the Republicans lacked a network of sympathetic clergy to promote the dissemination of their message.[62] Only the governor's voice might conceivably have checked the influence wielded by the legislature. However, quite apart from the effect that Lincoln's repeated humiliations at the hands of the legislature was having, he had impugned the authority of town meetings in his address to the General Court. This blocked him from issuing official answers to Republican towns that might have addressed him. Lincoln did reply to an address framed by the officers of the Third Division of the Massachusetts militia, which endorsed his orders to enforce the embargo. But instead of presenting himself as someone in command, he came across as a victim by complaining of having, along with the president and "the sovereignty of the Union" been "put under arrest, and on trial . . . before a grand legislative Court of Enquiry" that had condemned and sentenced them "unnotified, unheard and undefended." In addition, "the assertions, statements, and arguments in support of [these condemnations], and only these, have been transmitted to the people . . . for confirmation." Lincoln was clearly perplexed by where all this was leading: "Libels in every shape have assailed our government. Faults of every description have been urged against our rulers." But his warning that the "surrender of our government to excited discontents" could lead to "[s]ubmission to foreign domination" hardly seemed persuasive.[63]

Massachusetts Republicans fared badly in the state's 1809 spring elections. An electorate that expanded by 15 percent, from 79,293 in 1808 to 91,359, elevated Christopher Gore to the chair. The gubernatorial vote, in turn, proved an

accurate predictor of the balance of power in the new legislature. When it came
time to organize the House and Senate, Federalists were found to number 309 in
the House, Republicans 262, and 21 in the Senate, where Republicans held 18
seats.[64] As an added bonus to trashing the embargo and replacing it with a
non-intercourse law that favored Britain, the Federalists had managed to win
complete control of the Massachusetts state government.

However, this moment would prove to be a temporary high point in the
resurgence of the Massachusetts Federalists because of the course taken by the
nation's foreign relations. The Erskine Agreement temporarily removed all
reasons for worrying about the prospect of war with Britain.[65] During its spring
1809 session the Massachusetts legislature had very little to complain about
regarding the administration's foreign policy. Federalist scribblers were quick to
claim credit for the apparent rapprochement with Britain and pressed for a constitutional amendment limiting the duration of future embargoes.[66] But few
thought the moment was ripe for such an initiative because the Massachusetts
legislature had its hands full coping with a regional banking crisis created by the
disruptions that the embargo and non-intercourse had inflicted on New
England's economy. Nor did summoning the legislature back into emergency
session seem appropriate when word was received of the Erskine Agreement's
repudiation since trade remained lawful with Britain until the president's proclamation reimposed non-intercourse. Even then, the northern European trade,
opened to American vessels by Britain's Order-in-Council of April 26, 1809, was
exempt from non-intercourse's prohibitions.[67]

At least one federal district court in New England agreed with Madison's
Federalist critics, who had questioned his legal authority to reimpose non-
intercourse, creating a legal ambiguity of which local merchants readily took
advantage.[68] This would lead to an unsuccessful attempt in the next session of
the Eleventh Congress to waive the penalties incurred by importing British
goods.[69] Federalists construed the announcement that Jackson had been dispatched to Washington as an indication that a showdown with Britain was not
imminent, making a wait-and-see policy a better alternative than putting
Massachusetts to the expense of an additional legislative session before the New
Year. By then Jackson had been dismissed, and the Federal Congress had
endorsed Giles's resolutions. But attempts by Federalist commentators to represent the administration as bent on provoking a war with Britain fell flat.
Disgruntled Republican congressmen at least agreed with Macon that his
proposed measures were designed to avoid war.[70] In his January address to the
Massachusetts legislature Gore still argued that war was probable, but added that
since foreign affairs had been entrusted to the national government, the state
governments could only try to avert the calamity through resolutions and

memorials. His statement, while realistically recognizing the difficulties a state five hundred miles from the nation's capital would encounter in seeking to influence the nation's foreign relations, masked a new complacency.[71]

"Massachusettensis" responded with an alternative address to the legislature explaining why it was their duty to continue meddling in the Republic's foreign affairs.[72] In its reply to Gore's address, the House heeded "Massachusettensis" more than it did Gore by doing everything in its power to exaggerate the danger of war with Britain. Thus the House complained that negotiations with Britain had been broken off just when "all that can be reasonably expected from a successful war seemed to have been attainable by treaty." Though the House could hardly accuse the administration of actively seeking war and retain credibility, it worried that the government still might stumble into a conflict that would ally the United States with a power "whose friendship has proved fatal to so many republics."[73] The Senate, under Otis's presidency, rejected the idea that the administration was pursuing a neutral foreign policy.[74] Both houses then endorsed the lengthy report of a Joint Committee on Foreign Relations that argued a war with Great Britain would be "the greatest calamity that could befal [sic] the *United States*" because it would sweep the nation's vessels from the seas and expose all her seaports to British insult. The joint report also challenged the notion that the conquest of Canada could provide compensation for maritime losses. "It is morally certain, that *Canada*, conquered by the *United States*, would, under the patronage of *France*, become a northern hive, pouring forth successive swarms of Goths and Vandals, which, in alliance with savage tribes, would encompass the Union with a belt." The report concluded by proposing a resolve that measures hostile to Britain were "impolitic" because winning a war against her would leave the nation confronting France "unopposed."[75]

The winter session of the Federalist-dominated General Court declined to circulate this legislative report the way it had *The Patriotick Proceedings* of the preceding year. Instead it settled for publication in the Federalist newspapers throughout southern New England.[76] The hostile reception the report met with in the Republican press and in Republican towns may have exerted some influence here, though in the past the Federalists had been impervious to such pressures.[77] Perhaps the Federalists hoped Jackson, who seemed in no rush to return home, would accept Gore's invitation to visit Massachusetts and that the British envoy's presence would make a far deeper impact than any legislative report could.[78] The state legislature also could not escape the consequence of its peripheral relationship to the national government. What initiatives Congress took would remain unclear until well into the spring. Unless the Massachusetts Federalists were prepared to hold the state's legislature in continuous session until Congress adjourned—which would entail an expense that could not be justified—the best they could do was protest the warlike implications of the administration's policies, without knowing fully what these might be. The difficulty facing the legislature also seems to have inhibited county conventions and towns from acting as they had early in 1809.[79]

Associating the legislature's report with the concerns of Congregationalists remained the Federalists' best option. To this end the *New-England Palladium* inserted "An Appeal to Christians of all Parties, on our duty to preserve a Peace with England" by "Mather" in the same issue with the joint committe report. The appeal painted a picture of Britain as a land experiencing a *"rapid diffusion of pure Evangelical Religion"* and described the best of Nelson's crew at Trafalgar "as a little knot of *evangelical* sailors." It did so to make the point that war against Britain at the side of France would be "a GROSS IMPIETY" because Britain was protecting the rest of the world "from the more desolating taint and pestilence of French principles." This piece also attributed the difficulties the United States was experiencing with Britain to the nation's rebelling "against heaven" by electing Jefferson. "Mather" assured his readers that he was not actuated by "party spirit" because the happiness of all mankind was intimately connected with the destruction of France's "atheistical tyranny."[80] But Massachusetts Federalists exercised uncustomary restraint in scheduling the annual public fast for April 5, three days after the people cast their 1810 ballots to elect the governor and senators of the state, rather than just before. Though blatantly political sermons remained the order of that day, the Federalists felt they had done all they could do to reelect Gore without risking a hostile reaction.[81]

They had reason for acting cautiously. The gains the embargo had enabled them to make in other New England states like New Hampshire and Rhode Island had largely evaporated.[82] Beyond that, the Republicans had managed to persuade a popular revolutionary figure, Elbridge Gerry, to enter the gubernatorial contest, and William Gray, a wealthy Salem merchant and former Federalist who had supported the embargo, to be his running mate.[83] Gerry came with the wart that he had opposed ratification of the federal Constitution, though he had been a member of the Philadelphia Convention. But his revolutionary credentials before that were impeccable, and afterward he had served effectively as one of the American commissioners dispatched by John Adams to France in the crisis of 1798. He alone had stayed on in Paris after the humiliation to which Talleyrand's agents X,Y, and Z had subjected the American commissioners. By doing so he provided Talleyrand with a channel through which to pursue a rapprochement with the United States that led to the Franco-American Convention of 1800. After being defeated by Caleb Strong in the gubernatorial contest of 1802, Gerry had withdrawn from the partisan battles in Massachusetts, which now made him an attractive candidate to moderates of both persuasions. Gore, by contrast, had engaged in pompous, ceremonial processions as governor, first from his palatial residence in Waltham to Boston, and subsequently on a tour of the western part of the state that his supporters pretentiously orchestrated to resemble Washington's tour of New England in 1789.

No one was very surprised, then, when Gerry was elected governor in April 1810 by a margin of more than two thousand votes. As an added bonus Rhode Island also elected a Republican governor.[84] A group of Federalist gentlemen from Hampshire County nonetheless expressed shock at the electoral outcome in Massachusetts. "Such had been the system of policy originated and fostered by the democratic administrations, that no man would have anticipated an increase of democratic votes without . . . impeaching, in some degree, the intelligence or patriotism of the people." These gentlemen attributed the outcome to the electoral activity of the opposition together with "the high standing of its leading agents." But they were not prepared to concede defeat, though some, including John Marshall observing from distant Virginia, entertained "gloomy anticipations." Instead they stressed the importance of the legislative elections, particularly the House's, which had yet to take place. The two branches would jointly elect a senator to an evenly divided upper house as well as the executive council and decide whether Timothy Pickering would serve another term in the U.S. Senate. Accordingly they urged Federalist towns to send the largest delegation of representatives to which they were entitled under the constitution.[85]

Appeals like this simply inspired the Republicans to compete with them at the same game.[86] The question of who would hold the balance of power in the House would be decided by which party exerted itself most in expanding its delegations of representatives. The answer would not be known for certain until the legislature met to organize itself at the end of May. When it did so, the House was found to contain an unprecedented 639 members, the majority of whom chose a Republican as Speaker. The Republican majority in the House in turn gave them the power to choose the council and neutralize Federalist control of the state Senate by filling a vacancy from a district that had failed to produce a majority for any candidate. When Gerry addressed the legislature on June 7, 1810, he faced a situation very different from what either Sullivan or Lincoln had faced in the two preceding years. And he tried to consolidate the Republican victory by defining a moderate position designed to quiet the turmoil that had characterized the politics of the commonwealth for the past half-decade.[87]

Gerry proposed that "the mantle of friendship be drawn over past obnoxious measures, and our exertions be directed to prevent their repetition." The best defense against "the two gigantic combatants of Europe" was unity. Each had presented "itself at different times to United America, with the affected detachment of a disinterested admirer." But "when either merely suspects that [the

United States] favors the other," it was thrown into "a jealous frenzy . . . urging . . . American destruction." The federal government had "from the first burst of the Gallic Volcano, to this day" striven to occupy "the honorable ground of neutrality," though repeatedly confronted with a "choice of unavoidable evils." While mistakes may have been made, when balanced against what had been achieved "may we not with truth declare, that the Federal government have [*sic*] done well"? Gerry was confident his fellow citizens would resist attempts "prompted by imprudent zealots of any description, to hazard the irretrievable loss of all, or of any of [the nation's] inestimable blessings" once they compared the situation of the United States to that of Europe. Both houses then echoed Gerry's moderation.[88] Evidence of the partisan passions of the past survived only in the legislature's choice of Joseph Varnum rather than Pickering as the state's new senator and in the celebratory fêtes the Federalists simultaneously organized around Francis Jackson's visit to Boston in early June. At one of these Timothy Pickering offered as a toast "The world's last hope,—Britain's fast-anchored isle."[89]

The recovery of political control over the fourth-largest state in the Union that abutted Canada's maritime provinces decisively strengthened the administration's hand in dealing with Great Britain. Many had wondered whether the national government could effectively resist British pressure while Massachusetts opposed its policies, since experience demonstrated that commercial measures would be ineffectual without the state's cooperation.[90] Now that the spectacle of Massachusetts at loggerheads with the federal government and of her people refusing to obey federal laws no longer clouded the diplomatic horizon, it was more probable that foreign governments would take the nation seriously.[91] Additionally, Republican control of all the state governments in the region but Connecticut reassured the administration that it was in no immediate danger of forfeiting its good standing with the American people. And thanks to the adjournment of Congress and the state legislatures with the approach of summer, the executive could conduct diplomacy for the next few months free of domestic pressures.

Casting the Die

Though ostensibly neutral in form, the statute that evolved from Macon's Bill #2 to become law on May 1, 1810, offered a good deal more to France than to Britain, as some at the time realized.[92] Excluding the public vessels of both powers from American waters had little effect on France because, aside from an occasional French privateer, very few French public vessels had visited American waters since Trafalgar. More significant, Britain's control of the sea made the law's offer to reimpose non-intercourse against a belligerent that failed to follow the other's initiative especially inviting to France. Since France had no way of enforcing her decrees on the high seas, she had little to lose by renouncing them in return for United States cooperation in her efforts to strike at British commerce. The Erskine fiasco suggested that Britain valued the benefit she derived from her naval superiority more than she did her trade with the United States, so it was unlikely that she would reciprocate if France removed her decrees. Thus France could gain an advantage that would otherwise elude her by rising to the bait contained in the law of May 1.[93] Of course, there was no guarantee that Napoleon would do so. But he could be relied on to recognize the statute for what it was, and if he chose to oblige, the Republicans would be relieved of the burden of trying to treat both belligerents in the same way. The effort to be even-handed had sprung from the quest for domestic consensus more than neutrality in sentiment. And since it had produced neither domestic harmony nor an accommodation with the great powers, the Republicans found it easy enough to abandon because of another benefit they derived from doing so.

The ineffectiveness of the Republicans' restrictive policies kept leading them back to the alternatives of submission or war. Though every Republican agreed that submission was unacceptable, hostilities with both powers was laden with many difficulties. Such a "triangular war" would entail considerably more preparation and expense. For that reason it increased the risk that the nation would enlarge its debt to the point where it would become indistinguishable from a corrupt monarchy. Declaring war against both European powers also risked the possibility that the belligerents might combine against the United States. Though we know in retrospect that the Napoleonic Wars would last until one of the principal protagonists decisively defeated the other, that was not evident at the time. Instead rumors of peace negotiations circulated throughout these years.[94] Nor could anyone be entirely sure that in the event of a European peace, the principal powers might not then turn their combined forces against the source from which the revolutionary disease had first emanated.[95] Financial and political considerations, then, combined with strategic ones to dictate the selection of one adversary, which, in retrospect, some claimed was the intent of the May 1 law. And if that adversary were Britain, as the Republican majority assumed it should be, France might still provide a haven for American privateers without a formal alliance.

Playing to France, however, was fraught with difficulties because Franco-American relations had been problematic from the start. During the Revolution the language barrier had fed the conclusion reached by most French observers that shared traditions, culture, and religion would naturally lead the United States to gravitate back to Britain. Napoleon added a personal element to this larger problem by his reluctance to delegate authority.[96] One could conceive of a British minister plenipotentiary sorting out the difficulties between the United States and Britain in Washington. One could not conceive of that happening with a French ambassador or even an underling of Napoleon's in Europe. Only a personal arrangement with the emperor would suffice, and given Napoleon's preoccupation with European affairs and the marginal significance of the United States to that world, it proved difficult for any American minister to command his attention. On the other hand, if all one sought was the performance of a ritual, and the ritual cost the nation performing it very little, an underling claiming authorization from the emperor might just do.[97]

For once France obliged the administration, although only minimally and equivocally. At the beginning of July 1810 Madison had specified what he expected from each belligerent in order to get the United States to invoke non-intercourse against the other. Britain would have to withdraw all its orders as well as its blockade of the European coast initiated in May 1806. France would have to repeal its decrees and restore all U.S. vessels it had seized entering French ports after March 23, 1810, under the Rambouillet Decree, allegedly in retaliation for the way the original non-intercourse had favored Great Britain.[98] On August 5, the duke of Cadore notified Ambassador John Armstrong that France was taking the bait. Cadore's letter described the replacement of non-intercourse with the law of May 1 as ushering in a "new state of things." It then declared "that the decrees of Berlin and Milan are revoked, and that after the 1st of November they will cease to have effect; it being understood that, in consequence of this declaration, the English shall revoke their Orders in Council, and renounce the new principles of blockade . . . or the United States, comformably [*sic*] to the act you have just communicated, shall cause their rights to be respected by the English."[99] In other words, France was offering partial compliance with Madison's expectations, since Cadore had failed to mention the decree of Rambouillet, in exchange either for Britain's full compliance or non-intercourse being invoked against her. Even that partial compliance was compromised by two other developments. Danish privateers, licensed by a government allied with France, had indiscriminately seized and condemned American vessels in the Baltic, claiming they were British vessels in disguise. And France had imposed prohibitive duties on many American imports, effectively shutting them out of the Continental market.[100]

Madison understood the potential problems in Cadore's declaration, which first came to the American public's attention at the end of September.[101] For instance, official confirmation of the French government's offer might not be communicated to the administration until after November 1, when Cadore had indicated the agreement was to go into effect. The president also realized that the Federalists and British were likely to object to the authenticity of France's actions, as indeed proved to be the case.[102] Madison nonetheless did everything in his power to seal the bargain by issuing a proclamation on November 2 that gave Britain only three months, or until March 3, 1811, in which to revoke its orders and blockades.[103] If Britain failed to do so, the provisions of the non-intercourse law would then be revived against her.

Two days earlier Madison had announced that the United States was taking possession of West Florida. In 1808, Spain's once glorious empire in the Western Hemisphere had begun disintegrating in the wake of the upheaval touched off by Napoleon's attempt to place the Spanish crown on his brother's head. As Spain's colonial administration collapsed, power devolved to provincial juntas. In West Florida, recent immigrants from the United States formed a rump convention that declared independence from Spain on September 26, 1810. Many adherents of the convention openly favored annexation by the United States. With Spanish authority visibly evaporating in the area, Madison issued a proclamation authorizing Governor William Claiborne of Louisiana to occupy part of the province on October 27. The proclamation claimed that the designated territory—at least that portion west of the Perdido River—had been part of the Louisiana Purchase and that the United States had shown restraint since 1803 in allowing Spain to retain possession of it until the collapse of Spanish rule had endangered "the tranquility and security of our adjourning territories."[104] In actuality, the administration responded more to the fear that if it did not act, Great Britain would assert herself there. But Madison's two proclamations had in a short interval turned the Republic toward confrontation with Great Britain. Though hardly a warmonger, Madison was relieved to have settled on a course that at last promised "extrication from the dilemma, of a mortifying peace, or a war with both the great belligerents."[105]

Crosscurrents

When the Eleventh Congress reassembled for its third and last session in November 1810, the principal item on its agenda was the recharter of the Bank of the United States. A preliminary vote during the preceding session had suggested that the bank's supporters enjoyed a comfortable majority in both houses.[106] Several state legislatures had then stepped into the fray and instructed their senators and representatives against recharter. This provoked a debate in the Senate about the status of instructions as well as declarations from several congressmen, most notably by Timothy Pickering— now a congressional representative instructed by the Massachusetts General Court to oppose recharter— of their intention to ignore them.[107] The controversy over the bank had the welcome effect of distracting attention from divisions over the nation's foreign policy at the end of 1810. This in turn quieted the Federalist press. Though most Federalists supported recharter, so too did many Republicans, including the secretary of the treasury, Albert Gallatin. The recharter of the bank was ultimately defeated by paper-thin margins in both houses, and on March 3, 1811, the first Bank of the United States ceased being a national bank. Defeat, however, came without the bank becoming a strictly party struggle.

Many members of Congress noted this development with relief, even though the bank could not be entirely isolated from the conflict over the nation's foreign relations. Aside from the constitutional issue of whether chartering such an institution was a necessary and proper exercise of the powers delegated to Congress, the most significant objection to the bank related to the influence Britain might exercise over the United States through it.[108] Critics saw evidences of British influence that went well beyond Federalist support for the recharter and the bank's preference for dealing with Britain rather than France. Seventy percent of the bank's stockholders were foreigners, among them prominent members of the British aristocracy, including a former chancellor of exchequer, currently the duke of Northumberland. Supporters of recharter argued in vain that the foreign stockholders were precluded from becoming bank directors. The plea that the federal government would need a national bank if it ever found itself at war with a European power also carried little weight, despite repeated allusions to the services rendered by the Bank of North America at the end of the revolutionary war. In 1811 more than a hundred commercial banks, most chartered by the states with a total authorized capital of more than $65 million, dotted a landscape that during the Revolution had been devoid of state banks.[109] If war with Britain threatened, many felt that no national bank would be better than one that was mortgaged to if not controlled by the nation's adversary.

Utility did persuade some Republicans to lay aside ideological anxieties and vote with the Federalists for recharter, in the process incurring unfamiliar criticism from their ideological compatriots. In pursuing this course, the Republicans supporting the bank were careful to affirm their submission to the majority. Samuel McKee of Kentucky spoke for them in conceding that they could face defeat. But McKee noted that though "the affections of the people" might "on account of the frequent appeals made to their passions and prejudices, recede for a moment, from us . . . it cannot but be . . . a consolatory reflection, that we have discharged, with honesty and fidelity, our duty to our country." And he was confident that "when reason and reflection have resumed once more their empire, we will again be surrounded with the confidence and gratitude of the people."[110]

McKee's bow to the sovereignty of the people stood in marked contrast to the stance taken by Josiah Quincy in the debate over a bill authorizing the inhabitants of Orleans—that part of the Louisiana territory that eventually became the state of Louisiana—to draft a constitution and apply for statehood. Quincy was not the first Federalist to raise constitutional objections to Louisiana's admission to the Union, nor to point out that doing so would upset the balance between the original parties to the national compact. But he was the first member of Congress to declare before that body that if Congress made Louisiana a state, "the bonds of this Union [would be] virtually dissolved," and that it would be "the right of all . . . [as] it will be the duty of some, to prepare definitely for a separation—amicably if they can, violently if they must."[111] George Poindexter, delegate for the Mississippi territory in Congress with voice but without vote, accused Quincy of inviting a revolt against the government and threatening the dissolution of the Union. He questioned whether members of Congress should be issuing such invitations to the people, as the "*nursery of tory principles*," by which he meant New England, had done during the controversy over the embargo. And likening the threat to Aaron Burr's schemes for dividing the western part of the nation from its eastern part, he claimed that Quincy's language, "if accompanied by an overt act, to carry the threat that it contains into execution, would amount to treason."[112]

The issue of Louisiana's admission to the Union over which Quincy threatened secession would not come to a head before the Twelfth Congress met at the end of 1811. But in early February the Eleventh Congress was again riled by a Federalist-inspired attempt to repeal what remained of non-intercourse. Madison's proclamation of the preceding November promising to reinstate non-intercourse against Britain on February 2, should she fail to lift her restrictions affecting America's neutral rights, provided the occasion for the challenge. The British government had its work cut out for it if it wished to respond to the American ultimatum. The three-month interval between November 2 and February 2 corresponded to the season during which transatlantic communications normally slackened. Though messages moving from the United States to Europe could arrive in as little as three weeks, the return trip in the face of the winter westerlies might take months. Assuming it was prepared to reciprocate France's gesture, the British would be hard-pressed to meet the February 2 deadline in Washington. In this particular instance their ability to do so would be further compromised by one of George III's periodic bouts of insanity, a temporary regency, and the king's eventual resumption of his governing powers with a new ministry. Even without such complications, it seemed likely that Madison would not hear whether Britain intended to comply by February 2. That uncertainty, in turn, raised the question of how non-intercourse with Britain after February 2 would be executed.

Congress had been alerted to the problem by petitions from merchants seeking relief from the operation of the law before it went into effect. The simplest way to cope with that uncertainty was to repeal the law of May 1, 1810, as John Randolph proposed on February 2.[113] Randolph's motion opened up all the old wounds about pursuing commercial restrictions against the belligerent powers, but in a new context in which France's compliance with the terms of Congress's law came into dispute. Barent Gardenier accused Madison of issuing his November 2 proclamation on the basis of a French promise rather than proof of French action. Other Federalists joined Gardenier in pointing to reports that an American vessel, the *New Orleans Packet*, had been seized in France despite the alleged revocation of her decrees. Gardenier acknowledged that the report might be false, but argued that until confirmation could be obtained, neither Madison's November proclamation nor the reinstitution of non-intercourse was legal. Like Randolph, Gardenier favored repealing non-intercourse as the simplest solution to the problem.[114]

Since the Federalists had not objected when Madison had given Erskine the benefit of the doubt, the Republicans argued Congress should stand by the pledge the nation had made in the law of May 1. Though Republicans were disturbed by reports of continued French seizures, they noted that the detention of the *New Orleans Packet* could have occurred before the president's proclamation arrived in France. The United States certainly did not want to be caught reneging on a pledge to reimpose non-intercourse if it turned out that France had in fact revoked her decrees on the basis of a promise made by the United States. The effort to repeal the law of May 1, 1810, accordingly went down to defeat.[115]

But the issue of France's compliance quickly resurfaced when the House Foreign Relations Committee reported a bill exempting from the non-intercourse all vessels sailing from a British port before February 2.[116] James Emott of New York took this concession as the occasion to renew the dispute. He maintained that France had only promised prospectively and conditionally to revoke its Berlin and Milan decrees and had said nothing about the Rambouillet Decree of March 23, 1810, under which much American property remained sequestered. Emott also complained the French had canceled any benefit that America might derive from the revocation by prohibiting the importation of some American staples and subjecting the rest to outrageously high duties. He concluded, as Gardenier had, by questioning the legality of Madison's proclamation and declaring his opinion that non-intercourse was not then in force.[117]

Emott's intransigence drew from Robert Wright of Maryland the comment that "while Great Britain finds such able advocates on this floor, she will find no

necessity to redress our wrongs." Wright added the opposition's behavior was
hardly surprising given the way in which "the seditious clamors of certain arch
traitors in the Eastern States" had subverted the embargo.[118] However, now that
Massachusetts was safely back under Republican control, dredging up its past
seemed unnecessary if not counterproductive. Quincy's threat over Louisiana
might merit such a retort, but Emott's objections by themselves would hardly
have warranted so heavy-handed a response had not they pressed on another
exposed Republican nerve. This was anxiety about the imminent arrival of a new
French ambassador, Louis-Barbé-Charles Sérurier. Having just finished a term as
governor of Maryland, Wright knew all about the out-going French ambassador,
General Louis-Marie Turreau, who in March 1809 had set up an establishment
nearer to Annapolis than to the nation's capital.

After serving as a subaltern with the French forces in America during the war
for independence, Turreau had risen rapidly from the rank of captain at the
beginning of the French Revolution to lieutenant general, despite a mixed
record on the battlefield. In 1804 Napoleon had put him out to pasture as
ambassador to the United States after first ennobling him. Flamboyant in dress
and sumptuous in display, Turreau epitomized that "upstart insolence" which
Edmund Burke felt "inevitably . . . disgrac[ed] those who are the first acquirers
of any distinction."[119] This affected his dealings with everyone he considered his
inferior, which meant most Americans, as well as his wife whom he reportedly
beat. Known behind his back as "the butcher of the Vendée" for his vicious
suppression of a provincial revolt against Jacobin rule in the early days of the
French republic, he expressed ill-disguised contempt for the United States
throughout his diplomatic mission and did little to smooth Franco-American
relations.[120] Now that Madison needed some confirmation that France meant to
honor the duke of Cadore's pledge of August 5 as well as some clarification of the
status of American shipping and produce under French municipal regulations
and the Rambouillet Decree, the Republicans certainly did not want another
Turreau.

Sérurier arrived in Washington on February 14, 1811. At the presentation of
his credentials on February 20, the secretary of state gave him a series of queries
covering the issues the administration wanted clarified as an agenda for their
first meeting. Sérurier responded by assuring Smith about the repeal of the
decrees, but hinted strongly that the restoration of American property seized
under the Rambouillet Decree was contingent on the vigor with which the
United States pursued non-intercourse against Great Britain. He also pleaded
ignorance of France's municipal regulations since many had taken effect after his
departure from Paris.[121] Sérurier thus failed to provide the administration with a
weapon that might have silenced Federalist opposition in Congress just when it

most needed one, though his demeanor was far more acceptable to official Washington than his predecessor's had been.

The administration's visible disappointment led the Federalists in Congress to ratchet up their opposition to a bill for implementing non-intercourse against Britain. William Milnor of Pennsylvania protested that France's insulting suspension of its decrees had created no obligation requiring the United States to interdict commerce with Britain. Quincy used especially provocative language, characterizing Napoleon as "a princely pirate" covetous of his "plunder." He mockingly congratulated Napoleon on his success in manipulating the adminis-tration, which he described as "our . . . pen and ink gentry—parchment politicians" caught in "a paper fly trap, dipped in French honey." Other Federalist orators blamed France's confiscation of large quantities of American property on non-intercourse and pointed to the diminished revenue as evidence that the restrictive system was hurting Americans more than anyone else. The bill, subse-quently referred to as the Law of March 2, passed, but the reporter recording the debate noted he had omitted "many circumstances of trivial importance" that had contributed to the "warmth" of the proceedings.[122]

Resolving Uncertainties

The verbal barrage to which the Federalists subjected the Republicans in the third session of the Eleventh Congress failed to prevent them from overwhelm-ingly backing non-intercourse against Britain.[123] Madison took ambassador Sérurier's assurance that the decrees had been repealed at face value and con-strued Sérurier's response to the secretary of state's query about the Rambouillet Decree as reflecting distrust about "the stability & efficacy of our pledge to renew the non-intercourse agst. G.B." Madison feared that Napoleon's reluc-tance to trust the United States might authorize a parallel response from Britain and "defeat every arrangement between parties at a distance from each other . . . which is to have a future or continued execution."[124] Undoubtedly these thoughts were communicated to the Republican majority in Congress, which helped it to hold the line until Congress adjourned on March 3. Federalist attempts to split the Republican coalition over implementing restrictive measures against Britain had, for the moment, failed.

At the same time, Madison had the satisfaction of seeing attempts to inflame the people against the administration in both Massachusetts and Connecticut founder. In March, Boston's Federalists had organized a rally at Fanueil Hall to promote the candidacy of Christopher Gore, who was again running against Gerry. The meeting adopted a resolve proposed by John Lowell Jr.[125] and seconded by Harrison Gray Otis that denounced Congress's act of March 2 implementing non-intercourse against Britain as "tending to the ruin or impoverishment of some of the most industrious and meritorious citizens of the United States." The resolve had also endorsed "peaceable but firm" opposition to the "execution of laws which if persisted in, must and will be resisted."[126] Gerry's son-in-law, James T. Austin, had countered with a newspaper series for the Boston *Patriot* under the pen name of "Leolin" that attacked Otis rather than Lowell, whom he ignored as an irreclaimable extremist. Austin's "Leolin" letters, widely reprinted in other Republican papers and appearing in pamphlet form, censured Otis for allowing himself to be associated with resolves calling for resistance to the laws.[127] The tactic seemed to work as Gerry beat Gore handily in the April election and the Republicans recaptured decisive control of the state Senate. Boston did elect a delegation of forty-four Federalists as representatives, but that failed to confer on them control over the state House of Representatives.[128]

The defeat of the Massachusetts Federalists in the election of 1811 led Elbridge Gerry to shift political gears. Hitherto he had posed as a centrist in his efforts to separate well-meaning moderates from the more intransigent Federalist leadership. Now he tried to crush that leadership by launching a withering attack on them in his address to the legislature. Because Gerry's strategy ultimately backfired, ushering in a prolonged Federalist supremacy in the state, it is worth asking why he abandoned the political approach that had secured him his position in the first place. His modern biographer claims he was responding to the pressure of Republicans who chafed because Gerry had not been partisan enough in the distribution of offices to which they felt entitled.[129] Patronage certainly proved to be a double-edged weapon that Gerry and the council experienced difficulty in wielding effectively. But Gerry also recognized that Madison was moving toward a showdown with Britain and he wanted to discredit the Federalist extremists before a war with Britain provided them with a political boost. The Republican leadership of the state in turn went along with Gerry's initiative in ways that eventually led them to mirror the Federalists.[130]

In his speech of June 7, Gerry's address singled out Boston "where of late an 'assemblage' of a majority of her electors . . . passed 'unanimously' various Resolutions, too important, in their nature and tendency, to be unnoticed." While the reasons for Madison's reimposition of non-importation against Great Britain had eluded "the assemblage," both "the National Government, and generally the State Governments" understood that though Napoleon had not revoked all of his edicts, Great Britain had revoked none of her orders. Gerry asked whether "one part in four hundred of the federal electors [is] . . . to govern the whole" in condemning "our national government, whilst supporting our just claims," when by doing so they encouraged "a foreign power in unjust

demands. . . . Can it, on any ground, justify, or apologize for such impudent conduct?"[131] Gerry also accused "the assemblage" of making "a change of our government, or the alternative of force . . . convertible terms." If "every citizen . . . has a
right . . . to put his construction on any law . . . and to resist them by force, our
constitutions are nullities, our constituted authorities are usurpers, and we are
reduced to a state of nature." He argued that "those who have denounced the government of the United States as oppressive, tyrannical and unjust, and who have
declared an intention to resist the execution of their laws" were trying "to excite a
spirit of insurrection and rebellion." While Gerry was confident that the sovereign people of the United States would not commit "political suicide" by
rebelling "against their own sovereignty," he blamed the Federalists for cooperating with the government of Great Britain, whose " 'avowed object' " was " 'the
dismemberment of our Union.' " "Who can contemplate, without chills of
horror" the "civil war" such a dismemberment would produce? Americans knew
enough of the face of war to take seriously Gerry's caution that "[t]en foreign wars
are a luxury, when compared with one civil conflict."[132]

The *National Intelligencer* valued the political drama the Massachusetts sufficiently to reprint Gerry's address and the replies of the House and Senate, which
seconded his condemnation of the misdeeds of the Boston "assemblage" in their
entirety. The stance of the governor and state legislature also met with the approval
of prominent Republicans. Madison certainly appreciated the verbal drubbing
Gerry had administered to the state's Federalist leaders, and James Monroe explicitly congratulated Gerry on supplying the decisiveness and firmness that the "situation required." Former president John Adams, a longtime friend of Gerry's,
thought the governor's speech "a masterly Performance," while an anonymous correspondent, possibly John Randolph, conceded that the test of Republicanism taking place in Massachusetts had attracted the attention of Europe.[133]

With Massachusetts in safe hands, only Connecticut's government remained
in a position to challenge the administration's policies. In 1810 Connecticut had
recalled James Hillhouse, its most prominent figure in Congress, to sort out the
disarray into which the state's school fund, dependent on the sale of lands in its
Western Reserve, had fallen. In doing so Connecticut showed it valued husband-
ing its own resources far more than any influence it could exert over the nation's
government. That did not stop the New Haven town meeting from adopting a
series of resolves on May 4, 1811, in which Hillhouse undoubtedly had a hand.
The resolutions criticized all attempts to restrict commerce as "partial and
unjust," as well as "*inefficacious*" and "*mischievous*," and condemned the reimposition of non-intercourse as "unconstitutional." New Haven appealed to the
Connecticut General Assembly "to use their influence to obtain a repeal of
the . . . law" and to oppose "as far as their constitutional powers extend, every

attempt of the national government to restrain" the state's foreign commerce. The town also appointed a committee of seven headed by Hillhouse to petition the president to call Congress back into session so that it could reconsider its commercial measures, while the town's chamber of commerce sent circulars to other commercial towns in the state and beyond, urging them to follow New Haven's lead.[134] In many respects New Haven seemed to be acting like Boston.

But the results were very different. Though it would have taken a good deal more than a complaint from a Connecticut town of fewer than six thousand persons to induce Madison to recall the national legislature that had adjourned less than two months before,[135] he did take the trouble to answer the New Haven petition. The president approved of the manner in which the town had exercised "the right of freemen" so as to distinguish its behavior from Boston's.[136] There was little danger that in doing so Madison would encourage other Connecticut towns and merchants to follow New Haven's example, even though his reply was printed in most of the state's newspapers, as only a handful had petitioned the state legislature to act against Congress's commercial restrictions.[137] Nor was the state government likely to respond as New Haven requested after Connecticut's April elections in which the freemen had replaced the unpopular John Treadwell with a governor less intimately associated with the state's Congregational establishment. Though Roger Griswold had won notoriety in 1798 for his assault on the Republican Matthew Lyon in the House of Representatives and had subsequently been involved in the secessionist conspiracy of 1804, many Connecticut Republicans voted for him in 1811 as the lesser evil. His inaugural address to the General Assembly seemed to confirm the wisdom of their decision. Griswold did little more than note that "THE VITAL INTERESTS OF THE COUNTRY ARE ENDANGERED BY TEMPORIZING SYSTEMS OF POLICY, *and from the want of vigour—of national spirit, and of union at home.*" The General Assembly echoed the governor's moderation in its reply. Though the legislature affirmed its right to review the constitutionality of federal laws and condemned the use of commercial restrictions "to coerce foreign governments," it urged the people of Connecticut to "co-operate in support of a just, liberal, and magnanimous policy" for securing "the liberties and independence of the United States."[138] Madison clearly had little to fear from that sort of opposition.

More troubling for the administration was the loss of a direct diplomatic connection with both of the European belligerents. During his six-year tour as ambassador to France, John Armstrong had accomplished little apart from generating controversy among Americans claiming compensation for French spoilations under the Louisiana Treaty and demonstrating an inability to influence the French government in any way. Exasperated with the intransigence of Napoleon, Armstrong had come home at the end of 1810, pleading financial hardship.[139] William Pinkney followed in the spring of 1811, having become convinced after Jackson's dismissal that the British government intended neither to maintain reciprocal diplomatic relations with the United States nor to change its commercial policies toward the Republic.[140] Pinkney's departure did lead Spencer Perceval, who had become prime minister in 1810, to dispatch Augustus John Foster as a fully accredited ambassador to the United States in April 1811. However, Foster did not arrive in Washington until after Congress had adjourned.[141] In the meantime, Ambassador Sérurier continued to be of little help to Madison either in fathoming Napoleon's intentions toward the United States or in promoting communication between the two governments. Historian Bradford Perkins attributes Madison's procrastination in dispatching Joel Barlow, the chosen successor for Armstrong, to the "barrenness of Sécurier's communications."[142] The delay did little to address the difficulties of an administration that had lost diplomatic representation in the two capitals where it most mattered as it tried to play each power off against the other.

A rupture in the Madison administration between the president and his secretary of state, Robert Smith, further complicated relations with the great powers. The break had several sources. Most important, Madison lacked confidence in Smith's abilities and had taken upon himself responsibility for drafting many of the official communications Smith signed. Smith understandably chafed under Madison's micromanagement. He also was jealous of the influence that Swiss-born Albert Gallatin exerted as secretary of the treasury. Smith's brother, Samuel, an influential senator from Maryland, felt that he was as qualified, if not more so, than Madison to be president. Samuel had openly criticized non-intercourse, and Madison had reason to fear that Robert shared his views. In short, Smith was exactly the kind of secretary of state Madison did not need as the Eleventh Congress adjourned.

In mid-March Madison began sounding out James Monroe, his principal competitor for the Republican presidential nomination in 1808, who at the time was governor of Virginia, about replacing Smith. He then offered Smith the ambassadorship to Russia in exchange for his resignation as secretary of state.[143] Russia remained the only European power capable of acting independently of the two principal belligerents. After 1807 Jefferson and then Madison attempted to establish diplomatic relations with her. But isolationist sentiment in the Senate obstructed their efforts until John Quincy Adams's appointment as ambassador was confirmed in 1810.[144] Personal considerations led Adams to request that he be relieved of the post in 1811. Though a demotion compared to being secretary of state, an ambassadorship was by no means a disgrace, and Smith hesitated before eventually refusing. In the interval Madison signed Monroe's commission on April 2. Shortly thereafter, on April 5, the Philadelphia

Aurora, a paper sympathetic to the Smiths, announced publicly what Washington had known for some days, that Smith and Madison had come to a parting of ways.

Smith seized the initiative so as to make it appear as though policy differences between the two men had precipitated the rupture. He wrote a detailed criticism of Madison's presidency that appeared in June 1811 under the title *Robert Smith's address to the people of the United States*. Smith focused on the policy disagreements that had developed between the two men since March 1809. He asserted that Madison was the inspiration behind Macon's Bills #1 and #2, both of which he described as "unwise as [well as] humiliating." Smith also questioned whether Napoleon had revoked his decrees and claimed that the administration had received information prior to the passage of the recent non-intercourse law that no restoration of the property seized under the Rambouillet Decree could be expected. Smith concluded by producing a series of diplomatic letters he had drafted which he claimed Madison had disapproved of, modified, or suppressed.[145]

Smith's pamphlet went through four editions and appeared in the more important newspapers throughout the country, conveying the impression that Madison was as soft on the French as he was hard on Britain.[146] It played into the hands of those who sought to portray Madison as a weak leader prepared to do anything to avoid a showdown with France.[147] But there was little likelihood of Smith and his brother joining forces with the Federalists or even cooperating with them as John Randolph had in Congress. The Federalists had been too lavish in their assaults on Smith while he acted as secretary of state to make such an alliance likely. As a writer in the *Essex Register*, probably William Bentley, observed, they did not have in Smith "a sharp tool to cut with."[148] The real danger in Smith's *Address* was the evidence it provided of a serious split within the Republican Party. And because the *Address* came from a former secretary of state, it was likely to embarrass the government in its subsequent dealings with France and Britain.[149]

Smith's defection would have less effect than Madison had initially feared. "A Review of Robert Smith's Address to the People of the United States," by Joel Barlow, promptly appeared in the *National Intelligencer.*[150] Barlow contemptuously described Smith as perhaps the only person in the country unaware of his lack of qualification for the job of secretary of state and then proceeded to prove the claim by reference to Smith's diplomatic correspondence. But Barlow went beyond Smith's competence to another, more damning fault. He accused him of betraying government secrets by needlessly publishing documents that touched on "a point of national honour, with a rival power, jealous, haughty, [and] lavish in her insults" as she was "frugal in her acts of justice." Barlow claimed this marked "a turpitude of heart, or a blunted, muffled, wooden-headed power of penetration and feeling too disgraceful in itself to be able to disgrace the government it betrayed."[151] In addition to being reprinted or excerpted in many Republican newspapers, Barlow's review also appeared in two pamphlet editions. And the *National Intelligencer* followed Barlow's devastating assault by printing excerpts from other Republican papers that condemned Smith.[152] Though Smith's faction continued to pursue their vendetta against Gallatin, Madison didn't have to worry about a political challenge led by his former secretary of state.

After weathering the Smith imbroglio Madison gained a significant political advantage from Monroe's appointment. Since Monroe's return in 1807 from the diplomatic mission he had undertaken at Jefferson's behest, he was known to prefer accommodation to confrontation with Britain. Monroe's first response to Madison's feelers centered on this issue, and Madison had assured Monroe that he too preferred accommodation.[153] Consequently, Monroe's presence in the cabinet as secretary of state served as a warranty that every peaceful avenue for avoiding a conflict with Britain would be pursued.[154] Eventually that would prove useful in securing the acquiescence of those who were reluctant about pushing the nation's defense of its neutral rights to the point of a showdown with Britain.

5

THE STRUGGLE OVER
DECLARING WAR

After the abandonment of non-intercourse in 1810, Britain relaxed its surveillance of America's principal ports. With the reimposition of non-intercourse in 1811, Britain resumed inspecting American vessels entering and leaving home ports. Shortly after noon on May 16, 1811, the frigate USS *President,* forty-four guns, Commodore John Rodgers in command, was cruising forty miles northeast of Cape Henry when it sighted a man-of-war bearing eastward. As the *President* hoisted its colors, the man-of-war bore away to the south. Rodgers, wishing to identify her, ordered a chase. But because of diminishing winds the *President* could not close with the fleeing vessel until almost nightfall. When Rodgers finally hailed her to identify herself, he received a demand that the *President* identify itself, followed by the discharge of a gun whose shot cut a backstay and lodged in the *President*'s main mast. The *President* fired a shot of its own, which was answered by three quick cannon bursts, followed by a general discharge of the American frigate's broadside. The *President* and HMS *Lille Belt* of eighteen guns, at the time commonly rendered as *Little Belt,* then exchanged fire for more than an hour before the guns of the British sloop of war fell silent. By this time Rodgers realized that he had engaged a smaller vessel than his own, and on hailing again he learned of her identity. The two lay near each other for the rest of the night. The next morning Rodgers sent one of his lieutenants aboard the *Lille Belt,* who reported that the British sloop had sustained massive damage as well as more than thirty casualties, including nine dead. The *Lille Belt*'s captain denied that he had fired the first shot, but a subsequent U.S. naval court of inquiry acquitted Rodgers of all wrongdoing.[1]

Republican editors construed Rodgers's action as defending "the honor of the *American* flag."[2] Federalist papers, on the other hand, condemned Rodgers for having violated the law of nations by firing on the *Lille Belt* before identifying her. They worried that the incident would further complicate the already disturbed state of Anglo-American relations, leading to a rupture between the two countries. The incident clouded the mission of the new British ambassador,

Augustus Foster, who arrived in Washington in its wake. Foster had left Britain well before news of the encounter between the *President* and the *Lille Belt* was received, so he had to wait for supplementary instructions to discuss the matter. When they finally arrived in September, it became clear that the British government, unlike certain elements of the British public, wished to minimize the incident. Foster informed the administration his government expected little more than a "disavowal & reparation on the part" of the United States.[3] Because these were the terms the administration was prepared to accept in connection with the still unresolved *Chesapeake* incident, both nations could agree on separating the incidents from their other problems. The principal point in contention between the two countries remained the clash over Britain's orders and blockades. At this point impressment, though a factor, seemed peripheral to the dispute between them.

Setting a Course for War

Ambassador Foster's first communications with Monroe aggressively protested the reimposition of non-intercourse against Britain. He claimed that France had not repealed her decrees, and he asserted that Britain had no intention of lifting her commercial restrictions—described as "just measures of retaliation" adopted "in . . . defense"—until France renounced all her edicts. By this Foster seemed to mean not only those French decrees that affected the United States, but also those affecting Britain. Foster also hinted that non-intercourse was "a ground for retaliation" by Britain.[4] In addition to protesting that the United States was taking France's part in the war, his exchanges with Monroe came laced with allusions to Britain as "the only Power which stands up as a bulwark against . . . [Napoleon's] efforts at universal tyranny and oppression."[5] These phrases replicated those previously employed by Jackson and could be counted on to inflame the enmity between Federalists and Republicans when the correspondence was published. The unpromising outlook led Madison to call Congress back into session at the beginning instead of the end of November, after the administration leaked to the *National Intelligencer* just enough of what had transpired between Monroe and Foster to make the public aware of the seriousness of the situation.[6]

The continued tightening of British naval surveillance along the North American coast gave the administration additional anxiety. Throughout the summer of 1811 the Republican press carried reports of repeated boardings of American merchantmen as they entered or cleared American ports. The crew and passengers on these vessels were vulnerable to being impressed, and the vessels and cargoes could be sent to Halifax to be libeled in the vice admiralty court if they had cleared to or were coming from a non-British port. The British boardings and seizures often took place within sight of the coast, sometimes within the capes of the Delaware and Chesapeake.[7] The *National Intelligencer* challenged the Federalist press to explain why British cruisers were patrolling the coast when there were no French vessels in American ports.[8] The Federalists countered by pointing to the French seizure of American vessels in Europe and the effect her municipal regulations had on those that escaped seizure, hoping to establish the bogus nature of the claim that France had repealed its decrees.[9] The Republican press responded by distinguishing between municipal regulations and attempts to exercise control over American commerce on the high seas. France's municipal regulations might hurt American commerce, but how could the United States object without compromising her own power to regulate the trade entering U.S. ports? The Republican press also questioned the authenticity of the reports in the Federalist press. Because the incidents involving France usually occurred at a much greater remove from American shores than did British seizures and impressments, they remained abstract compared to the actions of British naval officers, who usually returned the passengers and crews of the vessels they seized—but did not choose to impress—immediately to land. That meant the incidents precipitated by British naval activity on the American coast yielded multiple, fresh eyewitnesses to what had happened.[10]

The naval pressure that Britain applied to the American coast during the summer of 1811 took a more ominous turn in early September with a report that a British squadron of four ships under the command of Sir Joseph Yorke was reinforcing its fleet in the western Atlantic.[11] Shortly afterward, Yorke's squadron was reported off New York. The information alarmed Secretary of the Navy Paul Hamilton sufficiently to order the nation's frigates to sea lest they meet with a fate similar to that of the Danish fleet at Copenhagen.[12] Madison had no reason to conclude that war was imminent, since reports from Europe suggested that no major new initiatives were in the works. But British naval power in the western Atlantic did bear on another problem that was festering between the United States and Britain.

The occupation of West Florida, which Madison had ordered in October 1810, had taken place peacefully, as intended, thanks to the success of William Claiborne, governor of the Territory of Orleans, in restraining local rebels from attacking the remaining Spanish posts. But the British chargé d'affairs, John Philip Morier, the highest ranking British official in Washington after Jackson's dismissal, wrote to Secretary of State Smith on December 15 protesting the occupation and warning that Britain, which now claimed Spain as an ally, could not view "with indifference any attack upon [Spain's] interests in America."

After assuring Morier that "no hostile or unfriendly purpose is entertained," Smith declined to correspond with him further, saying the matter had been referred to the American minister in London.[13] Pinkney, however, had departed for America before Smith's communication arrived, leaving the administration in the dark about how the British government would respond. Madison suspected that Yorke's squadron had its eye on securing East Florida from a fate similar to West Florida's.[14]

The autumn of 1811 failed to provide the administration with any encouragement that the other problems plaguing Anglo-American relations were moving toward resolution. Neither Foster nor the British papers gave any hint that Britain might lift its Orders-in-Council. Instead, rumors circulated that new restrictions on U.S. commerce, including the exclusion of all American vessels from British ports except those laden with wheat and flour, would soon be imposed.[15] Everything seemed to point to the British government's determination to resist U.S. commercial measures. Republicans suspected the hardening of Britain's stance stemmed from calculations about the weakness of Madison's administration derived from Robert Smith's dismissal and his subsequent *Address*. The British government must also have been aware of the flourishing trade being conducted in defiance of non-intercourse with Nova Scotia and New Brunswick in the North, Amelia Island in the South, and with Saint-Barthélemy in the West Indies, as well as with British forces in Spain.[16]

Britain's intractability invited unfavorable contrast with French policy. Declarations in the Republican press that France had indeed revoked its decrees accordingly gained a measure of credibility as the year progressed. The resolves of the Tammany Society of Newport, Rhode Island, on September 2 claimed that the Law of May 1, 1810, had "produced on the part of one [of the great belligerent powers] a manifestation of a more just and liberal policy."[17] Sérurier's repeated assurances to the administration also helped, though there was no denying that France's behavior still left much to be desired. French captures, which the Federalists made so much of, particularly in the Baltic, could not be ignored. But captures could be distinguished from condemnations, and until condemnation actually took place, it remained an open question whether the emperor intended to respect American property rights. *Niles's Weekly Register* printed reports from the American consuls in Paris and Copenhagen about their success in winning the release of some of these vessels.[18] At the same time the Republican press teemed with accounts of Britain's condemnation and sale of ships seized under her trade regulations and the legal decisions of William Scott, a British admiralty court judge, who cited the persistence of the French decrees in the judgments he rendered against American vessels.[19] The status of American property detained under the Rambouillet Decree also remained unclear.

However, France still offered more hopeful possibilities than Britain, especially as the administration's difficulties in sorting out French intentions could be attributed to the absence of an American ambassador in the French capital.

The Twelfth Congress has been known as the "War Hawk" Congress because it eventually declared war against Britain, allegedly in response to the demands of its constituents. The popular resolves, Independence Day toasts, and memorials produced at the time support such an interpretation, as does the substantial turnover that took place in the House of Representatives.[20] Four of New Hampshire's five representatives in the Twelfth Congress had not sat in the Eleventh Congress, roughly two-thirds of New York's and Tennessee's representatives were new, half of Vermont's, New Jersey's, North Carolina's, South Carolina's, Georgia's, and Kentucky's, approximately one-third of Pennsylvania's, and a quarter of Virginia's. In all more than 45 percent of the representatives were freshmen and the most prominent among these were under forty.[21] But some of the newcomers reflected the enlargement of the House after the census of 1810 as much as a political sea change in the public at large. Nor did the replacement of previous delegates, as was the case with Delaware's one representative, necessarily add to the Republicans' strength. Nonetheless, it was clear from the beginning that the Twelfth Congress would be very different from the Eleventh.

When Madison first addressed the new Congress, he could not have known the mettle of the Republican majority with the same clarity that retrospection has afforded. Indeed, some of the advice he was receiving from prominent Republicans, including one of his closest advisors, Albert Gallatin, opposed war. They questioned the capacity of the nation to survive a contest with Britain, particularly when the United States could expect to have little control over its duration, given the disaffection of the Federalist minority. A prolonged conflict risked dragging the Republic to its doom by two possible routes. Either the populace would respond to hardships by a change in administrations that would eventuate in a disgraceful peace or the nation would be transformed into a de facto monarchy.[22] As Madison contemplated his options in early November 1811, the road ahead looked neither easy nor promising. The only thing that seemed clear was that the chances for negotiating a peaceful settlement of outstanding differences with Britain were dimming.

Though the president carefully avoided calling for war, his address to Congress nonetheless charted a course that he had every reason to believe would eventuate in one. After portraying the Foster-Monroe negotiations as emblematic of British intransigence, Madison announced, "The period is arrived, which claims from the Legislative Guardians of the National rights, a system of more ample provisions for maintaining them." He called on Congress to put "the

United States into an armour, and an attitude demanded by the crisis." Madison made a number of suggestions about how the Congress might do this, but expected it to be governed by "the national spirit and expectations."[23] Few Republicans failed to construe these words as a call for a declaration of sentiments from the state governments to guide the Congress in gauging the popular temper.

Not all the states could be expected to speak in a timely fashion. Some legislatures were not sitting when Madison delivered his message. Governor Daniel P. Tompkins had prorogued the New York legislature to check the flood of new bank charters that it was approving, and it was not scheduled to reassemble until mid-January. This was a possible blessing because New York's legislature had for some time been at odds with the Republican sentiments of the state's governor.[24] The Republican-controlled Massachusetts legislature had also scheduled its next meeting so as to break what had become a habit of meddling in the nation's foreign affairs. Finally, no Republican expected anything positive to issue from Connecticut after Governor Roger Griswold, abandoning previous pretenses to moderation, had treated the General Assembly to a scathing critique of the administration's foreign policy on October 10, 1811.[25] But most other governors and state legislatures either anticipated Madison's guarded invitation or were receptive to it.

Though the state governments were not as unanimous or as resolute as might have been wished, their actions reassured Congress on one important point. There was general agreement that Madison was justified in focusing on Britain's violation of the nation's rights and postponing a reckoning with France until some future time. This agreement emerged despite the questions that Ambassador Foster, seconded by the Federalists, continued to raise about whether Napoleon had actually repealed his decrees and their attempts to paint France's behavior as qualitatively worse than Britain's. All of the state legislatures agreed that France at least had made some gesture in acknowledging the nation's neutral rights whereas Britain had made none. That agreement was important in confirming whom the nation's adversary should be. But it still left the Republican leadership with a formidable task of charting a course acceptable to a majority of Congress representing varied constituencies that had little acquaintance with each other.

Once again the House Foreign Relations Committee assumed leadership, though three weeks elapsed between Madison's address and the release of its report. The principal drafter was a freshman congressman from South Carolina, John C. Calhoun. After restating the case against Britain, the report declared that the time had come "when the national character, misunderstood and traduced . . . by foreign and domestic enemies, should be vindicated." To defend the "sovereignty and independence of these States" from deliberate and systematic violation, the committee proposed a six-point program: (1) adding a land bounty to the monetary bounty to bring the regular army to its authorized ten-thousand-man strength; (2) raising an additional ten thousand regular troops; (3) authorizing the president to accept up to fifty thousand volunteers into a reserve corps; (4) authorizing the president to order out detachments of militia as the public service required; (5) putting all naval vessels into active commission; and (6) arming merchant vessels and authorizing them to defend themselves under certain restrictions.[26]

Republican papers for the most part welcomed the committee's report. The Baltimore publisher, Hezekiah Niles, immediately endorsed both its tone and substance in his new but already influential *Weekly Register*. He assured the committee that the American people were "ripe for any thing but submission: and should this report be adopted, and immediately receive effect, congress will do nothing more than ratify the deliberate judgment and cool determination of their constituents."[27] In a subsequent issue, Niles published the speech of Peter Porter of New York, the Foreign Relations Committee's chair, in presenting the report to the House. The committee had concluded "that all hopes of accommodating our differences with Great Britain by negotiation must be abandoned." Though Porter accused Britain of using its Orders-in-Council to "cut up . . . about three-fourths of our best and most profitable commerce," the committee was more concerned about the "character of the country" than its economy. Porter likened the situation of the United States to "that of a young man just entering into life . . . who, if he tamely submitted to . . . intentional indignity, might safely calculate to be kicked and cuffed for the . . . remainder of his life" unless "he should afterwards undertake to retrieve his character." In that case he would "do it at ten times the expense it would have cost him at first to support it." The committee's recommendations were designed to prepare for war "in case Great Britain shall not have rescinded her Orders-in-Council, and made some satisfactory arrangements in respect to the impressment of our seamen."[28]

The behavior of Republicans in the Tenth and Eleventh Congresses led Niles and others to worry whether the Twelfth Congress had the "fortitude to give energy to [the resolutions] and persevere in them" or "whether they . . . will suffer their plans to be unhinged by the threats and menaces of a discontented minority?" Niles feared that "such another *retrograde movement* as the tenth congress made [when it abandoned the embargo], would . . . undermine the republican institutions of our country, by inducing the people to apprehend that government so constituted" lacked sufficient "energy to preserve its own dignity." While "much stress has been laid upon the political divisions prevalent among us" in England, Niles stated it as "*a fact,* that the whole number of the opponents of the present administration is far short of the number of the tories we had in the revolutionary war." And he believed that "when the question shall be put [to them], '*For America or for England?*' a very small and contemptible portion, indeed, will fail to rally round the standard of government." In addition, he predicted that a war would "not be without its blessings—*for it will weed our country of traitors.*"[29]

On one issue the Republicans had no trouble agreeing: if war were to be declared, the initiative should come from the House rather than the Senate. The new House was a far better embodiment of the sovereign people upon whom the burdens of the conflict would descend than was the Senate, only a third of whose members had been chosen by the state legislatures in the recent congressional elections. In addition, the greater transparency of House proceedings made it a better mirror of the people than the Senate. The *National Intelligencer* took pains to publish the major speeches delivered in the House. Though the results fell far short of the modern Congressional Record, every paper throughout the land was free to copy what it wanted to from the *Intelligencer.* When speeches delivered in the Senate appeared in print, they usually did so because the individual senator had seen to their publication. No paper carried a complete transcript of the House proceedings, but attentive members of the public had access to more of the drama taking place there than they did to the Senate's proceedings.[30] Everyone recognized that the Constitution required the Senate to concur in a declaration of war and that the final decision would have to be made in secret session, but leadership by the House was appropriately Republican.

The transparency of the House's proceedings, however, also raised questions about its ability to fulfill the role envisioned for it. On December 9, John Randolph, who had been appointed to the Foreign Relations Committee in the hope the assignment might tame his opposition, launched a fiery dissent against the committee's resolve calling for enlarging the army, thus destroying the impression of unanimity Porter had tried to convey. Randolph claimed the Republican Party had originally formed to resist a Federalist military establishment. He called on Republicans to reaffirm the principles of 1798, implying that failure to do so—rather than his dissent—threatened Republican unity. Randolph played on widely shared prejudices about standing armies. Were "seven millions of Americans . . . to be protected in their lives and liberties by . . . vagabonds who were fit food for gunpowder?" "The people of the United States could defend themselves, if necessary, and had no idea of resting their defense on mercenaries, picked up from brothels and tippling houses— pickpockets who had escaped from Newgate, &c."[31]

In a subsequent speech, Randolph touched on all the anxieties he knew his Republican colleagues entertained about a war. The American people would be unwilling to bear the direct taxes needed to finance the conquest of Canada because it would require many more troops than the administration contemplated. Nor would New England's merchants support such a war while their defenseless seaports remained vulnerable to British sea power. Turning to his fellow southerners, he warned that the same "habits of subordination" that had kept slaves from rising against their masters—despite repeated invitations from the British to do so during the Revolution—no longer prevailed. Instead the last decade had seen "repeated alarms of insurrection." Randolph attributed the change to the pollution of the French Revolution disseminated by "pedlars from New England and elsewhere." Though Randolph offered no apology for "the outrages and injuries" that England had inflicted on the United States, he urged his colleagues to reflect upon what they could expect if the French "were the uncontrolled lords of the ocean?" War against Great Britain threatened to make the United States "a partner in the wars" of one of the prime "[m]alefactors of the human race," on a par with "Attila . . . Zingis, Tamerlane, [and] Kouli-Kan."[32]

Felix Grundy, a young war hawk recently elected from Tennessee and appointed to the Foreign Relations Committee, responded that the committee's recommendations affirmed rather than repudiated Republican principles. Though he acknowledged that the course recommended by the committee would "ascertain by actual experiment how far our Republican institutions are calculated to stand the shock of war," he expressed more anxiety about whether Congress in general and the House in particular was up to meeting the challenge. "[S]hould this resolution pass, and you then become faint-hearted, . . . you [will] have abandoned your old principles, and trod in the paths of your predecessors." Grundy warned, "We now stand on the bank; one movement more, the Rubicon is passed . . . and we must march to Rome." The occasion called for resolution. If there was a Republican "member here not determined to go with us, to the extent of our measures, I prefer now to take my leave of him, rather than to be deserted when the clouds darken, and the storm thickens upon us."[33]

The exchange between Grundy and Randolph highlighted the potential that war still possessed for dividing the Republicans. It also fueled doubts as to whether a republic like the United States would be able to declare war in the face of the determined opposition of a minority.[34] These doubts had the effect of steeling the Federalists in their opposition. With a loose cannon like Randolph playing on the Republicans' ideological fears, Federalist congressmen were free to focus on the feasibility of war with Britain. Their most effective spokesman in this regard turned out to be Daniel Sheffey, a plain-speaking, backcountry Federalist representative from the Shenandoah Valley of Virginia. On January 3, 1812, Sheffey rose to oppose the House Foreign Relations Committee's recommendations.[35]

Though Sheffey did not deny that the nation had good reasons for going to war against Britain, he said "it would be the grossest folly to precipitate" one unless there was some prospect that "the waste of our blood and treasure" would yield substantial benefit. He denounced Britain's Orders-in-Council as destructive of her interests and condemned impressments. But he was unwilling to fight a war to "defend every person (even aliens) who shall sail under our flag." "The question" was "not what we want, but what, under all circumstances, it is possible we can get." Sheffey would not "consent to purchase national misery, even should it be accompanied with . . . national honor," at the expense of "its future destiny." A "Quixotic war . . . was not calculated to cure the evil which affected us," if at the end of a prolonged conflict "we shall be compelled . . . to acquiesce under the system against which the war is waged."[36]

Sheffey also questioned Republican assumptions about how a war against Britain would be waged. Certainly the United States could not hope to challenge Britain's control of the seas. Instead her naval supremacy made the nation's principal ports like New York and New Orleans vulnerable to attack if not to the prolonged occupations similar to those experienced during the revolutionary war.[37] Privateers offered some prospect of compensating for the damage the enemy might inflict by raiding the coast, since one did not need naval superiority to prey on an adversary's commerce. Nonetheless, the United States was unlikely to emerge with advantage in a contest with the world's foremost sea power, since Britain's naval preponderance ensured she would recapture many of the vessels that fell prey to American privateers.[38] Strategically the nation needed a way of striking at Britain that had some prospect of yielding a quick military decision.

That is why seizing Canada had come to seem so compelling. Canada was nearby and of sufficient value to Britain to make its loss grievous. Canada also seemed vulnerable. The United States was more populous, and Canada's European population was thought to fall into two groups: refugees from the Revolution, whom Americans still viewed with contempt because they had refused to fight for their rights, and people who were as restive under British rule as the majority of Americans had been in 1776. Taking Canada would also diminish the threat of British-inspired Indian wars on the northern frontier, such as the one William H. Harrison had been credited with recently suppressing at Tippecanoe Creek, and deprive British cruisers of the convenience of libeling their prizes before the vice admiralty court in Halifax.[39] But though conquering Canada made strategic sense, serious tactical obstacles stood in the way of accomplishing this objective. Sheffey, joined by other Federalists in Congress, took delight in pointing to them and in doing so often exaggerated them.[40]

The most obvious was the severity of the Canadian winter, which limited military operations to part of the year. Operations against lower Canada also required attacking strong points like Quebec city and Montreal, which were garrisoned by British troops. Military wisdom at the time held that an attacking force had to outnumber the defenders by a factor of three or four to one to succeed. That put a premium on launching the attack before reinforcements had a chance to arrive from Europe, in other words just after a spring declaration of war. Later on, twice the force levels would be required to secure the same objectives.[41] Operations against upper Canada presented fewer problems. But upper Canada was also less important to Britain.

If the nation was to go to war, the tactical requirements of mounting an attack across its northern border required that the army's strength be built up as quickly as possible. But everyone knew that enlisting, training, equipping, and provisioning a regular force would take time. Some even viewed proposals to enlarge the army by twenty-five thousand men, instead of the ten thousand men the administration had asked for, as precluding a campaign against lower Canada during 1812.[42] Most Republicans instead expected Canada to be conquered by volunteers. The "volunteers" they had in mind were not only individuals, but entire military companies already in existence. The early Republic had seen the organization of many such units outside the formal ranks of the militia, including numerous junior cadet corps. Their formation reflected an anxiety, particularly in the more populous areas, about the ability of the militia to preserve and transmit the military traditions of the Revolution. Volunteer units selected their members, whereas the militia in principle had to accommodate all comers. Volunteer units were also less vulnerable to the bitter partisan divisions that had prevented the Massachusetts militia from giving effective support to the federal government during the embargo crisis. Though volunteer units tended to form around local political affinities, their officers could force the resignation of objectionable members to preserve political reliability when necessary. Volunteer companies also armed and equipped themselves, usually with special uniforms that engendered unit pride, so they would be less expensive than regular troops.[43]

However, volunteer units also had disadvantages. During peacetime their principal function was to grace civic ceremonies such as Independence Day celebrations. Some also made political statements, usually by publicly tendering their services to an executive they wished to support.[44] Neither their equipment nor their training qualified most volunteer companies to spearhead an invasion of Canada. Some militia units, particularly those from less densely settled areas, possessed a homogeneity approaching that of the volunteer units. But they were less likely to be properly equipped or trained, and, in any case, doubts had arisen as to whether they could constitutionally be ordered out of the country. These doubts were shared by both Republicans and Federalists.[45]

The nub of the Republicans' dilemma that Sheffey bore down upon, however, was money.[46] Since Jefferson's election in 1800 the Republicans had prided themselves on cutting back public expenses and retiring the revolutionary war debt. Over the dozen years of Republican rule the domestic debt of the United States shrank to roughly half its original size thanks to the expansion of the nation's foreign trade and the rising yields from the impost. War with Great Britain could erase this achievement overnight by cutting off imports just as military expenditures increased. Thereafter the public debt could be expected to increase in direct proportion to the length of the war. Short of a quick, easy victory, the administration would have only two financial alternatives besides resorting to currency finance, which few were willing to contemplate after the disastrous depreciation of the continental currency during the Revolution.[47] These were borrowing or taxation.

Several obstacles stood in the way of financing the war through loans. The capital markets of Europe, hitherto a resource for the Republic, were unlikely to be accessible once the nation embarked on a war against Britain. The supply of capital in the United States had grown considerably since the Revolution, but most of the potential lenders, including the majority of state banks, were controlled by Federalists who opposed an "offensive war" against Britain.[48] That left the government with little it could rely on besides internal taxation, much of which would involve direct taxation. The experience of Massachusetts in 1786 and the federal government in 1799 pointed to the political hazards of resorting to such an expedient. On both occasions a rebellion had ensued. Even without a rebellion, direct taxation was likely to be economically self-defeating because collection would take considerable time and in the end consume much of the revenue raised. Many Republicans agreed with the Federalists that they had come to power in 1800 in part because of the political backlash generated by the direct tax of 1798. Their popularity since then derived from their success in retiring the revolutionary debt with taxes that the average American scarcely noticed. Federalist newspapers taunted the Republicans with the prospect that changing direction now might inflict on the Republicans the same political damage that Adams and his supporters had experienced in 1800.[49]

If the Republicans led an unprepared nation into a war and were humiliated, they would discredit the cause they sought to vindicate. Some Federalists openly relished this prospect, expecting to be the political beneficiaries of a Republican sponsored debacle. Others Federalists like Alexander L. Hanson, the aristocratic editor of the Baltimore *Federal Republican,* advocated raising the ante on the Republicans by endorsing "the war-like preparations" the Foreign Relations Committee had called for, "as far as they go." But Hanson added they were "materially inadequate" for conquering Canada. "Militia cannot be relied upon for operations of any great extent, or for services of a long duration.— Volunteers, such as can favorably be distinguished from militia, are not to be raised." Hanson also objected to the committee's recommendations for the Navy "which ought to be immediately enlarged or laid by as totally useless."

Hanson did endorse the committee's recommendation for arming merchant-men, but not for reasons Republicans found reassuring. He hoped it would enable American vessels to resist piracies sponsored by the continental navies. Hanson assumed Congress would try to restrain armed merchantmen "from exercising their power against any vessels but those of Great Britain." But he was confident the restriction could not be enforced because there were no British privateers and thus no British vessels "against which a merchantman could effec-tually defend herself." Instead he expected American vessels to use their arma-ments exclusively in defending themselves from the occasional "French freebooter or . . . piratical Dane." Hanson, for one, claimed he welcomed the prospect of war because the people would then "remedy [the] folly" of those in power and "purify the political atmosphere. . . . Idiots who bellow in public bodies will be sent to Bedlam, and imposters to the stocks."[50]

Josiah Quincy supported Republican efforts to achieve military preparedness in Congress.[51] Quincy guessed that Republican fears of expanding the debt—coupled with their dread of direct taxation—meant they were bluffing about embarking on hostilities. The regard that Federalists like Quincy had for the power of Great Britain led them to assume the Republicans would never be so rash as to go to war against her if insufficiently prepared. At the same time Quincy realized that the Federalists were unlikely to capitalize on the Republicans' disgrace unless they could shun the blame for what happened.[52]

Federalist support of defense measures aggravated the Republicans' preparedness dilemma, but it also ran the risk of contributing to—rather than deterring—a declaration of war the Federalists wished to avoid. Many Federalists were unwilling to play with such fire. They argued that Republican subservience to France constituted a potential counterweight to Republican timorousness. They feared that the nation might very well find itself involved in a war with Britain, and that the lack of adequate preparations would ensure "a degrading and deadly connexion with France." A debate took place in the columns of the *New England Palladium* in December 1811 about the wisdom of diverging from unambiguous opposition to all war measures.[53] It failed to produce a consensus, perhaps because, as a minority, the Federalists' only hope was to divide their opponents. Acting as provocateur and pacifist simultaneously had advantages. By attacking the Republican majority from both flanks, the Federalists would make it more difficult for the Republicans to unite against them.

Rising to the Challenge

The Republicans were not without resources in coping with the difficulties they faced. They knew that the United States was considerably more developed than it had been as a league of colonies in 1775. How much more developed, of course, remained anyone's guess. Some said the nation was three times more populous and in possession of four times the revenue; others claimed it had four times the population and ten times the wealth. But everyone realized that it had become a very different country by 1810 than it had been in 1775. The notion that a nation of seven million souls was powerless to defend itself against a European adversary seemed preposterous.[54] These claims, of course, did not address the key question of why a nation with such resources was so unprepared. John C. Calhoun had pointed to the lack of political resolve in previous Congresses. "[S]uch has been our past conduct, that [Britain] will still calculate on our patience and submission till war is actually commenced." The remedy was not more of the same, but action. Though the nation might not at the moment be prepared for war, nothing could be gained by refusing to take the first decisive steps in that direction.[55]

The majority of Republicans in Congress followed Calhoun's lead in waving aside the strategic, ideological, and prudential objections the Federalists raised against embarking on hostilities with Britain. The change took some members of the House by surprise. Richard Stanford of North Carolina, an "old Republican" inclined to follow where John Randolph led, asked, "If gentlemen will have it that this is the accepted time for war, how has it happened that we have not had it before?"[56] Few had to be told that the answer lay in a failure of will in the previous Congresses. But Henry Clay, the Kentucky senator who had chosen to stand for election as a representative in the Twelfth Congress and had been elected the House Speaker, provided the most compelling testimony of the new temper of Congress in a rousing speech delivered at the end of December on expanding the army.[57]

Clay dismissed the objection that enlarging the army by twenty-five thousand would preclude declaring war in 1812 because of the time and expense required to bring so large a force into the field as a prescription for national humiliation. It resembled the opposition urging the nation to "bear the actual cuffs of her [Britain's] arrogance, that we may escape a chimerical French subjection! . . . We are called upon to submit to disbasement, dishonor, and disgrace—to bow the neck to royal insolence, as a course of preparation for manly resistance to Gallic invasion! What nation, what individual was ever taught, in the schools of igno-minious submission, the patriotic lessons of freedom and independence?" Certainly not the United States. "[I]t was not by submission that our fathers atchieved [*sic*] our independence." They "saw, beyond the petty taxes . . . a long train of oppressive measures terminating in the total annihilation of liberty; and . . . did not hesitate to resist them." If yesterday the nation had been con-tending with Britain over the indirect trade, today it was the direct trade, and tomorrow, it would be the coastal trade. "Gentlemen say that this government is unfit for any war, but a war of [defense against] invasion. What, is it not equivalent to invasion, if the mouths of our harbors and outlets are blocked up, and we are denied egress from our own waters?"

Like most Republicans, Clay believed that without British support the Federalists would shrivel into an insignificant minority. So he tried to drive a wedge between Britain and her American allies by arguing "that the real cause of British aggression, was not to distress an enemy, but to destroy a rival." The commerce Britain had interdicted "was not of very vital consequence" to France and certainly of less value than Britain's trade with the United States. "Would she . . . for the sole purpose of depriving her adversary of this commerce, relinquish her valuable trade with this country" except out of the jealousy? "She sickens at your prosperity, and beholds in your growth . . . the foundations of a power which, at no distant day, is to make her tremble for naval superiority." Clay brushed aside the possibility that war with Britain would lead the people to replace the Republicans with the Federalists who "will make a disgraceful peace." He felt "the people saw . . . that war was the only alternative left to us by the injustice of one of the powers." But Clay was not to be deterred even if they had not. "What! Shall it be said that our *amor patriae* is located at these desks—that we pusillanimously cling to our seats here rather than boldly vindicate the most inestimable rights of the country?" As to the dangers such a war might pose to liberty, Clay dismissed them as chimerical. "[A] people . . . affording a physical power of about a million men capable of bearing arms, and ardently devoted to liberty, could not be subdued by an army of 25,000 men." The decentralized nature of the Republic made the nation invulnerable to subjugation either by American or European armies.[58]

Clay was careful to attack Federalist ideas rather than the Federalists themselves in the hope that some members of the opposition could still be reclaimed. But in reducing the Republicans' objective to a defense of the nation's honor, he had opened himself to two Federalists objections. One was Sheffey's caution against being led into a "Quixotic war" by abstractions; the other was the claim that France had offended the nation's honor as much if not more than Britain. Both were addressed by a crescendo of Republican voices. Joseph Desha of Kentucky affirmed that "the honor of a nation is its life. Deliberately to abandon it, is to commit an act of political suicide." Then focusing on the critical point of which power's actions posed the greater challenge, he argued that British behavior was more threatening than France's because of Britain's supporters in America. Desha pointed at "those minions of royalty concentrating in the East" who in connection with the embargo had "talked of the violation of the laws as a virtue." He reminded the House of how the Federalists had "demoralized the community by raising the flood-gates of civil disorder; they gave absolution to felons, and invited the commission of crimes by the omission of duty." They, as much as the British, were responsible for the choice now confronting the United States between war and national degradation.[59]

Representative David R. Williams of South Carolina summarized the sentiments of many Republicans more colorfully if not more forcefully than even Clay. "To avoid war, we have receded, step by step, until we have not one inch of honorable ground to stand on." Where would this lead? Would "unqualified submission . . . satisfy" Britain? Williams thought it would not. "A disposition to advance on a receding opponent marks her character." Williams warned that Britain was attempting to fasten "a gangrene at the heart of the nation, which will imposthumate in ruin and corruption." "To war there must be an end; to this there never will be." Representing Britain as "contending for the liberties of the world" made about as much sense as claiming "that the Devil had espoused the cause of Christianity." If experience had shown that a government resting on opinion could not enforce measures like the embargo and non-intercourse against external enemies in league with internal ones, then the only alternative was to meet force with force. Williams concluded with a biting parody of the Federalists. "It would seem we are destitute of resources; without means to support the war; even our physical force is inadequate; but, was it adequate, were the means ample, they must not be exerted; the Government would be subverted; the veil of the temple of the Constitution would be rent in twain. Although the best interests of this nation are crushed beneath the paw of the British lion, we must not resist; he then is wisest who can soonest bow, with all the stupid serenity of servitude, and take the yoke!"[60] The words of Williams, Desha, and Clay apparently persuaded a majority of the House, which voted ninety-four to thirty-four to expand the regular forces of the United States by twenty-five thousand men.[61]

Still, many reasons remained for doubting whether the Republican coalition in Congress favoring war could hold together. On one side, Randolph and the Quids continued to harp on the threat that armies and wars posed to freedom. On the other, the Federalists raised embarrassing questions about at the practicality of fighting Britain. In addition, the House had to contend with Randolph's repeated attempts to derail the Republicans from achieving their objective with nuisance motions. The Republican majority retained the option of moving the previous question, which—when agreed to—cut off debate. But they could not stop him from making the motions in the first place, and considerable time and energy were consumed in countering them. Then the Federalists exploited news that arrived in March that a French squadron in the Atlantic was seizing and burning all the shipping it encountered allegedly under authority of the Berlin and Milan Decrees. Federalist newspapers focused on the two American vessels so far victimized while the Federalists in Congress presented petitions from the owners and captains of the vessels involved. Though the grounds for these piracies could not be ascertained, they nonetheless lent color to the Federalist complaint that the Republicans were allowing themselves to be manipulated by the French into declaring war against Britain.[62]

Two developments sustained the Republican congressional majority as it moved toward war. The first was the awareness that most of the country was even more exasperated with Britain than they were. A number of representatives commented on the inversion that had taken place in the way they expected public opinion to form.[63] Rising public anger against Britain focused especially on the impressment of American seamen. Reports of Britain's "man stealing" tended to elicit a more intense response than did reports of seized vessels. The friends and relatives of those involved found it difficult to accept the loss of a fellow citizen's freedom. The seizure of a vessel, by contrast, only affected the property of merchants who in all likelihood were also guilty of violating the nation's commercial regulations. The public sentiment against impressment could be measured in proposals for retaliation that won endorsement from some state legislatures. In December 1811, a Pennsylvania Senate resolution, with which the House subsequently concurred, recommended that "for every impressed American citizen" the United States seize "a subject of his Britannic majesty, wherever such subject can be found" and subject him "to imprisonment and labor corresponding to the impressed American, on board of a British ship of war."[64]

The second development that helped steady the Republican majority was the Henry Affair of March 1812. John Henry, by birth an Anglo-Irishman, had immigrated to the United States in the 1790s. During the Quasi-War against France he had obtained a commission in the U.S. Army as captain of the artillery and had served briefly in forts defending Portland and a harbor near Boston. At the conclusion of the Quasi-War, Henry resigned his commission, bought property in Vermont near the Canadian line, and studied law. He subsequently came to the attention of the Governor General of Canada, Sir James Craig, after Henry's outspoken anti-Republican sentiments found their way into print. Craig recruited Henry as a spy and in the winter of 1809 dispatched him on a confidential mission to Boston to assess the political upheaval the Federalists were creating there. Craig's instructions to Henry noted that "if the Federalists of the Eastern States should be successful in obtaining . . . [a] decided influence . . . it is not improbable, that . . . they will . . . bring about a separation from the general Union." Henry was authorized to put the Federalist leadership in touch with British authorities should they desire assistance in pursuing that goal.[65]

Henry's first reported from northern Vermont that the embargo was so unpopular the people would join Massachusetts "should [she] take any bold step toward resisting the execution of these laws." But at the beginning of March, when Henry reached Boston, he saw the situation differently. The federal government had become sufficiently "alarmed, at the menacing attitude of the Northern States" so that the danger of war was diminishing. The only thing that could lead to hostilities was a belligerent response by Britain to non-intercourse. If war were declared, Henry predicted the Federalist leadership of Massachusetts legislature would call a Congress "to be composed of the delegates from the Federal States, and erect a separate Government for their common defence and common interest." Henry felt that the new government then "would . . . be in a condition to make or receive proposals from Great Britain," which would in all likelihood ripen into "a strict alliance." But Henry warned that the "project of withdrawing the Eastern States from the Union" was "a very unpopular" one and that the likelihood the Republicans would push matters to extremes was diminishing. Henry concluded that "[t]o bring about a separation of the States under distinct and independent Governments, is an affair of . . . uncertainty, and, however desirable, cannot be effected but by a series of acts and a long continued policy tending to irritate the Southern and conciliate the Northern people."[66]

Madison arranged to purchase Henry's correspondence with Craig for $50,000, using a Frenchman named Paul-Emile Soubiron—who posed as the Spanish count Edward de Crillon—and Ambassador Sérurier as intermediaries. Soubiron and Henry had split the money and were in the process of departing the country when Madison transmitted the Henry correspondence to Congress on March 9. The president claimed the documents "prove[d] that . . . the British Government . . . [had employed] a secret agent . . . in certain States, more especially at the seat of the Government in Massachusetts, in fomenting disaffection to the constituted authorities of the nation . . . for the purpose of bringing about resistance to the laws, and eventually, in concert with a British force, of destroying the Union."[67] The Senate responded to the president's communication by requesting the names of Henry's informants only to learn that Henry had screened their identities. The House referred the Henry correspondence to a select committee, which reported on March 19 that though they were convinced the documents were authentic, Henry's "careful concealment . . . of every circumstance which could lead to the discovery and punishment of any individuals . . . who were criminally connected with him" precluded further proceedings in the matter.[68]

Though the circumstances surrounding the Henry correspondence as well as the revelation that Soubiron was an imposter diminished the impact of the disclosure, it still amounted to more than the "dud" that most historians, following the lead of the British ambassador and the Federalists, have dismissed it as being.[69] The House committee's report endorsed the president's opinion that the papers constituted "conclusive evidence that the British Government . . . have been deliberately and perfidiously pursuing measures to divide these States, and to involve our citizens in all the guilt of treason, and the horrors of a civil war."[70] In the meantime Henry's correspondence, first published in the *National Intelligencer* on March 10 in a ten-column spread, had appeared in various regional papers, and was well known to the nation at large. A letter from Henry to Secretary of State Monroe dated February 20, 1812, accompanied Henry's letters to Craig. In it Henry alleged the United States had been badly treated because of the "opinion entertained by foreign states, '*that in* [responding to] *any measure tending to wound their pride, or provoke their hostility, the Government of this Country could never induce a great majority of its citizens to concur.*'" He also claimed his motive in tendering his correspondence was to produce "UNAIMITY AMONG PARTIES IN AMERICA."[71]

The Henry Papers failed to silence the Federalists. The *New England Palladium* dismissed the administration's action as a ploy designed to affect the outcome of the 1812 gubernatorial contest in Massachusetts. The Federalists picked up on Henry's admission that the ministry had refused to reward Henry as much as he thought his services were worth to argue that Henry had been unable to gather any information that the British government valued enough to pay for. They also accused Madison of squandering the public's money in purchasing tainted testimony.[72] In this way Massachusetts Federalists succeeded in neutralizing the local effect of the Henry correspondence. But the exposé had a major impact on Republicans throughout the rest of the nation.

Republican newspapers were discriminate in evaluating the credibility of Henry's revelations, noting that "his *treason to the hatchers of treason*" personally entitled him to little credit. However, the correspondence did demonstrate the perfidious intentions of the British government as well as the support Britain expected to receive from New England's Federalists. The committee of the House of Representatives had gone to the trouble of having the secretary of state verify that the signatures of British officials in the correspondence were authentic. Thus the Henry Papers supported the Republican conclusion that the challenge Britain—in association with the New England Federalists—posed to the nation required action rather than prudence. As the *National Intelligencer* subsequently noted, war had long ceased to be "a question of expediency. War or irretrievable disgrace appear to us to be the only alternatives in the choice of the American government."[73]

After consulting with the House Foreign Relations Committee, Madison sent Congress a brief message on April 1 recommending the adoption of a temporary embargo. Though Madison's official message made no mention of war and Monroe responded deviously when Foster queried him on the matter, Hezekiah Niles thought it was a "measure which all have considered as the necessary prelude to war."[74] Madison would have preferred a 120-day embargo as most likely to bring Britain to heel without hostilities, but after the fiasco of 1809 the Republicans could no longer afford to look as though they were hesitant to fight. Moreover, if Canada was to be the field of operations, the summer of 1812 offered the best chance for achieving a military decision before Britain had a chance to send reinforcements.[75] Madison accordingly asked for a sixty-day embargo. The House adopted the president's recommendation on the same day it was received. Objections in the Senate prevented that body from acting for two more days. It then voted for a ninety-day embargo, to which the House immediately acquiesced, lest any further delay send the wrong message by encouraging wholesale evasions. In addition, ninety days would allow the administration more time to prepare for the summer campaign.[76]

An Ominous Setback

News of the impending embargo leaked out even before Congress received the president's message. Josiah Quincy boasted to the House on April 3 that he, together with Representative Emott of New York and Senator Lloyd of Massachusetts, had dispatched an express to warn the merchants of Philadelphia, New York, and Boston on March 31. Quincy contended that in doing so, they "violated no obligation, even of the most . . . delicate kind" since the Foreign Relations Committee had informed various members of the House, one of whom had passed the information on to him. Quincy praised the committee's "patriotism" for enabling him with his Federalist colleagues "to give an opportunity for great masses of property to escape from the ruin our Cabinet was meditating for them. . . . [T]he jaws of the British lion, and of the French tiger . . . are places of refuge, of joy and delight, when compared with the grasp and fangs of this hyena embargo." Quincy pointed to the effect the news had had in Philadelphia where "the whole mercantile class was in motion . . . flying in all directions from the coming mischief, as if it were a plague and a pestilence." If anyone doubted his word, Quincy invited the members to look down the Potomac to Alexandria where they would see "poor seamen, towing down their vessels against wind and tide, anxious only to escape from a country which destroys under the mask of preserving."[77]

After the Henry disclosure the majority of Americans had no trouble locating Quincy's purple rhetoric squarely within the context of British intrigue. But the timing of Quincy's leak proved unfortunate for the Republicans in Massachusetts. Word of the ninety-day embargo of 1812 came just before the electorate went to the polls to choose the next governor and Senate. In retrospect it is tempting to attribute the Federalists' electoral triumph exclusively to Quincy's warning.[78] A full understanding of this pivotal Massachusetts election, however, requires one to look beyond the ninety-day embargo because the interval between when the public first learned of it and the election was very brief. As significant as the embargo or the play the Federalists were giving to recent French depredations were the difficulties the Massachusetts Republicans had made for themselves in trying to lead the state into a war with Britain.[79]

With Gerry's assault on the Boston "assemblage" at the spring 1811 meeting of the General Court, the Republicans had embarked on an extensive legislative program designed to curtail Federalist power in the state. Their most important measure was to transfer responsibility for the travel and living expenses of representatives from the towns to the state treasury. As one commentator observed, now that "Representatives of *all* the people . . . [were to be] paid by *all* the people . . . the towns who are represented as counties, and who . . . [elect]forty-four, or even twelve representatives [Boston and Salem respectively] shall no longer have it in their power to oppress small and distant corporations by an *overwhelming representation*."[80] The Republicans also expanded the suffrage and changed the law so that unincorporated religious societies would have access to funds raised by public taxation.[81] Finally, they reformed the state's judicial system. This involved replacing the old courts of common pleas with a new system of circuit courts, making the clerks of these courts serve at the pleasure of the governor rather than the court, and limiting the terms of sheriffs. At the end of October 1811 Gerry had even issued a Thanksgiving proclamation that admonished the clergy against preaching "under the guidance of passion, prejudice, and worldly delusion."[82]

The Federalists press denounced these Republican measures as self-serving. They objected especially to the new court system, construing it as an expression of Republican hostility toward the judiciary as well as a way of enhancing the patronage at the executive's disposal to secure the governor's reelection.[83] Judicial patronage, however, caused almost as much dissatisfaction among Republicans as it did among Federalists because of the difficulties the governor and council encountered in filling all the vacant offices. Part of the problem arose from lack of information about the qualifications and stature of candidates. But part also stemmed from a shortage of Republicans possessing the social qualifications associated with the exercise of judicial authority. This led to a continuing tension between Gerry and his council, exemplified at the end of 1811 by a deadlock over who should be appointed sheriff of Worcester.[84] Republican dissatisfaction with Gerry's appointments was no less debilitating for staying underground. Injured Federalists, however, proved to be very vocal.

Alden Bradford, one of court clerks affected by the reform, who would later emerge as a leading historian of the commonwealth, linked the loss of his position to a Republican attempt to monopolize power. Bradford reminded Gerry that he had been elected in 1810 as a moderate who promised relief from the vicious partisan politics to which the embargo had given rise. Bradford attributed his dismissal to Republican extremists and warned Gerry that he risked forfeiting the support of moderates from both parties if he backed the administration's policy of war with Britain. Bradford felt that Britain was behaving in a more conciliatory way than France and attributed the continued anti-British stand of the administration to French influence. Though himself a moderate, Bradford now identified unambiguously with the state's Federalist leadership. "[I]f our national Rulers . . . persevere in measures *ruinous to our trade and navigation* and calculated to further the schemes of the *mighty Despot* of continental Europe," he predicted, "the people of the *New England* states will . . . rise in their wonted strength, and with the *indignant feelings of* 1775, sever themselves from that part of the nation, which *thus wickedly abandons their rights and interests.*"[85]

Samuel Freeman, dismissed from a position that he had held since 1776 as clerk of the court of common pleas, linked orthodox Congregationalism and Federalist politics in precisely the manner Gerry had hoped to discourage. To the usual Federalists objection that the Republicans were partial to France, Freeman added an apocalyptic dimension by casting France as the Antichrist referred to in the Book of Revelation. He maintained that if the people of the United States had supported godly Federalists, the nation would have remained united and happy. Instead Freeman feared if the Republicans persisted in their present course, a civil war would ensue. He admitted that he might be mistaken in his beliefs, but finding fault with one's rulers was not a crime and he was doing no more than urging those who agreed with him to vote.[86] Freeman's diatribe had the virtue of making the subsequent protest of an unidentified Federalist clergyman look moderate, even reasonable. This cleric claimed the governor had insinuated that he and his Federalist colleagues were traitors, and he suggested that the allusion to their "passion, prejudice, and worldly delusion" applied more aptly to Gerry himself than to them.[87]

However, neither the squawks of disappointed officeholders nor Federalist attempts to exploit religious prejudices weakened the Massachusetts Republicans as much as Gerry's January 1812 address to the legislature did. Gerry intended a sermon about the evils of party that would separate moderate from extreme Federalists, whom he claimed had hijacked "the *name* of

Federalists . . . as a cloak . . . for avoiding . . . censure." But he undercut his effort to isolate the extremists with a polarizing description of Great Britain designed to justify the approaching war. Gerry accused her government of pursuing "a *system of rapine*," of seeking "to *degrade* these States to the level of *colonies*," and of literally enslaving American seamen by forcing them to serve on "*floating pandemoniums of the ocean*." He claimed a recent proclamation by the prince regent granting free entry and clearance from Halifax to U.S. vessels violating non-intercourse seduced "our citizens from their allegiance" and placed "his royal highness on a *level* with lawless smugglers." Though the British people were justly "celebrated for their religion, morality, love of liberty, literature, industry, and valour," Britain's government had been transformed by "a system of executive *influence*" into one of "*lawless* power" which he claimed had "ruined every . . . [nation that] has yielded to her policy." Gerry invoked his countrymen's former subordination to Britain for illustration, but argued that Britain's worst crime both then and in 1812 was employing writers and printers to "vilify . . . the members of Congress, and their principal officers."[88]

References to the revolutionary past were of questionable relevance in selling the Massachusetts public on a war with Britain while that nation remained locked in a death struggle with France. Gerry acknowledged that hostilities might "accelerate [Britain's] destruction." "This, which it is in her power to prevent, is not the object of the United States." In fact "they would deeply regret it." But so long as Britain persisted with her "*man stealing*" of American sailors, would not a failure to resist invite "acts more criminal; *to seize our landsmen, when requisite for her mines, or for defending her conquests in distant climes?*" Gerry asserted that the country's "existence, as an *independent* nation, depends on their maintaining their rights." If "at this momentous crisis" it shrank from the duty of self-preservation, it would next find itself petitioning the British Crown "to admit us again into his royal favor as penitent subjects." Since the choice was between "liberty and independence" or "reenslavement by Britain," it was time to "terminate [the] unnatural, dangerous, disgraceful *spirit of party*."[89] Gerry then undercut his pitch for unity by adding he had "received several anonymous threats of assassination, for having supported the national government." He saw these as "part of a system to paralyze the exertions, in the cause of our country" and had nothing but defiance for those who would deflect the Republicans from "their duty to . . . support . . . the national government." However, the only other person Gerry could point to that had been threatened was ex-president John Adams, who had been menaced "with *assassination* in his bed."[90]

Both houses of the legislature had dutifully reiterated the sentiments in Gerry's address, though the Senate managed to distance itself from his death-threat conclusion by expressing confidence "that the wretches who penned them stand isolated from the rest of society."[91] The House took the threats to Gerry's and Adams's lives seriously and used them as evidence "that the enemies of the U. States, have most of them, rendezvoused in this capital and vicinity." It also tried to intimidate extremist Federalists by accusing them of committing "mental treason." The House majority hoped "that their anticonstitutional principles bursting forth in practices little short of overt acts of treason" would not be sanctioned by the majority of well-meaning Federalists, and expressed confidence that Gerry's address would "arrest the bold career of [this] noon-day inceptive treason." Such allusions were intended as a reminder to the Federalists that the Republicans expected war against Britain would empower them to prosecute disloyal behavior.[92]

Gerry and his Republican followers made a serious miscalculation in harping on the prospect of war with Britain because Massachusetts had more reason to dread the eventuality than the rest of the nation. Halifax, Britain's largest military base in the western Atlantic, posed an immediate threat to the state, which possessed a longer, more accessible coastline than any other region with the possible exception of the Chesapeake. Hostilities with Britain could be expected to impose greater hardships on New England than elsewhere, quite apart from the damage it might do the region's commerce. The evils that Federalists claimed they saw in Republican policies, then, possessed an immediate, palpable quality that was lacking in the evils the Republicans alleged would result from their adversaries' electoral triumph. Massachusetts Federalists accordingly construed the exaggerations and veiled threats in the governor's address and the House reply as signs of political weakness and exploited them accordingly.

The Federalist press assaulted Gerry for his "intemperate" description of foreign governments and his domestic, political adversaries. A series of hostile editorials in the Boston *Repertory* dismissed Gerry's performance as a "monument of disgrace." The second editorial in the series likened Gerry's "mode of reasoning" to charging Christianity "with all the martyrdoms which attended the persecution of it." The final one accused him of appealing to the "credulity and prejudice of the community." The editorialist also observed, "If your Excellency were really in terrour for your life," that should be imputed "to the wild suggestions of a disturbed conscience, rather than to a depravity in the morals of your fellow citizens." The series described the address as "a record for posterity that Governour [*sic*] Gerry was a child in intellect—a tyrant in principle, and the slave of passions even worse than his own."[93]

Though the *Repertory* was the harshest on Gerry's person, a series of "Projected Answers" to his address in the *Columbian Centinel* proved more effective in drawing attention to the composition's all-too-evident contradictions. Was not Gerry's attempt to revive feelings about former differences in sentiment

1. James Sullivan (1744–1808) The Republican governor of Massachusetts during the embargo controversy. By H. Wright Smith after Gilbert Stuart. (This item is reproduced by permission of the Huntington Library, San Marino, California.)

2. Levi Lincolm (1749–1820) James Sullivan's lieutenant governor and successor. By William S. Lincoln in the possession of Mrs. J. W. Wetherall. (This item is reproduced by permission of the Huntington Library, San Marino, California.)

Timothy Pickering

Æt. 68.

3. Timothy Pickering (1745–1829) The controversial Federalist congressman from
    Massachusetts. By H. Wright Smith after Gilbert Stuart. (This item is reproduced
    by permission of the Huntington Library, San Marino, California.)

4. James Hillhouse (1754–1832) Timothy Pickering's roommate in Washington for many years and Connecticut's most prominent Federalist. Engraving by A. H. Ritchie. (Courtesy of Sterling Memorial Library, Yale University.)

5. Josiah Quincy (1772–1864) Federalism's most flamboyant spokesman in congress.
From an oil painting by Gilbert Stuart, 1824. (Photograph © 2004 Museum of
Fine Arts, Boston.)

6. Harrison Gray Otis (1756–1848) A leading Boston Federalist. From an oil painting by Gilbert Stuart, 1809. (Courtesy of the Society for the Preservation of New England Antiquities.)

7. Christopher Gore (1758–1827) A Federalist governor of Massachusetts. From an oil on panel by John Trumbull, circa 1802-1804. (Courtesy of the Massachusetts Historical Society.)

ELBRIDGE GERRY.

Engraved by J.B.Longacre from a drawing by Vanderlyn.

8. Elbridge Gerry (1744–1814) A Republican governor of Massachusetts and vice president of the United States. Engraving copy by Longacre, after Vonderlyn. (Courtesy of the Massachusetts Historical Society.)

9. Caleb Strong (1745–1819) The Federalist governor of Massachusetts during the War of 1812. From an oil on canvas by James B. Marston, 1807. (Courtesy of the Massachusetts Historical Society.)

at odds with his stated objective of quelling party strife? What was the propriety of Gerry's suggesting without any evidence that there were writers in the commonwealth in the pay of the British government? If the Republicans seriously desired peace with Britain, was it appropriate to label "the Sovereign" of that country a " 'Smuggler, Forger, and Incendiary?' " Finally, the insinuation "that your precious life is in danger" was a "calumny . . . on our country" since political assassination was unknown in "our happy and peaceful republic."[94]

Gerry made matters worse with his response to a Federalist taunt in the *Repertory* that he should act rather than complain about the licentiousness of the press. He obliged by ordering the state attorney and solicitor general to survey the Boston press for libels of elected officials. At the end of February 1812 a report appeared identifying 253 libels, twelve of which resulted in indictments by a Suffolk County Grand Jury. Ten of the twelve indictments were against the *Scourge*, a recent addition to Boston's Federalist press, and two were brought against the Republican *Independent Chronicle*. All had resulted either in guilty pleas or convictions. Gerry noted that because Massachusetts had no statute governing seditious libels, the trials had taken place under the common law. But a judicial ruling allowed those accused of libeling elected officials to plead the truth in their defense. This did little to calm political passions on the eve of the election, however, since the Federalists viewed the report and the message accompanying it as a clear signal that a Republican victory would muzzle their press.[95]

In early February 1812 Massachusetts Federalists nominated Caleb Strong for governor. After two defeats at Gerry's hands, they concluded that Gore was a liability. Strong had an unexceptional past, and his manner, unlike Gore's, was one of "unostentatious, republican simplicity." Fisher Ames had described Strong as someone who "calls hasty-pudding luxury." Born in Northampton in 1746, Strong had graduated from Harvard with the class of 1764. A bout with small pox had left his sight too impaired to permit military service. However, it did not prevent him from studying law with Joseph Hawley, western Massachusetts's leading revolutionary. Strong soon found himself serving on Northampton's committee of public safety and then representing the town in the state legislature. After playing a prominent role in drafting and securing the ratification of the Constitution of 1780, he had served as senator for Hampshire County in the new government until 1789. In 1787 he was an active member of the Massachusetts delegation to the Philadelphia convention, and unlike Gerry had exerted his influence to have the Constitution approved by the state ratifying convention. Appointed United States senator for a six-year term beginning in 1789, Strong supported Hamilton's fiscal program, sponsoring the bill to incorporate the Bank of the United States. After 1793 he backed Washington's efforts to come to an accommodation with Britain by voting for ratification of the Jay

Treaty. He retired from Congress in 1796 and only consented to reenter public life in 1800 when he was elected governor in a year of Republican triumphs. Thereafter Strong was reelected each year until Sullivan defeated him in 1807. In the midst of the growing acrimony between Federalists and Republicans, Strong managed to retain his reputation for moderation.[96]

The Federalist convention that nominated Strong also issued an "Address to the free and independent people of Massachusetts." It protested the legislature's recent decision to pay the town representatives in the House of Representatives because it would increase the size of the legislature, "already too unwieldy for the despatch of public business" to a point where "all fair deliberation" would become impossible. This would permit "the many to be led blindfold by the few." It accused the Republicans of trying to drive "the substantial and independent men of all parties" from government to make way for "the bold, aspiring, and unprincipled" to impose "Standing Armies" and a "whole system of Internal Taxes, including a LAND TAX and a STAMP TAX." It concluded with a declaration that "*the Metropolis and the Federal Party have been denounced, for stating what the whole people now realizes to be true,*" namely that Republican commercial restrictions had served no other purpose than to drain "the country of wealth, and render us less prepared for War," which it was neither to the nation's interest or honor to declare.[97]

Of the many complaints covered in the address, none proved more effective than criticism of the Republicans for redrawing the senatorial districts for the coming state election. The Republicans had divided several counties, which had previously constituted a single district, to form new electoral districts. The address denounced the scheme's disregard of "immemorial usage, geographic boundaries, local convenience, and 'the proportion of public taxes paid by the respective Districts.' " It accused the Republicans of seeking "the permanent ascendancy of [a] party, without respect to any change which the will of the people may effect in the other departments of the government."[98] The Federalist minority of 226 members of the House of Representatives protested the constitutionality of the legislature's actions. They denounced the Republicans' handiwork as an example of "the modern spirit of innovation, which . . . acts on political institutions *like vice upon the human heart. Its presence is hardly acknowledged, before it manifests the attainment of its object, and is prepared to found its right on usurpation.*"[99]

Senatorial redistricting provided the Federalists with their most potent weapon because of the difficulty the Republicans experienced in reconciling it with their principles. The Federalist press made as much as it could out of the Republicans' embarrassment on this score.[100] The campaign culminated with a political cartoon that appeared in the *Boston Gazette*. Pictorial matter in the newspapers of the period was rare and usually primitive in quality. This cartoon portrayed the new Essex South senatorial district as an elaborately rendered dragon. Beneath the picture appeared the deliberations of a learned doctor, described as "famous for peeping under the skirts of nature," in trying to classify the monster. After comparing it with a salamander, he christened it a "gerrymander."[101] The term, which has remained a part of our political language ever since, possessed then a telling specificity which it has subsequently lost. In availing themselves of humor in the midst of a struggle which partisans on each side viewed as anything but funny, the Federalists communicated far more effectively with the less committed middle of the political spectrum than Gerry did.

The result of Republican missteps and Federalist adroitness was Strong's election by a narrow margin, twelve hundred out of the more than one hundred thousand votes cast. Even before it was clear that Gerry would be defeated, Madison received reports that some of the larger towns that had previously sent Republican delegations to the state House of Representatives would be sending Federalist ones in 1812.[102] The political transformation of Massachusetts was much more threatening to the Republicans than the challenge DeWitt Clinton in New York would pose as Madison's rival for the presidency in 1812. Unlike his uncle, Vice President George Clinton (who died on April 20, 1812), DeWitt Clinton had never served as the governor of New York. Instead his political base was New York City, over which he presided as mayor. Though the younger Clinton was prepared to ally with northern Federalists in pursuing his presidential ambitions, his candidacy fed on hostility to Virginia's leadership more than to Republicanism itself. Clinton would run as a peace Republican after war was declared, but Madison knew in advance that he would never lead a regional insurgency that was prepared to threaten disunion in order to stymie the national government. During the spring of 1812, the congressional opponents of war with Britain construed Clinton's nomination for the presidency by a caucus of the New York legislature as a Republican setback comparable to the loss of Massachusetts. But they confused an effort on the part of New York to assert political preeminence with an ideological confrontation. Despite its rapid growth since the Revolution, New York lacked the resources to challenge Virginia's leadership of the Republican party.[103] Nor was New York likely to succeed in doing so while the Napoleonic wars continued. Instead the European conflict perpetuated the rivalry between the two largest states that had sponsored the Revolution, and by doing so helped to keep national politics polarized around a Massachusetts/Virginia axis that dated back to 1774.

The Final Plunge

As April gave way to May, Republicans had additional reasons besides the looming loss of Massachusetts to make them hesitate about going to war with Great

Britain. Despite repeated declarations that British force would be met with American force, very little had been done to implement the military program Congress had endorsed during the winter. Some progress had been made during the spring in raising the men authorized for the expanded army, but the flood of volunteers that had played so large a role in Republican calculations failed to materialize.[104] The only service that was remotely prepared was the navy, and it was ready only because there was so little of it. If the United States was to triumph, it would do so on land. But the force of twenty-four thousand men that Secretary of War Henry Dearborn calculated he needed to take Quebec as it was presently garrisoned clearly would not be ready before navigation on the St. Lawrence opened and reinforcements arrived from Europe. Upper Canada remained a feasible theater for operations; Dearborn thought that a force of five thousand men might subdue British posts in that region and two thousand could hold them.[105] But even this operation could not be delayed past midsummer if it was to avoid being overtaken by the Canadian winter. Long before the ninety-day embargo was due to expire, Madison and the Republican leadership in Congress realized that their hope for a speedy conquest of Canada was a pipe dream.

More disturbing than the lack of men and materials was the shortage of money arising from the disappointing response to the loan that had been opened to finance military preparations. Republican areas like South Carolina joined Federalist-dominated financial circles in the North in failing to take their full quotas of this loan.[106] The Twelfth Congress's determination to postpone the imposition of war taxes until war was declared further undermined the government's credit. Of course, the treasury had other options for raising funds, the most eligible being to issue interest-bearing treasury notes. Gallatin recommended this expedient when the federal loan came up almost $5 million short.[107] Reliance on treasury notes, however, stirred memories of revolutionary finance when the depreciation of the continental bills of credit had bankrupted the Continental Congress. And those with money to lend were not reassured by the token provision made for the continentals in Hamilton's fiscal plan for funding the consolidated revolutionary debt.[108]

The administration's problems with France also persisted. Madison entertained high expectations for Joel Barlow's mission to Paris that began in the autumn of 1811. Since 1788 Barlow had spent a total of sixteen years abroad, more than a dozen of them in Paris, where he owned a house and was well known to a wide circle of prominent men and women. Though Barlow's Parisian friends regarded the emperor as an upstart, Barlow still had unrivaled assets in working with the new imperial bureaucracy. He was one of a handful of Americans, including Washington, Hamilton, Jefferson, and Madison, who had been made citizens of France. He was also fluent in the language, as well as having a competence in German and Italian and a smattering of Spanish and Arabic. Most important, he had demonstrated his diplomatic mettle in 1796–1797 by managing, in the course of a perilous mission, to ransom 120 Americans from the Dey of Algiers and to conclude treaties with the North African pirate states of Tunis and Tripoli.[109] If anyone could extract advantage from unpromising circumstances, Barlow's track record suggested he could.

Unfortunately, Napoleon was not prepared to be obliging. Though Barlow was warmly greeted in France—he was personally received by the emperor, and the foreign minister was lavish in his verbal reassurances—Napoleon's ambitions in eastern Europe moved the United States, never at the center of his visual field, further to the periphery. Insofar as he was prepared to devote any attention to the Franco-American relationship, he did so only to injure Britain. From Napoleon's perspective the United States could best serve his purposes by declaring war against his adversary. Since the British cabinet based its refusal to modify its Orders-in-Council on France adhering to its decrees, Napoleon steered a course designed to give the United States only enough encouragement to persevere in its confrontation with Britain, without risking an Anglo-American reconciliation. When Barlow pressed the French foreign minister for clarification about the status of American vessels, which French cruisers were continuing to seize and burn, he was eventually handed a copy of a decree allegedly issued on April 28, 1811, at St. Cloud. This stated that the Berlin and Milan decrees no longer applied to American shipping, but it failed to explain why French depredations had continued after its issuance. It also failed to address the status of American vessels seized under the Decree of Rambouillet, about which the Federalists continued to clamor for clarification.

Federalist critics, seconded by John Randolph, played on the Republicans' multiple embarrassments as much as they could. At the beginning of May, when attendance in Congress had thinned after six continuous months in session, Representative Hermanus Bleecker of New York presented the petition of eight hundred Albany residents calling for the repeal of the ninety-day embargo. Bleecker justified his action on the grounds that an "active offensive war" in sixty days time was "wholly out of the question." "What is the state of your fortifications? Where are your armies, your navy? Have you money? No, sir, rely upon it there will be, there can be, no . . . active and offensive war, within sixty days." Bleecker then invoked Randolph as authority for the notion that embarking on hostilities "in our present unprepared state, would be little short of an act of treason." Congress had nothing to show for itself besides "paper preparations." "To go to war under such circumstances would necessarily bring upon us shame, disgrace, and defeat." Therefore, the only reasonable course was to repeal the embargo. Otherwise the Republicans would alienate the people and "You cannot go to war without the people."[110]

Randolph seconded Bleecker's argument, playing on the inconsistencies of the Republicans' behavior with unexcelled sarcasm. "Go to war without money, without men, without a navy! Go to war when you have not the courage, while your lips utter 'war' to lay war taxes!" Randolph claimed the public did not believe there would be a war "because the public are totally unaware of the high price at which this House holds its own consistency—that the ruin of the nation weighs nothing in the scale against it." Randolph accused Congress of misleading the nation with its behavior. "Passing resolutions to lay taxes by overwhelming majorities, and letting them lie on the table" while "relying on the scanty resources of borrowing, which has failed, proves that you have no system." Randolph warned the Republicans that "you cannot stem the current of popular sentiment; you cannot drive the American people into measures which they see and which they feel to be subversive of their best interests. They will speak, and you must hear."[111]

The Federalist onslaught seconded by Randolph left the Republicans little alternative but to affirm their determination to go to war regardless of the lack of preparations. Many spoke to this effect despite their private misgivings, in which subsequent historians have put far too much stock.[112] But the impassioned words of Felix Grundy exerted the most influence. He accused the opposition of attempting "to alarm us with" warnings about "a gathering storm in the East, which, they say, threatens destruction to the present majority of Congress, in the event of a war with Great Britain." Instead he insisted the "great body of the people . . . are only waiting to see the constituted authorities lead the way . . . in vindication of the nation's rights." Grundy was confident that "[w]henever war is declared, the people will put forth their strength to support their rights." The greater danger was vacillation: "if we *talk* of war, and *tamely submit*—then, indeed, public opinion will and ought to be against us. If one day you lay an embargo, and on the next repeal it, without any cause . . . public confidence must be withdrawn." Grundy acknowledged the nation could be better prepared, but held the congressional opposition responsible. Should "any national calamity . . . take place . . . from want of preparation," Grundy said "[t]he American people have intelligence enough to put down to each public man his due." He lamented the existence "in this country [of] an organized opposition" that had "admonished" the people "to withhold their resources from us." It was "no subject of congratulation to see a set of men combining together to weaken their own country, and thereby indirectly give advantage to the enemy." But Grundy predicted that if Congress stood firm in defending the nation's rights, the people "will go with you in every extremity." The House then voted fifty-seven to thirty-one to postpone consideration of Bleeker's petition until after the ninety-day embargo expired.[113]

That might as well have been the House vote to declare war but for the thin attendance in early May. Though Congress could have postponed the final decision until the end of June, other factors such as retaining an option for a Canadian campaign and intercepting Britain's annual fleet from the West Indies pointed to June as the best time to commence hostilities. On May 19, the USS *Hornet* arrived from Europe with dispatches that failed to convey any change in the diplomatic situation there. On June 1, Madison invited Congress to oppose "force to force in defense of their national rights."[114] On June 4, the House voted to declare war by a margin of seventy-nine to forty-nine, despite Randolph's continuing attempts to obstruct its proceedings.[115] The Senate then let itself be diverted for more than a week by proposals to limit hostilities to the high seas. When these failed, both because of the impracticality of challenging the world's foremost sea power to a naval contest and the improbability of limiting hostilities in the way intended, the Senate eventually agreed with the House, subject to minor amendments. On June 19 Madison finally issued a proclamation announcing that war had been declared.[116]

Unbeknownst to either the president or Congress, the British government was in the process of revoking its Orders-in-Council that had been a principal object of contention between the two countries. During 1811 non-intercourse had exerted more pressure on Britain than either the embargo of 1807–1809 or the original non-intercourse law that replaced it. Most of this effectiveness derived from the altered state of the Atlantic economy. Napoleon's subversion of the Spanish monarchy in 1808 had opened Latin America to British trade, taking up most of the slack in the demand for British exports created by the shrinking American market. In 1810, however, the Latin American market became saturated, setting off a severe depression in British industry and conferring new significance on the American market. Since non-intercourse still permitted American vessels to export to Britain, American merchants built up substantial sterling credits there. But they hesitated to purchase British manufactures despite their financial ability to do so while importation remained forbidden. British merchant-industrialists, seconded by laborers adversely affected by a poor harvest in 1811, brought increasing pressure to bear for a relaxation of the Orders-in-Council. The new government, which formed in the wake of prime minister Spencer Perceval's assassination at the hands of a madman, concluded it had enough on its plate without an unnecessary war with America and, prodded by the parliamentary opposition, finally revoked its orders on June 23.[117]

Americans remained completely in the dark about developments in Britain because of their dependence on the reports of charge d'affairs Jonathan

Russell, the highest-ranking U.S. diplomat in Britain after Pinkney returned home. Russell misread the confused political situation in Britain, and communication problems compounded Russell's error. Thus news of Perceval's assassination failed to arrive in Washington until after Congress had declared war, and the event's effect on future British policy took much longer. Modern technology might have delayed or even aborted hostilities for the moment, but it would not have resolved the problem the Republicans were convinced they confronted. For they saw the nation imperiled not just by Britain, but by Britain in league with a domestic faction. New England Republicans felt more threatened by their domestic opponents than did Republicans from other areas. Hence Henry Dearborn's anxiety about the encouragement the Federalists derived from the Senate's delay in accepting the House decision to declare war, and Gerry's jubilant response to the news of the eventual declaration: "God be praised, our country is safe."[118] But all Republicans agreed on the dual nature of the challenge they confronted, and this would complicate how the administration would respond to British peace overtures. While the Federalists remained such avid British partisans, few Republicans believed that British concessions were likely to be either meaningful or lasting.[119]

6

RESISTANCE TO THE WAR

Declaring war in the face of the determined resistance of a resourceful minority was one thing; triumphing over a foreign adversary thought to be allied with that minority was quite another. The complex challenge facing the Republicans helps explain both the extreme reluctance of Madison and other leading Republicans about commencing hostilities and their aversion to terminating them once begun. At a conference the president solicited with departing British ambassador Foster shortly after the declaration of war, Madison "expressed his regret" about the rupture that had taken place between the two countries, "giv[ing] it to be understood, that his desire was to avoid . . . pushing matters to extreme[s]." But the political difficulties the Republicans had surmounted to embark on war made Madison even more wary about bringing hostilities to a premature halt. When Foster asked what it would take to restore peace, the president had first replied that a revocation of the Orders-in-Council together with "a promise of negotiation . . . on the Question of Impressment . . . would suffice." But when Foster pressed for an armistice of three months to find out whether his government was prepared to change its policies in the wake of Prime Minister Perceval's May 11 assassination, Madison became evasive.[1] In a subsequent meeting Monroe again rebuffed Foster's proposal for an immediate three-month armistice, reinforcing the impression Madison had given the British envoy that the administration was reluctant to be precise about its terms for halting hostilities. Though the president and secretary of state clearly did not welcome war with Britain, they were even less enthusiastic about peace on the terms they thought Foster was likely to propose.[2] It is worth pausing for a moment to explore in greater detail the sources of their reluctance.

The Perils of Peace

In soliciting a three-month truce, Foster was asking for a great deal. Granting the request meant forfeiting any advantage the United States might hope to gain in Canada during 1812 and postponing offensive operations until 1813. A three-month truce would release the British government from any immediate pressure to relax its Orders-in-Council while providing it with ample time to reinforce Canada. Though, in fact, all three of the attempts to invade Canada during the remainder of 1812 ended in humiliating failure, Madison and Monroe could not have foreseen this at the beginning of the summer. Neither had they any reason to believe that the British ministry would withdraw its orders three days after Congress's declaration of war. The President knew that the poor harvest of 1811 and the need to provide for their forces on the Iberian Peninsula had put the British government under pressure. But he had no way of measuring what effect such considerations would have when weighed against the importance Britain attached to restricting the commerce of neutrals in her struggle with France. And it was anyone's guess how Perceval's assassination might affect British policy. News of this development reached Washington on the same day Madison proclaimed war had been declared. Since the prime minister had a reputation for being a hardliner on the American question, Foster hinted that his death might lead to improving relations between the two nations.[3] But the first reports that the new government had lifted the Orders-in-Council did not arrive in the United States until August 4, long after Congress had adjourned and most of what remained of the government had retired from the unhealthy heat of a Washington summer. Official notification took somewhat longer.[4]

By then the political threat posed by the Federalists had persuaded Madison and Monroe that they little choice but to continue hostilities despite Britain's belated concessions. Had Republican leaders enjoyed the backing of a united country, a different course might have beckoned. But experience had convinced them that although the British government might not wish for a full-scale war with the United States, it meant to assert as much control as it could over American commerce short of provoking war. Changes in administrations and the failure of ministers to honor commitments made by their predecessors had convinced Jefferson that the British were unreliable well before the Erskine fiasco showed that any concessions wrung from Britain at one moment might be revoked the next.[5] More significant, Britain's apparent treachery had failed to destroy the Federalists' attachment to her or to deter them from taking the part of her government against their own. Republican leaders also believed, correctly, that the Federalists were advising the British about how to undermine Republican resolve and strengthen the hand of their American friends. The Federalists, who counseled Augustus Foster that there would be no war because the Madison administration was bluffing, were mistaken.[6] But that error did not assuage Republican anxieties that their coalition was more fragile than the alliance they confronted between the Federalists and the British.

An Address . . . to their Constituents on the subject of the war with Great Britain, issued by the Federalist congressional minority in the House of Representatives, dramatized the Republicans' peril. On June 22 Madison warned Jefferson "that the Federalists in Congs. are to put all their strength and talents into a protest agst. the war, and that the party at large are to be brought out in all their force."[7] Stephen Snowden, a Federalist printer in Alexandria, Virginia, was the first to publish a thirty-five-page version of the eleven-thousand-word document signed by the thirty-four Federalist members of the House of Representatives in early July, but hardly the last. Twenty additional printings, suggesting a combined press run of well over twenty thousand copies, quickly appeared in twelve of the seventeen states. In addition, many of the nation's leading newspapers reprinted the *Address*, including leading Republican ones like the *National Intelligencer* and *Niles's Weekly Register*.[8] By early-nineteenth-century standards this was a media blitz comparable to that which had accompanied Timothy Pickering's notorious 1808 *Letter*. The *Address* rebutted each of the points Madison had made in his "war" message and in so doing summarized the debate that had raged between the Federalists and Republicans. However, few were under the illusion that the *Address* had been written with an eye to changing anyone's mind. Instead its function was to represent the Federalists as the party of peace.

The signers of the *Address* claimed they had "always been of the opinion . . . that a system of peace was the policy which most comported with the character, condition, and interest of the United States." The "prudential considerations" entertained by all "thoughtful men" about "the perils of . . . war" were strengthened by the "experimental" nature of the Constitution. Though peace was best suited to confirming the nation's "recent institutions," Americans "entered upon this war . . . as a divided people." The division proceeded both "from a sense of the inadequacy of our means of success," and "from moral and political objections."[9] The last phrase referred to doubts as to whether a republic could fight an offensive war and still remain a republic. The *Address* then asked how: "A nation like the United States, happy in its local relations: removed from the bloody theatre of Europe: with a maritime border, opening a vast field for enterprise: with territorial possessions exceeding every real want: its firesides safe: its altars undefiled: from invasion nothing to fear; from acquisition nothing to hope; . . . [could] look to Heaven for its smiles, while throwing away, as though they were worthless, all the blessings and joys which peace and a distinguished lot include?"[10] The signers of the *Address* hoped in this way to position themselves to benefit from any military reverses that might occur as well as any peace that might be concluded before the next presidential election.

The Republicans regarded Federalist claims that they were the party of peace as sheer hypocrisy. Had the Federalists not done everything in their power to trash the commercial alternatives to war sponsored by the Republicans and repeatedly advocated war with France?[11] Instead of promoting peace, the *Address* dramatized the political costs the Republicans would incur if they suspended hostilities. Not only would it confirm that the Republican leadership could not be "kicked into war," but it risked demoralizing if it did not entirely dissolve the Republican coalition that had declared the war. A truce would also permit the Federalist minority to coordinate measures with the British government as they were thought to have done against the embargo during 1808 and 1809. Wringing a declaration of war from Congress despite widespread misgivings about the nation's preparedness and the effects war might have on its political institutions had been too strenuous an achievement for the president and secretary of state willingly to repudiate at the first whiff of an accommodation.

The response of Massachusetts Federalists to the prospect of war reinforced the Republicans' conviction that the domestic foe they faced was as dangerous as their foreign enemy. On June 2, the Federalist majority of the newly elected Massachusetts House of Representatives had forwarded to Congress a resolution condemning "an offensive war against Great Britain" as "impolitic, unnecessary, and ruinous." On June 5 a lengthier memorial followed. Anticipating the congressional *Address*, the Massachusetts House claimed that "good policy" as well as "the duty of a nation to itself, forbids us to plunge into a war which desolates the European world, and from which it seems to have been the design of Almighty Providence to exempt us."[12] Countering the theme of national honor in the many legislative resolutions favoring war, the House asserted that the nation's character would not be "stained by yielding to circumstances which it cannot control." Nor would the conquest of Canada afford "indemnification, if achieved, for the losses to which we should be exposed upon our unprotected seaboard, and upon the ocean." Once begun, a war was likely to go on as long as the European conflict persisted, and the memorial predicted it would terminate "after years of disaster, incident to all wars, without accomplishing the object for which it was undertaken." The Massachusetts House undertook "this last respectful effort . . . to induce the National Government to pause," in response to the "dictates of self-preservation," out of "their attachment to the Union, . . . a persuasion of the invincible and growing opposition of the people to these measures, and . . . duty to themselves, to posterity, and to God."[13] The memorial reached Congress on June 12 while the U.S. Senate was still dithering over the declaration.

The day before, a Boston town meeting had appointed a committee of twelve to draft a report about the measures it should "adopt at this momentous crisis." The committee reported back on June 15 that the town could not "*of itself* " do anything to avert the imminent calamity. But "believing . . . that an immense majority of the people are invincibly averse from a conflict equally unnecessary and menacing ruin to themselves, and their posterity," the report hoped "a general expression of the voice of the people would satisfy Congress that those of their Representatives who have voted in favor of war, have not truly represented the wishes of their constituents." If Boston's declaration were ignored, it might nonetheless prove useful in "rescu[ing] the nation from ruin" by the "constitutional means of a change of men and measures," a pointed allusion to the approaching federal elections. The report urged the people to act with "energy and resolution" to have "[t]he public opinion respected," and to "unite without party distinction to save the country from a foreign war, and what is still worse to be dreaded, a *foreign yoke*." A set of resolves condemning war with Britain, calling on the United States to "ride out the storm which we cannot direct," and inviting other towns in the commercial states to join Boston in establishing committees "for corresponding or meeting with them" on the revolutionary model accompanied the report. Boston's town meeting adopted the report and the resolves and made provision for each town in the commonwealth to receive copies.[14]

Both in its inflammatory tone and substance Boston's report and resolves shaped the more elaborate "Address of the House of Representatives to the people of Massachusetts," at the end of June. This address paralleled in many respects the *Address . . . to their Constituents* emanating almost simultaneously from the Federalist minority in Congress. But the Massachusetts version sought local political advantage from holding the Republicans' responsible for the war. The "system deliberately adopted . . . for securing permanent power to a majority of the Senate, in defiance of the voice of the people" had compromised the state government's ability to avert "the ruinous consequences" of the conflict. The Senate and the state's Republican congressmen "exhibit[ed] you as a divided people." Political divisions within Massachusetts in turn persuaded the national government that the people would acquiesce in hostilities, however "unnecessary, unjustifiable, and impolitic." But a "war . . . so outrageous to public opinion, to the feelings and interests of this people, can be supported only by the violence which destroys the freedom of speech, and endangers the liberty of the citizen." The Massachusetts House proposed to speak its mind while it was still free to do so about three causes of the war that the Republicans refused to acknowledge. First and most important was "the embarrassment arising from the precipitate declaration of the President . . . that the French decrees . . . were repealed." Second was the desire "to aggrandize the Southern and Western States at the expence of the Eastern section of the Union." And finally there was the "spirit of jealousy, and competition with Great Britain" and the "mistaken belief that she [Britain] would yield to the pressure of the continental system established by the Tyrant of Europe." The address concluded that the Republicans were far too committed to "retreat without discredit." But Americans still possessed a peaceable remedy against a president who, having made war, was clearly "not qualified to make peace." The House majority exhorted them to "[d]isplay the Majesty of the people" in expressing their outrage, by forming a peace party and denying Madison reelection.[15]

The Federalist leaders of Massachusetts almost seemed to welcome war because it provided an opportunity to resume the political dance previously choreographed against the embargo. The protests of the Republican minority in the state House of Representatives together with the resolves of the Senate caused them little concern. Their adversaries were heavily outnumbered in the House, and the recent gerrymandering of the Senate's electoral districts undercut any claim that the narrow Republican majority there reflected the sentiments of the people.[16] Massachusetts Federalists did not expect much from Independence Day celebrations that year because July 4 followed so closely on the addresses of their partisans in the Congress and the state government. But at the request of the House, Governor Strong designated July 23 as a state fast day in coordination with Connecticut, giving the clergy an occasion to weigh in against the war.[17] In the meantime Boston tried to maintain political momentum after the legislature adjourned by summoning a mass meeting of the "friends of Union, Independence and Liberty of the U. States" on July 13. Newspaper accounts claimed that four thousand people attended, and endorsed, without a single dissenting vote, a set of resolutions that replicated the points made by the Massachusetts House in its address.[18]

Other Federalist towns in the commonwealth obediently mobilized to pass resolutions condemning both the justice and necessity of the war and endorsing the need to replace those in Washington who were responsible.[19] In addition, eighty-six delegates from Hampshire, Hampden, and Franklin counties, eighty-two of whom had been appointed by "regular town meetings," gathered at Northampton on July 21 to denounce the secret actions of Congress that had led to the declaration of war. During the following week the towns of Essex County met in convention to warn of the twin dangers of French influence and tyranny arising from standing armies and mob rule.[20] Finally peace conventions assembled in Plymouth, Barnstable, Middlesex, and Worcester counties during August to urge Madison's repudiation in the coming election. Because the Middlesex and Worcester county conventions met later than the others, they alluded to the lifting of Britain's Orders-in-Council in calling for a cessation of hostilities.[21]

The Transition to Wartime Politics

Because most of the state governments had voiced their support for war the preceding winter, the Federalist leadership of Massachusetts realized that the political revolution they desired would have to come from a spontaneous rising of the people beyond the state's borders. A few meetings and conventions outside Massachusetts appeared to respond to Boston's call for Americans to act as they had during the 1770s. One was an August 5 address, allegedly adopted by fifteen hundred "electors" at Rockingham, New Hampshire, strongly criticizing the official reasons given for the conflict. Since word had just been received that the British had withdrawn their orders, it concentrated on impressment. It wanted no part in fighting a war to protect foreign sailors in American vessels, especially when France's decrees remained unrepealed. The Rockingham meeting attributed the war to a "small and heated *Majority*" tyrannizing over a "large and respectable *Minority*" and vowed to resist any efforts to unite "the Republic of America, with the military despotism of France."[22] However, since southeastern New Hampshire was little more than an annex to neighboring Essex County in Massachusetts, its declarations hardly signaled the general disaffection that the Federalist leadership of the state had hoped for.

Slightly more gratifying was a rally of twenty-five hundred "Friends of Peace, Commerce, and the Constitution" that assembled in Hudson, New York, on August 18, during the height of the agricultural season despite "the exertions of the advocates of the war . . . to repress the attendance."[23] The state of New York possessed the political potential for restoring the Federalists to national influence, and many Clinton Republicans had joined the Federalists in voting against the declaration of war. Though Clinton had no intention of capitulating to Britain, his supporters portrayed him as more cognizant of the interests of commerce than were the southern Republicans and therefore more likely to bring the conflict to a speedy conclusion. Clinton won Federalist endorsement at a September convention of party leaders in New York City. But Federalist backing was something of a mixed blessing because Pennsylvania's electoral vote was needed in addition to New York's to defeat Madison. The Clintonians accordingly were wary of the Hudson peace convention—as it turned out, with good reason, because the revelation that the Federalists were supporting Clinton eventually helped Madison to carry Pennsylvania.[24] The Hudson peace convention reflected western Connecticut's and Massachusetts's influence in the Hudson River Valley more than New York's conversion to Federalism and failed to set off the groundswell of popular agitation in New York Federalist leaders wanted.

Developments in New Jersey initially seemed to offer greater promise. On July 4 a convention of Federalist delegates had assembled in Trenton to prepare a lengthy address. It condemned the "small majority in Congress" for declaring war in secret session despite "the Petitions and Remonstrances of every class and part of the community" and the sentiments of "a great majority of the delegates in Congress from *this* State, and by those of many other States." The address contrasted the advantages the nation had reaped from peace with the horrors now anticipated from war. These included the loss of all its seaborne commerce, the desolation of its coasts and ports, the raising of large, unproductive armies, the prostration of its public credit, the accumulation of burdensome debts, the "decay of agriculture [and] commerce," and a decline in "the morals of our people." All these evils were to be endured because of a specious notion of honor. The address thought it should rather "be *our honor to prevent* the introduction of standing armies—the increase of taxes and public debt—the distresses of private life." It urged all to unite in striving for peace by electing men who would revoke the declaration of war and deal with Britain "in the true spirit of peace and mutual concession."[25] The Trenton convention may have contributed to a subsequent electoral victory in New Jersey that gave the Federalists, in alliance with peace Republicans, narrow control over both houses of the state legislature.[26] The legislature then issued a declaration against the war, reversing its previous endorsement of hostilities, and later cast the state's electoral votes for Clinton.[27]

Federalist success in New Jersey, however, still fell short of the groundswell of popular sentiment that New England's Federalist leadership needed. Outside Connecticut, New Jersey, and Delaware, the Federalist voice remained a marginal one, confirming the Republican description of them as a factious minority. The steady stream of vituperation against the war issuing from the Federalist press counted for far less than the resolves of the state legislatures, of large and influential towns, or of conventions purporting to represent numerous constituents. In only one instance did a Federalist press manage to have a major influence on public opinion, and it did so as much because of what was done to it as because of what it said. The newspaper was the Baltimore *Federal Republican* published by Alexander C. Hanson.

Hanson had greeted the declaration of war on June 19 with such invective that a Republican mob destroyed his printing establishment the next day. This failed to silence Hanson, who resumed publication in Alexandria, Virginia, five days later, drawing on the resources of his prominent planter family and its gentry connections. He also resolved to defy the Baltimore mob and for this purpose recruited a number of Federalists from the surrounding countryside to assert the freedom of his press by force if necessary. After procuring a well-built brick house in the city that Henry Lee—a revolutionary hero and former governor of Virginia—pronounced militarily defensible, Hanson published the first Baltimore issue of the resurrected *Federal Republican* on July 27. It contained a stinging condemnation of the Republican mob, of the Republican newspapers that had warned the *Federal Republican* it risked violence if it continued its opposition after Congress's declaration of war, and of leading Republicans in the nation's government. The announcement that two dozen supporters were prepared to defend Hanson's right to publish with arms attracted a mob around "Fort Hanson" that evening. When shots from the house killed one person and wounded several others, the crowd commandeered a militia artillery piece against which "Fort Hanson" was defenseless. Rather than allow the violence to escalate, local authorities arranged for its Federalist defenders to surrender on the understanding they would be protected in the city jail. But on the evening of the July 28 a mob broke into the jail after the guard had retired for the night and ferociously assaulted the defenseless prisoners. The attack led to the death of one revolutionary militia general and the serious injury of many other people, including Lee.[28]

The savagery of the Baltimore mob gave the Federalists a better prospect for political advantage than their denunciations of the war had. Federalist martyrdom lent itself to many uses. Since the event resembled the excesses associated with the early phases of the French Revolution, it could be made emblematic of the Republicans' "Jacobin" inclinations. Connecticut's governor, Roger Griswold, assured his people that they could "rely on the protection of the laws, and the power and disposition [of the government] to execute them" when it came to securing "the rights of individuals . . . preserv[ing] internal peace . . . [and] promot[ing] order." The implicit comparison between riotous, Republican Baltimore and virtuous, Federalist Connecticut could not have escaped anyone.[29] Closer to home, the riots enabled Maryland Federalists to rally the countryside against the city in the next election and to recover control of the state's House of Delegates. Since under the Maryland constitution the governor was elected by both branches of the legislature, they also named the next governor, despite the numerically smaller Senate remaining under Republican control.[30] Maryland thus came closest to exemplifying the political chain reaction that the Federalist leadership had hoped the declaration of war would ignite. Finally, the Baltimore riots embarrassed the Republicans and forced them to be more scrupulous about the liberty of the Federalist press than they might otherwise have been.

However, Boston's attempt to capitalize on the incident revealed the limits of what could be extracted from it. On August 6 yet another town meeting assembled to condemn the riot. The preamble of the resolves it adopted hailed "this Bloody scene" as "a prelude to the dissolution of all free government, and the establishment of a reign of Terror." It noted that "Mobs . . . which volunteer professedly in support of Government are the most to be dreaded" because they threatened to set in motion a dynamic which would lead to "[t]he Government of the nation and the Mob Government chang[ing] places with each other." The resolves then condemned Madison for not taking appropriate steps to discourage the rioters. Though they avoided holding the president personally responsible for the disorders, the last resolve traced their source back "to the present wanton, impolitic and unjust war." It also referred to the riot as "a prelude to greater evils justly to be apprehended" from which there was no escape except by "a change of our present rulers."[31]

Boston's action was unlikely to carry much weight on the national scene, not only because of the inflated rhetoric but also because of the shrinking economic importance of the metropolis from which they emanated, at least relative to the nation's other major cities prior to the commencement of hostilities. That deficiency, however, could be overcome by having the committees of correspondence that Boston had previously called for meet in a statewide convention. The warrant for the town meeting mentioned "the expediency of choosing . . . *Delegates*, to correspond with, and meet with such other Delegates, as have or may be chosen in the different counties . . . to consult together for the common good." However, a motion to elect nineteen delegates met with opposition from Samuel Dexter, a Federalist who preferred forming an antiwar coalition with like-minded Republicans. Dexter's objections earned him the nickname of "Ambi" among Federalists who rejected a conciliatory strategy, but there was no inconsistency in his moderation.[32] After representing Massachusetts in the House and Senate during the 1790s, he had been appointed secretary of war after the forced resignation of McHenry, and then secretary of the treasury when Oliver Wolcott retired at the end of 1800. Though Dexter's challenge in the town meeting went down to defeat "by a large majority," the debate over it consumed the better part of a day because of the warning in the Henry Papers that such a convention might serve as prelude to secession. Boston Federalists overcame the objection, probably by showing that they were not the only town in the commonwealth that favored electing delegates at this time. But a convention on the scale of the Provincial Congress of 1774 failed to materialize, though it remained an option and was treated as such by the press of both parties.[33]

Instead of Federalist-sponsored agitation against the war rising to a crescendo throughout the land, it remained centered in New England. Even there, criticism became more subdued as summer gave way to autumn, despite William Hull's humiliating capitulation on August 16. Hull's attempt to invade upper Canada had ended in a retreat to Detroit and surrender of his army to an inferior enemy force without firing a shot. Within New England, leadership in opposing the war also passed from Boston and the Massachusetts House of Representatives to the government of Connecticut, even though Madison's war message had come just after the adjournment of the latter's May legislative session. That had precluded Connecticut's General Assembly from taking a stand against the war. But toward the end of June the state's Federalist leadership got a chance to assume a vanguard role.

On June 17 Governor Griswold had replied to an alert from the secretary of war, William Eustis, declaring that Connecticut was ready to respond to any requisition Henry Dearborn, now major-general in command of the northern theater, deemed "necessary for the defense of the sea-coast."[34] On June 29, however, Griswold declined to obey Dearborn's June 22 request for five companies of militia to man the fortifications at New London and New Haven. Instead he called upon his council to consider whether "the contingencies enumerated in the constitution" for placing the state militias under federal control actually existed. Framing the issue in this way invited the council to pursue the same route the state had taken in 1809 when Governor Jonathan Trumbull Jr. had refused to place the state's militia at the service of civil officers charged with enforcing the embargo. The council now denied that any "of the exigencies recognized by the constitution and laws of the united states" had transpired, though the Constitution specified that one function of the militias was to "repel Invasions." Griswold based his refusal on the council's finding, making Connecticut the first state officially to do so after the declaration of war.[35]

When, in mid-July, Eustis learned of the governor's decision, he expressed surprise that after the commencement of hostilities "against a nation possessed of a powerful and numerous fleet, a part of which were actually on our coast," there should have been any doubt as to whether the United States was " 'in imminent danger of invasion.' " Eustis naively assumed that assurances from the president that there was such a threat would dispose of the objection.[36] But he had not reckoned with Griswold's and the council's opposition to placing the state's militia under federal command. They feared that compliance would authorize transferring the militia "into the army of the United States" and deprive the state of the benefit of its military manpower.[37] When Dearborn learned of this latter objection in mid-July, he tried to meet it by allowing the four companies destined for New London to "be commanded" by one of the officers "detached with your State's quota." He added that the detached militia would replace the regular troops garrisoning the fortifications who were being withdrawn for "other objects."[38]

Dearborn's persistence forced Griswold to call another meeting of his council in early August. The council claimed that if the militia could legally be ordered to do garrison duty by Dearborn, it might also "be called to . . . march to any place in the United States, to perform the same duty." If Congress declared war before making provision for raising and supporting armies, "it does not follow that the Militia are bound to enter forts and garrisons to perform ordinary garrison duty, and wait for an invasion which may never happen."[39] On August 6, backed by this opinion, Griswold issued a proclamation that made public his refusal to comply with the requisition. He also summoned the legislature to meet in special session at the end of August. In his address to the legislators, Griswold reviewed the course he had pursued with the council's endorsement and in the process drew national attention to a controversy that until now had taken place largely behind the scenes.[40] The assembly responded by issuing a statement condemning the war "as unnecessary" and criticizing Congress for not having "*first counted the cost*" in declaring it. While Connecticut would "perform all their [constitutional] obligations," the assembly expressed its full "accord with the decision" of the governor not to comply with Dearborn's militia requisition.[41]

Dearborn had also requested forty-one companies from the Massachusetts militia at the same time he had asked for five from Connecticut. Some of the Massachusetts companies were to march to Newport, Rhode Island, to relieve the garrison of regulars there who had been ordered to the northern frontier. Governor Strong made less of a performance than Griswold did in refusing to comply, though the reasons he subsequently gave paralleled Griswold's. Only at the end of July, when Eustis seconded Dearborn's requisition, did Strong summon the Massachusetts council, which promptly endorsed his refusal. The governor and council then asked the state's supreme court to decide if state governors were empowered to determine whether "the exigencies contemplated by the constitution of the United States" (an invasion or rebellion) actually existed, and whether, if "the exigencies" did exist, detachments from the state militia could be commanded by someone other than a militia officer. Nonetheless, Strong and the Massachusetts council subsequently ordered three companies of the state's militia detached to the eastern frontier, as Dearborn had requested, adding that they would remain there "until the President should otherwise direct."[42] In their management of the militia requisition, Connecticut pursued a more confrontational course than Massachusetts because Connecticut remained obsessed with the possibility it would be stripped of manpower by federal requisitions, as had been its fate during the Revolution.[43]

Dearborn's attempt to requisition four companies of militia from Rhode Island also met with rebuff from Governor William Jones, who worried, as Connecticut had, about his state being drained of its militia should they be put under federal command. Rather than explore ways in which the state might cooperate with federal authorities, Jones used the occasion to demand the state's share of arms that the federal government had appropriated $200,000 to procure in 1808 to equip the state militias.[44] But Rhode Island's response to the federal requisition at least suggested there was room for negotiation. Both Massachusetts and Rhode Island also tried to avoid drawing unnecessary attention to the controversy. The course the war took in its earliest phase contributed to their comparative moderation.

During the summer of 1812 British authorities assumed that the revocation of their orders would bring a quick end to hostilities provided their forces remained on the defensive. British naval commanders were instructed to avoid seizing U.S. commercial vessels. Ships of war were another matter, of course, and in July 1812 the USS *Constitution* barely eluded the Halifax squadron after unwittingly sailing into its midst. But the *Constitution*'s August 19 capture of the HMS *Guerrièrre* failed to hurt the nation's overseas commerce. Britain continued to encourage American vessels to carry grain, on which it had become dependent, to its armies on the Iberian Peninsula, as well as supplies to Canada and the West Indies. At the same time Congress failed to bar this trade in the act it passed just after the declaration of war outlawing trading with the enemy.[45] The British government only authorized general reprisals against American shipping in mid-October after staggering losses to American privateers had precluded any easy way out of hostilities.[46] Even then, most incoming vessels that had not known about Congress's declaration of war before they had departed from overseas ports were allowed to proceed, and neutral shipping continued to pass unmolested, leading many merchants to re-flag their vessels. Contrary to the dire predictions of the Federalists, none of the region's ports were attacked, let alone destroyed. If anything, much of the East enjoyed a momentary flush of prosperity.

Though British warships hovered off most of the nation's ports looking for their public and private American counterparts, Britain waited until late December to institute its first strict blockade of the Chesapeake and Delaware.[47] The change would have little effect on the Northeast, which continued to enjoy the profitable commerce that had sprung up with Canada during the embargo and non-intercourse. Certainly there was little for the commercially oriented Federalists to complain about in the first half year of the conflict. Dampening their polemic against the war also maximized their chances of defeating Madison in the approaching presidential election. As long as the president insisted on rebuffing all offers of truce after Britain's withdrawal of its orders, the American people might be persuaded that he was the only obstacle to peace. In August, Dearborn, in personal command of the forces along the Canadian frontier, had agreed to a truce with his British counterpart, Sir John B. Warren, only to have the administration repudiate it. A subsequent feeler made to Monroe met the same fate because it failed to address impressment.[48] That gave the newly elected Federalist legislature of New Jersey the chance to protest "*the expense of American blood and treasure to protect* British subjects *on the high seas*" and to demand that the dispute be resolved by negotiations between the two governments.[49] However, Federalist leaders knew they could not defeat Madison on their own. At most they could only hope to contribute to the split that had emerged

between war and peace Republicans. The Federalists did not wish to risk
estranging the Clinton Republicans and the critical state of New York by appearing to take the lead when they would be fortunate to be accepted as followers.
Aggressive opposition also risked alienating moderate opponents of the war in
New Jersey, Delaware, Pennsylvania, and Maryland, whose support would be
equally crucial if Madison were to be defeated.

Massachusetts Federalists remembered the reactions their assault on the
embargo had provoked in 1809 when the response of the Republicans had
brought New England to the brink of civil war. More recently the competition
between Republicans and Federalists to maximize their respective delegations
had swollen the state's House of Representatives to 750 elected members.
Federalist leaders in Massachusetts and Connecticut were better equipped to
deal with their Republican adversaries at home than elsewhere because of the
advantage they derived from their superior wealth and social position magnified
by their association with Congregationalism. Federalism in both Connecticut
and Massachusetts grew stronger as the war progressed. But their success in making these two states Federalist bastions did not rest on popular endorsement.
Instead a selective migration of potential Republicans to the West and into the
army together with privateering, particularly lucrative at the beginning of hostilities, thinned the ranks of their opponents in southern New England.[50]
Federalist officials then did everything in their power to weaken the Republicans
who remained. In Connecticut, the General Assembly's passage of the "Standup
Law" in 1801 had eliminated the anonymity of written nominations for the
upper house. This, together with a transfer of authority over the admission of
freemen from elected selectmen to justices of the peace appointed by the
General Assembly, insulated the Federalists from effective political challenge.[51]

In Massachusetts, lingering elements of Republican power, particularly in the
state's Senate, forced the Federalists to attack their adversaries from below. Salem
provides an interesting illustration of how the Federalists proceeded. Along with
nearby Marblehead and Lynn, Salem had been Republican during the embargo
crisis and the years directly preceding the War of 1812. As the second-largest
town in the state, however, it attracted the special attention of the Federalists.
Coaching by prominent Federalists in the neighborhood, including Timothy
Pickering, allowed them to gain on their adversaries though never to displace
them before 1812. Republicans felt the pressure and attempted to secure their
position for that critical spring election by allowing all male inhabitants to vote
for town officials. The Republicans reasoned that since Salem was sending as
large a delegation as it could, everyone should have a voice in the selection of its
representatives. They also assumed the newly enfranchised, which included the

town's black adult males, would reciprocate by supporting the sponsors of this reform. Instead the Federalists managed to persuade many new electors to support their candidates and, on the basis of these votes, captured control of the town in March 1812.[52] Federalist officials then removed three to four hundred Republicans from the list of those entitled to vote in state elections on the pretext that they lacked the minimum property required under Massachusetts law. Procedures existed whereby the disenfranchised could win reinstatement, but many were reluctant to exert themselves in so unfamiliar and humiliating a situation. Nor was there time before the approaching election for most to do so. This enabled the Federalists to deliver a decisive majority for Strong in the gubernatorial contest and to elect a solid delegation of thirteen Federalists to the next House of Representatives. The Federalists also exerted pressure on the militia, by replacing Republican with Federalist officers, and through the courts by initiating prosecutions against townsmen protesting the manner in which the selectmen had conducted the April elections for governor and the Senate. Marblehead and Lynn successfully resisted takeover, but Massachusetts Republicans everywhere were placed on the defensive by their opponents' aggressiveness.[53]

The Federalists nevertheless remained a minority in the nation. Invoking extreme remedies against a war that a majority of the nation supported, at least at its outset, risked bringing down the wrath of the government upon them in the form of loyalty legislation similar to that which the Federalists had deployed against the Republicans in 1798. It was far better to let the Republicans answer for the mess they appeared to be making of the war than for the Federalists to act in ways that made them accountable for what was going wrong. In mid-October the American attempt to invade upper Canada from the Niagara frontier had been repulsed at Queenstown Heights, while further to the East time was obviously running out on Dearborn's stalled attempt to move against Montreal. Certainly enough Federalists remained in Congress to hold the Republicans responsible for the disasters the Federalists expected. At the same time, subtler strategies were available for derailing the war effort and replacing Madison as president. The Connecticut legislature attempted to sequester military resources from the federal government by recruiting politically reliable volunteers. Offering to pay them twice what federal recruiters could discouraged young men from joining the nation's army.[54] Added to this were the pressures that unfriendly local authorities could exert to counteract the appeal that recruiters exercised over young men thirsting for adventure and glory. These varied from personally admonishing the young to legally harassing recruiters with writs of habeas corpus to recover enlistees.[55]

Reversion to Form

Federalist restraint had limits. When it became clear that Britain's revocation of her Orders-in-Council together and the faltering Canadian invasion would produce neither the desired peace nor a change in the nation's leadership, Federalist congressmen in the lame-duck session of the Twelfth Congress renewed their former aggressiveness. The session began by considering proposals to stimulate enlistment in the army—which still was under its authorized strength—including a substantial raise in pay. On November 21, 1812, Quincy rose to denounce the measure, arguing that a deficiency in "moral motive" rather than in "pecuniary motive" accounted for the manpower shortage in the army. Quincy boasted that "the happy and wise yeomanry of New England . . . alone . . . [could] fill your armies with men worth enlisting." But they had no desire either to conquer Canada or to "be the tools of any man, or any set of men." These objections might not be appreciated in the South, where slaves performed all the labor. But he predicted that the states that felt injured by the war, would respond by applying "the old laws against kidnapping and manstealing" against the recruiters.[56]

Quincy provoked the usual chorus of objections from House Republicans. James Fisk of Vermont expressed his "astonishment" at Quincy's comments. Was it a crime "to defend our country"? He accused Quincy of inflaming regional jealousies in order to throw a "brand of discord . . . among us" and observed, "It is the division they have excited, and the hope of still greater, which has drawn this war upon us."[57] David R. Williams, who had introduced the proposal under debate, added that he hoped the House would not let itself be frightened "by the gentleman, from the prosecution of its true interest, as at the repeal of the embargo." If Massachusetts chose to resist the law and "contrary to our mutual interest, array herself against the General Government," Williams "for one," would "not hesitate to search for proof that she is only a component part of the Union—not its arbitress."[58]

Williams's defiant words failed to conceal Quincy's success in touching on Republican insecurities. Though they retained control of the White House and the new Congress, it was already evident, even before the results of the congressional elections in North Carolina, New Jersey, New York, Vermont, and Virginia were known, that Federalist strength in the Thirteenth Congress would increase dramatically.[59] That in turn influenced the way the Republican majority in the Twelfth Congress dealt with the vexing issue of merchant bonds.

Upon Britain's revocation of its Orders-in-Council on June 23, many overseas agents, acting on standing instructions from their American principals and assuming a suspension of non-importation would automatically follow, had dispatched cargoes of British goods to the United States. Estimated at between $16 million and $20 million dollars in value, the cargoes were seized as they arrived for violating the non-importation provisions of the non-intercourse statute. Importing merchants had then persuaded judges in several districts to release the seized cargoes after posting bond for the value of the goods and duties due on them. Lest the few profit at the expense of the many, the government put all the importers on a common footing. The importers then petitioned Secretary of the Treasury Albert Gallatin to recover their forfeited goods. Though Gallatin possessed the legal authority to decide each case individually, he referred the matter to Congress because so much was at stake. Gallatin recommended remitting half the forfeitures on the assumption that wartime conditions would enable the importers to recover their losses in the price the other half of the goods fetched in the market. But some Republicans urged exemption from all forfeitures to deny the merchants any excuse for using wartime conditions to gouge consumers. Exemption would also conciliate a group on whom the government would have to rely in financing the war through loans. Though many Republicans objected to treating violators of non-importation so leniently, after a prolonged debate a majority composed of Federalists as well as Republicans agreed to restore all goods shipped from Europe between June 23 and September 15.[60]

However, when the House turned back to a consideration of additional measures for prosecuting the war, the acerbity previously evident in the debate over recruitment quickly resurfaced. A proposal to add twenty thousand men to the army provided the occasion. Though one of their objections to declaring war against Great Britain had been lack of preparedness, the Federalists now opposed increasing the army's size on the grounds that the men would be used to invade Canada. Many Federalist congressmen participated in the rhetorical assault, but none put on the performance that Josiah Quincy did in a long, carefully prepared speech drenched in the sarcastic irony and claims of moral superiority that had become his elocutionary trademarks.

By the time Quincy took the floor of the House it was clear that all attempts at invading Canada during 1812 had failed. This did not surprise Quincy, who had discounted the likelihood that Canada would be conquered because of "the imbecility of the American cabinet, and the embarrassment of its resources." Madison's reelection, on the other hand, had shown even "the most molesighted how a nation can be disgraced, and yet a Cabinet attain its desired honors." That made it unlikely that the project of conquest would be laid aside despite the initial failures because Quincy admitted it was still feasible. All that was required was a temporary army large enough to accomplish the mission, since "thereafter they will [n]ever be deficient in resources. If they cannot obtain their pay by your votes, they will collect it by their own bayonets." Quincy predicted that

whenever an American standard was planted "on the walls of Quebec . . .
a dynasty [would be] established in that country by the sword" against which
New Englanders would have "to defend themselves." The only sort of people in
the "northern section of the United States" who approved of the war were those
"men whose fathers, brothers, and cousins, are provided for by the Departments;
whose full-grown children are at suck at the money-distilling breasts of the
Treasury . . . toads that live upon the vapor of the palace that swallow the great
men's spittle at the levees." The real purpose of seizing Canada was to prevent a
peaceful settlement with Britain and ensure that James Monroe would succeed
James Madison. Who was to command the enlarged army? "I say the
man . . . who is notoriously the selected candidate for the next Presidency."
Quincy conjectured that "with thirty thousand veterans at his heels" he would
not "be troubled with rivals" or have to "concern himself about votes." Instead a
president "elected under such auspices" could if he pleased be "a President for
life."[61]

Quincy's skill as a provocateur again drew down on him a torrent of condemnation from the Republicans. The most effective rebuttal, because it was the
most sensible, again came from Henry Clay. He accused the Federalists of having "unremittingly impeded" "the administration of the Government . . . for the
past twelve years." He declined to dwell on the embargo controversy beyond
alluding to its repeal as a "[v]ain and fruitless attempt to conciliate." Instead he
focused on the contradiction between Federalist resistance to peaceful responses
to meet foreign challenges and their subsequent opposition to war with a power
"emboldened by the very opposition here made" that refused to do the nation
justice. The only areas in which these "parasites of opposition" had been consistent
were their unremitting complaints about French influence and their "application
of every vile epithet, which our rich language affords, to Bonaparte." Clay then
turned to Quincy's allegation of "Cabinet plots": "I wish, sir, that another plot of
a much more serious kind—a plot aimed at the dismemberment of our Union—
had only the same imaginary existence. But no man, who had paid any attention
to the tone of certain prints, and to transactions in a particular quarter of the
Union for several years past, can doubt the existence of such a plot." Clay would
not impute "such a design" to the generality of the opposition. But he did
remind Quincy of another of his infamous phrases, "peacefully if we can,
forcibly if we must"—which had been spoken on the floor of the House shortly
before Henry's correspondence revealed a plan for "the neutrality and eventual
separation of that section of the Union" in the event of war with Britain. Clay
declined to dwell further on the matter beyond noting that British officers in
Canada were expecting New England to establish its neutrality. Instead Clay
"turn[ed] from one, whom no sense of decency or propriety could restrain," to

a substantive rebuttal of the Federalist claim that the Republic had no cause for quarreling with Britain.[62]

Turning Massachusetts to Account

Quincy's words had been designed principally for consumption in Massachusetts, where baiting the Republicans in the nation's capital earned one credit among a gentry leadership that defined itself by its alienation from the Virginia dynasty. There, the attacks on Massachusetts's loyalty that Quincy's vituperation inevitably provoked, such as Clay's reference to "the howlings of the whole British pack, set loose from the Essex kennel," ran no risk of neutralizing the effect of his words.[63] Boston's Federalist newspapers made Quincy's speech on the enlargement of the army into grist for the political mill they expected the Massachusetts legislature's winter session to set in motion. In addition, three pamphlet editions of the speech appeared, though only one of these was published in the state.[64] The immediate prize in contention was the Massachusetts Senate. If the Federalists succeeded in capturing the upper branch of the legislature, there would be nothing to stop them from pursuing a similar course to that taken against the embargo. The Federalists relied on Quincy's speech, echoed by denunciations of the war in the Federalist press, to compensate for the current divided state of the legislature.

Already on the defensive as a result of the loss of all but one congressional seat in the previous November's election, Massachusetts Republicans groped for a way to fight back. Aside from republishing Clay's speech rebutting Quincy,[65] the best they could manage was a ceremonial exchange on February 16, 1813, between the state's Republican senators and representatives and Elbridge Gerry. Though Gerry had been selected as Madison's vice president after losing the Massachusetts gubernatorial election in 1812, he had begged off going to Washington to be sworn in and so was locally available for the ritual. It nevertheless bore the mark of desperation, given Gerry's last addresses to the state legislature.

After celebrating Gerry's revolutionary credentials, the Republican legislators thanked him "for reprobating the conduct of those, whose inconsiderate resolutions had a direct tendency to dissolve" the Union, as well as for exposing the pretense of those who claimed for themselves "the exclusive appellation of federalists and friends of peace."

[Were] those persons . . . friends to the peace and honor of their country who attempt to rouse . . . the people to rebellion;—who draw geographical lines of hostile divisions between the northern and southern districts;—who endeavor to alienate the endearing tie of sister States, and instill the degrading idea that their embraces are more to be dreaded than the impositions of Britain, or the ravages of their indian allies;—who vindicate the impressment of our seamen . . . who behold with apathy the insults offered to our flag, the violation of our commercial rights, and who arrogantly exclaim amidst these complicated enormities, that "Britain does us no essential injury"?

Massachusetts's Republican legislators met Federalist complaints about southern dominance of the national government by pointing out that the South had helped to elect Gerry vice president. In the event of the presidency becoming vacated, "they will submit their political destinies to a citizen of Massachusetts," a circumstance the Republican legislators hoped would "forever confound those disturbers of the general harmony, who wish to excite a jealousy between the respective States."[66]

Since most of the heavy lifting had already been done, Gerry could have simply thanked his supporters, restated the objectives the Republicans were pursuing in the war, and called for national unity. Instead he tried to justify the course he had pursued toward "internal ostensible friends, but real foes of the people" while governor. Though he attributed "the political division of our citizens" primarily to "the unparalleled effrontery" of the British government, he blamed "those citizens whom Great Britain claims 'as her friends'" for putting the British up to it. Gerry argued that the British government, in league with her American friends, stood in the way of peace with Britain on terms of reciprocity. Why? Here Gerry invoked a recent speech by an opposition member of Parliament, who had accused the ministry of carrying on a piratical campaign against the shipping of other nations to secure the funds needed to control Parliament. Gerry expressed "deep regret and surprize, that any citizens of Massachusetts" should cooperate in such schemes and "foment divisions between [Massachusetts] and the southern states." He concluded by warning that Massachusetts would suffer far more than the southern states if she separated from the Union and inferred from the evident folly of such a course, just as Pickering had with respect to the embargo, that "foreign influence [w]as the probable" source of it.[67]

Political debate that involved a serious exchange of ideas had long since collapsed in Massachusetts. Only the *Boston Gazette* noted Gerry's reply, dismissing it as "rancorous invective against the British government, and vulgar abuse of the wise and honorable portion of his fellow citizens."[68] The *Columbian Centinel* directed its readers to a report in the state House of Representatives against a Republican motion calling on the state to build a seventy-four-gun line-of-battle ship and loan it to the federal government.[69] Both the *New England Palladium* and *Repertory* focused on a resolution proposed by Representative William

Austin of Charlestown which complained of the clergy "profan[ing] the Holy Sabbath, by introducing into their pulpits political discourses." Austin wanted to authorize "individuals, in a decent and orderly manner, to answer, correct, or explain, any part of" such discourses. The *Palladium* reported that the House refused his proposal "the ordinary respect of a commitment," charging that Austin's real objection was not to "the clergy's '*preaching politicks*, [so much] as to the *politicks which they preach*." It concluded, "We do not . . . recollect any thing equal to this motion, since those of Danton and Anacharsis Clootz [against organized religion] in the maddest moments of the French [Revolution]."[70]

Such purple rhetoric mirrored Quincy's and presaged an overwhelming victory for the Federalists in the state's spring election. Strong was reelected by a resounding majority, and the Federalists captured decisive control of the Senate as well as the House. That victory equipped them to turn their new, unchallenged dominance of the Massachusetts government to maximum account in influencing the Thirteenth Congress. Quincy had returned to Massachusetts after the dissolution of the Twelfth Congress in time to run for the state Senate and he contributed to a nineteen-vote majority the Federalists enjoyed in the upper house when the new state legislature assembled. He used his position as senator to guide the General Court in several directions.[71]

In early June, Quincy pushed for the creation of, and then got himself appointed to, a joint committee charged with examining the "extension of the territorial limits and forming [of] new states without the territorial limits of the United States." The committee issued a report that condemned both as "deliberate" violations of the Constitution amounting to "manifest usurpations." Though it might be thought inappropriate to raise such issues in wartime, the objection had no weight with the committee because "the particular subject of animadversion [was] independent of the principle of the war." The report concluded that the "admission into the union, of states, created in countries, not comprehended within the limits of the United States" was unconstitutional and that Massachusetts should oppose them as "tending to the dissolution of the confederacy." It also recommended that the state's congressmen be instructed to obtain the repeal of the act incorporating Louisiana into the nation. Quincy then signed the order transmitting this resolution to the state's congressmen in Washington.[72]

There was a quixotic quality to this effort, suggesting the difficulty Quincy experienced in moving from the national to a state arena. But he did succeed in recapturing the nation's attention, if only briefly, in another way. On June 1 James Lawrence, in command of the USS *Chesapeake*, had accepted a challenge to a naval duel with HMS *Shannon* off the Massachusetts coast. When the *Chesapeake* did not return, the Boston papers concluded she had been lost, and

Republican members in the Senate attempted to make the best of the situation by proposing a resolution commending Lawrence for his February 24 victory in the USS *Hornet* over HMS *Peacock* off the coast of Brazil. Quincy countered with an amendment that stated "in a war like the present, waged without justifiable cause, and prosecuted in a manner which indicates that conquest and ambition are its real motives, it is not becoming a moral and religious people to express approbation of military or national exploits."[73] Shortly after Quincy's amendment carried, word arrived that Lawrence had perished in the engagement and that his dying words were "Don't give up the ship."[74] Quincy's son and biographer, writing just after the Civil War, observed that the phrase "unbecoming a moral and religious people" drew the same vehement denunciations from Republicans as "peaceably if they can, forcibly if they must" had. He failed to add that the British had buried Lawrence with the full military honors that Quincy's resolution would have denied him. The younger Quincy also did not mention Quincy's other quip about Republicans who could not be "kicked into war," sensing in the wake of our bloodiest conflict that it would not have reflected credit on his father. When a Republican majority again recaptured control of the Massachusetts Senate in 1824, it expunged Quincy's 1813 amendment from its record.[75]

Governor Strong steered the state's legislature toward more effective forms of resistance by inviting it to focus on two other matters. The first involved the distribution of weapons procured under the 1808 congressional appropriation, already questioned by Rhode Island's governor, for arming the militia of the United States. At its previous meeting, the legislature had instructed Strong to solicit the state's share of these arms. Secretary of War John Armstrong had replied that very few had been procured and that the president had "deemed it most conducive to the general interest" to distribute those available to the "frontier states, and the militia who have come forward in the service of the country."[76] The allusion to the state's refusal to place its militia under federal command led a committee of the Massachusetts House to file an elaborate report on the subject.

This report argued that since Massachusetts had contributed a fifth of the revenue appropriated for the purposes mentioned, she was entitled to a corresponding proportion of the arms. Though the state was "capable of bringing into the field an effective force of one hundred twenty thousand free white citizens," it accounted for only one-tenth (seventy thousand out of seven hundred thousand) of the total enrolled militia. Still this should have entitled it to a tenth of the arms that had been distributed. Instead it had received none, though twenty-four thousand stand were contracted for in Massachusetts, 9,875 of which had been delivered to the arsenals of the United States. Eleven states, the

District of Columbia, and Illinois Territory had benefited while "the populous, respectable, and exposed state of Massachusetts" was denied all succor. The report asked how it could be "conducive to the general interest" to leave Massachusetts, possessed of a "militia inferior to none in the union," without the least share in the common stock of weaponry.[77] The House committee recommended that the adjutant general of the state request delivery of the arms to which the state was entitled. Should he be refused, the resolve directed "that such proportion of the money collected under the said act, as if invested in arms would of right belong to Massachusetts, should be held subject to the disposition of the treasurer of the commonwealth." Both branches of the legislature agreed to the recommendation, in effect authorizing the state to sequester federal funds.[78]

Governor Strong also invited the Massachusetts legislature to investigate the alleged causes of the war. While acknowledging the obligation all were under to obey the laws of the land, Strong had affirmed the "right and duty [of the legislature] to enquire into the grounds and origin of the present war" and to "endeavor, as far as our limited influence extends, to promote . . . an honorable reconciliation."[79] The legislature responded by appointing a joint committee that framed an elaborate memorial against the war in which Quincy undoubtedly had a hand.[80] The text was distinctive less for its substantive originality than for the Olympian wisdom it claimed to purvey. "[T]he certainty that time and prudent application of their resources would bring a seasonable remedy for any transient wrongs, would have induced a wise and provident administration, to overlook, any temporary evil, which . . . foreign powers might . . . have inflicted." Much of the memorial focused on France's role in precipitating the war through "the pretended repeal of [her] decrees." But it also harped on the ideological anomaly of the United States as "sworn foes to civil and religious slavery," cooperating "with the oppressor, to bind other nations in his chains." And it tried to paint Massachusetts's opposition to the expansion of the Republic as anti-Bonapartism. What really upset the Massachusetts legislature, though, was the "project of forming" new territories "into states, and admitting them to the union without the express consent of every member of the original confederacy!" It solemnly protested "[a]gainst a practice so hostile to the rights, the interests, the safety of this state, and so destructive to her political power."[81]

The elaborateness of this memorial begs the question of what the Federalists in the Massachusetts legislature thought they were accomplishing by framing it. Similar memorials for repealing the embargo and against declaring war had been futile. But it would be a mistake to assume the Federalists were totally impervious to experience. Instead the memorial represented an attempt to extend a technique perfected within the state to the nation at large. Just as the Federalists had tried to magnify the authority of the Massachusetts legislature by making it appear to echo the voice of the people articulated in town meetings and county conventions, they now hoped to magnify the influence of their spokesmen in the new Congress, which was assembling for a special session. Massachusetts Federalists also wished that their example would be copied by other states, though in this they were largely disappointed.

The Federalist Offensive in Congress

The retirement of Josiah Quincy and James Lloyd from national politics failed to change the political landscape of the Thirteenth Congress significantly. Because Lloyd had resigned before the expiration of his term, Governor Strong had been able to appoint Christopher Gore in Lloyd's place. With an overwhelming majority of Federalists in the state's delegation to the House of Representatives, Quincy's presence in Washington no longer seemed that essential. Were there a need for a Federalist enfant terrible in the House, Alexander C. Hanson—the publisher of the Baltimore *Federal Republican*—could be expected to step into the breech. Hanson had been elected to represent a "safely Federalist" district in Maryland "as a stick jabbed in the eye of Republican Baltimore."[82] The most noticeable absence from the new Congress, at least from the opposition's perspective, was John Randolph. Though Quincy continued to court Randolph's friendship in their mutual retirement, Randolph's eclipse was not of much account since no one could ever be sure what he would do next. Of more significance were the fifty-four votes garnered by the Connecticut Federalist, Timothy Pitkin, for Speaker of the House. Though only five more than the number of representatives who had voted against the June 1812 declaration of war, many in the previous year's minority had been Clinton Republicans whose loyalty to the Federalist version of "peace" remained unclear. The first vote of the Thirteenth Congress suggested that Federalism's strength had grown.[83]

Federalists in Congress were aware of the course their Massachusetts brethren were bent on pursuing. On June 3, Daniel Webster, the freshman representative from New Hampshire, confidently predicted that "the tone in Mass [would] be high" in response to Strong's invitation to pursue additional initiatives against the war.[84] Webster had good reasons for his confidence. Graduating from Dartmouth College in the class of 1801, he had become Christopher Gore's clerk just after Gore's return to Boston from London. In introducing Webster to the Suffolk County bar, Gore had predicted his protégé's future distinction. Webster remembered Gore's precise words on the occasion and resolved to fulfill his mentor's expectations as far as he was able.[85] Though Webster returned to New Hampshire to practice law, rising in the esteem of Federalists in the eastern part of his home state to the extent that they sent him to Washington as their representative, he remained closely tied to the Federalist leaders of Massachusetts. Senator Gore's simultaneous presence in Washington reinforced that connection.

On June 10, as if responding to Strong's cue, Webster proposed a set of resolutions calling upon the president to submit the information in his possession relating to France's revocation of her Berlin and Milan decrees. The resolutions were framed in language that left it to Madison's discretion as to whether "the public interest" forbad such disclosures. Five days later, Timothy Pitkin moved that the House investigate the manner in which federal arms had been distributed to the state militias. The parallel course being pursued by the government of Massachusetts and congressional Federalists was unmistakable.[86]

The Republicans experienced little difficulty in defusing Pitkin's motion. George Troup claimed it was "calculated to excite distrust and jealousy between the General and State governments" and demonstrated that neither Massachusetts nor Connecticut were alone in being denied federal arms. James Fisk added that both states had implied they were fully able to defend themselves when they resisted having their militias placed under federal command.[87] Webster's resolutions were to give the Republicans considerably more trouble because they threatened to undermine the moral basis that Republicans had established for embarking on the war.

The Federalist hand against the administration had been strengthened by the British ministry's decision to cite France's alleged revocation of her decrees as the pretext for lifting her orders on June 23, 1812. That opened up several possibilities. One was to argue that because Britain had lived up to her long-standing pledge, the basic cause for the war had vanished. In this view, Madison rather than Britain remained the principal obstacle to peace. One could—and some did— carry that theme further by suggesting that Madison had possessed proof of France's action for some time and had purposefully kept the information from Britain in order to go to war with her. Alternatively, if one did not want to accuse the president of outright mendacity, one could argue that France had duped Madison into declaring an unnecessary war by purposefully withholding the information.[88]

Either way played to reservations about the course of the war entertained by a growing number of Republicans as well as Federalists. William Henry Harrison's attempt to retake Detroit had led to a winter defeat at Frenchtown and a British invasion of western Ohio during the spring. Though American forces had succeeded in burning York (modern Toronto) in April, by May they had retreated to the Niagara where, during June, operations remained inconclusive. To the east,

American forces did manage to repulse a British assault on Sackett's Harbor, but efforts to move against Montreal continued to stall. Webster's resolutions thus increased the pressure to which the failure to make headway in seizing Canada necessarily subjected the Republicans.

Webster's resolutions also confronted Republican congressmen with a tactical dilemma. If they opposed them, they risked appearing afraid of the truth, which Federalists claimed the resolutions were designed to ascertain. Alternatively, supporting the resolutions might strengthen the hand of the Federalists in opposing the war by focusing public attention on France's devious behavior. Webster had the satisfaction of observing the confusion into which he had thrown the Republicans.[89] Some tried opposing the resolutions on the grounds that France's actions were irrelevant either to evaluating Britain's aggressions or to raising revenues to prosecute the war, which was the principal reason Congress had been summoned into special session. Others, like Calhoun, tried to counter Federalist charges by arguing Britain had lifted her orders out of regard for her commercial interests, which had been adversely affected by non-intercourse and would be even more so by war. Republicans taking this tack relied on the statements of the prince regent on April 12 and Ambassador Foster on June 10, 1812, both of which affirmed Britain's determination to revoke its orders only when France lifted all her decrees against the commerce of neutral nations, not just those that affected the United States. They claimed these statements showed Britain had required the United States to "make the continent of Europe a market for [Britain's] manufactures," a thing "we had no right to demand of the French Government, and England knew we could not obtain." But Republican congressmen showed more than confusion about which course to follow. Calhoun used language that several Federalists construed as threatening anyone who argued to the contrary.[90] And Felix Grundy, who announced he would support the resolutions because he was confident the information requested would show that Britain had not been prepared to modify its orders prior to June 23, 1812, accused certain Federalists of "moral treason."

Grundy absolved those opposing the war for "honest motives . . . and whose opposition is confined within reasonable and Constitutional bounds" from his accusation. Instead Grundy had in mind one "who professes himself to be a friend of this country, yet proves by his actions to be" otherwise. "I accuse him who sets himself to work systematically to weaken the arm of this Government by destroying its credit and dampening the ardor of its citizens." Since the war could not be carried on without men or money, Grundy asked: "Is not that man then subserving the interest of the enemy, who, to the extent of his power keeps money from our coffers, and men from our armies?" Who would dispute that a "citizen [who] goes over to the enemy and arms in his behalf" was a traitor? Was not the guilt of "the same citizen" who remained "amongst us and employ[ed] himself in aiding the enemy, by paralyzing the national energies . . . equally great?"[91]

If Grundy had hoped to tame the Federalist opposition in this manner, he was sorely disappointed. Instead of toning down their objections to the war, the Federalists escalated them. They had little difficulty dodging the accusation of moral treason, pleading instead that the Constitution and Christianity justified their actions.[92] But the arrival of the Massachusetts memorial shortly after Grundy's speech also aided them. On June 28, Christopher Gore presented it to the Senate. Joseph Varnum, the state's other senator, countered with a protest drafted by the Republican minority of the Massachusetts legislature. This protest expressed "extreme regret that the legislature of this state . . . [had] presented a remonstrance to congress . . . denouncing . . . the war as *improper, impolitic,* and *unjust*" and "excusing and justifying all the aggressions and outrages of Great Britain." They found it "impossible to conceive what *good* motive could induce" them to endorse a document "so treasonable in its origins, reprehensible in its language, erroneous in its facts and principles, and pernicious in its effect." A state government had no business telling the national government that it "ought to have resisted the *French decrees* agreeably to the demand of the British government," or that it had "*seduced* her seamen from their allegiance," and "invaded the territory of a *peaceable* and *unoffending* neighbor." The minority sought to dissociate themselves from a memorial that took "the *enemy's ground*" to "support their claims, and justify their aggressions."[93] On the basis of this protest the Senate declined even to commit the Massachusetts memorial for possible future consideration.

The House of Representatives pursued a different course. Timothy Pickering insisted on reading the memorial aloud on June 29 and concluded the lengthy process with a motion to refer it to a Committee of the Whole House on the state of the Union. By agreeing to such a motion, the House of Representatives would have recognized the memorial's allegations as being worth debating on their merits. There were immediate objections to such a reference, the most cogent questioning the right of a state legislature to challenge Congress in the exercise of its constitutional duties.[94] Instead of referring the memorial, the House agreed to let it lie on the table. A motion was then made to print it. A few Republicans supported this motion on the grounds that Pickering had failed to read the text with sufficient clarity to be heard. Some thought printing was the best way to ensure that the House refute its "treasonable" language. After a majority finally agreed to its being printed, the House disposed of it by postponing further consideration until Congress met again in its regular December session.[95] Then it would be lost in a welter of other more pressing matters connected with the conduct of the war.

Despite the success of the Republicans in burying the Massachusetts memorial, it reinforced the willingness of the Federalist congressmen to indulge in precisely those activities that Grundy had branded "moral treason." When the special session finally turned to the revenue, most Federalists claimed that while they were prepared to pay taxes lawfully levied, they drew the line at lending money to support a war of conquest.[96] They then did everything in their power to deny the administration the revenue it needed. Since current operations were being financed by three major lenders,[97] who had supplied the deficiencies in previously authorized federal loans at tremendous discounts, Federalist opposition focused on crippling the government's ability to borrow in the future. Pickering warned potential investors that war loans might never be repaid, pledging that he intended to oppose any measures for honoring debts contracted during hostilities.[98] That provided cover for the more cautious to declare they would consider making provision for the public debt only after the war stopped.[99] A few Federalists argued that the majority's aversion to taxation—evident in the Twelfth Congress's passing on of that responsibility to the Thirteenth—showed the Republicans had no intention of collecting the revenues provided for in the array of proposed new taxes. Instead they meant to abandon the creditors once the government had secured the funds it needed.[100]

The Republicans managed to pass most of the taxes that the secretary of the treasury had requested despite Federalist sniping. They also passed Webster's resolutions by a resounding majority. Secretary of State Monroe then wrote a nine-thousand-word defense of the administration's foreign policy since 1808. It was referred to the Foreign Relations Committee, which proposed a resolve approving the conduct of the executive. The committee acknowledged that it was unusual for the House to express either approbation or disapprobation of the executive, but the "language of . . . [Webster's] resolutions, and the motives avowed by their supporters, leave no alternative. To be silent would be to condemn."[101] Some Republicans wanted the House to adopt the resolution before the opposition had a chance to read Monroe's report to pay the Federalists back for what they regarded as Webster's ambush. However, the majority felt that doing so would only make a bad situation worse. Nor did they want to get bogged down in a fruitless debate at the height of the summer heat while more urgent matters continued to press upon them. Accordingly, when the matter came up again on July 20, the majority settled for simply publishing Monroe's lengthy report without official endorsement.[102]

Jockeying for Advantage

In early August 1813, as the first session of the Thirteenth Congress came to an end, congressional Federalists had reason to congratulate themselves. They had not only succeeded in embarrassing their adversaries with Webster's resolutions. The Republicans had also been forced to embrace a fiscal program involving new or higher duties on distilleries, refined sugars, sales of foreign goods at auction, retailer's licenses, carriages for personal transportation, bank notes and negotiable paper, imported salt, and foreign tonnage. The capstone of these fiscal innovations was a $3 million direct tax, which the opposition hoped would do the Republicans as much political damage as the federal direct tax of 1798 had done to the Federalists at the turn of the century.

Beyond Congress the Federalists could take heart from the course of the war along the Canadian frontier. Oliver Perry's mid-September naval victory over the British on Lake Erie had relieved enemy pressure on northern Ohio and Michigan and allowed William Henry Harrison to go on the offensive. In early October he defeated a British force at the Thames River in Ontario, thus securing the Northwest frontier. But American forces on the Niagara frontier had achieved little since June, and at the end of the year they abandoned their meager foothold in Canada, allowing the British to seize Fort Niagara and burn Buffalo. Further to the eastward, the efforts of James Wilkinson and Wade Hampton to coordinate an attack against Montreal again unraveled after the former suffered defeat at Chrysler's Farm and ordered the latter to retreat from the Chateaugay River.[103] By the end of the year a diplomatic resolution to the conflict seemed far more likely than a military one, especially as the principal matter in dispute between the two nations was impressment.

European developments certainly pointed toward a diplomatic resolution. At the close of 1812, the Russian czar, distressed that two nations with which he was on friendly terms should be at war, offered his services in mediating the conflict. Madison was receptive to the offer, and one item of business on the Senate's agenda during the special session of the Thirteenth Congress had been approving the appointment of the peace commissioners Madison had named. Among them was Secretary of the Treasury Albert Gallatin. When the Senate learned that Madison intended to retain Gallatin in his former position by having the secretary of the navy act in his stead while he was absent on diplomatic assignment, the majority insisted that Gallatin resign one office before accepting the other.[104] Federalists, who had no love for Gallatin, undoubtedly enjoyed watching him being attacked by his fellow Republicans. Only after Congress had adjourned did the administration learn that the Britain had refused mediation. In November, however, the British Ministry opened the door to direct negotiations, lending credence to the idea that the war could not last much longer.

That supposition drew its greatest strength from the new configuration of the European world. Napoleon's retreat from Russia at the end of 1812 had placed France increasingly on the defensive. In February 1813 Prussia, previously an ally of Napoleon's, joined forces with Britain and Russia in a Sixth Coalition, formally declaring war on France in March. Though both sides failed to achieve a decisive victory during the ensuing campaign in Germany and agreed to an armistice at the beginning of June, Napoleon's strength had been drained far more than had that of the allies. Realizing that the fate of his empire would be decided in central Europe, he withdrew French forces from Spain, abandoning Madrid on June 12, 1813. Their retreat paved the way for Wellington's decisive victory at Vitoria on June 21. With France's hold on Spain crumbling, it was only a matter of time before other central European powers elected to join the coalition, as Austria did in mid-August when the truce collapsed. Americans could not foresee the climactic battles that would take place at Dresden (August 26 and 27) and Leipzig (October 16–19), nor that one consequence of the latter— which involved more than half a million combatants—would be to force France to retreat from Germany. But they knew enough by the time the Thirteenth Congress adjourned to realize that Napoleon's power was on the wane. That, of course, meant that Britain's power was on the ascendancy. However, the principal rationale for British restrictions on the commerce of neutrals had also begun to fade as the European Continent progressively freed itself from the emperor's control. While the Republicans were less confident than the Federalists about Britain's intentions toward the United States, the European war was entering a new phase that pointed toward a general peace.

These developments failed to bestow much immediate political benefit on the Federalists at the state or local levels. Though they gained some political strength in the remoter districts of New England during 1813—particularly in Vermont, New Hampshire, and what would become Maine—and maintained their previous positions in states like New York and Maryland, they lost strength elsewhere in the Union, particularly in New Jersey and Pennsylvania.[105] The Federalist leadership of Massachusetts, which had hoped for something more decisive, attributed their disappointment to their acting as lone vanguard in resisting the war. Connecticut, though politically in sympathy with Massachusetts, had ceased taking the initiative because of her preoccupation with other problems. Governor Griswold had died on October 25, 1812, as the autumn legislative session came to a close, and the lieutenant governor, John Cotton Smith, would not feel fully empowered until he was elected governor in his own right the following spring. He also had a retiring temperament and urged the General Assembly to focus on preserving what the state had rather than on what it might become. In October 1813, he declared, "Our political system calls for no theoretical reforms; nor does our happy state of society depend on the multiplication of laws."[106] If Connecticut could not teach by example, it had no illusions about doing so in any other way. Such an approach had precluded producing anything like a strong second to the Massachusetts memorial of June 1813. In addition another problem consumed Connecticut's attention during the remainder of 1813.

At the end of May a squadron under the command of Stephen Decatur consisting of the USS *United States* and the recently captured HMS *Macedonian* was intercepted by two British seventy-four-gun line-of-battle ships and chased back into New London. The British seventy-fours were soon joined by an additional vessel of the line, three frigates, and several brigs. The Thames, one of the few rivers in Connecticut capable of accommodating deep-draft vessels, was flanked by high enough ground that it could be defended with heavy artillery. Decatur accordingly removed the guns from his frigates and sent his warships upriver. Though this discouraged the British from attacking, they took station at the mouth of the harbor to block Decatur from going back to sea.[107] The presence of a strong enemy force hovering off New London compelled Connecticut to cooperate with the federal government, particularly as British detachments in barges began to harass the coastal communities fronting on Fisher's Island Sound. Cooperation between the federal and state forces prevailed during the summer and autumn because each needed the other. Brigadier General Henry Burbeck, the ranking federal officer at New London, carefully avoided a confrontation with Connecticut authorities over who was in ultimate command while doing his best to have the Connecticut troops provisioned and paid by the national government.[108] So long as New London remained vulnerable to enemy attack, Connecticut had compelling reasons for avoiding provocative behavior.

Only Maryland's House of Delegates had joined Massachusetts, and then neither forcefully nor convincingly, since Maryland's Senate refused to concur in the House's resolves that faulted the federal government for failing properly to defend the state.[109] But despite their isolation, Massachusetts Federalists were still hopeful about the future because of the financial difficulties the federal government continued to encounter. The fiscal program finally enacted by the first session of the Thirteenth Congress did not address the government's immediate financial problems. In the middle of 1813 the treasury had to borrow an additional $7.5 million to cover expenses until the campaign of 1814 because the new taxes would not go into effect until the beginning of the following year.[110] And acting secretary of the treasury, William Jones, warned Congress that even then the United States would remain dependent on loans during the next campaign.[111] If the war continued as inconclusively as it had to date, eventually the cumulative debt would rise to a point where the political fortunes of those contracting it would be affected. Though the Federalists risked sharing in the accumulating burdens of the conflict, they might avoid them altogether if the Republicans could be ousted from power.

The financial embarrassment of the federal government gave New England Federalists a particular sense of empowerment because everyone concluded the secular and clerical opponents of the war had discouraged subscriptions to the public loans.[112] The geographical distribution of those who did subscribe confirmed the inference. Though Massachusetts did not wholly boycott the war loans, it declined to take a role commensurate with its financial resources, and Connecticut followed suit.[113] The private correspondence of leading Federalists shows that they were tempted by the high returns the federal government offered. But they took seriously the moral barriers Federalist leaders had erected against subscribing and behaved defensively when tempted to break rank.[114] Short of resorting to forced loans, there was little Republicans could do about this sort of resistance, except to point out that the more costly their opponents made the war, the more they would eventually suffer from it.

One reason the Federalist leadership remained unmoved by appeals to their long-term interests is that they had begun to sense an opportunity growing out of another feature of the war. In March 1813, Britain extended its "tight blockade" to the nation's principal ports and estuaries from New Orleans to New York. The following November they expanded it to include the entire coast to Rhode Island, closing Long Island Sound.[115] Though all American vessels that encountered a British man-of-war were now more likely to be seized and sent into Halifax, neutral vessels making for Massachusetts, Rhode Island, and New Hampshire were still exempt. This enabled their merchants to continue importing under neutral colors.[116] The possession of a British trading license offered additional insurance against capture. Massachusetts Federalists were not alone in utilizing these licenses, nor were Federalist merchants the only ones to trade with the enemy. Licenses were openly bought and sold in seaports along the entire length of the coast. Collusive captures and the ransoming of vessels detained by the British navy also facilitated evasion of the blockade. But all the devices for trading with the enemy could be used with greatest effect in Massachusetts Bay. It was a good deal harder to get around federal authorities in a blockaded port like New York, where the majority of people supported the war, than it was where local authorities condoned such activities and the political leadership excused them because the war was "unjust" and "unnecessary."[117] As a consequence, trade between northern New England and the rest of the world, particularly the British-controlled world, flourished through 1813, exceeding that of any other part of the nation.

Some of this trade contributed directly to British military operations. Again New England and Massachusetts were not alone in engaging in such activities. Commerce in provisions developed between the blockading squadrons of the enemy and other parts of the mainland, particularly around the Chesapeake and eastern Long Island. Significant amounts of American grain also ended up in Canada, the British West Indies, and the Iberian peninsula.[118] But more significant than the aid and comfort such a trade afforded the enemy was the effect it had on the banking system. After the charter of the Bank of the United States had expired, the nation's financial structure depended on state banks that were required by their charters to redeem their notes in specie. The nation had adapted quickly to replacing specie with bank paper since it was much easier to transport and protect than hard coin. Banks, moreover, could issue more paper than they had specie to redeem it with because it was unlikely that their outstanding bills would ever be presented simultaneously for redemption—unless, of course, their ability to pay in specie was called into question.

The "neutral" trade that developed during the first twenty months of the war made Massachusetts Bay the principal supplier of overseas imports to the rest of the nation. Foreign goods still came into other American ports, eluding the British blockade. But they did so at an additional cost. This meant that the supplies entering eastern ports could compete with goods entering to the south despite the additional transportation costs they bore. Massachusetts merchants, accepting out-of-state bank bills from purchasers, placed New York's banks—and, through New York wholesalers, the rest of the nation's banks—at the mercy of the Boston banks, which received their bills as deposits. In this way Massachusetts acquired unique leverage over the financial structure of the rest of the nation.[119] By presenting out-of-state bank notes for redemption, Massachusetts banks and the merchants controlling them could drain the rest of the nation of its specie and force the banks to the West and South to choose between curtailing credit or defaulting on their notes. This was not a card that the Federalist leadership of Massachusetts was prepared to play casually. But in the right set of circumstances, it could give them leverage over events should the Republicans refuse to make a timely peace with Great Britain.

7

TOWARD THE HARTFORD CONVENTION

Congress, though concerned from the beginning of the war about trade with the enemy, had been slow to tighten the laws against such trafficking. In March 1813, during the last session of the Twelfth Congress, the Senate deferred to the Thirteenth Congress consideration of a bill that would make possession of a foreign license and the change of registry in midpassage as much grounds for condemnation in a court as trading directly with the British. When the bill finally became law in mid-August 1813, it failed to have much effect on the clandestine trade in Massachusetts Bay because British men-of-war had orders to protect American vessels with licenses.[1] Some Massachusetts Federalists even celebrated the British capture of American privateers because they were more likely to seize vessels trading with the enemy than revenue cutters or naval vessels were.[2]

Madison had denounced British efforts to encourage the New England trade from the beginning. In his second inaugural address he had referred to an October 26, 1812 circular directing the lieutenant governor of Bermuda to restrict U.S. imports to vessels coming from the New England states as an attempt "to disorganize our political society" and to "dismember our confederated Republic."[3] When the Thirteenth Congress proved almost as inattentive to the problem as its predecessors had, the president asked for a temporary embargo to last from the end of July 1813 until Congress reconvened in November. Though the House obliged, the measure again failed in the Senate.[4] But during Congress's recess the evidence of continued abuses increased so much that when Madison renewed his request at the beginning of December, the legislature finally obliged with an embargo that was to run until January 1, 1815, unless the war ended before then.[5] The Federalists, true to form, tried to stall passage of the measure as long as possible to promote evasion. *Niles's Weekly Register* claimed a printed version of the embargo bill had been available in Boston long before it became law.[6]

The Embargo Revisited

The embargo of December 1813 fueled New England's opposition to the war. In his January 12, 1814, address to the Massachusetts legislature, Governor Caleb Strong questioned the act's constitutionality. Two days later, Massachusetts congressman Cyrus King proposed a resolution to the U.S. House of Representatives that declared the embargo to be beyond Congress's constitutional powers. King's proposal lent moral support to those determined to evade the measure and threatened to divert the House from the more urgent matter of filling the army's ranks. For both reasons House Republicans refused to consider it. On January 27 King tried to get them to change their minds by rephrasing his original motion. It now joined the assertion that the "people and . . . the respective states" had a right "to a free . . . coasting trade" with a declaration that Congress could not "consistently with the provisions of the constitution and the nature of our government, refuse to consider any resolutions offered by [a] representative." But the Republican majority again rebuffed him.[7]

Republican stonewalling in Congress, however, played into the hands of Federalist leaders in Massachusetts who hoped to bring the state's politics to the same fever pitch it had reached early in 1809. In replying to the governor's address, the Massachusetts House branded the embargo as "an instrument of slavery rather than of mutual defense and security." Not only was the measure clearly unconstitutional, it also "was worse than useless for the objects of war, as it destroys the resources which are indispensable for its success." The House reply declared the embargo "absolves from the obligation of citizens, all those who are disqualified by its arbitrary provisions from enjoying their rights, or fulfilling their duties as citizens." It concluded ominously "that the time has arrived [for the people] . . . to decide whether these burdens are not too grievous to be borne; and to prepare themselves, for the great duty of protecting . . . their unalienable rights, and of securing for themselves . . . the . . . privilege of mutual intercourse by water." The Senate reply took broader aim at the war and Republican policies than the House had, but endorsed the notion that the provisions "interdicting the trade coastwise, between different parts of the same state" called for "legislative interposition, in behalf of our injured citizens." The allusion to the 1809 bill potentially making it a state crime to obey a federal statute was unmistakable.[8]

The two replies of the Massachusetts legislature provided the signal for the Federalist towns and counties of the commonwealth to follow suit. One town had acted even before the legislature assembled. On January 3, Amherst, with Noah Webster acting as moderator, instructed its representatives "to take the most vigorous and decisive measures, compatible with the Constitution, to put an end to this hopeless war." Newbury, the first town to respond to the legislature's cue, questioned the constitutionality of an embargo that extinguished commerce "under a pretended right to regulate commerce." It urged the General Court to pass measures "to secure to us . . . our undoubted right of trade within our State," appropriating Josiah Quincy's words when it promised "to aid you . . . to the utmost of our power, '*peaceably* if we can, *forcibly* if we must.' "[9]

Federalist efforts to mobilize the commonwealth's towns received a boost from the seizure in New York of a consignment of specie for the Bank of New England in Boston. The federal collector in New York had acted as authorized under the new embargo on the suspicion that the money was destined for the thriving illicit commerce along the nation's northeastern frontier.[10] The stockholders of the Bank of New England responded by petitioning the Massachusetts General Court to intervene, and an outraged legislature requested Governor Strong's assistance. Strong had little trouble securing release of the specie after the state Senate published an abstract of the financial condition of the state's twenty-six banks. It showed that Boston's Federalist banks had accumulated almost $7 million of specie in their vaults, about twice the amount needed to redeem all their outstanding notes. This kind of liquidity meant they could pressure out-of-state banks for specie without fear of retaliation. If the Bank of New England were denied its due, the Federalist banks of eastern Massachusetts could increase their demands on banks outside the region, especially New York banks, leading them to suspend specie payments just when the government would need funds for the war.[11]

By the end of the legislative session thirty-four other towns had joined Newbury in passing resolutions, as did "sundry inhabitants" in three others. The only anomaly in what had by now become a political ritual was the silence of Boston. In this case the town's leaders may have been willing to let the General Court assume the vanguard role that Boston had so often taken upon itself because of a quandary confronting the Federalist leadership. Though some would have liked to have the state officially defy the embargo, they did not feel that Massachusetts could act without the support of its neighbors. That pointed toward the calling of a convention, but such a course might be construed as the first step in severing the Union. Neither Boston nor the majority of the legislature were prepared to take that step without further authorization from the people. In late February 1814, the joint committee, to which the town memorials had been referred, came up with another strategy in a report to which Harrison Gray Otis, by then a member of the state House of Representatives, affixed his name as chair.[12]

The report claimed that although the town memorials "testified to an ardent attachment to the *union* . . . the basis of that union [since 1800] had been destroyed by a practical neglect of [the Constitution's] principles" resulting in

"abuses, privations, and oppressions." The report held "the southern and western sections of the Union" responsible, claiming they were impelled by "an open
and undisguised jealousy of the wealth and power of the commercial states."
They had seized on the routine friction "naturally arising between rival nations"
as a pretext for going to war against "the greatest commercial nation on the
globe" at the same time they adopted "the system of [commercial] exclusion
maintained by her great enemy." The committee linked the nation's "descent
from national greatness, [to] a determination to harass and annihilate that spirit
of commerce which has ever been the handmaid of civil and religious liberty."
The report concluded menacingly: "A power to regulate commerce is abused
when employed to destroy it, and a manifest and voluntary abuse of power
sanctions the right of resistance as much as a direct and palpable usurpation. . . .
The question [of resisting] is not a question of power or right with this
Legislature, but of time and expediency."[13]

Over the previous decade Americans had grown used to threatening words
from Massachusetts. The *National Intelligencer* warned its readers in advance of
the "SEASON OF BRAVADO" that was likely to ensue while the state's legislature was
in session and advised them not to be alarmed by "seditious blusterings" because
the Boston Federalists were not mad enough "to pull their own house over their
heads."[14] Aware that Federalist credibility was wearing thin, Otis's report considered several remedies for the grievances it identified. It rejected remonstrating
with Congress, because in the past that had produced no effect other than an
"increase to the evils complained of." Passing laws protecting "the citizens of this
Commonwealth in their persons and property" had considerable support, but
the report rejected this course as well, at least for the moment. Instead, it turned
to calling a convention despite the connection the Henry Papers had alleged
between such a meeting and secession. The report met that objection by arguing
that a convention of "the wise and good of those states, which deem themselves
oppressed" provided the most eligible way for amending the Constitution,
"whenever they find that the practical construction given it by the rulers for the
time being, is contrary to its true spirit." Nonetheless, the report recommended
postponing a convention until representatives "soon to be returned for the next
General Court" were elected. They would "come from the people . . . more fully
possessed of their views and wishes" as well as "better acquainted with the . . . dis-
positions of other states, suffering alike with [Massachusetts]." The legislature
thus left its options open should the embargo persist. By mid-May it would also
have a much better sense of where the diplomatic initiatives under way in
Europe were leading than the General Court possessed in the depths of winter.
One hundred seventy-eight of the 221 members in the House then endorsed
Otis's report, as did a majority of the Senate.[15]

The assertiveness of the Maryland House of Delegates undoubtedly encouraged the Massachusetts Federalists in their expectations for the future. Since the spring of 1813 many Maryland inhabitants had felt the threat posed by the presence of a British naval squadron in northern Chesapeake Bay.[16] But despite destructive enemy raids on Frenchtown and Harve de Grace, Maryland's Federalists had succeeded, with help from the lingering effect of the Baltimore riots, in solidifying their hold on the lower house of the legislature. A memorial adopted by the House of Delegates on January 28, 1814, argued that the state's vulnerability derived less from its exposed coastline than from its proximity to Washington, which it feared the British would attack "to distract and frustrate the views of [our] rulers in their avowed plan of foreign conquest." After again complaining that the federal government had failed to provide for the state's defense, the Maryland House went out of its way to plead Massachusetts's case in terms almost identical to those being used in the Bay State. It likened the recent embargo to "the Boston port bill of 1774" and pointed to "the still greater miseries of the people of New England" deriving from "the formation of new states out of the limits of our ancient territory" that deprived them of their rightful "influence in the national councils."[17]

The alliance that seemed to be ripening between the Maryland House of Delegates and the Massachusetts legislature provoked a lengthy denunciation of the *"madness* of faction" from Hezekiah Niles, the publisher of the influential *Weekly Register*. But Niles focused his wrath more on the Massachusetts source of the disease than on its homegrown manifestations. Far from following where George Washington had led, Federalist leaders were repudiating everything Washington stood for.

> Little did that great man believe that in ten or fifteen years after his death, men in *Boston*, "the cradle of the revolution," should coldly sit down and *calculate a separation of the states.* Less did he suppose that in the *legislature of Massachusetts*, the *expediency* of that diabolical measure should become a question of debate! Much less did he believe that the faction which proposed, supported and encouraged such notions, would fasten upon *his* name, and cloak *their* baseness with *his* virtues. Unmanly hypocrites! Thus to abuse the memory of the dead; and, as far as in you lies, to ascribe to the deceased a depravity that he would have looked into annihilation!

Niles condemned the "*British* gazettes at *Boston*, and some other towns in *Massachusetts*" for discussing the "right and expediency of *separating from the union*." "The most barefaced lies and outrageous misrepresentations" were being "diligently used to excite state jealousies and partial sympathies" to malign the nation's government, while "all that was *religious . . .* and *magnanimous*" was associated with Britain. Niles accused the Massachusetts Federalists of trying to "cheat the public feeling" by "*manufactur[ing]* petitions and remonstrances, as in a mill by wholesale." They then "sent them to the (falsely called) leaders of *their* 'peace party' in many of the little towns of the state, where by any sort of chicanery, they might assume the form of a document, and be 'returned from whence they came,' as the VOICE OF THE YEOMANRY!"[18]

Others outside New England joined Niles in condemning and belittling the Federalists. The *Aurora* of Philadelphia, in an article titled "Treason Exploded," dismissed Otis's report as a "new plan of panic" that would come to naught because of New England's dependence on the rest of the nation.[19] The legislature of New Jersey, which now had a Republican majority, countered the memorial of the Maryland House of Delegates with a joint resolution that directed "contempt and abhorrence" at "the ravings of an infuriated faction, either issuing from a legislative body, a maniac governor, or discontented or ambitious demagogues."[20] The Pennsylvania legislature also joined in the fray, though it chose to focus on the possibility that Massachusetts would intervene in a dispute between the governor of Vermont and federal authorities.

In the autumn of 1813, shortly after becoming Vermont's governor, Martin Chittenden had ordered elements of the state's militia serving with federal forces in northern New York to return home, and had dispatched a militia brigadier to take charge of the state's troops there. On his arrival in camp, the brigadier was arrested. Twenty-two of the officers in the recalled detachment then publicly challenged the lawfulness of Chittenden's order. A Republican representative from the state supported them by introducing a resolution in Congress urging that Chittenden be prosecuted for "entic[ing] soldiers in the service of the United States to desert." Harrison G. Otis countered by proposing the state's legislature declare it to be "the duty of . . . Massachusetts to aid the Governor of Vermont" and to pledge "effectual support" whenever the legislature of Vermont should request it.[21] Though the General Court never adopted Otis's proposed motion, it attracted a great deal of attention. The Pennsylvania legislature expressed their "high disapprobation" of both Otis and Chittenden, arguing their actions embodied principles that threatened "civil war" as well as the prostration of "the only free government on earth." Pennsylvania's legislature then resolved "to the utmost of our power . . . [to] support the general government in all lawful and constitutional measures to bring to justice infractors of the laws and constitution of the United States."[22]

Legitimate versus Illegitimate Opposition

Republicans heaved a collective sigh of relief when the Massachusetts legislature finally adjourned at the end of February. For all its bluster, the state government had avoided doing anything directly to obstruct the war effort beyond denying the federal government the use of its prisons in accommodating prisoners of war.[23] However, the dissolution of the General Court failed to provide more than passing encouragement to the Republicans because of the debate that raged in Congress through the winter and into the spring of 1814 over the prosecution of the war. Republican measures for filling the army and financing operations through loans continued to encounter stout Federalist resistance. Initially congressional Republicans celebrated these exchanges as examples of what political debate should be.[24] They too assumed the war would end with the pacification of Europe, which seemed to be proceeding apace. They also assumed that as a minority the Federalists' capacity for mischief was limited. But as it dawned on them that a European peace was just as likely to empower Britain in conjunction with the Federalists to act against them, some Republicans began to lose their composure.[25]

In mid-January James Fisk, who had sponsored the motion for prosecuting Governor Chittenden, exploded in response to Cyrus King's denial that his opposition to a bill increasing the incentives offered enlistees impeded the recruiting service. Fisk claimed that in parts of New England "No sooner is a young man asked to enlist, than you see ten or a dozen around him dissuading him from doing so." Fisk then rebutted King's accusation that the Republicans were solely responsible for the miseries and disasters accompanying the war by applying Felix Grundy's notion of moral treason to King. "They are to be charged to those who have weakened the arms of their country; who have divided the opinions of the people; who have refused to defend the rights of their country. If that American feeling had prevailed everywhere which ought to animate the bosoms of every man, we should have had no occasion to go to war. . . . But for the Opposition, we should never have been at war."[26]

Daniel Webster responded by summarily rejecting the notion that "owing to opposition . . . war became necessary; and, owing to opposition, also that it has been prosecuted with no better success." Since the Federalist resistance to Republican measures dated from 1807, he reasoned war would have been declared long before 1812 had the Federalists really been its cause. Instead, a Republican thirst for conquest had ignited the conflict. If the Republicans hoped to check the Federalists' "freedom of inquiry, discussion, and debate," it would not work because their opposition was "Constitutional and legal." He added that the Federalists were "not of a school, in which insurrection is taught as a virtue," nor would they "seek promotion through the paths of sedition." Though a majority of Republicans might support the war, Webster warned that more than party backing was needed "to sustain the country through a long, expensive, and bloody contest."[27]

Webster's denial that the Federalists were in any way responsible for the war and its failures led John C. Calhoun to attempt to distinguish between legitimate and illegitimate opposition. Calhoun acknowledged that opposition might be "both innocent and useful" when "confined within those bounds which love of country and political honesty prescribe." But harnessed to "faction and ambition" it was "the first of political evils." Calhoun thought the Federalist opposition "factious and dangerous" because of its "settled and fixed character . . . to embarrass and weaken Government" by throwing "impediments in the way of every measure" so as to "destroy public faith, and deliver the country unarmed to the mercy of the enemy." Calhoun questioned whether critics of the war were acting within their constitutional rights, pointing out that no article in that document "authorized [their] dangerous and vicious species" of opposition. Certainly the fact that what they were doing was "not expressly forbidden" by the Constitution carried little weight since that logic would also justify violating "the whole decalogue."[28]

Yet Calhoun could not deny that the Constitution severely limited Republican options in dealing with their opponents. No Republican in Congress was prepared to defy the First Amendment as the Federalists had in 1798 with the Sedition Act. Charles J. Ingersoll of Pennsylvania, accordingly, tried to take a different tack in drawing the line between legitimate and illegitimate opposition. "The press, and exposure out of doors, debate, and contradiction by speeches and votes within this Assembly, public sentiment in short, in all its elements, is the theater for the operations of a minority." While the minority observed the regulations of Congress and adhered to the Constitution, no one would "strive to interrupt or suppress the agitations of opposition." But when these limitations were exceeded they could expect to meet with censure. "The gentlemen of the minority enjoy very great privileges and exercise them. They may put us all out. I promise them, if they do, that we will never ask to manage their measures, as they persist in their efforts to control ours. . . . We will never entreat them when they fairly get into power, as they now ask us, when they have fairly got themselves out of it, to forego [*sic*] all the rights of a majority, and in a republican Government to suffer the minority to rule."[29]

Congressional Federalists summarily dismissed the distinctions Calhoun and Ingersoll had attempted to advance. Zebulon Shipherd of New York noted that thinking, speaking, and acting against the war were not the only activities the Republicans objected to. "Indeed if you omit to support it, by loans, by advice, by encouraging your friends to enlist, by loud applauses and earnest commendations, you are smutted with 'moral treason.' " Shipherd also argued that submitting to Republican criticism would result in "an alarming encroachment upon the prerogatives of religion." Someone who believed that "offensive wars originate in the vilest passions of the depraved human heart" would "incur guilt of a serious kind if he contribute[d] to their prosecution." Should a man be "condemned as guilty . . . because he obeys the dictates of his conscience?" If pleading "the cause of humanity" meant one was guilty of moral treason, Shipherd preferred "to be called a moral traitor." Who could deny the immorality of conquering Canada, whose inhabitants were being "despoiled of their property" and slaughtered "in defence of those rights which Americans hold dear and sacred?"[30]

Manpower shortages, though acute, posed less of a problem for the Republicans than finance. By the end of 1813 they could take heart from the knowledge that the sons of some prominent Federalists were defying their parents and seeking commissions in the army.[31] Congressional Republicans realized they were much more vulnerable when it came to raising money because of the treasury's continued reliance on loans. In early February 1814, John W. Eppes, the chairman of the House Ways and Means Committee, had proposed financing the forthcoming campaign through a loan of $25 million and the issuance of $5 million in treasury notes. Eppes noted that "[t]he sum to be borrowed is much larger than any loan hitherto authorized in this country," but he argued that it was within the nation's means because past experience showed "the funds . . . in times of peace, will enable us to pay [it] off, within a reasonable period." Eppes's proposal provided a target for the Federalists to shoot at during the remainder of the month. In this instance the Republicans felt they had little choice but to indulge the opposition in "unlimited debate" lest they alienate moderate Federalists whose funds were needed to complete a loan of this size.[32] But the results were not encouraging.

Abijah Bigelow of Massachusetts opposed the loan because the money was to be used "to prosecute a war of invasion and conquest." Daniel Sheffey argued that "the present" was "the best moment to arrest" the war. He confronted head-on whether "certain acts done out of this House, tending to defeat the measures of Administration," such as "persuading persons not to enlist in the army, or not to loan money to the Government," constituted "moral treason." Sheffey himself had never engaged in such acts because "[t]hose who enlisted where I am acquainted, were generally persons who rendered a service to their neighborhood by leaving it," while his constituents had very little money to lend. Sheffey was unmoved by pleas for national unity because "union in accelerating [the nation's] ruin is worse than any division." Instead he felt it was his "duty to impede, rather than accelerate your progress in this downhill course of ruin."[33]

Felix Grundy responded to Sheffey's and Shipherd's comments by trying to clarify the concept of "moral treason" so as to separate extreme from moderate, well-disposed Federalists. "Moral treason" applied neither "to those who exercise their Constitutional privilege of opposing measures before they are adopted by the constituted authorities," or even to those "who shall . . . after their adoption, deliver their sentiments freely against them," nor even "to those who fail to join the Army themselves, or decline to loan their money." Instead it applied to "those who . . . exert their influence to prevent others from enlisting and . . . combine together for the purpose of preventing loans from being filled." To illustrate his point Grundy drew on language from the first section of the Sedition Law of 1798, which had made it unlawful for "any person . . . [to] combine or conspire together, with intent to oppose any measure . . . of the Government of the United States." But the Republicans had no intention of sponsoring a similar statute or of trying "to hide their conduct from public view and scrutiny" as the Federalists had in administering it. "All that is wished for is, that those who are opposed to them should so act as to not injure the public service. . . . We wish to effect our object, not by fines and imprisonments, as our predecessors did, but by making it disreputable in the public estimation to injure the country by indirect means."[34]

The Federalists refused to buy such notions. William Gaston of North Carolina claimed that the majority in Congress had adopted procedures "by . . . which every privilege, except that of thinking, is made to depend on the pleasure of . . . the majority." As an example, Gaston cited the House's refusal to consider a resolution he had proposed several weeks before, " 'that pending our negotiation with Great Britain, it is inexpedient to prosecute a war of invasion and conquest of the Canadas.' " Gaston conceded that "opposition may exceed all reasonable bounds and a minority become factious." But a factious government was infinitely more pernicious: "Faction out of power is a demon enchained! Faction, vested with the attributes of rule, is a Moloch of destruction." If the majority really wished to mitigate party rancor, they should "uphold [their] measures by force of argument . . . [rather than] denunciation. Stigmatize not opposition to your notions with offensive epithets."[35]

John Forsythe of Georgia protested that the Federalists were not showing "either that moderation or . . . liberality" in their "strictures upon the majority" for which Gaston asked. Forsythe welcomed Daniel Webster's declaration that the Federalists intended neither sedition nor rebellion. But how was this disclaimer to be squared with threats issued against customs houses and their officers in the eastern states? Forsythe also pointed to the "conduct of a portion of the Legislature of Massachusetts, the direct tendency of which has been to lead to a separation of the Union. Inflammatory resolutions, violent complaints of the injustice and oppression of the General Government have been heaped upon each other, to stimulate public prejudice, to prepare the public mind for stronger and more decided steps." Following the lead of the Republican press, Forsythe professed not to fear the consequences of such actions because "[t]he leaders of these factious spirits are prevented from carrying their wishes fully into operation by . . . interest and fear." If they ever did, Forsythe predicted an orgy of destruction would result from the ensuing civil war.[36]

Forsythe's denunciation of the Federalists received the warm endorsement of the *National Intelligencer,*[37] but it did little to quiet partisan passions in Congress. William Baylies of Massachusetts maintained that the common-wealth's legislature had "passed no act which they had not a Constitutional right to adopt." He went on to assert that Massachusetts still had "a few survivors of the good old Revolution high in the councils" of the state "who, in the path of duty, will be as little dismayed by the glitter of hostile steel as by the glitter of the tinselled invective of the honorable gentleman from Georgia."[38] In other words, the Federalist minority was not about to be intimidated inside or outside of Congress by personal insults or threats.

The matter before the House, however, was not who could call the other the worst names, but whether money could be raised to sustain the war effort. Calhoun tried to refocus attention on this task by asking "[w]ith what counte-nance . . . our opponents [could] withhold supplies for expenses incurred by their own votes?"[39] Pointing to the support that Federalists like Quincy and Emott of New York had given to the expansion of the army in 1812, he asked: "Was their object to embarrass and finally to put the majority out of power? Will they dare to make an avowal so disgraceful to their party?" Though Calhoun was unable to provide an "intelligible limitation" for governing the opposition's behavior, he backed away from advocating blanket proscriptions just as Grundy had. "We propose no law; no restraint on the conduct of the minority. We appeal to the virtue and intelligence of the community only. On the people must finally fall the ruinous effects of erroneous and dangerous principles" Calhoun instead called on the "upright citizen . . . to do no act, whatever he might think of the war" that "put his country in the power of the enemy."[40]

In taking this tack Calhoun played to a division that had begun to emerge in the ranks of the Federalists outside Congress. On February 14, Samuel Dexter had penned a public letter from Washington restating his opposition to the war and to the way it was being conducted. But Dexter's letter also criticized the Federalists for their "indiscriminate opposition" and their attempts "to paralyze public energy by degrading the resources . . . of our country, and exaggerating those of Britain." While he was not currently a member of Congress, Dexter's moderation had already attracted the attention of Republicans.[41] His com-plaint that Federalist behavior "diminish[ed] the chance for a speedy and hon-orable peace" and "endanger[ed] the union of the states" recommended him as a gubernatorial alternative to Strong. Though Dexter asserted that the right of every citizen "to examine . . . rulers is unquestionable," he reminded the public that this right could also be abused. "What good effect is to be expected from creating division when engaged in war with a powerful nation . . . ? Why make publications and speeches to prove that we are absolved from allegiance to the national government, and hint that an attempt to divide the empire might be justified?" Dexter maintained there was a distinction between exposing "the errors of government" and "preaching sedition."[42]

Neither the boost the Republicans derived from Dexter, nor their willingness to indulge the Federalists with an unlimited debate, nor even Congress's $5 million appropriation of U.S. stock to settle the claims of northern investors—many of them leading Federalists—in the Yazoo lands succeeded in attracting sufficient subscribers to the $25 million loan Congress eventually authorized.[43] The *National Intelligencer* blamed the loan's failure on the Federalists and condemned them for refusing to finance expenses already sanctioned by Congress. Surely in doing so, they crossed the boundary between legitimate and illegitimate opposition that both Calhoun and Dexter invoked.[44] Yet Federalist resistance to government loans hardened in the face of such criticism during the remainder of 1814. Some Federalists had subscribed to the loans of 1812 and 1813 despite their hostility to the war because of the high rates of interest. They justified their actions on the grounds that peace was in the offing. A year later the bar had risen to where they now insisted peace be a certainty. Some still subscribed despite their political professions, but most Federalists abstained.[45]

Though the Federalists acquired little honor with this resistance, the Republicans had left them with very few legitimate ways in which to oppose the war. Arguing that Federalist dissent alone stood in the way of an advantageous peace with Britain barred most public disagreement. Republicans were also altogether too ready to attribute extremist views—such as suggestions that additions to the national debt entailed by the Louisiana Purchase or the War of 1812, be repudiated—to all Federalists indiscriminately.[46] It is easy to see why the Republicans reacted as they did. The new situation in Europe meant that the alternative to concluding a peace with Britain was facing her full military power alone. That was hardly a comforting prospect for those who suspected the Federalists were still in league with the British government. It impelled some Republicans to liken the Federalists to Benedict Arnold. "Of what denomination then," asked "Virginiensis" writing in the *National Intelligencer*, is an "offence which puts in jeopardy, if it does not totally destroy the freedom of a nation, by persuading its citizens to yield their freedom to a foreign power?"[47] But being told one resembled the most despised traitor of the American Revolution hardly offered the Federalists an identity they cared to embrace.

The Federalist determination not to let the Republicans escape responsibility for an unsuccessful war, however, contributed as much to the failure to agree on a boundary between legitimate and illegitimate opposition as Republican defensiveness did. The flip side of the Federalists' growing confidence that the

European conflict would soon end was a fear that the Republicans would do everything in their power—including refusing to make peace when they should—to avoid disgrace. Considerations like these led the Federalists to cling to behaviors their opponents were anxious to discourage so as to limit Republican options as much as possible.

Backing Away from the Precipice

For the moment the confused state of Europe diffused some of the tensions between the Federalists and Republicans both inside and outside Congress. No one could be sure where European events were moving until after they learned that Napoleon had abdicated in early April 1814.[48] The news took two months to reach the United States, but it hardly came as a surprise after Napoleon was driven back to the ancient limits of France at the end of 1813.[49] That decisively broke the hold he had exerted for a decade over central Europe and rendered his "continental system" defunct. Aside from heralding the end of more than twenty years of warfare, it created circumstances in which the Republican leadership was able to rethink the embargo and their entire "restrictive system."

Many Republicans had entertained reservations about commercial restrictions from the start because of the political costs associated with them. The initial appeal of an embargo as an alternative to fighting simultaneously the two most powerful nations in the world had long since vanished, and nonintercourse directed against Britain had few enthusiasts. Because Napoleon had been less interested in cultivating a commercial relationship with the republic than in manipulating her into war, it had done little to open up commerce with continental Europe. At the commencement of hostilities, Britain continued to exert a stranglehold over the nation's commercial potential through its blockade of most of the European coast as well as portions of the American coast. The emergence of Europe from Napoleonic domination led Britain to lift its blockade of the liberated areas on the continent, freeing neutrals to resume exploring commercial opportunities overseas. Though Britain's expanding blockade of the American coast eliminated some of the commercial possibilities resulting from the narrowing of her blockade in Europe, Americans had plenty of experience with eluding naval patrols in home waters, especially when badly needed supplies were available in nearby neutral entrepôts. Opening the nation's ports could also help to replenish a bare treasury. The embargo stood in the way of reviving yields from the impost long after there was any chance it could adversely affect Britain.

The new state of affairs led John C. Calhoun, as chair of the Foreign Relations Committee, to call for an end to all the restrictive measures affecting the nation's commerce. The case Calhoun made for repeal stressed the advantage America could reap from aligning itself with other neutral nations who favored free trade. "[I]t would not be decorous or wise for the United States standing up for freedom of trade, to pursue a course of policy calculated to irritate those nations with whom we have common cause." Conversely, lifting the nation's restrictions on commerce would force on Britain the "awkward and perplexing" dilemma of acting against the neutral trade or "modify[ing] her system of paper blockade in favor of all neutrals. Will not a persistence in her present illegitimate blockade, and capture at sea of neutral vessels destined for the United States, irritate and vex those nations, and detach them from the cause of Great Britain?" If Britain "modifie[d] her blockade in their favor . . . we may carry on a lucrative trade to the continent of Europe, not beneficial to England, but very much so to the United States." Calhoun was confident that the dilemma in which the British government would find itself could contribute more to producing peace "than ten years continuance of the present system," now that "the prospect of its producing any [economic] pressure has become so very faint."[50]

While many congressional Republicans agreed with Calhoun, some felt uncomfortable about surrendering so familiar a way of resisting British power. Had not the succor British forces in North America derived from the illicit trade been the principal reason for laying an embargo four months before? Others were worried about the effect repeal might have on the nation's nascent industries, many of which had sprung up since 1808. Nonetheless, the proposal turned out to be one of the few measures considered by the Thirteenth Congress on which the majority of Republicans and the Federalists could agree. Both the embargo and what had survived of non-intercourse, namely non-importation, were repealed on April 14.[51] Any reservations Republicans entertained about lifting the embargo were at least partially assuaged by the almost simultaneous news that Britain was extending its blockade of the American coast to include all of New England.[52]

Unfortunately, the abandonment of the restrictive system did little to strengthen the Republicans in Massachusetts. It came too late to affect the gubernatorial election, which Caleb Strong won handily by a margin of more than eleven thousand votes.[53] After two years of bruising defeats the state's Republicans were so demoralized that many had emigrated to friendlier environments.[54] The willingness of those who remained to throw their support to Samuel Dexter in turn discouraged Federalists from accepting Dexter as an alternative to Strong.[55] The claim that any opposition in the state legislature diluted the influence the Federalist leadership could exercise nationally had proven efficacious.[56] When it came to the election of state representatives, Boston Federalists felt sufficiently confident to continue reducing the size of the town's delegation in the Massachusetts House that they had tentatively begun in 1813.[57] The Federalists emerged from the state elections of 1814 stronger than they had been the year before, or for that matter since 1804.

The election results could have been construed as endorsement of the previous legislature's qualified call for a convention, but the leadership declined, at least for the moment, to pursue such a route. Governor Strong, for one, went out of his way to strike a moderate pose in his June address to the General Court. Though he acknowledged that "a great proportion of the people in this state" viewed the war "as unnecessary and unjustifiable," he cautioned against pushing matters too far: "if we appear solicitous for our own advancement, or endeavor by unfair methods to ensure the success of a party we belong to, our fellow citizens may well doubt our sincerity when we pretend to an anxious concern for the public good." Instead "[t]he real patriot . . . wishes that the state and nation may prosper, whoever directs their affairs, and is content with his own proportion of the public happiness."[58]

The House in its reply reviewed the unconstitutional features of the recent embargo before recommending abstention from all voluntary acts that supported the war. But it also urged obedience to the laws. It hailed the new situation in Europe as opening the possibility for peace, but expressed apprehension "that our relations have been too intimately combined with those of one of the contending powers." Though House Federalists forbore saying that "our Government have been in alliance with that of France," it nonetheless accused the administration of "pursuing similar objectives by similar means, and . . . cooperat[ing with her] in fact if not in form." Such observations, however, fell far short of a call for a convention that might have been expected from the Federalists' recent electoral triumph.[59]

The Senate, to which Otis had again returned to join Quincy, was more strident in its reply. It approved the petitions and memorials received by the previous legislature demanding "an interposition . . . as would not only relieve them from present suffering, but secure them against future oppression, and restore to them [the people of Massachusetts] that constitutional weight and influence, of which they had been unjustly deprived." The Senate rejoiced "that the tremendous conflict which has so long spread havoc and carnage through the earth, is closed," and gave thanks to God that "[t]he gigantic despotism which had nearly exterminated freedom from the earth . . . is at length overwhelmed." Was it "not only right, but the duty of a people, mindful of what they owe to themselves, their country and their God, to oppose by every peaceable and constitutional effort a war thus declared, and thus prosecuted?"[60]

Ordinarily the reply of the Senate carried less weight than the reply of the House because the Senate, possessing fewer members, was considered to speak with less authority. So the added aggressiveness of this particular reply would normally have passed without attracting special notice. What ensured that instead it got national attention was an alternative reply proposed by one of the Senate's Republican minority, John Holmes of York, Maine. Holmes had recently defected from the ranks of the Federalists to assume informal leadership of the Massachusetts Republicans. That might have qualified him for a seat in Congress, but Massachusetts Republicans needed him too much to send him to Washington.[61] Nonetheless, his speeches in the state Senate were widely republished in the Republican press both inside and outside the commonwealth. After the war he would assume leadership of the movement leading to Maine's statehood.[62]

Holmes challenged the Senate majority's views with telling directness. His reply regretted that the recent embargo "so necessary to restrain unprincipled men from aiding the enemy . . . should have been made a theme of invective and abuse, and that the executive and legislature of a former general court should have encouraged opposition, to the verge of insurrection and civil war." Holmes then attacked the Federalists' moral posturing over the war: "However you may be disposed to yield to Great Britain the right of deciding on our property and our citizenship, and however much you may be attached to the opinion, that the capture and confinement of an American citizen at pleasure, is a British right, *and ought not to be resisted*, the people of this state have long exploded such opinions, and have united in justifying the war, by applauding its successes, exalting at its triumphs, and rewarding the heroes who have achieved the victories." Holmes urged the Senate "to encourage the people to rejoice at the successes of the arms and enterprizes of the United States." If they did, "we may safely expect a glorious result. Then might we look to the God of battles for his protection and blessing. Then we should again triumph over the enemies of our country. . . . Then would Massachusetts resume the rank from which she has descended, and put on her robes of righteousness."[63]

Holmes's allusions to "applauding [the nation's] successes, exalting at its triumphs, and rewarding the heroes who have achieved the victories" would carry a lingering sting. Though directed specifically at Josiah Quincy's attempt the year before to discourage public approbation of American victories, Holmes's words applied equally to the ostentatious celebrations with which the Federalists were greeting the news of Napoleon's abdication as it arrived in the United States. Hartford Federalists organized the first such event attended by "a large number of the citizens." In addition to the ceremonial toasts, they listened to Theodore Dwight, publisher and editor of the *Connecticut Mirror*, declaim on the significance of Britain's victory. Dwight welcomed "the assurance we now feel, that our own country is delivered from the fear of vassalage to the worst of tyrants." But he lamented that America's rulers had "considered it expedient to involve our concerns with those of the great enemy of national freedom" in such a way as to make it uncertain how the United States would "be affected."[64] Newburyport's Federalists seconded Hartford by expressing "their joy and gratitude for the astonishing and glorious events" which had taken place in Europe, by displaying the colors "from the naked stumps, of our few remaining shipping" and by ringing the church bells and firing two salutes. They also illuminated the town hall, adorning it with what was described as "a beautiful transparency" of "ALEXANDER THE DELIVERER," the Russian csar.[65]

Not to be outdone, Boston's Federalist leadership orchestrated the most elaborate celebration in the region. They modeled their event on a ceremony they had previously organized to commemorate Napoleon's retreat from Russia in March 1813.[66] A committee of thirteen, including Christopher Gore, George Cabot, Harrison Gray Otis, Thomas Handysed Perkins, and John Lowell Jr., invited William E. Channing (also a member of the committee) to pronounce a discourse commemorating "the Goodness of God in delivering the Christian World from Military Despotism." The celebration took the form of a religious service that featured hymns, readings from the Bible, and the performance of several compositions of sacred music, including a rendition of Handel's "Hallelujah Chorus." Unlike the previous year's celebration that had occurred after the adjournment of the General Court, this event was graced by the governor, lieutenant governor, the council, and many members of the Senate and House.

Channing addressed the question of "the propriety of our expressions of joy on the deliverance of Europe." After noting that Napoleon's "disastrous influence has already blighted our prosperity," Channing echoed Dwight in lamenting that "[a]s a nation, we cannot gather round the ruins of the fallen despotism, and say, We shared in the peril and glory of its destruction." To the published version of Channing's oration the Federalist committee appended a series of resolutions hailing Alexander as "the Deliverer" of "Christendom and celebrating the restoration of the Bourbons in France as being favorable to "liberty" because it "check[ed] anarchical propensities . . . restrain[ed] ambition, foster[ed] morals and religion; and protect[ed] property." The celebration concluded with an illumination of the State House authorized by the legislature and a display of fireworks.[67]

The Federalist leadership in both state capitals hoped to set a standard that would be followed by lesser towns as well as by the numerous Washington Benevolent Societies they had been busy establishing since 1809. And to some extent their expectations materialized. Several towns in the commonwealth copied their example while Federalists in others turned their Independence Day festivities into celebrations of Napoleon's defeat.[68] These observances spread beyond Massachusetts and Connecticut to Rhode Island and New Hampshire in New England, to New York City, New Jersey, and Maryland.[69] Their Federalist sponsors did not seem the least embarrassed about celebrating the triumph of a nation with whom their own country was at war. A Fourth of July oration by the New Haven Federalist, David Daggett, who had recently been elected to the U.S. Senate after a long career in Connecticut's legislature showed how the Federalists managed this problem.

Daggett had established his reputation as an orator fifteen years earlier with a satire of the French Revolution's attempt to replace tradition with reason titled, "Sun-beams May be Extracted from Cucumbers, But the Process is Tedious."[70] Daggett's 1814 address relied on pathos in depicting the crimes Napoleonic France had inflicted upon humanity. "Not less . . . than 20 millions of the human race . . . have miserably perished by it." However, in Daggett's judgment, its "influence on the moral world has been unspeakably more fatal. The lessons of fraud, falsehoods, treachery, oppression, cruelty, revenge, rapine, and murder, which it has read and taught, in the face of Heaven, transcend all the world had before witnessed." Daggett likened Napoleon's abdication to Lucifer's expulsion from heaven and hailed the news as being "more glorious than any which have been proclaimed to the world, since the appearance of the Angels to the Shepherds of Bethlehem." But "those who term themselves enemies of Kings and Tyrants," by which he meant the Republicans, were not rejoicing. Instead the glorious news had been met "by a ridiculous fabrication . . . of his [Napoleon's] triumphs in Paris." The Republican papers had eagerly disseminated the misinformation: "Their presses groaned to issue—their types swelled to magnify *this glorious news.*" Why were they so anxious to reassure the public that Napoleon was still in power? Was it, he asked sarcastically, "[t]o prostrate the power of Russia and England—to annihilate Spain and Portugal and then to teach *us* that we are 'a nation without energy and honour'—to compare our government to a Jamaica Assembly [as the duke of Cadore had], and finally to give us a king of the blood of the august Napoleon? Do these *pretended* republicans believe, that in the event of the conquest of Europe, he would not have made a second Holland of the United States?"[71]

Some Federalists nevertheless got into trouble celebrating Napoleon's downfall. On June 29, 1814, Gouverneur Morris spoke to a gathering of New York City Federalists marking the restoration of the Christian kings that France had deposed during the past quarter-century. Morris had been an influential member of the Continental Congress during the American Revolution. He had also attended the Philadelphia convention where he had done more to shape the felicitous wording of the Constitution's text than any other delegate. Subsequently he became deeply prejudiced against the French Revolution while serving as ambassador to France during its most radical phase. Morris now hailed the restorations as a deliverance from a savage democracy that had reduced "the virtuous and wise to [its] level of folly and guilt" and thus precipitated Europe into convulsions of violence and rapine. Peace became possible again only when Europe's Christian kings through God's providential intervention replaced Napoleon. Morris concluded his oration by urging his "abused, self-murdered country" to rejoice with Europe at the restoration of the Bourbons—America's true "friends"—to the throne.[72] Sympathetic Federalists then reprinted Morris's oration as a pamphlet in New York, and Salem, Massachusetts, and republished it in several newspapers.[73]

Morris's juxtapositon of benign monarchies with murderous democracies proved too ideologically provocative to go unchallenged. The *National Intelligencer* republished two long critiques of the address that had appeared in New York's *National Advocate*. And Hezekiah Niles penned his own denunciation of Morris for striving "to condemn the spirit of *revolution*, and maintain the idea of unquestioned right in kings to govern, in hereditary succession." Niles claimed that "[t]here was not one dynasty in Europe . . . that was not established by *revolution* or *force*," citing William III's accession to the English throne by way of example. The British monarchy, which Morris so admired, made a fifth of its people paupers, and Niles opposed " 'legitimate princes and *christian* kings' " because they "CANNOT EXIST BUT IN THE MISERY OF THE PEOPLE."[74]

Most Federalists proved more adept at extracting political advantage from Napoleon's defeat than Gouverneur Morris. A widely followed strategy, exemplified by the Reverend Samuel Cary, was to mix of religion with politics while eschewing any endorsement of monarchy. In the 177th annual sermon preached before Boston's Ancient and Honorable Artillery Company, he portrayed France as a "more ferocious and more extensive" despotism "than the soundest politicians had believed could have existed in an advanced and enlightened state of society." Cary argued that Napoleon had established a power beyond the challenge of mere humans by appealing to the "corrupt passions and sympathies of mankind," and he accused the Republicans of contributing to this tyranny in order to attain immoral advantage. Recent developments suggested the Republicans would have been better advised had they relied on divine Providence as the arbiter of nations and remembered that war was Providence's principal means for effecting human improvement.[75]

But purely secular approaches could work almost as well. William Jones, the governor of Rhode Island, thought Napoleon's abdication proved that the expectations leading the Madison administration to declare war against Great Britain had been "fallacious, and the supposed objects of the war . . . unattainable." Writing in the *New England Palladium*, "Camillus" drew a parallel between Bonaparte and Madison, likening the former's refusal to respect the territorial and cultural diversity of Europe to the latter's disregard of a people's natural inclination for commerce. "Camillus" also condemned the Republicans for trying to expand the size of the Republic in "presumptuous disregard of the admonitions of history." Was it any surprise that Madison was now threatened with Napoleon's fate? "One of the People" gloated in the same newspaper that "[p]eace therefore (an inglorious peace for the warhawks, but not so for the country in general)" would have to take place.[76]

In their exaltation over the distress Napoleon's defeat caused the Republicans, the Federalists revealed more about themselves than they realized. By repeatedly accusing the Republicans of predicating their foreign policy on the assumption that a corrupt, monarchical Britain was doomed to defeat in its struggle with Napoleonic France, they projected on their adversaries a mode of thinking to which they were far more prone. Hezekiah Niles better epitomized how Republicans viewed the two belligerent powers when he denied there was any difference between "the spirit of the government of *Great Britain* and the spirit of the government of *Bonaparte*." Though Niles acknowledged the importance of the European balance of power to America's future, he did not prefer "the continuance of the power of *Napoleon*, as well as that of *Great Britain*," to "*the extinction of both*." He had always maintained that French violations of American rights "were good causes of war; and only regretted that we had not power to punish *France* and *Great Britain*, at once." The Republicans had sought to settle scores with England first because it posed the more immediate threat. Nor, as a commentator in the *National Intelligencer* noted, were the Republicans prepared to conclude that with Napoleon's fall Britain had become all powerful.[77]

If anyone had been overwhelmingly guided by the assumption that one of the European powers would triumph over the other because of the superiority of its form of government, it was the Federalists. Their conviction that Britain would outlast France had always owed more to ideological conviction reinforced by religious and cultural prejudice than to reasoned analysis.[78] That is why the Federalists could scarcely conceal their exaltation now that events seemed finally to be vindicating their vision of the world. However, the support they derived from empirical fact didn't make them any less dependent on their ideology. Instead they behaved like triumphant ideologues, insisting that Jefferson's followers had turned all of Europe away from Republicanism by their craven courting of France. These Federalists also claimed they alone were true republicans.[79]

To the Precipice

Federalist exaltation over Napoleon's fall preceded a full realization of how it would shape Britain's North American campaign during 1814. Freed from having to sustain operations on the continent of Europe, yet fully mobilized, the British government decided to redeploy substantial forces in North America to teach the United States a lesson. The first reinforcements from Europe came too late to be of direct use in repelling an American invasion along the Niagara frontier in July. But Britain's redeployment did permit sending reinforcements to upper Canada from lower Canada to counter American successes at Chippewa and Lundy's Lane. It also powered a new British strategy of conquest, the first component of which was the seizure of Eastport, Maine in mid-July. Then on August 9 and 10 the British launched an attack on Stonington, Connecticut from a large fleet of warships in Gardiner's Island Sound.[80] That served as preview for a campaign in the Chesapeake beginning in mid-August that led to the burning of Washington and the plundering of Alexandria after the town had placed itself at the mercy of the enemy. Baltimore escaped both fates by the resistance of a well-entrenched militia in the field and the determined defense of Fort McHenry—memorialized in our national anthem.[81]

Britain's primary objective was compelling the United States to relinquish a substantial portion of northern Maine. She hoped to achieve this end by invading northern New York along Lake Champlain and seizing the Massachusetts coast from Eastport to the Penobscot. In early September a British force of two thousand occupied Castine, Maine while Sir George Prevost led a large British force of recently arrived, European veterans toward Plattsburg. On September 11 Commodore Thomas Macdonough decisively defeated the British naval force on Lake Champlain. Without control of the lake Prevost had no choice but retreat.[82] Shortly afterward, Admiral George Cockburn withdrew the British expeditionary force from the Chesapeake. New England Federalists took little comfort from American successes because the British still held much of the region's northeastern coastline and were blockading the remainder of its coast. The concentration of British force in Massachusetts Bay ensured that the alarm previously confined to the maritime communities south and west of the Race at the eastern end of Long Island Sound would spread to the rest of the New England. The first rumors that the British commissioners at Ghent were demanding harsh concessions as the price of peace arrived just after the British had succeeded in burning Washington. At the same time Madison's September 1 Proclamation warning that Admiral Cochrane had authorized the indiscriminate destruction of coastal towns alerted them to a new peril from which the experience of Stonington suggested New England would no longer be exempt. The anxieties entertained by the Federalists at the commencement of hostilities about the vulnerability of their seaports to enemy depredations seemed on the verge of becoming reality.[83]

Massachusetts Federalists responded to the intensification of the war by calling for Madison's resignation instead of rallying to defend the nation.[84]

Some Federalists elsewhere charted a different course. On September 19, 1814, Martin Chittenden, who had tried to recall detachments of Vermont's militia from New York in 1813, proclaimed that the war had become "almost exclusively defensive." In the wake of the victory at Plattsburg he urged all party considerations be laid aside and appealed to his fellow citizens to unite in defense of their country.[85] On learning of Britain's peace terms, a caucus of Federalist congressmen voted "that supplies ought to be granted for the defence of the essential rights of the nation," and Alexander C. Hanson ostentatiously called on his Federalist colleagues to support the war now that the existence of the nation was at stake. According to Caleb Strong, the report of Hanson's turnabout caused a "considerable sensation" among the Federalists of Massachusetts.[86] Strong need not have been perplexed; the way Hanson and most of his Federalist colleagues followed his recommendation would leave their Republican counterparts in the House wondering whether there was any difference between their outright opposition and their professed support.[87] Still the declaration was worth something, and in the case of New York's Senator Rufus King could be important. At the beginning of September he pleaded for unity in meeting the common threat, and at the end of the year he threw his considerable influence behind an administration proposal for a $6 million direct tax to finance the war effort. Though King had disapproved of the conflict, he now supported the direct tax because it "promised to revive and support the public credit."[88] If Chittenden, Hanson, and King could change course during 1814 in response to circumstances, the Federalist leadership of New England could have as well, especially now that all possibility of Napoleonic conquest or subversion had vanished.[89]

However, instead of pitching in to save the nation, New England's Federalist leaders seized on the occasion to explore two additional ways for prostrating their Republican adversaries before the British. Their most damaging course was also the least visible one and for that reason the most difficult to track. There had been nothing devious about Federalist opposition to war loans. "The Examiner" complained in the *Independent Chronicle* of the "pains . . . taken to excite every suspicion against our fiscal resources" and the attempts by Federalists "to persuade many well disposed persons, that the loan of money was an immoral act . . . unbecoming a moral and religious people." He accused Timothy Pickering and "the *Boston Rebel*," John Lowell Jr., of going beyond persuasion "by threatening . . . creditors that the debt never would be provided for by the federalists."[90] But the activities of the nation's banks were far more significant than the activities of individuals because of their greater collective resources. Many of the state governments had borrowed their portions of the $3 million direct tax levied in 1813 from state banks to qualify for the discount the treasury offered for prompt payment. Nor would the syndicate that had completed the government's loan that year have been able to do so without support from banks.[91] However, during the summer of 1814 the Bank of Boston turned down the application of a syndicate for money to subscribe to a national loan on grounds that the collateral offered—securities from the last national loan (to the full amount of the current loan, if necessary)—was unacceptable.[92] Then, in August 1814, coincidentally with the intensification of British military pressure on the Republic, all the banks outside New England, as well as some within it, were forced to suspend redeeming their notes in specie.

Hezekiah Niles and Matthew Carey were not alone in tracing the banking crisis to the flow of specie toward Massachusetts throughout 1814.[93] Others have subsequently blamed it on a general loss of confidence in the government resulting from the burning of Washington.[94] Though the suspension occurred immediately after the destruction of the capital, this explanation would be more compelling had not bankers throughout the country complained well before the British assault on Washington of the pressure the Boston banks were exerting on banks outside their region by presenting their bills for payment in specie. As early as March, Governor Snyder of Pennsylvania referred to the drain of specie to the Northeast when vetoing an omnibus banking bill passed by the legislature. And by summer the New York banks were feeling acute pressure.[95] In addition, it is hard to see why only the banks of eastern New England, with the exception of the Republican State Bank of Boston, were exempt from the suspension unless Niles and Carey were onto something.[96] Distance from Washington should not have accounted for New England's good fortune if one considers Massachusetts's proximity to Halifax.

No one disputed that the New England banks possessed superior reserves. But contemporaries attributed their financial strength to the region's exemption from the British blockade until 1814. This enabled them to drain the rest of the nation's banks of their specie and to thrive at everyone else's expense.[97] Bank notes that could not be redeemed in specie only circulated locally. As a consequence, the federal government was forced to issue treasury certificates to meet many of it expenses. Doing so raised the specter of a repetition of the paper money disaster that had accompanied the Revolution and precluded reestablishing a national bank whose notes could be backed by specie.[98]

State Bank, which had become the national government's fiscal agent in Boston after war was declared, alone experienced liquidity problems. In exchange for receiving all customs revenues as deposits, it had loaned the federal government $1.2 million at the beginning of the conflict. In late September 1814 State Bank experienced an extraordinary run on its specie reserves.[99] Shortly afterward the *Boston Gazette* reported State Bank had tendered all quarterly interest payments over $100 due on United States bonds in treasury notes at par. Massachusetts, which had $200,000 coming to it from its bond holdings, refused the tender because the market value of the notes was well below par. Instead the state treasurer demanded that State Bank lend Massachusetts $50,000 in specie equivalents, as it was obliged to by its charter. When none of the Federalist banks were willing to help State Bank comply, the Massachusetts legislature ordered an investigation that depressed the value of the bank's stock well below that of Boston's five other banks.[100] From the Republicans' perspective, Federalist boasts about their power to create a financial debacle from which they exempted themselves provided an apt illustration of how "the federal faction . . . systematically pursued a line of conduct, exactly calculated to produce the evils . . . complained of."[101] Twentieth-century historians have held the Republicans responsible for the banking debacle because they embarked on war without a national bank, but contemporaries had reason enough to see the matter differently.[102]

No one disagrees that the Hartford Convention constituted the Federalists' most visible challenge to the nation's survival. The Massachusetts legislature initiated the convention movement in an emergency session that took place in the first week of October. The timing seems odd, since apart from the banking crisis, the nation's determination to resist Britain appeared to be rising after victories at Baltimore and Plattsburg.[103] But the British seizure of Castine in early September provided a plausible pretext for Governor Strong to call the legislature into session earlier than was customary. Though his address to the General Court omitted reference to a convention, he complained that the United States was making heavy requisitions on the Massachusetts militia just as it withdrew most of its troops from the state in its hour of need. Strong had complied with a request for eleven hundred men in July, but an additional requisition in September had led him, with the advice of the council, to insist that any new detachment remain under the command of state officers. In doing so, Massachusetts pursued a course that Connecticut was simultaneously charting.[104]

Connecticut's uneasy cooperation with federal authorities during 1813 collapsed during 1814. Enemy harassment of the state's shoreline led to constant requests for military protection which the governor and council thought the state could ill afford. They sought to limit the state's responsibility for defense by arguing that protecting commerce was the national government's job. If the appropriate protection was not forthcoming from Washington, merchants should withdraw their property to a safe haven. Dickering between state and national authorities over who would pay for small units stationed along the coast led to the dissolution of the militia detachment manning a fort at the mouth of the Connecticut River during the winter of 1814. On April 8 the British attacked Pettipaug Point (modern Essex) eight miles up the river at a location previously thought to be secure. The raid destroyed twenty-six vessels worth $150,000 that had taken refuge there at the cost of no British casualties. It dramatized the state's vulnerability and strengthened the determination of its government to retain control of its military resources in defending itself. In August a confrontation between federal and militia officers took place in the wake of the British attack on Stonington that led to the collapse of all cooperation between them.[105]

Connecticut was not the first New England state to stop cooperating with federal commanders during 1814. In May, well before the Stonington raid, the executive authorities of New Hampshire had refused to reinforce the six hundred federal servicemen guarding from possible British attack a ship of the line under construction in the navy yard at Portsmouth. As in Connecticut the question turned on whether the state's militia would be paid by the nation while remaining under state command. At the end of the summer Massachusetts followed New Hampshire's lead in responding to Commodore Bainbridge's request for assistance in protecting the USS *Constitution* and USS *Independence*, as well as a ship of the line on the stocks at the Charlestown Navy Yard, from an expected British assault. A deputation from the governor and council responded that the area would be safer if Bainbridge stationed his naval vessels below the forts defending Boston harbor. Compliance would have invited attack by a vastly superior British force hovering off the coast and resulted in almost certain capture or destruction. When Bainbridge declined to oblige, the committee hinted that Boston might not assist him beyond lending a few cannon. Bainbridge replied that he intended to defend the vessels under his command as best he could, adding that Boston would be on its own if it failed to cooperate with him. Agitated townsmen then forced the calling of a town meeting about the military emergency, which under Otis's leadership "(nearly) unanimously" adopted resolves that expressed "undiminished confidence" in the state's defense measures. By pledging to "cheerfully and cordially co-operate" with Strong in defending the capital, they also forced the Republican first regiment of the town, which was threatening to cooperate with Bainbridge, back into line.[106]

Reassured that the Federalists were still in political control of Boston, Strong now used a new militia requisition issuing from Washington as the occasion for formalizing the separation between national and state defense efforts that was taking place throughout much of New England. Strong asked Monroe, who had become secretary of war, what reimbursement Massachusetts could expect from the national government for defending itself. He argued that as a consequence of having paid taxes to the federal government the state was now unable simultaneously to provide for itself and comply with the demands of the national administration. Pleading incapacity just after the state's banks had forced the rest of the nation's banks to suspend specie payments hardly seemed convincing, and Monroe replied that Massachusetts would be compensated only for troops placed under federal command.[107] When Strong relayed Monroe's message to the legislature in early October, it dispensed with the usual format of replying to the governor's address and instead formed a joint committee of both houses that produced yet another report written by Harrison Gray Otis. This report folded Strong's call for the state to assume responsibility for defending itself into the larger agenda of summoning a convention. The departure from established procedures was dictated by the need to recruit the other New England legislatures, particularly Connecticut's, into the convention movement before they adjourned.

The dramatic reversal in expectations about the likelihood of peace impelled those favoring a convention to take decisive action. Official confirmation of Britain's terms would not be available until mid-October, but the Federalists had enough advance warning so there were few surprises.[108] Peace would require the cession of northern Maine as well as a large segment of the Republic's northwest to form an Indian buffer state under British protection. To secure that buffer Britain demanded a monopoly of naval forces on the Great Lakes and free navigation of the Mississippi. Finally the United States would be required to surrender the right to take fish in British waters and dry them on British territory, enjoyed since the Peace of 1783.[109] No American government could accept such demands and survive, and the Federalists rightly concluded that the Republicans would fight to the finish rather than surrender. It suddenly seemed as though the war would continue indefinitely.[110]

In addition, Americans had become aware that the British meant to attack New Orleans, a city that many Federalists felt was indefensible. Some also assumed that if Britain ever established control over the mouth of the Mississippi, she would refuse to relinquish it because of the command it would give her over the continent west of the Appalachians.[111] But it was premature to conclude that the West had already been lost or that a dismembered United States would necessarily have to reconstitute itself around the thirteen original states, much as some Federalists would have welcomed this development. Their determination to call a convention derived more from the Federalists' exalted estimate of Britain's military capabilities and their low opinion of the Republic's military power than anything else. The presumption of national weakness also led the Federalists to call for a regional convention, as John Henry's reports to Sir James Craig had predicted they would, though as it turned out more with the aim of playing the Republicans off against the British than in moving to outright secession.[112]

It is worth noting that the Massachusetts legislature was presented with an alternative. Before Governor Strong had a chance to address the General Court, a state representative from Maine named Low had moved that a committee be appointed to confer with the other New England states. This committee would secure their cooperation before repairing to Washington to demand Madison's resignation or at least the removal from office of those responsible for the conduct of the war. Subsequently referred to by the Republican press as the "Low motion" (pun no doubt intended), it was designed to secure a major Federalist objective while avoiding any suspicion that they sought secession. The Boston *Patriot* took the proposal seriously enough to counter with the threat of a convention of delegates from "*all the Republican* counties in New-England" to demand Strong's resignation or the removal from office of those "who have by their nefarious plans ruined the *Nation of New England*."[113]

They need not have bothered. Low's motion never seriously competed with a convention because Federalist leaders realized that a committee representing the region's legislatures would have no chance of effecting its purpose. It would be dwarfed in numbers and authority by Congress and the federal administration claiming to represent the majority of the people. A delegation from a convention representing the New England states acting under the authorization of their respective legislatures, however, was another matter, insofar as it could claim to speak for the collective interests of a strategic, pivotal region.

On October 8 Otis's report appeared, echoing Strong's complaint that the national government had left Massachusetts entirely on her own in defending herself. While the report did not question the state's capacity to do so, it claimed Massachusetts was incapable of also responding "to the heavy and increasing demands of the national government." Given a choice between "submission to the enemy, or the control of their own resources, to repel . . . [that enemy's] aggressions," a people "determined to defend themselves," would not hesitate in choosing the latter course. The report claimed "this disastrous condition of public affairs" had been "forced upon Massachusetts" because of the federal government's insistence that "the patriotic citizens of this great State [are] tainted with disaffection to the Union and with predilection for Great Britain." The administration had "lavish[ed] . . . the public treasure in vain attempts to fix, by evidence [the Henry Papers], this odious imputation." The report concluded that "the Constitution of the United States [had] failed to secure to this Commonwealth, and . . . to the eastern section of this union, those equal rights and benefits, which were the great objects of its formation." The appropriate remedy was to amend the document, for which the framers had wisely made provision. But if Massachusetts followed the "ordinary mode," it would be too late "to prevent the completion of [the nation's] ruin." Since "a proposition . . . for a convention [to amend the Constitution] from a single State would probably be unsuccessful, and our danger admits not of delay," the report called for the appointment of delegates to meet with their counterparts from the other New England states to consult about their mutual defense, and "to take measures . . . for procuring a convention of Delegates from all the U. States . . . to revise the constitution thereof."[114]

Otis's report drew predictable fire from Massachusetts Republicans. The minority in the Senate and House sought to reinforce the objections of individuals writing under pseudonyms with formal protests. Thirteen senators questioned whether the state legislature had not "assumed an authority" the people had never delegated to it in summoning a convention of some of the states to amend the Constitution without Congress's sanction. They claimed a combination of the New England states taking control of regional resources for the purpose of defense amounted to "a resistance of federal authority" that could only benefit "a powerful and vindictive enemy." The British government would make proposals for a separate peace, which if accepted would lead to civil war, alliance with Britain, and eventually the "subjugation of *both sections* of the country" to her power.[115]

Seventy-five members of the Republican minority in the House also attempted to have their protest recorded in the House journal, but the majority rejected the request as "disrespectful." That meant that any newspaper in the commonwealth publishing it risked being held in contempt of the lower house. The protest of the House Republicans initially came to light because the *National Intelligencer* reprinted it, though the Republican Boston *Yankee*—which had been prosecuted on charges of libeling the legislature the previous winter—quickly followed suit. Since the House minority had hoped to have their protest entered into the record, its tone was less strident than the Senate protest and addressed only two issues. First it objected to the cost of raising a state force independent of federal command because "the expence of [the] Troops [would] . . . fall exclusively upon the State." Massachusetts could not constitutionally absolve herself from contributing to the common defense of the nation, and trying to do both would unnecessarily burden the people. Second, since the Constitution explicitly forbade any one state from entering into a compact with another without Congress's express permission, the convention could not constitutionally form a self-defense compact among the New England states. Nor was it appropriate to attempt amending the Constitution in this manner while other procedures were in place. The minority concluded "that more must be designed" in the legislature's call "than is distinctly avowed." It noted "the alarming assumption . . . that the Constitution has failed . . . and the people of Massachusetts [were] absolved from their allegiance," and it declared that the "other States" would interpret the resolutions of the

Massachusetts legislature as saying "that *Massachusetts shall govern the administration, or the government shall not be administered in Massachusetts.*"[116]

The protests of the Senate and House minorities concentrated on the constitutionality and consequences of the course the Massachusetts legislature proposed to follow. It remained for John Holmes, a signer of the Senate protest, to expose the logic of Otis's report. In a carefully prepared speech, which the *Independent Chronicle* reprinted in toto, Holmes assaulted the report's critique of the war as unjust by observing, "[I]f our cause is unjust *now*, it was much more so at the beginning of the Revolution." The British now were taking American men without their consent, whereas then they were merely taking American property. If the injustice of the war authorized the Federalists to refuse contributing to its conduct, what right had the New England states to raise an army to defend themselves against Great Britain? Holmes denied the distinction between offensive and defensive war, noting that American attempts to invade Canada had served to divert British forces from attacking the United States. States that refused the national government "the means to repel" the enemy had no right to "complain that you are left *defenseless.*" "The truth" was that the Federalists had "expected that *submission* would tempt the enemy to forbearance. . . . [D]isappointed in this, you *face about.*" Gentlemen who had before "placed great reliance on the magnanimity of Great Britain," excusing her every injury as "no cause of war," now suddenly change their tune. Holmes thought the only reason the Federalists were so urgent about amending the Constitution was it "operates to keep the *minority* from controuling the *majority.*" He predicted they would not be satisfied until the entire administration resigned. Only then would the Federalists transform themselves from the peace party into the war party in order to "take all the profit, honor and glory of an equitable peace" upon themselves. Short of that eventuality, they were determined to encourage the enemy by threatening civil war.[117]

Neither Holmes's assault, nor the chorus of condemnations issuing from the Republican press, nor the protests of the minorities of both houses deflected the majority of the Massachusetts legislature from issuing an invitation to the other New England states to send delegates to the proposed convention.[118] But only the legislatures of Connecticut and Rhode Island responded favorably. The Connecticut General Assembly endorsed by a large majority a report similar in its conclusions to Otis's report and named seven delegates, of whom James Hillhouse and Chauncey Goodrich were the most prominent, to join the dozen delegates Massachusetts had selected. The assembly's report claimed Connecticut had no choice but to defend itself since the federal government was unable to and saw a meeting "combining the wisdom of New-England, in devising . . . a proper course to be adopted, consistent with our obligations to the United States" as congruent with that end.[119] Otis's report had omitted all reference to "obligations to the United States," but the phrase had appeared in the letter from the president of the Massachusetts Senate and the Speaker of the House transmitting the summons to the other New England legislatures.[120] It reflected sensitivity to the reservations smaller states might have about directly challenging the federal government. The General Assembly also invoked the state's favorite conceit that Connecticut had brought republicanism as close to perfection as was humanly possible. Its report contrasted the French Revolution's "corruptions" that had "tainted . . . every State and province in Christendom . . . [with] its baneful influences," to "the pure principles" that Connecticut had "inherited from our fathers, conducive at once, to the preservation of liberty and order." Now that Connecticut's exceptionalism was threatened by the nation's involvement "in an odious and disastrous war," a convention was the appropriate remedy.[121] In addition the Connecticut legislature expressed concern about a proposal for a national draft that had surfaced in Congress. But for now it simply authorized the governor to call the assembly back into emergency session should the measure become law.[122]

Rhode Island responded to Massachusetts's invitation by focusing more on the defenseless condition the state had been left in by the federal government than on the mendacity of the Republican administration or the significance of the its peculiar social and political institutions. Rhode Island cast its appointment of delegates to the Hartford Convention as an act of prudence rather than defiance. The legislative resolve authorized its four delegates to confer "upon the best means of cooperating for our mutual defense against the common enemy, and upon the measures which it may be in the power of said states, consistently with their obligations to adopt, to restore and secure to the people thereof, their rights and privileges under the constitution of the United States."[123] The Rhode Island legislature saw the numerous regional conventions the state had participated in during the revolutionary war as the model for the Hartford Convention, though these conventions had sought to supplement rather than compromise the authority of the Continental Congress.

New Hampshire's legislature had already adjourned by the time Otis's summons arrived. John Gilman, the Federalist governor, declined calling it back into session for the purpose of appointing delegates because a majority of the council opposed a convention. But two delegates appointed by Federalist county conventions attended independently. Vermont's legislature voted unanimously against naming delegates, though one county sent one anyway. The absence of legislatively sanctioned representatives from these two states seriously compromised the Hartford Convention's claim to speak for New England as a whole, but by then it was too late for the conventioneers to retreat.[124]

8

DENOUEMENT

Few doubted that the Convention, which gathered at Hartford on December 15, 1814, intended to obstruct the authority of the federal government. Because of the Henry Papers and previous Federalist threats, the convention also raised the possibility that it portended the dissolution of the Republic.[1] Madison and other prominent Republicans suspected that New England's Federalist leaders lacked the resources to attempt secession on their own, but the possibility of their securing "foreign co-operation" continued to make New England's withdrawal from the nation a real possibility.[2] The administration assumed that the region's Federalist leaders were in contact with British officials in Canada and Madison would not have been surprised to learn that Caleb Strong did dispatch an emissary in November 1814 to explore the possibility of concluding a separate peace with the British governor of Nova Scotia, Sir John Coape Sherbrooke. Sherbrooke immediately relayed the proposal to his superiors in London, and the British government took it seriously enough to supply him with elaborate instructions about how to respond. But having just signed a peace treaty at Ghent with the American commissioners, the ministry did not feel that Strong's overture, which had raised the issue of direct military assistance, could be acted upon. Sherbrooke was instructed to assure Strong of British military supplies and naval support only if the American government rejected the terms agreed to at Ghent. The ministry drew the line at committing land forces to New England because they feared they would prove counterproductive in securing the Federalists' objectives.[3]

That New England's Federalist leaders ever seriously considered secession as a possibility has been discounted for several reasons. Every New England state, and particularly Connecticut—which would forfeit its stake in western lands—stood to lose far more by secession than they could hope to gain either alone or in association with Great Britain.[4] In addition, the organizers of the meeting made sure that Federalist firebrands like John Lowell Jr., who had published a series of articles in the *Boston Daily Advertiser* advocating secession, as well as Timothy Pickering and Josiah Quincy, were conspicuous by their absence.[5] Afterward those most closely associated with the convention's proceedings produced a voluminous literature of justification denying any disloyal intentions, which their descendants reiterated.[6] Finally, the convention failed to lead to the ominous consequences the Republicans feared. The result has been widespread acceptance of the idea that the convention served to calm a potentially volcanic situation. And since the United States subsequently followed the Federalist blueprint in its future development more closely than it did the Republicans', the latter have been saddled with more than their share of responsibility for producing the volatility, which the Federalists allegedly quieted.

There are major problems with such an interpretation. In the interval between Massachusetts's summoning the convention to meet in secret session and the delegates' adjournment in early January 1815, most Federalists in Congress, despite disclaimers to the contrary, continued to do everything they could to deny the government the resources it needed to invade Canada and bring the war to a successful conclusion. Disagreements among Republican congressmen certainly contributed to Congress's failure to take decisive action, particularly when it came to rechartering a national bank. But trying to reestablish the nation's credit was not made easier by the Federalists in Congress insisting that the new bank's notes be redeemable in specie while their compatriots outside Congress engineered a widespread suspension of specie payments.[7] As the end of the year approached and New England positioned itself to conclude a separate peace with Britain, the prospects of bringing the war to a successful conclusion looked almost as remote to the supporters of the administration as they did to the New England Federalists. Madison summed up the Republican view when he observed that "the conduct of the Eastern States is the source of our greatest difficulty in carrying on the war, as it certainly is the greatest, if not the sole, inducement with the enemy to persevere in it."[8]

In these circumstances the Republicans had good reason to be alarmed about the political threat the convention posed. They realized that a separate peace with Britain would subvert the nation as effectively as outright secession. Not only would it vastly complicate waging war against Britain, but it could also strengthen New England's hand in relation to the rest of the union. The Federalists had made no secret that their terms for reentry would involve giving New England more power in relation to the South and West than it currently enjoyed. What remained to be seen was how far the New England Federalists were prepared to exploit the difficulties of the nation in pursuing their objective.

Contention over the Convention

The administration saw no alternative to preparing for the worst. It did so by withdrawing troops from New York's border with Canada and stationing them at Greenbush, near Albany, where they could move into either Massachusetts or Connecticut should the authority of the federal government be contested. In addition, Secretary of War Monroe ordered several New England regiments back to the areas from which they had been recruited. These regiments had participated in the Niagara campaign of the previous year, the most credible operation of the army to date, despite its inconclusiveness. Though they would officially spend the winter recruiting, they could also maintain surveillance and provide a nucleus around which those loyal to the Republic could rally should the Federalists carry matters to extremes. Republican observers on the spot reported that most leading Federalists seemed more interested in controlling the federal government than in destroying it. But the administration could never be certain that the extremist minority might not gain the upper hand and prevail upon some of the New England states to declare their independence under British protection. The army regiments in the region had standing orders to secure the Springfield arsenal at the first hint of such a development. The Federalists may have commanded a majority of the voters in New England, but supporters of the national government remained confident that a majority of the fighting men would rally behind them.[9]

So long as the Federalists pursued a strategy short of secession, the Republicans settled for a public relations offensive directed at the convention.[10] In early November the Philadelphia printer Matthew Carey launched a personal crusade to rally moderate Federalists to the administration's cause with his pamphlet *The Olive Branch*. In it Carey tried to define the ground on which all patriotic Americans should unite by detailing the unacceptable ways in which the Federalist leadership was subverting the war effort. The threat to the union posed by the approaching convention at Hartford ranked at the top of his list, closely followed by trading with the enemy, their manipulation of the banking system, and the political preaching of the Congregational clergy.[11] Even John Randolph joined the chorus of voices condemning Massachusetts for its threatening behavior in the hour of the Republic's peril.[12] But many suspected that reasoning with Federalists was beside the point. William Eustis felt the presses of the nation had become so politicized that he despaired of any Federalist reading *The Olive Branch*.[13] Something more dramatic was required if the dangers implicit in the convention were to be avoided.

On the eve of the convention's meeting, the administration proposed an ambitious military expedition to expel the British from Maine and take Halifax. Monroe appealed to Strong for both Massachusetts's manpower and money, knowing full well that both were unlikely to be forthcoming.[14] But the project at least undercut any claims the convention might make that New England's welfare was being ignored by the national government. More immediately Colonel

Thomas Jesup, the thrice-wounded hero of Chippewa and Lundy's Lane and commander of the Twenty-fifth Infantry recruiting in Connecticut, had his men stage noisy parades within earshot of the Hartford state house while the convention delegates deliberated. Jesup also ostentatiously flew the British flag at half-mast under the American flag at his headquarters. At night he contrived to have his officers attend local balls organized by Republicans where their recent military accomplishments as well as their wounds would be on display, hoping in this way to court the sympathy and loyalties of the town's young women.[15] Connecticut's Federalists countered Jesup's tactics by trying to organize a public fast on the eve of the convention. When this idea fell flat, they attempted a public thanksgiving while the convention sat. But giving thanks ran counter to the delegates' intention of portraying the Republic as brought to the verge of destruction by the Republicans. Rumors circulated that the convention was even having difficulty procuring clergymen to offer prayers at the opening of its sessions. Jesup and his subordinates counted it a minor victory that the local population seemed indifferent to the convention's proceedings and that neither the delegates nor local leaders responded with hostility to his assertiveness while it sat.[16] Such behavior suggested a Federalist concern to defuse the notion that dissolution of the Union was imminent and demonstrated the lingering effects of the Henry Papers.

Meanwhile, the Federalist press reacted defensively to Republican criticism. "A.B.," writing in the *New England Palladium*, tried to rebut the charge that the Convention was treasonous by affirming the people's right to inquire whether the general government was protecting them. That right was especially important when a government claimed powers it was not entitled to for the purpose of waging an offensive and unjust war, "possibly, with a design to enslave us."[17] "A Citizen" argued a convention was necessary because of the "enervated state of the General Government" and the danger that posed to "our liberties." He attributed the nation's difficulties to the federal government's devotion to the interests of "the common enemy of the civilized nations," and charged the Republicans with having compounded a moral error with a strategic one when they chose Great Britain as their adversary. He lambasted the conduct of the war, arguing that the only thing the Republicans had to show for the expenditure of millions of dollars was naval supremacy on Lake Erie, where it least mattered. He accused the administration of having put "the achievements of an arduous revolution" at risk with its ill-advised measures and concluded that only the talents of the Federalists could ensure against "sinking again to a colonial dependency" on the one hand or "falling under the dominion of an active and exasperated faction" on the other. "A Free Citizen," responded to Republican criticism by paring down the list of constitutional amendments

Otis's report had suggested to the abolition of the three-fifths clause, which counted slaves as the equivalent of three-fifths of a free person in apportioning congressional representation and direct taxes among the states, and the exclusion of new states beyond the original boundaries of the nation.[18]

Given the palpable difficulties the convention created for the Federalists, it is worth asking why they persisted with it. They certainly were aware that it would be construed as a preliminary to secession. Did they not foresee the risk of precipitating a crisis beyond their control, as their opponents repeatedly warned them? The countermeasures taken by the administration against any attempt to dissolve the Union could not have escaped their notice, sending as they did the clear signal that secession would be met with force. But the Federalist leadership played down the possibility that their actions would lead to civil war. Their often-expressed contempt for the incompetence of the national administration and their conviction that slavery compromised the military potential of the South contributed to their bravado.[19] Nor did they feel they had reason to fear the New England Republicans since Federalist control of the region, at least as measured by the number of Federalist representatives the New England states would send to the Fourteenth Congress, had increased.[20] Few agreed with John Lowell Jr. that a separate peace, even one that had to be supported by British forces, would be instantly popular.[21] But there were other reasons why the danger of a civil war failed to deter the Federalists. They had become convinced that Britain would never yield what the Republicans needed to end the conflict without disgrace and, as a consequence, the war was likely to continue indefinitely unless the Federalists ratcheted up the pressure for peace.

New England's Federalist leaders had also become prisoners of their previous actions. The considerable time and effort they invested in developing a political weapon with which to repeatedly threaten their adversaries had acquired, as is often the case with threats, a momentum of its own. Most Federalists had hoped to achieve their ends without actually resorting to a convention, just as many Republicans had hoped to silence the Federalists and win concessions from Great Britain without actually declaring war. However, there were limits to the willingness of the Federalist rank and file to respond to the leadership's cues for public demonstrations and petitions. In 1812 the Republicans had finally been "kicked into war" by the realization that if they postponed hostilities any longer, they would lose all credibility both at home and abroad.[22] By the autumn of 1814, the Federalists had maneuvered themselves into a similar position. If they failed to call a convention after the elaborate preparations that had been going on for the better part of a year, not only would their threat cease to be credible, but they hazarded "refrigerating the popular zeal" they had been so busy cultivating.[23] Federalist leaders still had enough of the vanguard mentality characteristic of revolutionaries to shoulder the risks associated with preserving the credibility of their strongest political weapon.[24]

The autumn of 1814 also presented them with the political windfall of conscription.[25] In late September, Madison asked Congress to institute a new system for "classing and disciplining" the militia to fill the ranks of the army.[26] A full month elapsed before the House Military Affairs Committee presented its recommendations. James Monroe, acting as secretary of war, had recommended two approaches for the committee's consideration. One divided the free male population of the nation between eighteen and forty-five into classes consisting of 100 men. Each class in turn would be responsible for furnishing one man to the army for the duration of the war. If a class failed to produce its recruit within a specified time period, it would be subjected to "a draught on the whole class," though anyone "draughted" would have the option of hiring a substitute. The second plan divided the nation's militia into three classes defined by age and gave the president authority to call up "any portion . . . of these classes" for two-year terms of service. Monroe felt the second plan competed with filling the ranks of the regular army and thus precluded offensive operations that stood the best chance of bringing the war to a speedy end. He expressed his strong preference for the first plan, which he noted resembled the classing system that had been used during the Revolution after volunteers for the Continental Army had dried up. Monroe justified the adoption of such measures on the grounds that the nation was "contending for its existence against an enemy powerful by land and sea, [and] favored in a peculiar manner by extraordinary events."[27]

The House Military Affairs Committee produced a plan that resembled Monroe's preferred option, but replaced a "draught on the whole class" with a fiscal penalty. In the meantime the Senate approved a bill structured around Monroe's second option that empowered the president to call out portions of the militia for two-year tours. But those drafted could only serve in the state from which they were drawn, and, instead of three large classes, each state's militia would be divided into as many classes as corresponded to their proportional share of the total force to be raised. To prevent this plan from competing with army recruitment, every three classes that furnished two recruits would be exempt from the president's orders.[28] By now the season was sufficiently advanced that if action were not taken quickly no men would be available when the next campaign began. The House accordingly tried to strengthen the hand of the army in attracting recruits by eliminating exemptions from militia detachments and doubling the land bounty from 160 to 320 acres that an enlistee would receive after completing his term of service and being honorably discharged. In addition, the House measure permitted free males between the age of eighteen and twenty-one to enlist without the permission of their parent, guardian, or master. Thanks to the Senate's objections, the only action for increasing the nation's military strength Congress managed to agree on was that authorizing the recruitment of minors.

Though enlisting minors was only peripherally related to conscription, the Federalists, sensing Republican desperation, carried their opposition in Congress to new rhetorical extremes. Thomas Grosvenor of New York denounced the Republicans for plunging "their country, defenseless and naked, into that lake of blood where she is yet swimming." Cyrus King accused the administration of attempting "to impose upon the people a military despotism and French conscription." He subsequently suggested that anyone refusing to resist such a system would resemble a slave.[29] The conflation of the enlistment of minors with Napoleon's notorious *levée-en-masse* had more plausibility at this point than it had possessed when Quincy had first tried associating the two at the end of the Twelfth Congress, because classing and detaching from the militia continued to be live options until the war ended. But the actual law the Federalists objected to included a provision for a four-day grace period during which a minor was free to withdraw from the army. It also diverted portions of the bounty money, which a recruit received, to his master if the recruit was an apprentice.[30]

"Conscription" had not figured among the original reasons given for summoning the Hartford Convention because the committee of the Massachusetts legislature chaired by Otis had issued its call before Monroe's proposals became public. The prospect of "conscription," however, proved useful in parrying the hostility that greeted the call to meet at Hartford. Forced repeatedly to disavow secession as their objective, the Federalists risked ending up with little justification for a convention besides the claim that it shouldn't be feared because it would not do any harm and might even do some good.[31] Such a posture hardly promised to build political momentum either inside or outside the region and, as a dissident federalist extremist observed, augured ill for the convention's yielding any significant result.[32] Conscription enabled the Federalists to reiterate their claim that the Republicans were leading the nation to disaster by threatening to transform the republic into a military despotism.

If the war had been popular or successful, such a measure would never have been necessary. It was necessary now only because the Republicans had chosen to declare war against "the most powerful nation on earth" and the one most able to harm the United States. Republican imprudence had led to a situation in which the nation was without allies, its commerce completely destroyed, its credit in tatters, and oppressive taxation its only apparent recourse. To cap these calamities, there were reports that the American peace commissioners had broken off negotiations with Britain. An administration reduced to such straits could not make peace and could make war only through French coercions. Juxtaposed with the abominable *levée-en-masse*, a convention seemed like a reasonable, even a hopeful, alternative.[33]

Republican commentators sensed phoniness in the fuss the Federalists were making over the draft. They accused the Federalists of using "affected horror" to conceal from themselves and the public the hole into which they had backed themselves.[34] There were substantial risks in justifying the convention as the only alternative to a hopeless war that went beyond the Federalists having done everything in their power to deny the government the resources it needed to defend the nation. They had also to bet on developments taking place in the future over which they would have little influence. In particular they assumed that the British would not make peace with the Republicans, though there were other rumors from abroad that the negotiations at Ghent were back on track.[35] The Republicans taunted them with the possibility that the British had learned from the Revolution that "their professed friends [in America] are their real enemies."[36] Outside New England, Federalists like Washington Irving worried about any relationship with Britain not founded on mutual respect.[37] In the meantime, New Englanders were committed to a convention in which only three states, in aggregate no more populous than New York, were officially represented.[38] Their challenge to the authority of the federal government would depend entirely on the Federalists' pessimistic assessment of the Republic's prospects being borne out by events. But New England's Federalist leadership— barred from directly shaping national policy for the past fourteen years and encouraged by the way events seemed to be confirming their ideological assessment of how the European struggle would turn out—resolved to persevere with the convention anyway.

Consequences

The Hartford Convention was good to its sponsors' word in avoiding outright attempts at secession. In that sense the meeting could be said, in historian Samuel Eliot Morison's phrase, to have rallied the extremists to "moderation."[39] However, it was scarcely less subversive. The convention proceedings, ostentatiously endorsed by the legislatures of Massachusetts and Connecticut, proposed a series of amendments to the Constitution designed to magnify the influence of the "commercial states" in the federal government. It joined these constitutional changes with a thinly disguised threat to conclude a separate peace with Britain if they were rejected.[40] This was moderation only compared to the froth into which Federalists leaders—after six years of agitation—had managed to whip their southern New England followers. Many indicators suggested grassroots sentiment would have supported more radical measures than those adopted by the convention. One had only to look at the resolves passed by the town of Reading, Massachusetts, on January 5, just before the convention's proceedings became available. After rehearsing the familiar Federalist litany against the war, the town affirmed its determination to resist paying any federal taxes that might be assessed upon them and vowed not to "aid, inform or assist any officer in the collecting" of them.[41] Even before the convention met, the initiative for resisting federal authority seemed to be passing to the localities. That was a prescription for disaster that its leaders understandably hoped to head off.

But they were only partially successful in doing so, as became evident after the convention adjourned. In October, 1814, the Hartford town meeting had complained to the Connecticut legislature about disorders that had accompanied the recent arrival of elements of the Twenty-fifth Infantry regiment. The call for a convention issued by the Massachusetts legislature just before the veterans returned had led to friction between them and local Federalists that had bordered on a riot. The General Assembly responded by passing a law empowering Connecticut's four "incorporated Cities," of which Hartford was one, to make ordinances "regulating military parades and rendez-vous . . . [and] the marching of military companies, or parties with music in the streets," and "to inflict penalties for the breach of such by laws and ordinances."[42] While the convention sat, the town patiently endured Colonel Jesup's repeated demonstrations so as to avoid provoking a confrontation, which under the circumstances might be interpreted as initiating a civil war. But after the convention disbanded, the town took its revenge. On January 13 and 19 the Common Council considered two ordinances, which were approved by a small majority of the freemen on January 20. The ordinances prohibited military files accompanied by flags and music from parading or rendez-vousing in the town and subjected any officer violating the prohibition to a $34 fine for each infringement.[43]

Colonel Jesup claimed that the ordinance would make recruiting impossible. Though Chauncey Goodrich, the mayor of Hartford and member of the convention, suggested the Hartford Common Council was prepared to negotiate, Jesup was no more willing to have a town compromise the supremacy of federal laws than he was to tolerate a state's doing so.[44] In any case the confrontation was also about a state law since Hartford acted under an authority conferred upon it by the legislature. The tiff between Jesup and the town coincided with a special session of the General Assembly Governor Smith had summoned in response to Congress's passage of a law authorizing the enlistment of minors.

This session lasted for little more than a week between January 25 and February 3, during which the legislature did only three things of note. It incorporated the report issued by the Hartford Convention into the state legislature's record; it appointed state commissioners to join those named by Massachusetts to go to Washington; and it passed a law designed to block the execution of Congress's act permitting the recruitment of minors within the state's boundaries. The new law pronounced "the power assumed by Congress of removing the legal disabilities of minors to make contracts, and investing them with that capacity . . . to enlist . . . into the army of the United States" as "repugnant to the spirit of the constitution of the United States." It subjected anyone guilty of attempting to "purswade" [*sic*] a minor "to depart from this State, with intent to enlist" in the U.S. Army "without the consent of his parent, guardian and master," or actually enlisting a minor, to a fine of up to $500 or a year in jail. And it subjected anyone who wrote, printed, or otherwise displayed an invitation to minors to enlist in the army without the consent of their parents, guardians, and masters to a fine not exceeding $100 or three months in jail.[45] Colonel Jesup speculated that acquiescing in this challenge to national authority would "embolden the unprincipled faction who rule [Connecticut] . . . to commit greater outrages" such as raising the age of minority to twenty-five or thirty. He also reported that members of the Connecticut General Assembly were advancing the doctrine that the measure of a federal law's constitutionality was not whether it was consistent with the United States Constitution but whether it conformed to the laws of the state of Connecticut.[46]

Connecticut may have avoided pronouncing the act for enlisting minors "null and void," but it had gone about as far as was possible in rendering a federal law a nullity within its jurisdiction. In doing so it set itself in opposition to the majority of the American people who were no more prepared to endorse doctrines of crypto-nullification than they were to embrace other facets of Federalism in the winter of 1814–1815. Despite the additional political inroads made by the Federalists in the New England states during 1814 and the footholds they retained in Delaware and Maryland, it had been clear since the end of October that the Fourteenth Congress would remain under Republican control.[47] Nor, short of a humiliating military defeat, was the rest of the nation likely to become convinced that the Federalists were the only alternative to the indefinite prolongation of a disastrous war. The last session of the Thirteenth Congress has been criticized for all the things it failed to do, but a majority consensus did emerge in it, to which moderate Federalists contributed, for waging defensive war until Britain tired of the struggle.

National catastrophe alone could authorize the Federalists to resume control over the destiny of the Republic and that seemed less than likely given the tactical advantage possessed by the defense in warfare. Even in catastrophe the Federalists would not have much to offer beyond arranging an accommodation with Britain in accordance with the humiliating terms her peace commissioners demanded. Some Federalists argued that these terms were better than a continuation of the war. What was the cession of territories and a British protectorate over the Indians compared to national bankruptcy arising from an unpayable debt? Of course, the principal reason Federalist spokesmen could contemplate such a peace was because its humiliations could be blamed on the Republicans.[48] Federalists also hoped that such a peace treaty would turn out as the Jay Treaty had. Though not initially regarded as favorable, it had nonetheless benefited the country. Left unstated, but clearly understood by all, was what would happen if neither the rest of the nation nor its government yielded as New England's Federalists felt they should. In that case they were prepared to sit back and wait for them to be beaten into their senses by Britain's superior power. Though the Federalists might avoid taking an active role in chastising their fellow countrymen, entering into a neutral understanding with Great Britain would not be that much different from acting in alliance with her.[49]

The commissioners appointed by the Massachusetts and Connecticut legislatures to press for the Hartford Convention's amendments to the Constitution and to arrange for New England's autonomy in defending itself arrived in the nation's capital just as the first reports of Jackson's victory at New Orleans and news of the Treaty of Ghent restoring the prewar status quo, to which the prince regent had already affixed his signature, were received. The British surprised their American friends by unexpectedly abandoning the hard line initially taken with the peace commissioners in Europe. They did so to address challenges that were emerging in Europe as a consequence of the political instability engendered by Napoleon's abdication. In this Britain served her own interests well, but left her American allies in the lurch. Nothing could have undercut the Hartford Convention's proceedings more effectively than a peace with Britain that got the administration off the hook with honor. Instead of looking like patriots proffering the only salvation available to a desperate nation, the Federalists now looked like a disloyal minority intent on promoting their own interests at the nation's expense. Rather than accepting the administration's surrender, the commissioners were forced to return to New England empty-handed after being summarily laughed out of town.[50] Federalist protests that the peace had settled neither the issue of impressment nor Britain's attempts to control the nation's commerce earned them little credit because the European peace had for the moment laid these matters to rest. In addition, most Republicans felt that the war would never have been declared had the Federalists not acted in concert with the British, a conviction that wartime commentary in the British and Canadian press did much to reinforce.[51] Under these circumstances it was victory enough for the Republic to have survived such a challenge to its existence.

From a narrow legal perspective, no prominent Federalist had actually been guilty of treason. Attempts were made to prosecute the few who actively aided and abetted the enemy, though I am unaware of anyone being convicted let alone executed for the crime of treason.[52] By confining their political activities to speech and publication, most Federalists put themselves safely beyond the reach of existing law, which did not embrace acts of "moral treason." Some high-ranking Massachusetts Federalists, most notably Quincy, had used British diplomatic channels to urge adherence to the Orders-in-Council so as to force Madison to choose between humiliation and war.[53] Caleb Strong's emissary to the British commander in Nova Scotia had conducted a treasonous correspondence with the enemy in which he had predicted that the Hartford Convention would destroy what little was left of the Republic's credit.[54] The governments of Massachusetts, Connecticut, and Rhode Island had made no secret of their attempts to obstruct the federal government's conduct of the war by denying it access to their militias and by discouraging enlistments. All three states were guilty of sequestering their military resources from the national government. Connecticut on one occasion and Massachusetts on several had used the official organs of their state governments to subvert federal embargoes. Finally Hartford and the Connecticut legislature had in the last weeks of the war more directly obstructed the execution of a federal law than the Massachusetts Federalists had in the bill they drafted to counter the Enforcement Act of 1809. Connecticut's General Assembly in some respects even surpassed the South Carolina's legislature in 1832, which left merchants free to pay the federal tariff a state convention had nullified should they so choose.[55] Federalist merchant bankers had also done everything in their power to push the government into bankruptcy in its hour of peril. By giving quasi-legal status to the assemblage of delegates at Hartford and, in Massachusetts and Connecticut's case, explicitly sanctioning their proceedings, the states embracing barely a seventh of the nation's population had attempted to gain an advantage over the majority by threatening to come to terms with Britain.[56]

What is surprising is how ready the rest of the nation was to forgive the Federalists.[57] No one was legally prosecuted for his opposition to the war, Republican threats to the contrary notwithstanding. Those associated with the Hartford Convention forfeited all subsequent claim to national prominence, and Massachusetts was punished financially in two ways: Secretary of the Treasury Alexander J. Dallas favored the banks that had been forced to suspend specie payments at the expense of Boston's banks in his recovery program, and Massachusetts failed in its initial efforts to secure compensation from the federal government for its defense expenditures during the conflict.[58] But the few conventioneers that ventured to Washington after the peace were not socially ostracized, though they were denied positions of honor.[59] On the other hand, Federalists who managed to distance themselves from the Convention, including Rufus King, Daniel Webster, Roger Taney, and James Buchanan, went on to achieve future eminence in the federal government.

The national Republicans found it easy to forgive the Federalists once they no longer posed a threat, because they shared many of the Federalists' ideological anxieties. This had been the basis of the cooperation between the Tertium Quids and the Federalists after 1806. Nor were the old Republicans that ideologically removed from majority, mainstream ones. The affinity between them in Congress helps explain why a Republican majority failed to coalesce in the third session of the Thirteenth Congress to charter a national bank or to support offensive war. Settling instead for defensive war catered to the military strengths that republics were thought to possess and minimized the risk that the United States would evolve as France had after 1793, or spiral into hopeless bankruptcy. For those suddenly released from the burden of such shared concerns, it was enough that the Federalists endured the humiliation of betting against the nation's survival when, contrary to their expectations and those of some Republicans as well, it had endured. The simultaneous news of Jackson's triumph at New Orleans and the peace underscored just how mistaken Federalist assumptions had been about the Republic's impotence in the face of Britain's military power.[60]

In addition, the outcome of the war decisively changed the circumstances of the Republic, despite Federalist claims that nothing permanent had been settled between the United States and Great Britain. When the two nations next clashed, as many assumed was inevitable, the United States would no longer be hobbled by a domestic faction intent on proving the inadequacy of its government. This constituted triumph enough for the vast majority of Americans. The *National Intelligencer* in its jubilation urged the Federalists to rejoice that "your opposition has been unavailing in checking the measures of your government." For who could doubt that the Republic's future was at last secure? No one proposed to punish the Federalists publicly because their loss was too clearly the rest of the nation's gain.[61]

The Aftermath

Varied fates awaited New England's Federalist leaders after the war. Though the conflict had helped strengthen their hold over the states they controlled, the disgrace flowing from the unexpected peace inevitably generated countermovements to displace them. In Connecticut, Oliver Wolcott provided challengers with a welcome leader. Though a close associate of men like Pickering and Hillhouse in the 1790s, Wolcott had moved to New York City in 1802 and there become a prominent banker. Even before the war was declared, Wolcott had concluded that "[s]ubmission to the British system is out of the question." Thereafter he supported the war effort, though not necessarily Madison's management of it, and became increasingly critical of his former Federalist colleagues.[62] After moving back to Connecticut at the conclusion of the war, Wolcott headed up a reform movement that sought two related goals. The first was religious toleration through the disestablishment of the Congregational Church; the second a revision of the state's constitution, which, aside from cosmetic changes, was little more than the royal charter of 1662. It took Wolcott's coalition of democrats, dissenters outside the Congre-gational establishment, and disenchanted former Federalists several years before they were in a position to call a constitutional convention. But in 1818 they finally succeeded in framing a new form of government that put all religious sects on an equal footing. This constitution, narrowly ratified by the people, provided the framework for the state's government until the U.S. Supreme Court mandated another constitutional revision in 1965. The constitution of 1818 permitted Connecticut to develop in a manner that, though not fully in synch with the emergence of new national parties in the 1830s, at least was not actively at odds with them.[63]

The extremes that had characterized Federalist behavior in Massachusetts both before and during the war made the state's adjustment to the postwar era more traumatic. Instead of yielding gracefully to a new postwar order, Massachusetts' Federalist leaders dug in. They were assisted in their efforts by the stranglehold the eastern population centers continued to maintain over the state's government under the Constitution of 1780. The separation of Maine from Massachusetts as part of the Missouri Compromise in 1820 strengthened them because the Republicans had drawn more support from Maine than the Federalists had. Some Federalists hailed the dismemberment as "giving us a snug little Federal state for the rest of our lives."[64] The Federalists could even tolerate a constitutional convention in 1820, which framed nine amendments to the Constitution of 1780, because they were able to block any reforms that seriously compromised their power.[65] Nor was the leadership initially much changed by the inroads that incapacity, illness, and death would eventually make on its ranks. With the exception of Strong, who died in 1819, and the chairman of the Hartford Convention, George Cabot, who died in 1823, the state's Federalist leaders proved surprisingly long-lived.[66]

However, the dismembering of the state did dramatize an issue that challengers could hold the leaders of the past decade and a half responsible for.[67] And Federalist resistance to the principle that the president had exclusive power over when and whether the state militias should be called into federal service became controversial during the depression of 1819 and its aftermath. Congress continued to insist upon a formal renunciation of the legal grounds that Massachusetts invoked to justify withholding its forces before the state would be entitled to receive any compensation for her defense costs. The political insurgency arising from both sources eventually worked its way from the periphery to the center of Federalist power in Boston.

Ironically, Quincy, who had been passed over for a seat in the Hartford Convention and who opposed the separation of Maine from Massachusetts, made the most successful adjustment to democratic currents in the new postwar order. In 1821 Boston adopted a charter that transferred the powers formerly exercised by the selectmen and town meeting to a board of aldermen and common council. A mayor presided over this new government, but with few formal responsibilities beyond appointing committees. John Phillips, the first to hold that office, tried to minimize the effect the change in the city's governance would have, disappointing a growing body of residents who expected more from the recent reforms. Quincy's distance from the Federalist leadership now proved an asset. In 1823 he replaced Phillips and proceeded to make Boston one of the most progressive municipalities in the country by mobilizing an expanding electorate against anyone who opposed him. Eventually his aggressive style of leadership backfired, and in 1828 he withdrew from city politics. But the next year Harvard selected him to serve as its fifteenth president, and despite a tempestuous administration he remained there until the end of his active career.[68]

Less pleasing political fates awaited other Federalist leaders. Jackson's victory at New Orleans converted Pickering into someone who sounded like a Republican nationalist. But his constituents denied him election to the 15th Congress and he spent the rest of his life in retirement settling old scores with his enemies in the public prints. Otis fared even worse. Efforts to rehabilitate his reputation on the floor of the U.S. Senate, to which the state legislature sent him in 1817, led him to publish *Letters Developing the Character and Views of the Hartford Convention* in the *National Intelligencer*. They met with so hostile a response that Otis withdrew to Massachusetts. This failed to protect him from criticism for rejecting the terms that Congress insisted on if the state was to receive reimbursement for its defense expenditures. Instead he was forced to defend the Hartford Convention on his home turf. When he tried running for governor in 1823, he was decisively beaten by Madison's former secretary of war, William Eustis, becoming the first Federalist nominee to lose to a Republican since Gore's loss to Gerry in 1810 and 1811. Many objections were raised against Otis during the campaign, but the election ended up being a referendum on the Hartford Convention.[69] It took another year for the Republicans finally to gain control of the state legislature. With that victory the Federalist Party began to dissolve, and before long a Federalist caucus had ceased nominating either a gubernatorial candidate or Boston's delegation in the General Court.[70]

The Hartford Convention remained a whipping horse in Massachusetts politics into the 1840s. During the presidential election of 1828, John Quincy Adams revived the memory of Federalist threats to dismember the Union to counter accusations brought by former Federalists, who now supported Andrew Jackson, that Adams had deserted the party in 1808 to advance his own career. Some of Adams's opponents responded by forming a ticket of presidential electors consisting of five former members of the Convention pledged to Adams. It is a fair bet that this ticket, which received a grand total of 156 votes, alienated many more voters than it attracted. In 1830, Levi Lincoln Jr., now the governor of the state, joined both branches of the legislature in the repudiation required by the federal government that the Supreme Court had unanimously sanctioned in *Martin v. Mott* (1827). In return Massachusetts began receiving belated compensation for roughly half the sum the state claimed it had expended during the war on its defense, the remainder going to Maine.[71] During the presidential election of 1840 the state's Jacksonians accused many Whigs of being former Federalists and backers of the Convention, in an effort to prejudice the electorate against them.[72]

At least Massachusetts made a more graceful adjustment to the new order than Rhode Island, which clung until the 1840s to a form of government with a restricted franchise inherited from the colonial period. When frustrated reformers created a rival government under the leadership of Thomas Dorr in 1841, the governor under the old charter branded them as rebels and proclaimed martial law. Both sides then appealed to the federal government. A constitutional revision liberalizing the franchise eventually resolved the impasse, but not before the Dorrites had unsuccessfully attempted to seize a state arsenal. The insurgency came to an end after Dorr was tried, sentenced to life imprisonment, and then granted full amnesty.[73]

Reform after 1815 could for the most part proceed at a leisurely pace because, with the pacification of Europe, the issues agitating national politics lost the urgency they had possessed during the Napoleonic Wars. Peace in Europe defused the antagonism that had pitted Federalists against Republicans for two decades. With neither great power pressing remorselessly on the nation's interests, foreign disagreements could be worked out through diplomatic means, no matter how long that might take. And domestic concerns ceased to be seen as dimensions of a larger contest between revolutionary republicanism and its alternatives. The only dark cloud on the horizon of the Republic's future was slavery. It first surfaced in national politics during the agitation over the admission of Missouri to the Union in 1819, providing northern Federalists with a convenient means for refurbishing their morally tarnished credentials. It did not help to restore their political fortunes, though, because the next national parties would shun moral issues in the interests of maximizing their adherents. The second party system coalesced around controlling the expanding spoils of the federal government, particularly the postmasterships that proliferated with the spread of settlement.[74] Though the competing parties did take opposing positions on monetary policy, neither the quest for office nor attitudes about inflation inspired the passions that had driven the previous party rivalry. Not until the relentless expansion of slavery forced the nation to confront the fundamental moral issue posed by racial servitude did the second party system dissolve and the republic again face a challenge to its existence. This time the threat of secession was acted upon, leading to the most catastrophic war in our history.

To the mortification of Massachusetts, the South Carolina fire-eaters adopted many of the techniques pioneered by the New England Federalists between 1808 and 1815. In 1833, Levi Lincoln Jr. denounced South Carolina's nullification ordinance as "*treason against the people.*" Instead of challenging Lincoln's statement, the General Court of the commonwealth supported it by appointing several legislative committees to report on the constitutional issues involved. South Carolina had also called for a convention to revise the U.S. Constitution, a proposal that some other southern states had endorsed. The Massachusetts legislature condemned nullification and rejected a constitutional revision in no uncertain terms. The General Court also collected and published the proceedings of all the states responding to South Carolina's actions.[75] Healing the wounds the Federalists had inflicted upon the state's civic culture would cost Massachusetts much more in blood and money than this legislative gesture in the mid-1830s. In April 1861, the Commonwealth was the first state to put its forces in the field in response to President Abraham Lincoln's call for seventy-five thousand three-months volunteers that followed the firing on Fort Sumter. But by the beginning of the Civil War, Massachusetts had at least recovered some of its former identity as "a city upon a hill" to which the nation might again look for moral and political guidance.[76]

POSTSCRIPT

Though some will see in the foregoing account little more than a Republican indictment of the New England Federalists, my purpose has been to show modern readers how the Federalists appeared to their contemporaries. In the perspective of their times they, much more than their Republican counterparts, emerge as failed leaders. But describing Federalist behavior has always been subsidiary in my mind to explaining it, even though attempts at explanation beg the question of whether Federalism constituted a sufficiently homogeneous entity to be comprehended under any coherent hypothesis. My account has repeatedly distinguished between moderates and extremists as well as leaders and followers. But the problem is obviated by the surprising convergence of Federalist sentiment in their press, in the pronouncements of the state governments they controlled, and in the speeches of their spokesmen in Congress. Had Federalist leaders addressed the problem, they would have attributed this cohesion to the clash of the commercial interest with the manufacturing and agricultural interests. Such a scheme, however, serves better as a crude shorthand for their identity than as a convincing explanation for their unity. The contest between Federalists and Republicans in New England mobilized a far larger proportion of the electorate than is customary today. In the process the parties drew on the commitment of individuals from all three interests.[1] The New England Federalists were no more exclusively commercial in their occupations than their Republican counterparts were exclusively agricultural or industrial in theirs. At the same time both parties relied more than is currently the case on the willingness of their adherents to follow their gentry leaders. The black hole in the historiography of this period has been the bond that existed between leaders and led.

At the most fundamental level, the force uniting each party was the belief that their opponents threatened revolutionary achievements. When one considers the mass mobilizing revolutions of the modern world, of which the American was arguably the first, this should not surprise us. All modern revolutions have led to bitter internal struggles about their meaning. The United States fared better than most in this regard because the principal enemy was external to American society and because, after British rule had been eliminated, the regional elites that replaced imperial authorities lacked both the resources and the moral justification for dominating one another. Unlike the Jacobins in France or the Communist parties of Russia and China, there were no centralized institutions to which the American revolutionary elite could lay claim. Instead local leaders had to start almost from scratch in forming national institutions. The Continental Congress had little precedent in the political culture of British North America, and it barely succeeded in getting the revolutionaries through the war. Nor did the Articles of Confederation, which went into effect in March 1781, represent much of a departure from the improvisations that had preceded it. The revolutionary leaders quickly realized how inadequate the confederation was for solving the problems they confronted after the war, and in due course they provided the United States with a plan for a central government that would have powers and functions resembling those of a European state.[2] But though this government claimed superior legitimacy to its European counterparts, it could not, at first, pretend to equal power. The Constitution was only a blueprint for a government that began with little more influence than the Continental Congress had formerly possessed.

Nonetheless, the new government quickly acquired prestige, even among suspicious critics, because of its success in lightening the burden of the revolutionary debt. But that achievement in turn complicated the management of the nation's relations with the warring European states during the next two decades because most of the revenue derived from duties paid on British imports. The nation's vulnerability to pressures exerted by the belligerents led the regional elites to disagree about which of the great powers offered the Republic the best refuge in a war-torn world. Though they were not prepared to admit it, initially each favored aligning the United States with the power it thought, for ideological reasons, would win the European war. The Republicans thought France would triumph because it was a republic, while the Federalists thought Britain would be victorious because it was a monarchy. We can infer that the obsession was a common one because each accused the other of underestimating the resources of the nation with which the accuser sought alignment and of overestimating the resources of the nation the accuser feared. The first party system arose in the 1790s out of the divergent ways, reflecting their different ideological orientations, the Republican and Federalist leaderships proposed to address this strategic anxiety.[3]

Other modern revolutions have turned terror and purges on their own children. The European war fed impulses in the United States, similar to those that emerged in the France, Russia, and China, for repressing one's domestic adversaries. But in the North American case, the weakness of the regional elites in relation to one another left them with few opportunities for giving vent to these impulses even when they commanded the highest offices in the land. After John Marshall stymied Jefferson's attempt to have Burr convicted of treason, every member of the gentry realized that the nation's fledgling legal system could not be used to eliminate political opponents.[4] That left those seeking to guide the Republic in a dangerous revolutionary world with few options besides address-ing ideological appeals to the political nation at large. Because the Republicans initially enjoyed a clear advantage over their adversaries in this competition, the Federalists' only alternative was to try manipulating public opinion. When this failed them in 1800, some of their leaders went beyond using secession as a private threat in Congress to talking about it publicly. All recognized secession was a desperate remedy because, aside from the complementarity of the nation's regional economies, it invited interference from Europe that the Revolution had sought to eliminate. But that enhanced its power as a manipulative device.

With the advent of the nineteenth century the strategic anxiety that had divided the gentry during the preceding decade became the disproportionate obsession of the Federalists.[5] The asymmetry arose because the ideological orien-tation of each gentry coalition was also a projection of itself within the new nation. In the late eighteenth century the Republican leadership of the South and much of the West could take the dominance they enjoyed within their regions far more for granted than the New Englanders could. Southern Republicans had little reason to feel threatened by Federalist dissidents in their midst, since even when they dominated a state like Delaware, the Federalists invariably were minorities within the Republicans' regional hegemony.[6] The "Revolution of 1800" confirmed the Republican leadership's assumption that the constitutional majority of the political nation saw the world as they did, and that went a long way toward enabling the Republicans to look beyond their ideology in responding to European developments. Though some disgruntled Federalist leaders protested the legitimacy of the Republicans' triumph on grounds that it derived from the three-fifths clause, over the years the Republicans' political supremacy enabled them to develop a more realistic view of the nation's interest vis-à-vis the great powers than the Federalists possessed.

After the Louisiana Purchase the Republicans saw Britain rather than France as posing the greatest threat to the nation's future. They also attached greater significance to the growth of the Republic than the Federalists did and realized that the revolutionary past no longer provided a reliable guide to the present. It occurred to them long before it dawned on the Federalists that a war with one of the great European powers might not require direct military dependence on the other. Finally they believed that the forty-year success of their republican experiment made it unthinkable that the United States would evolve the way France had. The Republican rank and file knew that neither Jefferson nor Madison, whatever their other limitations, entertained Napoleonic ambitions, and that the vast dimensions of the Republic, together with its decentralized structure, was guarantee enough against a tyrannical central government emerging in the foreseeable future.

These advantages failed to immunize the Republicans from Federalist assaults on their ideological identity. When pushed by repeated humiliations that the Federalists thrust upon them, the Republicans were capable of taking desperate risks such as declaring war against Britain without adequate preparation. Nonetheless, they avoided sacrificing their central objective of preserving republicanism to the repression of their opponents. Instead they were prepared to honor the republican experiment by adhering to the principles of representative government agreed to in the Constitution even if that meant defeat at the polls. One can discount their resolve by saying they had little choice since doing otherwise would have been self-defeating. But that is simply to say that in the last analysis they retained a clearer view of the situation than their adversaries did. This point has eluded recent critics of Madison who take him to task for failing to act as a modern executive would. However, the Republicans had other objectives in the War of 1812 besides triumphing through the most efficient means. To defeat their Federalist adversaries they also had to show that the nation could declare a war and survive it without repudiating its republicanism.[7] Both Madison and his subordinates did a far better job pursuing this objective, considering the obstacles the Federalists put in their way, than they currently receive credit for doing.

The Federalists, by contrast, suffered from the disadvantage of being less secure than the Republican, not just within the nation at large but also in their regional hegemony. Though the election of 1800 signaled the end to Federalist control over the federal government because the future of the expanding nation seemed clearly to belong to the South and West, the social characteristics of New England society also threatened them. New England Federalists could not count on the same disparities in wealth, reinforced by the racial hierarchy of slavery, that made the southern leadership socially invulnerable. In addition they had to contend with dynamic changes taking place beneath their noses. These included the first phases of what subsequently became known as the transportation and industrial revolutions, the expansion of markets, and the uncertainties those participating in these processes were subjected to by surges and declines in commercial activity and the shocks of war.

William Bentley, the Republican clergyman-turned-journalist from Salem, Massachusetts, noted in his diary how common it had become for New Englanders to travel beyond the localities where they had been born. When Bentley was young most people expected to spend their lives in their birth communities. He also noted how the growth of travel had led to hotels along the new turnpikes and canal routes of New England. He chronicled the emergence of small-scale industry as he toured Essex and Suffolk counties and southern New Hampshire, and the rash of failures that sometimes afflicted these enterprises.

Bentley did not approve of all he saw. But he observed in a way that allowed him to pick and choose from the new order.[8]

By contrast Federalist ideologues saw themselves as defenders of a traditional, commercially oriented economy against the alleged assaults of the national government, even though many Federalists were deeply involved in promoting the early phases of the industrial revolution. They adopted this stance because the changes transforming northern society empowered new elites to speak against established religious and social leaders. Since there was no way to hide from the threat, Federalist leaders responded atavistically to the economic dynamism of their region. They certainly could not take consolation in geographical expansion in the way the southern leadership could. At the same time they were not of an ilk to acquiesce quietly in the emerging new order. Instead they resorted to the desperate expedient of democratizing their gentry-centered political movement. The elaborate political charades that became characteristic of Federalism after 1808 relied on the energies and commitment of a great many participants.[9] In the process the Federalist leadership developed an idiom that gave voice to both the political and religious concerns of those who felt threatened by the changes taking place within their society. It was a heroic response, but one that barely compensated for the leaders' sense of local vulnerability while doing little to address their declining national influence.

The Federalists' chronic sense of powerlessness eventually led them to see alignment with a foreign government against the Republicans as reasonable. How else could a minority in the nation, if not the region, hope to check the disastrous consequences of Republican rule, which they convinced themselves had world historical if not apocalyptic implications? Though the Federalist leaders prided themselves on their realism, they sacrificed crucial dimensions of reality to their ideology. One significant measure of their blindness was the importance they attached to French influence. When the United States was young and weak, foreign influence was legitimately feared as a threat to independence. Both parties were suspicious of it, though each saw the threat as emanating from a different source. The Federalist polemic held that French influence was the guiding force that set Jefferson and Madison against Britain. Republican commentators took the allegation seriously enough to refute it. They pointed out that few Americans were of French ancestry, that most could not speak the French language, and that the limited immigration from France inspired by the Revolution had ceased by the end of the 1790s. By contrast the majority of Americans, particularly New Englanders, traced their ancestry back to Britain, and almost all used a language and participated in a culture that was shaped disproportionately by Britain. In addition, large numbers of recent British immigrants had access to the American political system through the printed word if not directly through the ballot. Federalist anxieties about French influence seemed far-fetched, especially after Napoleon's fall. The Republicans had considerably more reason to suspect that their adversaries would never have taken Britain's part against their own government had they not been under British influence.[10]

The Federalists' ideology affected more than just their perception. The preceding narrative has described how they managed to push the Republicans in directions the Federalists least wanted them to go. The war the Federalists so vehemently objected to might never have happened had they refrained from appearing to cooperate with Britain in humiliating the Republicans. If the Federalists had avoided contributing to the embarrassments that Britain seemed determined to inflict upon the nation, can there be any doubt that the Republicans would have preferred muddling through as they had before 1812 to risking the achievements of the Revolution in a conflict with a great power? Only the perception of a disloyal domestic opposition waiting in the wings to capitalize on their humiliation and repudiate what had been achieved forty years before can explain the Republican willingness to embark on war totally unprepared. It was not Britain by herself that impelled the Republicans to take such a desperate course. Rather Britain in conjunction with the Federalist minority persuaded them they could not continue as they had from 1808 to 1811 without debasing the republican experiment in the eyes of successor generations beyond possibility of redemption.[11]

Once the Federalists had pushed the Republicans into an unwanted war, there was no turning back without admitting the hopeless inadequacy of the Federalist vision as it applied both to the past and future. Because they had left themselves no alternative besides abandoning their political identity, the Federalists became prisoners of their past actions. The irreversibility of the course chosen explains why they persisted in seeking every conceivable way to hobble the war effort against Britain, even when doing so exposed them to British depredations. It also explains why they used celebrations of the fall of Napoleon to cover their efforts to bankrupt the national government when they should have been cooperating with their countrymen in resisting British attempts to dismember the Republic. And finally it explains why they were caught seeking political advantage for themselves at the Republic's expense, at the very moment of the nation's triumph.

Federalist leaders clung to their distinctive identity even in defeat. They claimed they were retiring from national politics because the Republicans had finally learned the political lessons the Federalists had been trying to teach them about the need for a strong central government. The legal and philosophical dispute over how the Constitution should be construed, however, had always been peripheral to the core controversy between the two parties. Federalist claims that it was central gained plausibility only because the pacification of Europe conveniently removed the linchpin around which the first party system had formed.[12] The subsequent evolution of the nation, particularly since the Civil War, has also made the Federalists seem like the prophets of the modern state. But their contemporaries would remember them more for the challenge they had posed to the nation's republican institutions than anything else.

Historians today nonetheless have difficulty forgiving the Republicans for their involvement with racial slavery. Garry Wills's recent celebration of Timothy Pickering as an opponent of the slave power demonstrates the power of contemporary commitments to shape our perception of the past.[13] But despite the eagerness with which many former Federalists subsequently espoused aspects of the emerging antislavery movement, there was a big difference between Federalist hostility to South's slaveholding aristocracy and the eradication of slavery. Some Federalists who fantasized about reconstituting the Republic around the thirteen original states would have been as willing to keep the three-fifths clause in 1815 as northerners had been willing to accept it in 1787.[14] Nor were those who had allowed their ideological perceptions in conjunction with their hatred of the southern aristocracy to overpower their republicanism qualified to cleanse the nation of slavery's curse. William Lloyd Garrison, abolitionist scion of Newburyport and Pickering's disciple, yielded to a Federalist penchant for reducing politics to moral righteousness and ended up putting separation from the slaveholding South ahead of abolishing racial servitude.[15] Slavery was a political force as well as a moral challenge that the Federalists had neither the will nor the capacity to master. Nor for that matter was its abolition within the grasp of any group while the nation's republicanism remained in question. Slavery only fell in the 1860s when the majority of the politically and militarily preponderant North finally came to see it as incompatible with republicanism. The political agenda of early-nineteenth-century Federalism had little to contribute to the emergence of a northern majority willing and able to subdue a southern, slaveholding minority.

Instead of misunderstood harbingers of the future, I see the Federalists as offering a caution against becoming the prisoner of any ideology, whether secular or religious. That may strike the reader as a surprising legacy to derive from a revolutionary movement that was so deeply ideological in nature. Many of the core principles of our civic culture that I would not wish to repudiate come directly from the ideology of the American Revolution. But it is one thing to derive the organizing values of the society—responsible, representative government, equality under the law, and the separation of church and state—from an ideology and quite another to turn those values against themselves as was the tragic fate of the Federalists. The world they lived in was already dangerous enough so that there was no reason to make it more so with fantasies about American Jacobins and Napoleons. Without such illusions the Federalist minority might have felt less compelled to attempt dominating the majority in a manner that repudiated the basic premises of republicanism. Though the capacity to see the world as it is provides no guarantee against disaster, it does diminish the likelihood of our victimizing ourselves. Both the Republicans and the Federalists fell into this trap during the 1790s. After 1800, when alternatives began to emerge, the Federalists continued to do so far more than the Republicans with the unhappy consequences delineated in this book. My hope is that the successors of both, who are much more masters of their fate than the founders of our nation ever were, may be more prescient.

ABBREVIATIONS

Locations

AAS	American Antiquarian Society, Worcester, Massachusetts.
BPL	Boston Public Library
CHS	Connecticut Historical Society, Hartford, Connecticut
HL	Huntington Library, San Marino, California
LC	Library of Congress, Washington, D.C.
MHS	Massachusetts Historical Society, Boston, Massachusetts
NYHS	New York Historical Society
NYPL	New York Public Library
NA	National Archives, Washington, D.C.

Publications

AC   *The debates and proceedings in the Congress of the United States: with an appendix, containing important state papers and public documents, and all the laws of a public nature: with a copious index* (Washington, D.C.: Gales and Seaton, 1834–1856), listed by Congress and session when all the sessions do not appear in a single volume.

AM   *American Mercury* (Hartford)

ASP:FR   *American state papers, Documents legislative and executive, of the Congress of the United States. Selected and edited under the authority of Congress* (Washington, D.C.: Gales and Seaton, 1832–1861). The first six volumes pertain to foreign relations.

BG   *Boston Gazette*

BTR   Registry Department of the City of Boston, *A Volume of Records relating to the Early History of Boston containing the Boston Town Records, 1796 to 1813* (Boston, 1905). The Department's thirty-fifth report.

BTR2   Registry Department of the City of Boston, *A Volume of Records relating to the Early History of Boston containing the Boston Town Records, 1814 to 1822* (Boston, 1906). The Department's thirty-seventh report.

CC   *Columbian Centinel* (Boston)

CJ   *Connecticut Journal* (New Haven)

CM   *Connecticut Mirror* (Hartford)

CSR   C. J. Hoadley et al., eds., *The Public Records of the State of Connecticut* 17 vols. (Hartford: Case, Lockwood & Brainard Co., 1894–).

CtC   *Connecticut Courant* (Hartford)

DWB   *The Diary of William Bentley, D.D. Pastor of the East Church Salem, Massachusetts* (Gloucester, Mass.: Peter Smith, 1962), 4 vols.

ER   *Essex Register* (Salem)

IC   *Independent Chronicle* (Boston)

LCRK   *The Life and Correspondence of Rufus King; comprising his letters, private and official, his public documents, and his speeches. Ed. by his grandson Charles R. King.* 6 vols. (New York: G. P. Putnam's Sons, 1894–1900)

LLGC   Henry C. Lodge, *Life and Letters of George Cabot* (Boston: Little, Brown and Co., 1878)

NEP   *New England Palladium* (Boston)

NH   *Newburyport Herald*

MS   *Massachusetts Spy* (Worcester)

NI   *National Intelligencer* (Washington, D.C.)

NWR   *Niles Weekly Register* (Baltimore)

P   *Patriot* (Boston)

PDW   Charles M. Wiltse., ed., *The Papers of Daniel Webster: Correspondence* 14 vols. (Hanover, N.H.: University Press of New England, 1974–1989)

PHC   James F. Hopkins ed., *The Papers of Henry Clay* 10 vols. (Lexington: University Press of Kentucky, 1959–1991)

PJC   Robert L. Meriwether ed., *The Papers of John C. Calhoun* 27 vols. (Columbia: University of South Carolina Press, 1950–)

PJM   Herbert A. Johnson, and Charles F. Hobson eds.. *The Papers of John Marshall* 10 vols. (Chapel Hill: University of North Carolina Press, 1974–)

PJM: PS   Robert A. Rutland and J. C. A. Stagg eds., *The Papers of James Madison: Presidential Series* 4 vols. (Charlottesville: University Press of Virginia, 1984–).

R   *Daily Advertiser and Repertory* (Boston)

SG   *Salem Gazette* (Salem)

SS   Ralph R. Shaw and Richard H. Shoemaker, comps., *American Bibliography. A Preliminary Checklist 1801–1819* 19 vols. (New York: Scarecrow Press, 1958–1966).

WJM   Gaillard Hunt, ed., *The Writings of James Madison comprising his public and private papers and his private correspondence, including numerous letters and documents now for the first time printed* 9 vols. (New York: G. P. Putnam's Sons, 1900–1910)

WTJ   *The Writings of Thomas Jefferson collected and edited by Paul Leicester Ford* 10 vols. (New York: G. P. Putnam's Sons, 1893–1899)

Y   *Yankee* (Boston)

NOTES

Introduction

1. Robert H. Weibe, *The Opening of American Society; From the Adoption of the Constitution to the Eve of Disunion* (New York: Alfred A. Knopf, 1984), first proposed using the term as the foundation of his analysis of the period. See also Stanley Elkins and Eric McKitrick, *The Age of Federalism: The Early American Republic, 1788–1800* (New York: Oxford University Press, 1993); and more recently Bernard A. Weisberger, *America Afire: Jefferson, Adams, and the Revolutionary Election of 1800* (New York: William Morrow, 2000).

2. Marshall Foletta, *Coming to Terms with Democracy: Federalist Intellectuals and the Shaping of American Culture* (Charlottesville: University Press of Virginia, 2001); see also John L. Brooke, "To Be 'Read by the Whole People': Press, Party, and the Public Sphere in the United States, 1789–1840," *Proceedings of the American Antiquarian Society* 100 (2000): 82; and Mark Noll, *America's God: From Jonathan Edwards to Abraham Lincoln* (New York: Oxford University Press, 2002), 33ff.

3. See George Dangerfield, *The Era of Good Feelings* (New York: Harcourt, Brace, 1952); Shaw Livermore, *The Twilight of Federalism; the Disintegration of the Federalist Party, 1815–1830* (Princeton, N.J.: Princeton University Press, 1962); Linda K. Kerber, *Federalists in Dissent: Imagery and Ideology in Jeffersonian America* (Ithaca, N.Y.: Cornell University Press, 1970); Garry Wills, *James Madison* (New York: Times Books, 2002) and *"Negro President": Jefferson and the Slave Power* (Boston: Houghton Mifflin Co., 2003).

4. Seymour M. Lipset, *The First New Nation: The United States in Historical & Comparative Perspective* (Garden City, N.Y.: Doubleday, 1963) and Paul Goodman, "The First American Party System," in *The American Party Systems: Stages of Political Development*, ed. William N. Chambers and Walter D. Burnham (New York: Oxford University Press, 1967), 56–89, helped set this agenda. Richard Hofstadter, *The Idea of a Party System* (Berkeley: University of California Press., 1969) lent it his considerable prestige.

5. Livermore, *The Twilight of Federalism*, 16ff; David H. Fischer, *The Revolution in American Conservatism: The Federalist Party in the Era of Jeffersonian Democracy* (New York: Harper & Row, 1965), chap. 9.

6. See Doron Ben-Atar and Barbara B. Oberg, eds., *Federalism Reconsidered* (Charlottesville: University Press of Virginia, 1998), especially essays by Rogers M. Smith, Rosemarie Zagarri, and Paul Finkelman.

7. James Banner, Jr. *To the Hartford Convention: The Federalists and the Origins of Party Politics in Massachusetts, 1789–1815* (New York: Alfred A. Knopf, 1969).

8. Most notably Fischer, *The Revolution in American Conservatism.*

9. See Nathaniel Macon to Joseph Nicholson, April 6 and 8, 1808, in Joseph L. Nicholson Papers, LC.

10. Elkins and McKitrick's *The Federalist Era* is the best exemplar of this tradition. See also Banner, *To the Hartford Convention.* The recent commercial success of Joseph J. Ellis, *Founding Brothers: The Revolutionary Generation* (New York: Alfred A. Knopf, 2000) testifies to the popularity of the approach.

11. See "Deference or Defiance in Eighteenth-Century America?" in *Journal of American History* 85 (1998), 13–97.

12. Larry E. Tise, *The American Counter Revolution: The Retreat from Liberty, 1783–1800* (Mechanicsburg, Pa: Stackpole Books, 1998).

13. Ben J. Wattenburg, ed., *A Statistical History of the United States, from colonial times to the present* (New York: Basic Books, 1976), section A; *World Almanac and Book of Facts* (New York: Press Pub Co., 2002), 378.

14. By 1810 Philadelphia had grown to 111,210, New York to 96,373, Baltimore to 46,555, while Boston had reached only 33,787, according to Donna Andriot, ed., *Population Abstract of the United States* (McLean, Va.: Documents Index, Inc., 1993). For the economic function of gateway ports, Richard Buel Jr., *In Irons: Britain's Naval Supremacy and the American Revolutionary Economy* (New Haven, Conn.: Yale University Press, 1998), 107–13.

15. Noble E. Cunningham, Jr., *The Process of Government under Jefferson* (Princeton, N.J.: Princeton University Press, 1978), 148, 326.

16. *WJM*, 7: 190–96; *PJM: PS*, 1: 102–104; Sanford W. Higginbotham, *Keystone to the Democratic Arch: Pennsylvania Politics, 1800–1816* (Harrisburg: Pennsylvania Historical and Museum Commission, 1952), 183–98 contains the most complete discussion of the complex ramifications of the case.

17. I diverge here from Sandra Gustafson, *Eloquence Is Power: Oratory and Performance in Early America* (Chapel Hill: University of North Carolina Press, 2000), 233ff.

18. Richard D. Brown, *Knowledge Is Power: The Diffusion of Information in Early America, 1700–1865* (New York: Oxford University Press, 1989), 13, 218, 272.

19. Marshall Smelser, "The Federalist Period as an Age of Passion, *American Quarterly*, 10 (1958): 391–419; John R. Howe, "Republican Thought and the Political Violence of the 1790s," *American Quarterly* 19 (1967): 147–65.

20. Roger Brown, *The Republic in Peril: 1812* (New York: Columbia University Press, 1964), 181–82.

21. Frank Luther Mott, *American Journalism; A History of Newspapers in the United States through 260 years: 1690 to 1950* (New York: Macmillan, 1950), 46; Weisberger, *America Afire*, 38; Lawrence C. Wroth, *The Colonial Printer* (Portland, Me: The Southworth-Anthoensen Press, 1938), 80.

22. Clarence S. Brigham, *History and bibliography of American newspapers, 1690–1820* (Worcester, Mass.: American Antiquarian Society, 1947), Vol.1, 606–706.

23. Richard R. John, *Spreading the News. The American Postal System from Franklin to Morse* (Cambridge, Mass.: Harvard University Press, 1995), 36–37; Robert E.

Shalhope, *A Tale of New England: The Diaries of Hiram Harwood, Vermont Farmer, 1810–1837* (Baltimore, Md.: The Johns Hopkins University Press, 2003), 27.

24. Isaiah Thomas, *The history of printing in America* (Worcester, Mass., 1810), Vol. 2: 515–24, 527.

25. Brooke, "To Be 'Read by the Whole People,'" 68.

26. See Doron S. Ben-Atar, *Trade Secrets: Intellectual Piracy and the Origins of American Industrial Power* (New Haven, Conn.: Yale University Press, 2004), 125–26, 140–41.

27. Michael Warner, *The Letters of the Republic: Publication and the Public Sphere in Eighteenth-Century America* (Cambridge, Mass.: Harvard University Press, 1990), 17; see also Edward Bangs to Nathaniel Howe, December 22, 1807, in Edward Bangs Papers, AAS; Brown, *Knowledge Is Power*, 110, 126, and 157.

28. David Waldstreicher, *In the Midst of Perpetual Fetes: The Making of American Nationalism, 1776–1820* (Chapel Hill: University of North Carolina Press, 1997); see also Len Travers, *Celebrating the Fourth: Independence Day and the Rites of Nationalism* (Amherst, Mass.: University of Massachusetts Press, 1997), 70–83.

29. Their views reached the people either though publication in the newspapers and pamphlets or through the circular letters that congressmen from less settled areas addressed to their constituents. See Noble E. Cunningham, Jr., *Circular Letters of Congressmen to Their Constituents, 1789–1829* 3 vols. (Chapel Hill: University of North Carolina Press, 1978).

30. James Roger Sharp, *American Politics in the Early Republic: The New Nation in Crisis* (New Haven, Conn.: Yale University Press, 1993); Wiebe, *The Opening of American Society;* Joanne B. Freeman, *Affairs of Honor: National Politics in the New Republic* (New Haven, Conn.: Yale University Press, 2001); Lance Banning, *The Jeffersonian Persuasion: Evolution of a Party Ideology* (Ithaca, N.Y.: Cornell University Press, 1978).

31. For instance, Maximillian Godefray, *Military reflections, on four modes of defence, for the United States, with a plan of defence, adopted to their circumstances, and the existing state of things* . . . (Baltimore, 1807), 11–23.

Chapter 1

1. Richard Hofstadter, *The Idea of a Party System: The Rise of Legitimate Opposition in the United States, 1780–1840* (Berkeley: University of California Press, 1969); Bernard A. Weisberger, *America Afire: Jefferson, Adams, and the Revolutionary Election of 1800* (New York, William Morrow, 2000), 299–300.

2. Richard Buel Jr., *Securing the Revolution: Ideology and Politics in the New Nation 1789–1815* (Ithaca, N.Y.: Cornell University Press, 1972), 236–40; Weisberger, *America Afire*, 229ff.

3. The standard authority on the use to which the Federalists put the Sedition Act is James Morton Smith, *Freedom's Fetters; The Alien and Sedition laws and American Civil Liberties* (Ithaca, N.Y.: Cornell University Press, 1956); see also Buel, *Securing the Revolution*, 235–36 and chap. 11.

4. James Madison, "Report of the Committee to whom were referred the Communications of the various States," in *WJM*, 6: 352.

5. Weisberger, *America Afire*, 229, 238–40.

6. *AC*, 6th: 922, 952.

7. "A Republican" in *New York Journal*, June 15, 1793; "Cato" in *New York Journal*, January 8, 1794; unsigned in *National Gazette*, April 24, 1793; "An Old Soldier" in *National Gazette*, June 12, 1793; unsigned in *National Gazette*, June 15, 1793; "Virginius Americanus" in *National Gazette*, July 10, 1793.

8. Buel, *Securing*, 54–55.

9. Ibid., 65–66.

10. Ibid., 140.

11. Alexander DeConde, *The Quasi-War: the Politics and Diplomacy of the Undeclared War with France, 1797–1801* (New York: Charles Scribner's Sons, 1966).

12. Frederick C. Leiner, *Millions for Defense: The Subscription Warships of 1798* (Annapolis, Md.: Naval Institute Press, 2000).

13. *WTJ*, 7: 296; Madison, draft of "Resolves" and "Report of the Committee," in *WJM*, 6: 326–31; 341–406; Buel, *Securing*, 217–23.

14. Most recently David G. McCullough, *John Adams* (New York: Simon & Schuster, 2001), 523ff.

15. Stanley Elkins and Eric McKitrick, *The Age of Federalism* (New York: Oxford University Press, 1993), 614–41.

16. "The Public Conduct and Character of John Adams, Esq., President of the United States (1800)," in *The Papers of Alexander Hamilton*, ed. Harold C. Syrett, (New York: Columbia University Press, 1961–87), Vol. 25: 186–234.

17. Though formal notice of the Franco-American Convention of 1800 arrived just before the election (Weisberger, *America Afire*, 249), it had become clear before that some kind of agreement was in the works.

18. For the seeds of these attitudes see George Cabot to Oliver Wolcott, July 20, to Christopher Gore, September 30, 1800, and to Rufus King, July 9, 1803, in *LLGC*, 282, 292, 332.

19. Richard Buel Jr., "The Public Creditor Interest in Massachusetts Politics, 1780–1786," in *In Debt to Shays*, ed. Robert A. Gross (Charlottesville: University Press of Virginia, 1990), 55–56.

20. See Frederick Wolcott to John Cotton Smith, May 4, 1796, in John Cotton Smith Collection, CHS; George Cabot to Rufus King, August 14, 1795, in *LLGC*, 85.

21. James S. Young, *The Washington Community, 1800–1828* (New York: Columbia University Press, 1966), 22–28, 41–48.

22. The most recent treatment of the Adams-Hamilton relationship is Joanne B. Freeman, *Affairs of Honor: National Politics in the New Republic* (New Haven, Conn.: Yale University Press, 2001), 105ff.

23. Timothy Pitkin, *A Statistical View of the Commerce of the United States of America, including also an account of banks, manufactures and internal trade and improvements* (New Haven, Conn., 1835), 333.

24. Douglas C. North, *The Economic Growth of the United States 1790–1860* (Englewood Cliffs, N.J.: Prentice-Hill, Inc., 1961), 40.

25. Carl Seaburg and Stanley Paterson, *Merchant Prince of Boston, Colonel T. H. Perkins, 1764–1854* (Cambridge, Mass.: Harvard University Press, 1971), chap. 18; *LLGC*, passim.

26. Merrill D. Peterson, *Thomas Jefferson and the New Nation; a biography* (New York: Oxford University Press, 1970), 676.

27. In Salem Federalist vindictiveness extended to excluding Republicans from their dancing assemblies, see *DWB*, 3: 201. See also Mercy O. Warren to Elbridge Gerry, August 16, 1812, and Gerry to an unidentified child, June 28, and July 8 and 16, 1813, in Elbridge Gerry Papers, MHS.

28. *William Plummer's Memorandum of Proceedings in the Senate of the United States*, ed. Everett S. Brown (New York: The Macmillan Co., 1923), 8–9.

29. [William Plummer], *Address to the Electors of New Hampshire* (n.p., 1804), 7–8.

30. George W. Stanley, *An Oration delivered at Wallingford, August 18, 1805. In Commemoration of the Independence of the United States* (New Haven, Conn., 1805), 4, 7; see also *NEP*, November 11, 1803.

31. The most commanding Federalist critique of the Twelfth Amendment was Uriah Tracy's speech in the Senate, reprinted in *CtC*, February 22, 1804; see also *NEP*, January 24, 31, and February 3, 1804, and *CtC*, April 24 and June 12, 1805. In private, Federalists entertained darker assessments of its implications, see George Cabot to Timothy Pickering, January 10, 1804 and Pickering to Cabot, January 29, 1804, in *LLGC*, 336, 338. For the moral spin the Federalists put on their predicament, see Fisher Ames, *The Works of Fisher Ames* (Boston, 1809), 275, 277.

32. Richard E. Ellis, *The Jeffersonian Crisis: Courts and Politics in the Young Republic* (New York: Oxford University Press, 1971). For Pennsylvania, Raymond Waters Jr., *Alexander James Dallas: Lawyer-Politician-Financier 1759–1817* (Philadelphia: University of Pennsylvania Press, 1943), 124–32.

33. Lynn W. Turner, *William Plummer of New Hampshire, 1759–1850* (Chapel Hill: University of North Carolina Press, 1962), 133–50, is the best account of the plot. John Kukla, *A Wilderness So Immense: The Louisiana Purchase and the Destiny of America* (New York: Alfred A. Knopf, 2003), 60–64, 289ff, traces New England secession schemes back to the 1780s.

34. George Cabot to Rufus King, March 17, 1804, in *Documents Relating to New-England Federalism 1800–1815*, ed. Henry Adams (Boston: Little, Brown, and Co., 1877), 363; *LLGC*, 345–46.

35. Richard Purcell, *Connecticut in Transition: 1775–1818* (Middletown, Conn.: Wesleyan University Press, 1963), 139.

36. Paul Goodman, *The Democratic Republicans of Massachusetts: Politics in a Young Republic* (Cambridge, Mass.: Harvard University Press, 1964), 131–32; Alan Taylor, *Liberty Men and Great Proprietors: The Revolutionary Settlement on the Maine Frontier, 1760–1820* (Chapel Hill: University of North Carolina Press, 1990), 229–32.

37. *DWB*, 3: 80.

38. Ibid., 118, 126.

39. *BTR*, passim.

40. See Ezekiel Bacon to Wilson C. Nicholas, June 1, 1808, in Wilson Cary Nicholas Papers, LC; *BTR*, 197, 213–14, 232; also *ER*, April 16, 1808.

41. *NEP*, May 10 and 27, 1808.

42. *ER*, May 14, 1808.

43. Jacob M. Price, "Economic Function and the Growth of American Port Towns in the Eighteenth Century, in *Perspectives in American History* 8 (1974): 176.

44. Donna Andriot, *Population Abstracts of the United States* (McLean, Va.: Documents Index, Inc., 1993); North, *Economic Growth*, 43.

45. Concord provides a good example, see Robert A. Gross, *The Minutemen and Their World* (New York: Hill and Wang, 1976), chap. 7.

46. Walter M. Whitehill, *Boston: A Topographical History*, 2nd. ed. (Cambridge, Mass.: Harvard University Press, 1968), 50–72; *DWB*, 3: 83.

47. *DWB*, 3: 148

48. Ibid., 119.

49. Richard L. Bushman, *From Puritan to Yankee: Character and the Social Order in Connecticut, 1690–1765* (Cambridge, Mass.: Harvard University Press, 1967), 16.

50. Peter S. Field, *The Crisis of the Standing Order: Clerical Intellectuals and Cultural Authority in Massachusetts, 1780–1833* (Amherst, Mass.: University of Massachusetts Press, 1998), 22, 33–46.

51. Oscar Handlin and Mary Handlin, *The Popular Sources of Political Authority: Documents on the Massachusetts Constitution of 1780* (Cambridge, Mass.: Harvard University Press, 1966), 442–43.

52. Richard Buel Jr., *Dear Liberty: Connecticut's Mobilization for the Revolutionary War* (Middletown, Conn.: Wesleyan University Press, 1980), chap. 6.

53. See David D. Field, *A statistical account of the county of Middlesex, in Connecticut* (Middletown, Conn., 1819), 30; Jedidiah Morse, *Compendious History of New England* (Charlestown, Mass., 1804), 367.

54. Stephen A. Marini, *Radical Sects of Revolutionary New England* (Cambridge, Mass.: Harvard University Press, 1982); *DWB*, 3: 133, 193.

55. DWB, 3: 172–73.

56. Ibid., 146, 154.

57. Field, *Crisis*, 69–70, 76.

58. Marc M. Arkin, "The Force of Ancient Manners: Federalist Politics and the Unitarian Controversy Revisited," *Journal of the Early Republic* 22 (2002): 591ff.

59. Field, *Crisis*, 163–64.

60. Ibid., chaps. 4–6.

61. Benjamin Silliman, *A Journal of Travels in England, Holland and Scotland, and of Two Passages over the Atlantic, in the Years 1805 and 1806* (New York, 1810), Vol. 1: 167, 242, 305, 320; Vol. 2: 36.

62. Bentley complained bitterly of the clergy's political activities and suspected the Federalist leadership was urging them on; see *DWB*, 3: 124, 145, 154, 170, 193.

63. Ibid., 20, 28, 33, 45, 153, 175, 198.

64. Seaburg and Paterson, *Merchant Prince*, 172–75; *DWB*, 3: 242, 266, 268, 270.

65. *NEP*, January 3, 1806.

66. *DWB*, 3: 190–91.

67. Anna C. Clauder, *American Commerce as Affected by the Wars of the French Revolution and Napoleon, 1793–1812* (Philadelphia: University of Pennsylvania Ph.D. thesis ([1930], 1932), 80–81.

68. Texts of the memorials can be found in *AC*, 9th, 2nd: 805–19, 824–43, and 890–912.

69. Ibid., 894, 898.

70. *WJM* , 7: 204–375; *SS*, #10776.

71. *AC*, 9th, 1st: 72–73.

72. Ibid., 413.

73. Ibid., 449–51.

74. Ibid., 90–91, quotes 91. John Quincy Adams, Massachusetts's other senator, was absent.

75. Ibid., 1259–62. Congress subsequently suspended its operation until July 31, 1808, see *AC*, 9th, 2nd: 126.

76. *DWB*, 3: 180.

77. The text of the treaty can be found in *ASP: FR*, 3: 147–51.

78. Bradford Perkins, *Prologue to War: England and the United States 1805–1812* (Berkeley: University of California Press., 1961), 121–33.

79. Clauder, *American Commerce*, chap. 3.

80. Shortly after the *Chesapeake* incident the entire crew of a tender delivering dispatches to the British consul in New York City deserted; see *NEP*, September 11, 1807.

81. Documents relating to the incident were republished in *NWR*, 1: 49–52. In this particular case a British fleet anchored within the capes of the Chesapeake was watching for two French frigates that had taken refuge at Annapolis.

82. Burton Spivak, *Jefferson's English Crisis: Commerce, Embargo, and the Republican Revolution* (Charlottesville: University Press of Virginia, 1979), 85ff.

83. Henry Adams, *History of the United States of America during the Administrations of Thomas Jefferson* (New York: The Library of America, 1986), 998, 1002–1003, 1040–41.

84. See Worthington C. Ford, ed., *The Writings of John Quincy Adams* (New York: The Macmillan Company, 1913–1917), Vol. 3: 224–25.

85. *AC*, 10th, 1st: 2814–15.

86. *NEP*, December 29, 1807. Perkins, *Prologue to War*, 160, exaggerates the extent of this form of evasion, though there was considerable leakage at distant New Orleans.

Chapter 2

1. For instance, *NEP*, August 7, 14, 18, 21, 25, September 18, October 6, November 6, and December 25, 1807; for the diplomatic context, see Irving Brant, *James Madison. Secretary of State 1800–1809* (Indianapolis: Bobbs-Merrill Co., Inc., 1953), chap. 29.

2. Bradford Perkins, *Prologue to War: England and the United States 1805–1812* (Berkeley: University of California Press, 1961), 196–97.

3. Brant, *Madison. Secretary of State*, 413ff.

4. Gordon S. Wood, "Is There a 'James Madison Problem?' " 23–25, author's mss cited with permission.

5. See John Marshall to Charles C. Pinckney, September 21, 1808, in *PJM*, 7: 183; "Thoughts on the Embargo," in *ER*, February 13, 1808.

6. *AC*, 10th,1st: 2815–17, 2839–42, 2870–74.

7. *NEP*, August 18, September 1, October 16, November 6, 27, and December 25, 1807; *New York Evening Post*, January 2 and 4, 1808; *SG*, January 1 and 5, 1808; *CtC*, December 30, 1807, and January 6, 1808.

8. "Of Embargoes" and other untitled pieces in *NEP*, December 29, 1807. Also untitled commentary in *NEP*, January 5, 1808, and "Chatham" in *NEP*, February 9.

9. Cf. *NEP*, July 25 and August 26, 1806; also August 13, 1813.

10. Tabulated in Leonard W. Levy, *Jefferson and Civil Liberties: The Darker Side* (Cambridge, Mass.: Harvard University Press, 1963), 59.

11. For the Federalist harassment of the Republican press in Connecticut, see (Litchfield) *Witness*, March 5 and September 7, 1806; *AM*, March 17, 1808; for the prosecutions of Federalist newspapers in federal courts, *NEP*, October 6, 1807.

12. *AC*, 9th, 2nd: 248.

13. See "Chatham" for the Federalist obsession with French influence, in *NEP*, January 29 and February 2, 1808. For their strategic assessment of Britain's role, "Impartialis," in *NEP*, July 28, 1807.

14. Cf. Edward Bangs to Nathaniel Howe, November 2 and December 22, 1807, in Edward Bangs Papers, AAS.

15. The only full biography of Sullivan is Thomas C. Amory, *Life of James Sullivan: with selections from his writings* 2 vols. (Boston: Phillips, Sampson and Co., 1859); the best biographical sketch is in Ronald P. Formisano, *The Transformation of Political Culture: Massachusetts Parties, 1790s–1840s* (New York: Oxford University Press, 1983), 69–72. See also John Adams to Benjamin Waterhouse, September 13, 1813, in *Statesman and Friend: Correspondence of John Adams with Benjamin Waterhouse 1784–1822*, ed. Worthington C. Ford (Boston: Little, Brown, and Co., 1927), 110.

16. *A dissertation upon the constitutional freedom of the press in the United States of America* (Boston, 1801).

17. In *NEP*, June 5, 1807.

18. Ibid., January 12, 1808. Also James Sullivan to Jefferson, April 2, 1808, in Thomas Jefferson Papers, LC.

19. *NEP*, January 19 and February 2, 1808.

20. *IC*, February 1, 1808.

21. See *NEP*, March 18, 1808.

22. *IC*, January 21, 1808; quotes from *DWB*, 3: 337; see also Edward Bangs to Nathaniel Howe, February 10, 1808, in Edward Bangs Papers, AAS.

23. Hervey Putnam Prentiss, *Timothy Pickering as the Leader of New England Federalism, 1800–1815* (New York: Da Capo Press, 1972), chap. 1; Gerald H. Clarfield, *Timothy Pickering and the American Republic* (Pittsburg, Pa.: University of Pittsburg Press, 1980).

24. Charles J. Ingersoll, *Historical Sketch of the Second War between the United States of America, and Great Britain, declared by Act of Congress, the 18th of June, 1812, and Concluded by Peace, the 15th of February, 1815* (Philadelphia, 1845–49), Vol. 1: 60.

25. *DWB*, 3: 29.

26. George Cabot to Timothy Pickering, March 3 and 9, 1808, in *LLGC*, 379–80. The following account of Pickering's actions differs radically from that recently advanced in Garry Wills, *"Negro President": Jefferson and the Slave Power* (New York: Houghton Mifflin Co., 2003), chaps. 11–13.

27. [Abraham Bishop], *Some Remarks and Extracts, In reply to Mr. Pickering's Letter, on the subject of the Embargo* (New Haven, 1808), 13, noted that Pickering and the other senators who claimed information was being withheld from the public were the minority.

28. *A Letter from the Hon. Timothy Pickering, a senator of the United States from the state of Massachusetts, exhibiting to his Constituents, a view of the imminent danger of an unnecessary and ruinous war* 2nd ed. (Boston, 1808), quotes from 11, 12, 15.

29. Timothy Pickering to Rufus King, January 2, 1808, Christopher Gore to King, December 8, 1808, and King to Gore, April 9, 1809, in *LCRK*, 5: 47, 110, 152.

30. Henry Dearborn to William Eustis, March 19 and April 17, 1808, and Samuel Mitchell to Eustis, March 28, 1808, in William Eustis Papers, LC; Jefferson to Levi Lincoln, March 23, 1808, in Thomas Jefferson Papers, LC; Ezekiel Bacon to Joseph Story, March 24, 1808, in Joseph Story Papers, LC.

31. *NEP*, March 15, 1808.

32. *Interesting correspondence between His Excellency Governor Sullivan and Col. Pickering; in which the latter vindicates himself against charges made against him by the governor* (Boston and Newburyport, 1808); *SS*, # 15307–09.

33. *SG*, March 15, 1808 and *EG*, March 19, 1808, though bitter rivals, agreed on how aggressively it was being distributed. For the separate pamphlet editions, *SS*, # 15922–35, #15943; see also *A review of political affairs during the last half year by a Republican of Massachusetts* (Boston, 1808), 5. Pickering's *Letter* also appeared in such publications as *An address to the people of the United States* (Northampton, Mass., 1808).

34. Brant, *Madison. Secretary of State*, 450; also *ER*, April 23, 1808.

35. Quotes from New Haven ed., 8, 9.

36. See *ER*, March 26, and April 2, 16, 20, 23, 1808; *SS*, # 14265–83.

37. See *SG*, 15, 19, 22, 29; also [William Coleman], *Remarks and criticism on the Hon. John Quincy Adams Letter to the Hon. Harrison Gray Otis* (Boston, 1808); [Harrison Gray Otis], *A letter to the Hon. John Quincy Adams, occasioned by his letter to Mr. Otis* (Boston, 1808).

38. William Eustis to Nicholas Gilman, February 11, 1808; Daniel Kilhan, Nathan Weston, Levi Lincoln, Benjamin J. Porter, Samuel Rowles, Thomas Hazard Jr., and William Widgery to Eustis, March 7, 1808, and Eustis's reply, March 9, 1808; Barnabas Bidwell to Eustis, April 11, 1808, in William Eustis Papers, LC.

39. Edward Bangs to Nathaniel Howe, March 3 and May 16, 1808, in Edward Bangs Papers, AAS.

40. John Lathrop, *We rejoice with trembling. A discourse delivered on the day of the publick thanksgiving* (Boston, 1808), 17–18.

41. Cf. [Bishop], *Some Remarks*, 19.

42. See *A review of political affairs*, 7; "On the Massachusetts Elections," in *IC*, June 3, 1808.

43. Herman V. Ames, ed., *State Documents on Federal Relations: The States and the United States* (Philadelphia: Department of History, University of Pennsylvania, 1906), 18.

44. Prentiss, *Pickering*, 59.

45. First printed in the *NEP*, May 31, 1808, proposed in the House of Representatives, June 2, and reprinted in *NEP*, June 10, 1808.

46. A portion of the debate was reprinted in *NEP*, June 7 and 17, 1808.

47. James Sullivan to Jefferson, April 2 and April 5, 1808, in Thomas Jefferson Papers, LC.

48. Jefferson to Madison, May 24, 1808, in *WTJ*, 9: 196; Amory, *Sullivan*, Vol. 2: 303 and fn., 314; also *DWB*, 3: 401.

49. From *NEP*, June 10, 1808.

50. Henry Dearborn to William Eustis, June 16, 1808, in William Eustis Papers, LC. Eustis concurred, see his letter to Dearborn, June 21, 1808, in Henry Dearborn Papers, MHS.

51. Taken from *NEP*, June 10, 1808.

52. Ibid., June 14, 1808.

53. See William Blackstone, *Commentaries on the Laws of England. A Facsimile of the First Edition* (Chicago: University of Chicago Press, 1979), Vol.1: 159, 162.

54. See *NEP*, May 24, 1808. Of the recently elected representatives, 476 voted for Speaker of the House with the Federalists winning 255 to 221. After losing the initial contest many Republicans went home.

55. *IC*, June 13, 1808; *ER*, June 15, 1808.

56. Amory, *Sullivan*, Vol. 2: 300–303, quote from 302.

57. Winfred E. A. Bernhard, *Fisher Ames: Federalist and Statesman 1758–1808* (Chapel Hill: University of North Carolina Press, 1965) passim, especially 332–34; Jeffrey L. Pasley, *"The Tyranny of Printers": Newspaper Politics in the Early American Republic* (Charlottesville: University Press of Virginia, 2001), 240.

58. *CC*, July 9, 1808.

59. *NEP*, July 8, 1808.

60. *CC*, July 6, 1808; cf. Sandra M. Gustafson, *Eloquence Is Power: Oratory and Performance in Early America* (Chapel Hill: University of North Carolina Press, 2000), 235–46.

61. *Review of the Works of Fisher Ames* (Boston, 1809), 2–3, 5, 7–8.

62. *MS*, July 13, 1808; (Hampshire) *Federalist*, July 7, 1808; *NH*, July 8, 1808.

63. Cabot to Pickering, March 3, 1808, in *LLGC*, 379.

64. *SG*, June 24 and July 12, 1808.

65. *CC*, June 22, 1808; also [Pedro de Ceballos], *An exact and impartial account of the most important events which have occurred in Aranjuez, Madrid, and Bayonne* (New York, 1808); and *Exposition of the practice and machinations which led to the usurpation of the Crown of Spain* (Boston, 1808).

66. *SG*, August 16, 1808.

67. *AC*, 10th, 1st: 2859–60.

68. *SG*, August 9, 1808; *BTR*, 238–39. See also Richard D. Brown, *Revolutionary Politics in Massachusetts; The Boston Committee of Correspondence and the Towns, 1772–1774* (Cambridge, Mass.: Harvard University Press, 1970).

69. *IC*, August 15, 1808; *ER*, August 31, 1808.

70. *IC*, August 15 and 25, 1808.

71. Ezekiel Bacon to Joseph Story, August 22, 1808, in Joseph Story Papers, LC.

72. *NH*, September 30, 1808, lists them. Many more towns participated in this wave of petitioning against the embargo than Pickering's *Letter* had inspired during the preceding spring. See Louis M. Sears, *Jefferson and the Embargo* (Durham, N.C.: Duke University Press, 1927), 152–53.

73. *ER*, August 24, 27, 31, and September 3, 17, 1808; Jefferson to Madison, September 5, 1808, in Thomas Jefferson Papers, LC.

74. *IC*, September 8, 1808; *ER*, September 21, 1808.

75. Jefferson to S. H. Smith, September 9, 1808, in Thomas Jefferson Papers, LC. For the New Haven address, see *NEP*, September 6, 1808.

76. Albert Gallatin to Jefferson, September 16 and October 5, 1808, in Thomas Jefferson Papers, LC.

77. *ER*, July 30, and August 27, 31, 1808.

78. *NI*, September 30, 1808.

79. Albert Gallatin to Jefferson, July 15, 1808, Jefferson to James Sullivan, July 16, 1808, Sullivan to Jefferson, July 21, July 23, July 30, and August 24, 1808, Jefferson to Henry Dearborn, August 9, 1808, in Thomas Jefferson Papers, LC.

80. *NEP*, July 15, 26, and August 30, 1808.

81. Madison to Jefferson, September 14, 1808, in Thomas Jefferson Papers, LC.

82. *ER*, July 30, 1808; *NEP*, July 26, 1808.

83. *SG*, September 13, 1808. "Hampden" originated in the Boston *Repertory* on September 6, and subsequently was republished in the *Columbian Centinel* and the *Newburyport Herald* in its entire three installments, and in the *Massachusetts Spy* partially.

84. *SG*, September 16, 1808, from *NH*, September 9, 1808.

85. As *NI*, August 19, 1808, pointed out.

86. *SG*, September 27 through October 11, 1808. See also the *CC*, September 10, 14, 17, 24, and October 1, 1808; and the *MS*, September 28, and October 5, 12, and 19, 1808. Several leading Federalist newspapers, including the *Boston Gazette;* the *New England Palladium*, the *Repertory*, and the *Newburyport Herald*, did not run the "Falkland" series.

87. *SG*, October 4 and 11, 1808.

88. John Kukla, *A Wilderness So Immense: The Louisiana Purchase and the Destiny of America* (New York: Alfred A. Knopf, 2003), 60–64; Gaillard Hunt, ed., *Disunion Sentiment in Congress in 1794* (Washington, D.C.: W. H. Lowdermilk, 1905); *CtC*, November 21 and December 12, 1796.

89. *Essex resolutions: At a meeting of delegates from the several towns in the county of Essex, at Topsfield, Oct. 6, 1808* (Newburyport, Mass., 1808), 5, 7, 8, 9–10.

90. *IC*, November 21, 1808, gave a good overview of the federal elections that had recently been held in the states. See also *IC*, November 7 and 16, 1808.

91. James H. Broussard, *The Southern Federalists 1800–1816* (Baton Rouge: Louisiana State University Press, 1979).

92. *CC*, July 20, 1808.

93. Amory, *Sullivan*, Vol. 2: 314.

94. Ibid., 311–12; *CC*, November 15 and 18, 1808; the Senate Protest in *IC*, November 21, 1808.

95. *SG*, November 22, 1808.

96. Amory, *Sullivan*, Vol. 2: 313; *IC*, November 21, 1808. The committee report and resolves were presented to Congress on November 25, *AC*, 10th, 2nd: 128–30.

97. *ER*, December 14, 1808.

98. "Electioneering Fabrication" in *IC*, March 14, 1808.

99. Ezekiel Bacon to Joseph Story, March 24, 1808, in Joseph Story Papers, LC.

100. *NI*, June 3, 1808; also Ezekiel Bacon to Wilson C. Nicholas, June 1, 1808, in Wilson Cary Nicholas Papers, LC; Edward Bangs to Nathaniel Howe, June 14, 1808, in Edward Bangs Papers, AAS.

101. *NEP*, January 6, 1809.

102. *IC*, August 11 and 15, 1808.

103. *ER*, October 1 and 5, 1808.

104. *NH*, November 25, 1808.

105. *Resolutions of the Republican Citizens of Boston* (Boston, 1808), 3; William Eustis to Jefferson, December 24, 1808, in Thomas Jefferson Papers, LC.

Chapter 3

1. *NI*, November 7 and 16, 1808. *NI* did note the "disgraceful proceedings" of the Massachusetts legislature on November 25, and it published a copy of a seditious broadside that had been circulated in Newburyport by an "Enemy of Tyrants" on November 30.

2. William Patterson to Wilson Cary Nicholas, May 11, June 3, December 1 and 10, 1808; quote from unsigned correspondent in Philadelphia to Nicholas, November 16, 1808, in Wilson Cary Nicholas Papers, LC.

3. *ER*, September 13, 1808.

4. Larkin Smith to W. C. Nicholas, August 30, and Spencer Roane to W. C. Nicholas, sometime between mid-December 1808 and the following March, in Wilson Cary Nicholas Papers, LC.

5. Nathaniel Macon to Joseph H. Nicholson, November 15, 1808, in Joseph H. Nicholson Papers, LC. *NI* had concluded that the election of Madison was assured on September 12.

6. G. W. Daniels, "American Cotton Trade with Liverpool under the Embargo and Non-intercourse Acts, *American Historical Review* 21 (1916): 280; Herbert Heaton, "Non-importation, 1806–1812, *Journal of Economic History* 1 (1941): 191.

7. *AC* 10th, 2nd: 16, 20–29.

8. John Q. Adams to William B. Giles, December 10, 1808, in *Writings of John Quincy Adams*, ed. Worthington C. Ford (New York: The Macmillan Co., 1914), Vol. 3: 263–64.

9. *AC*, 10th, 2nd: 530.

10. Ibid., 855.

11. *An Oration, pronounced July 4, 1798 at the request of the inhabitants of Boston* (Boston, 1798) met with enough favor to go through two editions and three printings.

12. Norman Risjord, *The Old Republicans: Southern Conservatism in the Age of Jefferson* (New York: Columbia University Press, 1965), chap. 3.

13. Other Federalists concurred in Quincy's assessment of Randolph. See Archibald Lee to Timothy Pitkin, May 31, 1808, in Timothy Pitkin Papers, HL.

14. The phrase is taken from Robert A. McCaughey, *Josiah Quincy 1772–1864: The Last Federalists* (Cambridge, Mass.: Harvard University Press, 1974), title to chap. 3.

15. *AC*, 10th, 2nd: 535–52; *SS*, #16030–31.

16. Lyman Beecher, *The Remedy for Duelling. A Sermon delivered before the Presbytery of Long-Island, at the opening of their session at Aquebogue, April 16, 1806* (New York, 1809), 25 and 30.

17. *AC*, 10th, 2nd: 855.

18. McCaughey, *Quincy*, 52.

19. Excerpt from Josiah Quincy to his wife, December 17, 1808, in Edmund Quincy, *Life of Josiah Quincy. By his son* (Boston: Little, Brown, and Co., 1891), 160; Pickering was among them, see Charles Royster, *A Revolutionary People at War: The Continental Army and American Character, 1775–1783* (Chapel Hill, N.C.: University of North Carolina Press, 1979), 209.

20. *AC* 10th, 2nd: 520–21, 894–95.

21. Ibid., 232–36; 1798–1804.

22. Giles undoubtedly had access to the reports that Gallatin had solicited from collectors on November 16 about violations of the embargo in their respective districts, pursuant of a resolution of the House of Representatives calling for this information. See Gallatin Papers, microfilm edition (Carl A. Prince and Helene H. Fineman, eds.), reel 18.

23. *AC*, 10th, 2nd: 257–76, quotes from 275–76.

24. The other speeches were delivered on November 24 and December 2. See William B. Giles to William Eustis, December 6, 1808, in William Eustis Papers, LC; Joseph White to Joseph Story, December 25 and 28, 1808, in Joseph Story Papers, LC. Eighteen pamphlet editions of these speeches appeared, at least eleven issuing from Massachusetts presses, *SS*, #15105–16, and 17622–25, 17627–28.

25. *AC*, 10th, 2nd: 282–98; *SS*, #15229, 17748.

26. *AC*, 10th, 2nd: 915–30; *SS*, #18626–27.

27. *AC*, 10th, 2nd: 937, 938; *SS*, #15560.

28. *AC*, 10th, 2nd: 946.

29. Ibid., 946–50, quotes from 947, 950; *SS*, #17601–02.

30. *AC*, 10th, 2nd: 950–60, quotes from 954, 956, and 957; *SS*, #14950.

31. *AC*, 10th, 2nd: 968–69. The resolution failed to lead to congressional action, though.

32. Ibid., 1024–25.

33. Ibid., 904.

34. Ibid., 304–305.

35. Ibid., 976–78, quote 976. See also R. Kent Newmyer, *Supreme Court Justice Joseph Story: Stateman of the Old Republic* (Chapel Hill: University of North Carolina Press, 1985), 62.

36. See John Q. Adams to Ezekiel Bacon, November 17, 1808, to Samuel L. Mitchell, December 14, 1808, and to Orchard Cook, December 19, 1808, in *Writings of John Quincy Adams*, Vol. 3: 250, 266–67, 273. Joseph Story to Joseph White, December 31, 1808, and January 4, 1809, in William W. Story, *Life and Letters of Joseph Story* (Boston: C. C. Little and J. Brown, 1851), Vol.1: 173, 174.

37. *AC*, 10th, 2nd: 977–78, quote 977.

38. Ibid., 978–79, quote 978.

39. Ibid., 1032.

40. Ibid., 1032–47 passim, quote 1057. Story's role in inadvertently revealing a deep fissure within the Republican congressional coalition provided Jefferson with a far

more compelling reason for being angry with him than the one Jefferson eventually gave. See Newmyer, *Story*, 59–60.

41. *AC*, 10th, 2nd: quotes 1040; also 1051–52, 1048–49, 1065. Also see Nathaniel Macon to Joseph H. Nicholson, December 4, 1808, in Joseph H. Nicholson Papers, LC.
42. *AC*, 10th, 2nd: 1078–80, 1808.
43. Joseph Story to Samuel P. P. Fay, January 9, 1809, in Story, *Life and Letters of Joseph Story*, Vol. 1: 178–80.
44. *AC*, 10th, 2nd: 1112–13, quote 1112; *SS*, #18471–72.
45. *AC*, 10th, 2nd: 1114–15.
46. Ibid., 1121, 1121–22, 1130–31, 1134. For a personal assessment of Quincy's speech, see Ezekiel Bacon to Joseph Story, January 22, 1809, in Joseph Story Papers, LC.
47. *AC*, 10th, 2nd: 1117, 1121–22, 1127, 1128, 1132, 1133, 1138, 1150, 1163.
48. It was subsequently referred to six times in the second session. See *AC*, 10th, 2nd: 1127, 1163–64, 1284, 1368, 1445, 1525.
49. Ibid., 1172.
50. Ibid., 1232.
51. Quotes from Jefferson to Thomas Mann Randolph, February 7, 1809, in *WTJ*, 9: 244, and to Alex McCrae [?], February 8, 1809, in Thomas Jefferson Papers, LC.
52. See correspondence received by Gallatin from November 16, 1808 to February 25, 1809, Gallatin Papers, microfilm edition, reel 18. See also John Q. Adams to William B. Giles, December 26, 1808 and January 16, 1809, *Writings of John Quincy Adams*, Vol. 3: 284, 287.
53. I rely on Ezekiel Bacon to Joseph Story, February 5, 1809, in Joseph Story Papers, LC, for my account of the disagreement within the Republican congressional caucus. For evidence of Congress's awareness of what was happening in New England, see *AC*, 10th, 2nd: 1117, 1121, 1128, 1134–35, 1152 1155, 1272, 1277–78, 1306, 1319; for the particular consequences feared by southern Republicans, see 1268, 1270, and 1319.
54. See John Cotton Smith to Timothy Pitkin, December 31, 1808, in Timothy Pitkin Papers, HL.
55. Collected as *A Farmer's Letters to the people* (Salem, 1802); also *Address pronounced at Worcester, Mar. 4th, 1803* (Worcester, 1803).
56. Transcripts of his letters to Jefferson during 1808 are in the Levi Lincoln Sr. Papers, AAS.
57. *P*, March 3, 1809; *ER*, March 26, 1809.
58. See Allan R. Pred, *Urban Growth and the Circulation of Information: The United States System of Cities 1790–1840* (Cambridge, Mass.: Harvard University Press, 1973), 52–53. "*The CONSTITUTION gone!!*" appeared in boldface in the original.
59. *NEP*, January 13, 1809, took the lead among Boston's Federalist papers in inciting opposition to the Enforcement Act.
60. *BTR*, 243.

61. *NI*, February 7, 15, and 17, 1809.

62. *NEP*, January 27, 1809.

63. The letter had been drafted by Jefferson on January 17 and dispatched from Dearborn's office on January 18. See *WTJ*, 9: 237–38.

64. *NEP*, February 3, 1809; *CC*, February 25, 1809.

65. *NEP*, February 7, 1809. The reports do not appear to have been fabricated; see Heaton, "Non-importation, 1806–1812," 191.

66. *NEP*, January 27, 1809, for this and what follows.

67. Reprinted in *NI*, February 7, 1809.

68. Samuel E. Morison, *The Life and Letters of Harrison Gray Otis, Federalist* (Boston: Houghton Mifflin Co., 1913), Vol. 2: 11; the text of what follows is from *NEP*, February 7, 1809.

69. These went beyond the running critique of Lincoln's address that had appeared in the *CC* under the pen name "Cratippus" on February 4, 11, 15, and 25, 1809.

70. Text from *NEP*, February 7 and 10, quotes from February 7, 1809.

71. Text from *R*, February 7, 1809; also in *CC*, February 4, 1809. The bill only contravened sections 10 and 11 of the Enforcement Act.

72. *CC*, March 8, 1809.

73. *NEP* and *NI*, February 10, 1809.

74. For evidence of the nervousness, see *AC*, 10th, 2nd: 1302–1303; Charles Warren, *Jacobin and Junto or early American politics as viewed in the diary of Dr. Nathaniel Ames 1752–1822* (Cambridge, Mass.: Harvard University Press, 1931), 233. For the reasons behind it, see Richard Buel Jr., *Securing the Revolution: Ideology in American Politics, 1789–1815* (Ithaca, N.Y.: Cornell University Press, 1972), 203–13, 236–40. Cf. also Winfield Scott to James Monroe, January 7, 1811, in James Monroe Papers, NYPL.

75. *AC*, 10th, 2nd: 345.

76. Ibid., 353–83, quotes from 354, 381, and 382; *SS*, #17626–27.

77. *AC*, 10th, 2nd: 421; Bayard's speech received more attention than Lloyd's, *SS*, #16956–61.

78. *AC*, 10th, 2nd: 426, 432–33, 435.

79. Ibid., 1438–39.

80. Ibid., 1439.

81. Ibid., 1440; *NEP*, January 6, 1809.

82. *NI*, February 15, 1809.

83. Helen R. Pinkney, *Christopher Gore Federalist of Massachusetts 1758–1827* (Waltham, Mass.: Gore Place Society, 1969), 3–112 passim; Gore's name appeared as the Federalist nominee in *NEP*, February 10, 1809.

84. The text, of which there are several variants, is from *CC*, February 4, 1809.

85. See *NI*, February 10, 15, and 17, 1809.

86. SS, # 18041–18042; the report together with excerpts of the debate over it also appeared in *The Patriotick Proceedings of the Legislature of Massachusetts, during their session from January 26 to March 4, 1809* (Boston, 1809), 64–71, 71–99.

87. *AC*, 10th, 2nd: 1447.

88. *CSR*, 14: 385–86.

89. Ibid., 124.

90. Ibid., 381–84, quote 382; *AM*, November 10, 1808.

91. *CSR*, 14: 386.

92. Only New Haven and Brooklyn imitated Boston to the extent of pronouncing the Enforcement Act unconstitutional; at least one other town had tried and failed. See Elisha Tracy to Madison, February 20, 1809, in James Madison Papers, Ser. 1, LC. Others, like Bethlehem and East Haddam, settled for inviting the legislature to do so. See *CJ*, February 2, 1809; *CtC*, February 8, 1809; *CG*, February 15, 1809.

93. Jonathan Trumbull to Henry Dearborn, February 4, 1809, in *CSR*, 14: 389.

94. *CSR*, 14: 187–88; for the legislature's address, 189–93.

95. *NI*, December 12, 1808, and January 6, 1809; *CJ*, February 9, 1809; *AC* 10th, 2nd: 1304–1305.

96. *AC*, 10th, 2nd: 1206–1207, 1248–49, 1299, 1367–68.

97. Ibid., 1444–45.

98. Ibid., 1437, 1438.

99. Ibid., 1481; also see Gardenier in 1460.

100. Ibid., 1452–59, 1476–77, 1489, 1500–1501.

101. Ibid., 1460.

102. Ibid., 1465.

103. Ibid., 1507, 1510, 1523–24, 1531.

104. *To the honourable the Senate and House of representatives of the United States. The memorial and remonstrance of the legislature of Massachusetts* (Boston, 1809), 11, 13, 14, 15.

105. *AC* 10th, 2nd: 444–50; 1538–39.

106. Ibid., 451–52, 1541, 1829.

Chapter 4

1. *ER*, February 22 and April 15, 1809; Address of the Republican delegates of Hancock County to Jefferson and Madison, February 23, 1809, in James Madison Papers, Ser. 1, LC; Elbridge Gerry to James Madison, March 26, 1809, in *PJM: PS*, 1: 80.

2. In *PJM: PS*, 1: 41–42.

3. In ibid., 12.

4. In ibid., 50.

5. In ibid., 125–26.

6. Cf. "Communication" I and II in *NEP*, April 28 and May 2, with *ER*, April 29 and May 2, 1809.

7. *SG*, July 18, 1809; *PJM: PS*, 1: 299–300.

8. *PJM: PS*, 1, 320–21.

9. Ibid., 310.

10. *ER*, August 9 and October 7, 1809.

11. Ibid., August 5, 12, and 23, 1809.

12. Ibid., July 26, 1809; Gallatin to Madison, July 31, 1809, in *PJM: PS*, 1: 313.

13. For the relevant documents see *SG*, September 15, October 6, November 3, 1809, and *ER*, August 2, 1809; William Pinkney to Madison, May 3, 1809, in the Rev. William Pinkney, *The Life of William Pinkney* (New York: D. Appleton and Co., 1853), 235–36.

14. See *SG*, July 28 and August 1, 1809.

15. *ER*, August 5, 1809.

16. Ibid., August 19 and 30, 1809.

17. *SG*, August 15, 1809; *ER*, August 30, 1809.

18. Republished in *SG*, August 15, 1809.

19. *AC*, 11th, 1st and 2nd: 2109.

20. Ibid., 2109, 2113.

21. Ibid., 2133: Smith to William Pinkney, November 23, 1809.

22. *AC*, 11th, 1st and 2nd: 743, 2123–24.

23. Madison to Pinckney, October 23, 1809, in *PJM: PS*, 2: 27, 28.

24. *ER*, November 22 and 25, 1809.

25. *PJM: PS*, 2: 90–94.

26. *NI*, December 4 and 6, 1809; also Jackson to Smith, October 23, 1809, in *AC*, 11th, 1st and 2nd: 2105; *PJM: PS*, 2: 10.

27. *NI*, November 20, 1809.

28. *SG*, November 24 and 30, 1809; *CM*, December 18, 1809; *NEP*, December 26, 1809.

29. *SG*, December 12 and 15, 1809.

30. *ER*, November 22 and December 6, 1809; "Marblehead" in *ER*, December 2, 1809; "Timoleon" in *ER*, December 20, and 23, 1809.

31. *NEP*, December 26 and 29, 1809.

32. Ibid., September 15, and November 7, 14, and 24, 1809. Aaron Ogden to Timothy Pitkin, February 5, 1810, in Timothy Pitkin Papers, HL.

33. *PJM: PS*, 2: 90–94, quotes 93.

34. *AC*, 11th, 1st and 2nd: 481.

35. Federalists made much of Giles's error. See Sully, *Remarks on the Report of the Legislature on our Foreign Relations* (Boston, 1810), 5, 7, 10.

36. *AC*, 11th, 1st and 2nd: 485–86, 509, 511.

37. Ibid., 757–58, quote 759; also 805–806, 808, 812–17.

38. Ibid., 762; also 825–27, 936, 942–43, 959–60, 1048, 1061–62, 1084, 1131–32, 1141, 1143.

39. Ibid., 769; *SS*, #19915; also *AC*, 11th, 1st and 2nd: 1056.

40. *AC*, 11th, 1st and 2nd: 794, 795; *DWB*, 3: 364.

41. *AC*, 11th, 1st and 2nd: 855. See also 1036, 1087–88, 909, 935.

42. Ibid., 893, 894; for Johnson, 802; for Ross, 825–26, for Macon, 861, 864. See also 871–72, 878, 887–88, 912–14, 1000–1001.

43. Ibid., 1102–103, 1121. See also, 1067, 1068.

44. Ibid., 1161–62. See also 1193, 1276–78, 1281, 1284.

45. For comments about avoiding war, see *AC*, 11th, 1st and 2nd: 1167, 1189, 1190, 1191, 1230; for the effect of British retaliation, see 1187, 1266, 1283; for its compatibility with continued negotiations, see 1279, 1280; for objections about its weakness, see 1164, 1165–66, 1249; for violations of non-intercourse, see 1636, 1639–40; for defenses of non-intercourse, see 1309, 1311, 1323.

46. For comments about avoiding war, see *AC*, 11th, 1st and 2nd: 577, 609. See also 608, 610.

47. William E. Dodd, *The Life of Nathaniel Macon* (New York: B. Franklin, 1970), 256; Raymond Walters, Jr., *Albert Gallatin: Jeffersonian Financier and Diplomat* (New York: The Macmillan Co., 1957), 230–32.

48. *AC*, 11th, 1st and 2nd: 1442, 1446, 1447–48, 1452–53.

49. Ibid., 1463, 1484–85, 1492, 1493, 1495–96.

50. John Randolph, *The letters of Mutius*[*sic*] *addressed to the president of the United States* (Washington, D.C., 1810); *PJM: PS*, 2: 175–76, 208.

51. *AC*, 11th, 1st and 2nd: 1609–16, 1703.

52. Ibid. 1709, 1712.

53. Walters, *Gallatin*, 233.

54. *AC*, 11th, 1st and 2nd: 1763.

55. Ibid., 1772–73, 1887, 1892–93, 1894–1900, 1908.

56. Ibid., 1786, 1788, 1825, 1827, 1869, 1913, 2051–52.

57. Theodore Dwight to Timothy Pitkin, March 8, 1810, in Timothy Pitkin Papers, HL.

58. Text from *NEP*, March 7, 1809.

59. *SS*, #18020–24.

60. Preface, *The Patriotick Proceedings of the Legislature of Massachusetts, during their session from January 26 to March 4, 1809* (Boston, 1809).

61. Texts of all the documents appeared in *IC*, March 2, 1809.

62. Cf. Manasseh Cutler to Timothy Pickering, January 5, 1809, in William P. Cutler and Julia P. Cutler, *Life, Journals, and Correspondence, of Rev. Manasseh Cutler by his Grandchildren* (Cincinnati, Ohio: Robert Clarke & Co., 1888), Vol. 2: 314–16.

63. Text from *IC*, March 16, 1809.

64. Ibid., June 3, 1809.

65. *NEP*, May 19, 1809.

66. Ibid., April 28, May 5, and June 9, 1809.

67. Ibid., June 13 and July 18, 1809.

68. *SG*, August 18 and 25, and September 5, 1809. Joseph Story, a Madison appointee to the Supreme Court, subsequently upheld the decision of the district court, see R. Kent Newmyer, *Supreme Court Justice Joseph Story: Statesman of the Old Republic* (Chapel Hill: University of North Carolina Press, 1985), 87–88.

69. *AC*, 11th, 1st and 2nd: 1917–26.

70. *NEP*, January 9, 16, and February 2, 1810.

71. Ibid., January 26, 1810.

72. Ibid., February 6, 1810.

73. Ibid., February 9, 1810.

74. Ibid., February 13, 1810.

75. Ibid., February 9, 1810.

76. Theodore Dwight to Timothy Pitkin, February 10, 1810, in Timothy Pitkin Papers, HL.

77. See *Remarks on the Report of the Legislature on our Foreign Relations* (Boston, 1810), 12; for Republican criticism, *ER*, February 15, 24, 28, and March 10, 1810. See also the "Quintus Curtius" series in the *New York Public Advertiser*, March 3, 7, and 11, 1810.

78. Henry Adams, *History of the United States during the Administrations of James Madison* (New York: The Library of America, 1986), 151–52.

79. I have found reference to only one county convention during the winter session of the legislature; see *NEP*, March 13, 1810.

80. Ibid., February 9, 1810; for the Republican response, see *ER*, March 7, 1810.

81. *DWB*, 3: 507; Isaac Braman, *Union with France a greater evil than union with Britain. A Sermon preached in Rowley, West Parish, at the annual fast, April 5th, 1810* (Haverhill, Mass., 1810).

82. *NEP*, March 23, 1810.

83. Joseph White to Joseph Story, February 19, 1810, in Joseph Story Papers, LC.

84. *NEP*, April 10, 1810; *ER*, April 25 and June 2, 1810.

85. *NEP*, May 8, 1810; John Marshall to Josiah Quincy, April 23, 1810, in *PJM*, 7: 242.

86. *ER*, May 1, 1810.

87. Text taken from *NEP*, June 7, 1810.

88. Ibid., June 15, 1810.

89. Adams, *History of Madison's Administrations*, 153.

90. *AC*, 11th, 1st and 2nd: 1026.

91. As members of the Eleventh Congress had predicted. See *AC*, 11th, 1st and 2nd: 1237, 1240.

92. The Republicans saw this statute as compensating for the bias toward Britain in the original non-intercourse law. See *AC*, 11th, 1st and 2nd: 884. Also Madison to Caesar A. Rodney, January 16, 1810, and Madison to Jefferson, May 7, 1810, in *PJM: PS*, 2: 183, 335.

93. See Madison to William Pinkney, May 23, 1810 in *PJM: PS*, 2: 349; also Robert Smith to John Armstrong, June 5, 1810, in ibid., 366–67.

94. Henry Dearborn to William Eustis, April 17, 1808, in William Eustis Papers, LC; Adams, *History of Madison's Administrations*, 21.

95. See the "Republican motion" drafted by Elbridge Gerry for a Cambridge, Massachusetts, town meeting, January 27, 1809, in Elbridge Gerry Papers, MHS.

96. Jefferson to John W. Eppes, September 20, 1808, in Thomas Jefferson Papers, LC.

97. Madison to William Pinkney, May 23, 1810, in *PJM: PS*, 2: 348.

98. Ibid., 403: draft of Robert Smith to John Armstrong, July 5, 1810.

99. *AC*, 11th, 3rd: 1236; John Armstrong to Madison, August 5, 1810, in *PJM: PS*, 2: 460.

100. William Montgomery to Madison, August 28, 1810, and George Joy to Madison, September 2, in *PJM: PS*, 2: 514, 521.

101. Ibid., 554.

102. *NEP*, October 2, 5, 26, and December 18, 1810.

103. *PJM: PS*, 2: 612–13.

104. Ibid., 595–96.

105. Ibid., 565: Madison to Caesar A. Rodney, September 10, 1810.

106. *AC*, 11th, 3rd: 778.

107. Ibid., 172, 194–95, 199, 269.

108. See Samuel Carswell to Madison, January 28, 1811, in *PJM: PS*, 3: 137.

109. J. Van Fenstermaker, "The Statistics of American Commercial Banking, 1782–1818," *Journal of Economic History* 25 (1965): 401, 404.

110. *AC*, 11th, 3rd: 825.

111. Ibid., 525; *SS*, #23775–76

112. *AC*, 11th, 3rd: quotes from 558, 567; also 563–64.

113. Ibid., 863–65.

114. Ibid., 875–78.

115. Ibid., 861, 862, 871, 894–95.

116. Ibid., 909–10.

117. Ibid., 916–17, 921–22, 927, 932; *SS*, #22764.

118. *AC*, 11th, 3rd: 952, 955.

119. The quote is from Edmund Burke, *Reflections on the Revolution in France*, ed. J. C. D. Clark (Stanford, Calif.: Stanford University Press, 2001), 185.

120. Joseph Fr. Michaud, *Biographie universelle, ancienne et moderne: ou, Histoire, par ordre alphabétique, de la vie publique et privée de tous les hommes que se sont fait remarquer par leurs écrits, leurs actions, leurs talents, leurs vertus ou leurs crimes* (Paris, 1843–65?), Vol. 42: 300–302.

121. *PJM: PS*, 3: 175n.

122. Quotes from *AC*, 11th, 3rd: 1011, 1024; also 1000–1005, 1017, 1045, 1046, 1060, 1095.

123. Ibid., 1095–96, 1338–39.

124. Madison to Jefferson, March 18, 1811, in *PJM: PS*, 3: 224, 225.

125. The John Lowell Jr. (1769–1840) referred to here and subsequently was the son of John Lowell (1743–1802) and brother of Francis Cabot Lowell (1775–1817). He should not be confused with his nephew John Lowell (1799–1836), who also was referred to as John Lowell Jr. within the family.

126. *NEP*, April 5, 1811.

127. *Resistance to the Laws of the United States: considered in four letters to the Honorable Harrison Gray Otis, Esq* (Boston, 1811). See also William Eustis to James Austin, July 20, 1811, in William Eustis Papers, LC.

128. See *BTR*, 285.

129. George A. Billias, *Elbridge Gerry: Founding Father and Republican Statesman* (New York: McGraw Hill Book Co., 1976), 315; Edward Bangs to Nathaniel Howe, September 21, December 22, 1810, and April 24, 1811, in Edward Bangs Papers, AAS.

130. See Bangs to Howe, May 20, 1811, in Edward Bangs Papers, AAS.

131. *Speech of his excellency the Governor . . . before the Gentlemen of the Senate, and the Gentlemen of the House of Representatives, on Friday, June 7, 1811* (Boston, 1811), 2, 4, 5, and 9.

132. Ibid., 7, 8, 8–9, 10, 11, 12, 13.

133. *NI*, June 15, 22, and 29, 1811; Madison to Elbridge Gerry, June 21, 1811, in *PJM: PS*, 3: 345; James Monroe to Elbridge Gerry, June 14, 1811, William Eustis to Gerry, June 20, 1811, and "A distinguished Public character" [Randolph?] to Gerry, June 30, 1811, in Elbridge Gerry Papers, MHS; *Statesman and Friend: Correspondence of John Adams with Benjamin Waterhouse 1784–1822*, ed. Worthington C. Ford (Boston: Little, Brown, and Co., 1927), 55.

134. *CJ*, May 9, 1811. The New Haven resolves described "non-intercourse" as a "non-importation" that Congress had made part of the law; see *AC*, 11th, 3rd: 1338–39.

135. In 1810, New Haven was the largest town in the state with a population of 5,772; see Donna Androit, ed., *Population Abstract of the United States* (McLean, Va.: Documents Index Inc., 1993), 82.

136. Madison to the Inhabitants of New Haven, May 24, 1811, in *PJM: PS*, 3: 316–18, quote from 318.

137. *CtC*, May 29, 1811; *CJ*, May 30, 1811.

138. *CJ*, June 6, 1811.

139. C. Edward Skeen, *John Armstrong, Jr., 1758–1843. A Biography* (Syracuse, N.Y.: Syracuse University Press, 1981), 57–116.

140. Bradford Perkins, *Prologue to War: England and the United States 1805–1812* (Berkeley: University of California Press, 1961), 310–11.

141. Ibid., 279.

142. Ibid., 294.

143. Madison to Jefferson, April 1, 1811, in *PJM: PS*, 3: 239.

144. Madison to the Senate, June 26, 1809, in *PJM: PS*, 1: 266–67.

145. *Robert Smith's address to the people of the United States* (Baltimore, 1811), quote from 8; also 9–10, 12–15, 16–29. *SS*, #23949 is the edition used.

146. *SS*, #23947–50.

147. *NEP*, June 28, 1811.

148. *ER*, July 10, 1811.

149. Memorandum on Robert Smith, April 11?, 1811, in *PJM: PS*, 3: 262–63; also George Joy to Madison, August 15, 1811, in *PJM: PS*, 3: 417.

150. *NI* ran Smith's "extraordinary" address on July 2, and Barlow's reply on July 4, 6, 9, and 11. For the attribution, which Barlow was anxious to conceal, see James Woodress, *A Yankee's Odyssey: The Life of Joel Barlow* (Philadelphia: Lippincott, 1958), 280.

151. *NI*, July 11, 1811. Madison and Barlow agreed on both points, see Memorandum on Robert Smith, April 11?, 1811, in *PJM: PS*, 3: 257ff.

152. *SS*, #22201 and #23808. For a reprint, see *ER*, July 13, 17, 20, 24, 1811; for excerpts, see *IC*, July 18, 1811; also *NI*, July 11, 13, 16, and 23, 1811.

153. Monroe to Madison, March 23, and Madison to Monroe, March 26, 1811, in *PJM: PS*, 2: 230, 235.

154. *NI*, July 4, 1811; cf. also John G. Jackson to Madison, April 1, 1811, in *PJM: PS*, 3: 241.

Chapter 5

1. *NWR*, 1: 33–38.

2. Ibid., 38.

3. Madison to William Eustis, September 8, 1811, in *PJM: PS*, 3: 452.

4. *AC*, 12th, 1st: 1782–1807, quotes 1792; Madison to Richard Cutts, July 23, 1811, in *PJM: PS*, 3: 389.

5. *AC*, 12th, 1st: 1787, 1790, 1791, quote 1792.

6. Proclamation of July 24, 1811, in *PJM: PS*, 3: 392–93; *NI*, July 23, 1811; *ER*, July 31, 1811.

7. *IC*, June 20, 27, and July 4, 8, 22, 1811; *NI*, June 13, 25, 27, and July 11, 1811; *ER*, July 6 and Aug. 28, 31, 1811.

8. *NI*, July 4, 1811.

9. *NEP*, June 25 and July 19, 1811.

10. *IC*, July 29, August 8, 15, and September 9, 26, 1811.

11. *NEP*, September 3, 1811; *NWR*, 1: 39; Samuel Smith to William Eustis, August 31, 1811, in William Eustis Papers, MHS; Eustis to Madison, September 2, 1811, in *PJM: PS*, 3: 438–39.

12. Paul Hamilton to Madison, September 9, 1811, in *PJM: PS*, 3: 453.

13. Ibid., 3: 95n.

14. Ibid., 3: 221: Harry Toulmin to Madison, March 14, 1811.

15. Ibid., 539 fn; *NI*, September 6, 1811.

16. Charles Holmes to Madison, July 27, 1811, and Albert Gallatin, Treasury Department Circular, October 7, 1811, in *PJM: PS*, 3: 393–94, 476–78; see Gerald S. Graham, "The Gypsum Trade of the Maritime Provinces: Its Relation to American Diplomacy and Agriculture in the Early Nineteenth Century," *Agricultural History* 12 (1938): 209–23.

17. Quote from *PJM: PS*, 3: 439; also *PJM: PS*, 3: 495–96, and *NWR*, 1: 103.

18. *NWR*, 1: 209–13, 215; the consuls were Jonathan Russell and George Erwing, respectively. Madison also received reports of the condemnation of some captured American vessels; see George Joy to Madison, October 18, 1811, in *PJM: PS*, 3: 490–91.

19. *NWR*, 1: 207; *ER*, August 7, 11, 1811; *NI*, July 23, 1811.

20. Address from the Inhabitants of St. Clair County, Illinois Territory, September 6, and from the Cambridge Light Dragoons, October 5, 1811, Cambridge, South Carolina, in *PJM: PS*, 3: 446–47, 475.

21. Cf. *NWR*, 1: 355; Robert A. Rutland, *The Presidency of James Madison* (Lawrence: University Press of Kansas, 1990), 86.

22. See William Eaton to Madison, August 29 and October 25, 1811, in *PJM: PS*, 3, 434, 499–500; Memorandum from Albert Gallatin, November 1, 1811, in *PJM: PS*, 3: 535.

23. Ibid., 4: 3.

24. For example see *CM*, February 19, 1810.

25. *NWR*, 1: 128.

26. Report in *AC*, 12th, 1st: 373–77, quotes from 376.

27. *NWR*, 1: 250.

28. Quotes from *AC*, 12th, 1st: 414, 415, 417; *NWR*, 1: 267–69.

29. *NWR*, 1: 250–51.

30. William E. Ames, *A History of the* National Intelligencer (Chapel Hill: University of North Carolina Press, 1972), 112–13.

31. *AC*, 12th, 1st: 422, also 525, 541–42.

32. Ibid., 441–55, quotes from 450, 451, 453, 454; reprinted in *NWR*, 1: 315–20.

33. Quotes from *AC*, 12th, 1st: 423, 424; reprinted in *NWR*, 1: 313–14.

34. Cf. John Adams to Thomas McKean, July 6, 1815 in *The Works of John Adams, second president of the United States: with a life of the author, notes and illustrations, by his grandson Charles Francis Adams.* (Boston: Little, Brown and Co., 1850–1856), Vol. 10: 168.

35. *AC*, 12th, 1st: 619, reprinted in *NWR*, 1: 346–49; see also *SS*, #26726.

36. *AC*, 12th, 1st: 620, 623, 625–26.

37. Ibid., 628, 631. Republicans like Giles assumed that Britain would first move against these strategic locations; see *AC*, 12th, 1st: 40.

38. *NWR*, 1: 327.

39. *AC*, 12th, 1st: 415–16, 450, 457–58, 490, 652.

40. Ibid., 629–30; for the tendency of Federalists to exaggerate, see 145, 492, 521, 605.

41. Ibid., 43, 55, 69, 616.

42. Ibid., 55, 60, 67, 630.

43. Ibid., 56, 58, 60–61, 68, 69, 77, 603, 656, 701, 702. Cf. Lawrence D. Cress, *Citizens in Arms: The Army and the Militia in American Society to the War of 1812* (Chapel Hill: University of North Carolina Press, 1982), 144–45.

44. *DWB*, Vols, 3 & 4, passim; Thomas Jefferson to a Georgia volunteer company, March 12, 1808, and to the Warrior Run Volunteers (Pa.), April 3, 1808, in Thomas Jefferson Papers, LC; also *PJM: PS*, 4: 68, 119, 452, 486–87.

45. *AC*, 11th, 2nd: 1471–1514; 12th, 1st: 728–800. See also C. Edward Skeen, *Citizen Soldiers in the War of 1812* (Lexington: University Press of Kentucky, 1999), 13–15.

46. Randolph joined Federalists in inflating the estimated costs; see *AC*, 12th, 1st: 632, 712.

47. *AC*, 12th, 1st: 632–33; see also 146, 543, 663, 714.

48. Report of the secretary of the treasury, November 22, 1811 in *NWR*, 1: 232; also *AC*, 12th, 1st: 700.

49. *NEP*, May 5, 1812.

50. In *NWR*, 1: 251, 252. See also *NEP*, February 7, 1812, and *AC*, 12th, 1st: 527–28.

51. Edmund Quincy, *Life of Josiah Quincy. By his son* (Boston: Little, Brown, and Co., 1891), 240. For Hanson, see Jeffrey L. Pasley, "*The Tyranny of Printers": Newspaper Politics in the Early American Republic* (Charlottesville: University Press of Virginia, 2001), 241–48.

52. My interpretation goes beyond that of Robert A. McCaughey, *Josiah Quincy 1772–1864* (Cambridge, Mass.: Harvard University Press, 1974), 72, which is based on a letter from Quincy to Harrison G. Otis, November 25, 1811, in the Harrison Gray Otis Papers, MHS.

53. Quote from *NEP*, December 3, 1811; see also December 6, 1811.

54. *AC*, 12th, 1st: 46, 82, 475, 658, 689.

55. Ibid., 483.

56. Ibid., 514. For Stanford, see Norman K. Risjord, *The Old Republicans: Southern Conservatism in the Age of Jefferson* (New York: Columbia University Press, 1965), 29, 62, 77, and 97.

57. *PHC*, 1: 471, 484, 594.

58. Ibid., 605, 607–608, 609; also in *AC*, 12th, 1st: 598–99, 600, 601, 602, republished in *NWR*, 1: 332–35.

59. *AC*, 12th, 1st: quotes from 485, 489; see also 508–509, 518–19, 659.

60. Ibid., 681, 682, 688, 690–91, republished in *NWR*, 1: 349–51; see also *SS*, #27559.

61. *AC*, 12th, 1st: 691.

62. Ibid., 139–42, 207–208; *R*, March 10, 1812; *NEP*, March 13, April 21, and June 5, 1812.

63. *AC*, 12th, 1st: 563; see also *NWR*, 2: 29–30.

64. *NWR*, 1: 299.

65. *AC*, 12th, 1st: 1164–1165, quote 1165; also 1222.

66. Ibid., 1167, 1170, 1171, 1172: "A.B." to the Governor General, February 14, and March 7, 13, 1809.

67. *PJM: PS*, 4: 235.

68. *AC*, 12th, 1st: 1220; *NWR*, 2: 45.

69. Richard Beale Davis, *Jeffersonian America. Notes on the United States of America Collected in the Years 1805–6–7 and 11–12 by Sir Augustus Foster, Bart* (San Marino, Calif.: The Huntington Library, 1954), 70–78; Rutland, *Presidency of James Madison*, 90; Garry Wills, *James Madison* (New York: Henry Holt and Co., 2002), 95.

70. *AC*, 12th, 1st: 1220.

71. *NI*, March 10, 1812.

72. *NEP*, March 17, 20, and 27, 1812; the text of Henry's statement is taken from *NWR*, 2: 20.

73. Quotes from *NWR*, 2: 31; *NI*, March 24, 1812; also *AC*, 12th, 1st: 1220.

74. *AC*, 12th, 1st, 186–87; *NWR*, 2: 86; *PJM: PS*, 4: 279.

75. Madison to Jefferson, April 3, 1812, and Henry Dearborn to Madison, April 6, 1812, in *PJM: PS*, 4: 287, 301.

76. *AC*, 12th, 1st: 1589–98.

77. Ibid., 1603.

78. See Elbridge Gerry to Madison, May 19, 1812, in *PJM: PS*, 4: 398. Gerry subsequently discounted the embargo's effect, Elbridge Gerry to Madison, May 20, 1812, in *PJM:* PS, 4: 403.

79. See Christopher Gore to Rufus King, February 7, 1812, in Rufus King Papers, NYHS.

80. From *P*, June 29, 1811.

81. *NEP*, August 6 and 13, 1811.

82. Ibid., October 29, 1811.

83. Ibid., August 20, 27, and September 6, 1811.

84. Edward Bangs to Nathaniel Howe, July 24, September 10, and December 16, 1811, and February 24, 1812, in Edward Bangs Papers, AAS; Elbridge Gerry to the Council, August 14, November 27, and December 17, 1811, in Elbridge Gerry Papers, MHS.

85. *NEP*, October 29, 1811.

86. Ibid., November 29, 1811.

87. Ibid., December 3, 1811.

88. *Speech of His Excellency the Governor of the Commonwealth of Massachusetts, at the session commencing on the second Wednesday in January, 1812* (Boston, 1812), 6, 10, 11; *SS*, #26028.

89. *Speech of His Excellency*, 13, 14, 15.

90. Ibid., 19. Gerry had previously drafted a proclamation offering a $500 reward for information about the person who had threatened to burn his house. Elbridge Gerry, Proclamation, December 11, 1811, in Elbridge Gerry Papers, MHS.

91. *R*, January 24, 1812.

92. From *P*, January 18, 1812; also *R*, January 21, 1812, and *CC*, January 22, 1812; Elbridge Gerry to Madison, May 19 and 20, 1812, in *PJM: PS*, 4: 398, 403.

93. *R*, January 17, 21, 24, and February 4, 1812.

94. *CC*, January 18, 25, and February 1, 5, 1812. Quotes from February 5.

95. *R*, January 24, 1812; *Message from His Excellency the Governor. February 27, 1812* (Boston, 1812), 9–12; *BG*, March 5, 1812.

96. The best short sketch of Strong's life outside the standard biographical reference works is Ronald P. Formisano, *The Transformation of Political Culture: Massachusetts Parties, 1790s–1840s* (New York: Oxford University Press, 1983), 62–63, quotes from 63 and Ames to Christopher Gore, March 5, 1800, in *Works of Fisher Ames. With a Selection from his Speeches and Correspondence*, ed. Seth Ames (Boston: Little, Brown and Co., 1854), Vol.1: 277–78. Formisano's account relies heavily on Alden Bradford, *Biography of the Hon. Caleb Strong* (Boston, 1820) and Henry Cabot Lodge, *Studies in History* (Boston: Houghton, Mifflin Co., 1884), 224–62.

97. Dated February 7 and first published in *R*, February 11, 1812, and *CC*, February 12, 1812; then issued as the pamphlet, *Address to the free and independent people of Massachusetts* (Boston, 1812), 5–7.

98. Ibid., 5.

99. *Protest. In the House of Representatives of the Commonwealth of Massachusetts*, appended to the *Address to the free and independent people*, 9.

100. *BG*, February 13, 24, and March 9, 1812.

101. Ibid., March 26, 1812.

102. Richard Cutts to Madison, April 8, 1812, in *PJM: PS*, 4: 305.

103. Steven E. Siry, *DeWitt Clinton and the American Political Economy: Sectionalism Politics, and Republican Ideology 1787–1828* (New York: P. Lang, 1990), chap. 6; also *AC*, 12th, 1st: 1390, 1401; William Plummer to John A. Harper, April 7, 1812, in William Plummer Papers, NYHS.

104. Donald R. Hickey, *The War of 1812. A Forgotten Conflict* (Urbana: University of Illinois Press, 1989), 77.

105. Henry Dearborn to Madison, April 6, 1812, in *PJM: PS*, 4: 299–300.

106. See William Turpin to Madison, May 29, 1812, in *PJM: PS*, 4: 422–23.

107. See Elbridge Gerry to Madison, May 19, 1812, in *PJM: PS*, 4, 398; *AC*, 12th, 1st: 1432.

108. Edwin J. Perkins, *American Public Finance and the Financial Services 1700–1815* (Columbus: Ohio State University, 1994), 98.

109. James Woodress, *A Yankee's Odyssey. The Life of Joel Barlow* (Philadelphia: Lippincott, 1958), chap. 7.

110. *AC*, 12th, 1st: 1380–81.

111. Ibid., 1388, 1389.

112. Ibid., 1390, 1391, 1398.

113. Ibid., 1407, 1408, 1410, 1412, 1413–14.

114. *PJM: PS*, 4: 432–38, quote 437.

115. *AC*, 12th, 1st: 1637.

116. Ibid., 1682; *PJM: PS*, 4: 489–90; J. C. A. Stagg, *Mr. Madison's War: Politics, Diplomacy, and Warfare in the Early American Republic, 1783–1830* (Princeton, N.J.: Princeton University Press, 1983), 111–15, provides the best analysis of the struggle in the Senate over declaring war.

117. Herbert Heaton, "Non-importation, 1806–1812," *Journal of Economic History* 1 (1941): 194–97; Bradford Perkins, *Prologue to War: England and the United States 1805–1812* (Berkeley: University of California Press, 1961), chap. 9.

118. Henry Dearborn to James Monroe, June 18, 1812, in James Monroe Papers, NYPL, and Elbridge Gerry to James Madison, July 5, 1812, in Gerry-Townsend Papers, NYPL.

119. For the view that modern communications might have permanently averted war, see Hickey, *War of 1812*, 42.

Chapter 6

1. Memorandum of a Conversation with Augustus J. Foster, June 23, 1812, in *PJM: PS*, 4: 501–502.

2. Ibid., 503–504 fn.

3. Ibid., 493, 496: Madison to John G. Jackson, June 21, and to Jefferson, June 22, 1812; Richard B. Davis, ed., *Jeffersonian America. Notes on the United States of America Collected in the Years 1805–6–7 and 11–12 by Sir Augustus John Foster, Bart* (San Marino, Calif.: The Huntington Library, 1954), 102.

4. *NEP*, August 4, 1812.

5. Jefferson to Thomas Digges, August 10, 1808, in Thomas Jefferson Papers, LC.

6. Davis, *Jeffersonian America*, 88ff.

7. Madison to Jefferson, June 22, 1812, in *PJM: PS*, 4: 496.

8. *NWR*, 2: 309–15 managed to compress the *Address* into six pages using very small print; *SS*, #24535–55.

9. *AC*, 12th, 1st: 2198, 2199.

10. Ibid., 2219.

11. *NWR*, 3: 133; also *Review of an Address of the Minority in Congress to their Constituents, on the Subject of the War with Great-Britain* (Trenton, N.J., 1812), 6ff.

12. *AC*, 12th, 1st: 259, 260.

13. Ibid., 261. For the resolves outside New England stressing the nation's honor, see *PJM: PS*, 4: 36–37, 156; *PJC*, 1: 110, 119, 121–22.

14. *BTR*, 316–17, 318, 319, 320.

15. Text from *CC*, July 7, 1812.

16. *NWR*, 2: 207–208, 308–309.

17. Cf. *SS*, #25445, #25824, #26146, #26354, #26830–2, #26812, #27418 with the moderate #25733. On this occasion Connecticut's published fast sermons were less political, see SS, #26431 and #26820.

18. *NEP*, July 17, 1812; *CtC*, July 21, 1812.

19. Ipswich in *CtC*, July 7, 1812; Newbury, Long Meadow, Northampton, Newburyport, and Plymouth in *NEP*, July 3, 7, 10, 24, and August 7, 1812; also *SS*, #26321.

20. *NEP*, July 21 and 24, 1812.

21. Ibid., July 31, and August 7, 14, and 18, 1812; *SS*, #25407, #25355, #26074, #26322, #27624. A Norfolk county convention in October focused on a congressional race; see *SS*, #26308.

22. *NEP*, August 14, 1812; *SS*, # 26825–26.

23. *CtC*, August 4, 1812.

24. Rufus King memo, summer 1812, in *LCRK*, 5: 269; Steven E. Siry, *DeWitt Clinton and the American Political Economy: Sectionalism, Politics, and Republican Ideology, 1787–1828* (New York: P. Lang, 1990), 164–75.

25. *CtC*, August 11, 1812.

26. For a tabulation of the results, see *NWR*, 5: 136.

27. Ibid., 3: 144, 160, 179; *New Jersey Journal*, November 17, 1812.

28. Donald R. Hickey, *The War of 1812: A Forgotten Conflict* (Chicago: University of Illinois Press, 1989), 57–68 devotes more attention to this incident than to the other ways in which the Federalists sought to influence public opinion; cf. also Jeffrey L. Pasley, *"The Tyrany of Printers": Newspaper Politics in the Early American Republic* (Charlottesville: University Press of Virginia, 2001), 246–47.

29. *NWR*, 3: 5.

30. Ibid., 96.

31. *BTR*, 321–24, 325.

32. David Hackett Fischer, *The Revolution of American Conservatism: The Federalist Party in the Era of Jeffersonian Democracy* (New York: Harper & Row, 1965), 259.

33. *BTR*, 325. Also Timothy Pickering to John Lowell Jr., November 7, 1814, in *LLGC*, 539.

34. *CSR*, 16: 89.

35. Ibid., 90, 92. Trumbull had then pronounced the Enforcement Act unconstitutional whereas Griswold simply asked the council to certify that the constitutional conditions for mobilizing the state militia under federal command did not exist.

36. Ibid., 96.

37. Ibid., 92.

38. Ibid., 98.

39. Ibid., 99, 100.

40. *NWR*, 3: 4–5.

41. Ibid., 22–24; *CSR*, 16: 106–12.

42. *NWR*, 3: 116–18.

43. Richard Buel Jr., *Dear Liberty: Connecticut's Mobilization for the Revolutionary War* (Middletown, Conn.: Wesleyan University Press, 1980), chaps. 3–6.

44. *NWR*, 3: 179–80.

45. William S. Dudley, ed., *The Naval War of 1812: A Documentary History* (Washington, D.C.: Naval History Center, Department of the Navy, 1985), Vol. 1: 202–203, 526–27, 566, 638. The statute against trading with the enemy was drawn ambiguously and generously interpreted, see *AC*, 12th, 1st: 2355.

46. Hickey, *War of 1812*, 282–83; at the end of September, Hezekiah Niles claimed American armed vessels had captured 176 British prizes, *NWR*, 3: 48.

47. Dudley, *The Naval War of 1812*, 1: 633–34.

48. J. C. A. Stagg, *Mr. Madison's War: Politics, Diplomacy, and Warfare in the Early Republic, 1783–1830* (Princeton, N.J.: Princeton University Press, 1983), 245; Joseph Warren to James Monroe, September 30, and Monroe to Warren, October 27, 1812, in *ASP: FR*, 3: 595–97.

49. *NWR*, 3: 179.

50. Ibid., 4: 148, and 6: 207, 320; *DWB*, 4: 101, 103, 104, 105; Samuel E. Morison, Frederick Merk, and Frank Freidel, *Dissent in Three American Wars* (Cambridge, Mass.: Harvard University Press, 1970), 4.

51. Richard Purcell, *Connecticut in Transition: 1775–1818* (Middletown, Conn.: Wesleyan University Press, 1963), 139, 153.

52. *DWB*, 4: 16, 90.

53. Ibid., 90, 91–92. See also 93, 94, 95, 96, 97, 108; Mercy Otis Warren to Elbridge Gerry, August 16, 1812, and Gerry to Nathan Tudor, August 17, 1812, in Elbridge Gerry Papers, MHS; *ER*, April 1, 4, and 8, 1812.

54. *CSR*, 16: 134–36.

55. Stagg, *Mr. Madison's War*, 172–73, 264.

56. *AC,*, 12th, 2nd: 167–73.

57. Ibid., 173–74.

58. Ibid., 175, 177.

59. *NWR*, 3: 232.

60. *AC*, 12th, 2nd: 218–451 passim; 1251–55, 1258, 1316.

61. Quotes from ibid, 543, 544, 549, 550, 560, 566, 569.

62. Ibid., 660, 661, 662, 664, 665; *SS*, #28158–60.

63. *AC*, 12th, 2nd: 663.

64. *NEP*, January 12, 1813; *R*, January 26, 1813; *CC*, January 30, and February 3, 6, 1813; *BG*, February 1 and 4, 1813; *SS*, # 29614–16.

65. *IC*, February 18 and 22, 1813.

66. Ibid., February 22, 1813.

67. Also in *IC*, February 22, 1813.

68. *BG*, March 15, 1813.

69. *CC*, February 20, 1813.

70. *NEP* and *R*, February 16, 1813.

71. *BG*, May 10, 1813.

72. *NWR*, 4: 285–87, quotes 285 and 287; Robert A. McCaughey, *Josiah Quincy 1772–1864. The Last Federalist* (Cambridge, Mass.: Harvard University Press, 1974), 77.

73. *NWR*, 4: 287.

74. *P*, June 5, 19, 26, and July 3, 1813.

75. Edward Quincy, *Life of Josiah Quincy. By his son* (Boston: Little, Brown, and Co., 1891), 325.

76. *NWR*, 4: 233, 236.

77. Ibid., 251–52.

78. Ibid., 253.

79. Ibid., 233.

80. *AC*, 13th, 1st and 2nd: 333–41; *NWR*, 4: 297–301; McCaughey, *Quincy*, 77.

81. *AC*, 13th, 1st and 2nd: 334, 337, 338.

82. Pasley, "*A Tyranny of Printers*," 247.

83. *AC*, 13th, 1st and 2nd: 106.

84. Webster to Charles March, June 3, 1813, in *PDW*, 1: 144.

85. Ibid., autobiography, 19.

86. *AC*, 13th, 1st and 2nd: 150–51, 158.

87. Ibid., 159–62.

88. Ibid., 178–82, 185–219, 229–65.

89. Webster to Charles March, June 21, 1813, in *PDW*, 1: 151.

90. *AC*, 13th, 1st and 2nd: 176, 221–22, quotes 222. Calhoun was accused of speaking with "unnecessary warmth"; see *AC*, 13th, 1st and 2nd: 177, 188.

91. Ibid., 225–26.

92. Ibid., 236.

93. *NWR*, 4: 301.

94. *AC*, 13th, 1st and 2nd: 341–42.

95. Ibid., 343, 347, 348, 349, 404–405, 618; see also *AC*, 12th, 1st: 254–55.

96. *AC*, 13th, 1st and 2nd: 235.

97. *NWR*, 4: 131.

98. *NEP* March 16, 19, 23, 26, 30, and April 6, 1813; *DWB*, 4: 161.

99. *AC*, 13th, 1st and 2nd: 406.

100. Ibid., 461.

101. Ibid., 435.

102. Ibid., 438, 439, 470–71.

103. Hickey, *War of 1812*, 127–44.

104. *AC*, 13th, 1st and 2nd: 83ff.

105. *NWR*, 3: 288; 4: 250–51, 430; 5: 278.

106. Ibid., 5: 122.

107. Ibid., 4: 232, 273.

108. The uneasy collaboration is documented in the John Cotton Smith Papers, *Collections of the Connecticut Historical Society* (Hartford, 1948–49), Vols. 25 and 26.

109. *NWR*, 4: 220, 280.

110. Hickey, *War of 1812*, 49–50, 118, 122, 123.

111. *NWR*, 4: 237.

112. See for instance, [Matthew Carey], *Examination of the pretensions of New England to commercial pre-eminence* (Philadelphia, 1814), 73–74; Matthew Carey, *The Olive Branch: or, Faults on Both Sides, Federal and Democratic. A Serious Appeal on the Necessity of Mutual Forgiveness and Harmony* 10th ed. (Freeport, N.Y.: Books for Libraries Press, 1969), chap. 52; Charles J. Ingersoll, *Historical Sketch of the Second War of Independence between the United States of America and Great Britain, declared by Act of Congress, the 18th of June, 1812, and concluded by Peace, the 15th of February, 1815* (Philadelphia, 1845), Vol.1: 52–56.

113. *AC*, 12th, 1st: 2102; James Lloyd to Harrison Gray Otis, May 10, 1814, in Harrison Gray Otis Papers, MHS.

114. Israel Thorndike to Harrison Gray Otis, April 23, 1814, in Harrison Gray Otis Papers, MHS.

115. Dudley, *Naval War of 1812*, Vol. 2: 78–79, 262–63.

116. *AC*, 12th, 2nd: 212; *NWR*, 5: 351.

117. *AC*, 12th, 2nd: 212; 13th, 1st and 2nd: 549; *NWR*, 5: 343, 351.

118. *NWR*, 5: 330.

119. Carey, *Olive Branch*, chap. 53.

Chapter 7

1. *AC*, 12th, 2nd: 121; 13th, 1st and 2nd: 2777–79.

2. *DWB*, 4: 110; for an example of a license signed by the British Consul in Boston, dated September 3, 1812, see the Harrison Gray Otis Papers, MHS.

3. *WJM*, 8: 234, quote 237.

4. *AC*, 13th, 1st and 2nd: 98–101, 500–504.

5. Ibid., 549–50; J. C. A. Stagg, *Mr. Madison's War. Politics: Politics, Diplomacy, and Warfare in the Early American Republic, 1783–1830* (Princeton, N.J.: Princeton University Press, 1983), summarizes some of the abuses.

6. *NWR*, 5: 317; *AC*, 13th, 1st and 2nd: 549, 1993, 2780–88.

7. *AC*, 13th, 1st and 2nd: 938–39, 1154–57, quotes 1155; *NWR*, 5: 343, 378–79.

8. *NEP*, January 25 and 28, 1814.

9. Ibid., February 1 and 4, 1814; also "A Friend to Peace" in *NEP*, January 25.

10. *AC*, 13th, 1st and 2nd: 2785.

11. *NEP*, February 1 and 15, 1814; *NWR*, 5: 380; *AC*, 13th, 1st and 2nd: 1379–80.

12. Samuel Putnam to Timothy Pickering, February 17, 1814, in Timothy Pickering Papers, MHS.

13. *NEP*, February 22, 1814.

14. *NI*, January 17, 1814, responding to an excerpt from *BG* it had republished on January 15.

15. *NEP*, February 22, 1814; Samuel Putnam to Timothy Pickering, February 11, 1814, in *LLGC*, 532–33.

16. *NWR*, 4: 164–65.

17. Ibid, 5: 376, 377, 378.

18. Ibid., 6: 1–3. Niles appears to have relied on reports in *P*, January 29, and February 9, 12, and 26, 1814 for his local information.

19. Reprinted in *NI*, March 1, 1814.

20. *NWR*, 6: 11.

21. Ibid., 5: 204, 212, 214, 251, 264; *AC*, 13th, 1st and 2nd: 859; Samuel E. Morison, *The Life and Letters of Harrison Gray Otis* (Boston: Houghton Mifflin Co., 1913), Vol. 2: 64–65.

22. *NWR*, 5: 423; *P*, January 29, 1814; Morrison, *Otis*, Vol. 2: 65.

23. *NI*, March 7, 1814.

24. Ibid., January 17, 1814.

25. See Daniel Webster to Isaac P. Davis, January 6, 1814, in *PDW*, 1: 159–60.

26. *AC*, 13th, 1st and 2nd: 932, 933–34.

27. Ibid., 942, 944, 946; *SS*, #33018–22.

28. *AC*, 13th, 1st and 2nd: 998, 1000–1001, 1002: *SS*, #31068.

29. *AC*, 13th, 1st and 2nd: 1008; *SS*, #31799.

30. *AC*, 13th, 1st and 2nd: 1019, 1021, 1022; Shipherd had taken a similar stand in the previous session, see 235–37.

31. Charles J. Ingersoll, *Historical Sketch of the Second War between the United States of America and Great Britain, declared by Congress, the 18th of June, 1812, and Concluded by Peace, the 15th of February, 1815* (Philadelphia, 1845–1849), Vol. 2: 235; William Phillips to Caleb Strong, October 28, 1813, in Caleb Strong Papers, MHS.

32. *AC*, 13th, 1st and 2nd: 1271, 1405; *NI*, February 15, 1814.

33. *AC*, 13th, 1st and 2nd: 1274, 1298, 1325, 1327, 1328, 1329; *SS*, #32756.

34. *AC*, 13th, 1st and 2nd: 1534–36; *SS*, #31622.

35. *AC*, 13th, 1st and 2nd: 1545–46, 1573, 1575, 1576, *SS*, #31560–62.

36. *AC*, 13th, 1st and 2nd: 1591, 1601, 1609; *SS*, #31504; comment in *ER* republished in *P*, February 16, 1814.

37. *NI*, February 24, 1814.

38. *AC*, 13th, 1st and 2nd: 1657.

39. Ibid., 1690.

40. Ibid., 1690–91; *SS*, #31069.

41. *NI*, February 1, 1814.

42. *NWR*, 6: 9–10.

43. *AC*, 13th, 1st and 2nd: 1925, 2817–22: C. Peter Magrath, *Yazoo: Law and Politics in the New Republic. The Case of Fletcher v. Peck* (Providence, R.I.: Brown University Press, 1966), 97–100.

44. *NI*, January 28 and February 15, 1814.

45. David Parish to Harrison Gray Otis, April 12, 1813; Israel Thorndike to Harrison Gray Otis, April 23, 1813; James Lloyd to Otis, May 10, 1814, in Harrison Gray Otis Papers, MHS; Morison, *Otis*, Vol. 2: 67, 75–76.

46. *NI*, March 12, 1814.

47. Ibid., February 26, 1814.

48. James Monroe to Henry Clay, February 13, 1814, in *PHC*, 1: 866.

49. See *SS*, #31648–50.

50. *PJC*, 1: 246–47.

51. AC, 13th, 1st and 2nd: 2000–01, 2830; for the Republican opposition to repeal, see Stagg, *Mr. Madison's War*, 384.

52. *NWR*, 6: 182–83.

53. *NEP*, April 19, 1814.

54. *P*, March 5, 1814.

55. Elijah Brigham to Dwight Foster, March 28, 1814, in Dwight Foster Papers, BPL; Lucius M. Sargent, *Reminiscences of Samuel Dexter. Originally Written for the Boston Evening Transcipt* (Boston: Henry W. Dutton & Son, 1857), 89–90.

56. See *NEP*, April 22, 1814.

57. *NEP*, May 13, 1914; *BTR2*, 7. Over two years the delegation declined from 44 to 36.

58. *NWR*, 6: 250–51.

59. *NEP*, June 10, 1814.

60. *NWR*, 6: 273–74.

61. Cf. *IC*, November 21, 1814, explaining why the Republicans had withheld their support for Holmes's bid for Congress.

62. See *P*, February 2 and 19, and March 5, 1814; *NI*, February 9, June 23, and July 1 and 4, 1814.

63. *NWR*, 6: 274–75; *SS*, #31746–48.

64. *CM*, June 13, 1814; *NEP*, June 17, 1814.

65. *NEP*, June 21, 1814.

66. See *R*, March 27, 1813.

67. William E. Channing, *A discourse, delivered in Boston, at the solemn festival in commemoration of the goodness of God in delivering the Christian world from military despotism* (Boston, 1814), quotes from 4, 5, 8; *NEP*, June 17, 1814; *R*, June 16, 1814.

68. *NEP*, June 24, and July 1, 5, 8, 12, 15, 19, and 26, 1814; *SS*, #30951, #31287, #31663, #31881, #32973, #33671.

69. *NEP*, July 5 and 8, 1814; *SS*, #31371, #31563.

70. *Sun-beams may be extracted from cucumbers, but the process is tedious. An Oration pronounced on the Fourth of July, 1799, at the request of the citizens of New-Haven* (New Haven, 1799).

71. *CtC*, July 26, 1814; Daggett referred here to erroneous information that had appeared in *NI*, June 2 and 6, 1814.

72. *NWR*, 6: 313.

73. Morris's speech was republished in *NI*, July 19, 1814; *SS*, #32171–72.

74. *NI*, July 21, 23, 28, 1814; *NWR*, 6: 362, 363, 365.

75. Samuel Cary, *A Sermon preached before the ancient and honourable artillery company, in Boston, June 6, 1814* (Boston, 1814), 4–5; reprinted in *NEP*, June 21 and July 1, 1814.

76. *NEP*, July 1 and 12, 1814.

77. *NWR*, 6: 361, 362, 364; also *NI*, June 13 and 17, 1814.

78. See George Cabot to Oliver Wolcott, March 26 and June 9, 1798, Cabot to Christopher Gore, March 27, 1800, Cabot to Rufus King, July 1, 1803, Cabot to Timothy Pickering, September 5, 1799, February 14, 1807, and March 12, 1808, in *LLGC*, 152, 160, 235, 270–71, 331, 372–73, 383; Timothy Pickering to Rufus King, January 2, 9, 25, 1808, and February 10, 1810, in Rufus King Papers, NYHS.

79. *NEP*, August 12, 23, 1814.

80. *NWR*, 6: 415, 428; James Tertius De Kay, *The Battle of Stonington: Torpedoes, Submarines, and Rockets in the War of 1812* (Annapolis, Md.: Naval Institute Press, 1990), chaps. 9–12.

81. *NWR*, 6: 444; 7: 3–4.

82. Ibid. 7: 32, 41–44, 51–52.

83. *WJM*, 8: 304–306: *DWB*, 4: 281.

84. *NEP*, July 1, 29, and August 30, 1814; for the first hint of Britain's terms, see *NWR*, 6: 369, 422.

85. *IC*, September 29, 1814.

86. *LCRK*, 5: 423; Caleb Strong to Timothy Pickering, October 7, 1814, in Timothy Pickering Papers, MHS.

87. *AC*, 13th, 3rd: 381–82, 420, 435–37, 440, 506–10.

88. *LCRK*, 5: 412–13; *DWB*, 4: 280. There was a dispute about what King actually said in the Senate debate over the direct tax bill on January 5. *NI* reported that though King had disapproved of the war, he was now prepared to support giving "the executive

men and money to carry it on," and *NWR*, 7: 318, reprinted the story. A different account appeared in the New York *Evening Post*, January 13, 1815, which I have adhered to. Both are reproduced in *LCRK*, 5: 449–53. Nonetheless King failed to vote for the bill he said he supported; see *AR*, 13th, 3rd: 160.

89. *NI*, June 14, 1814.

90. *IC*, November 24, 1814; also *IC*, November 3, 1814; see also [Matthew Carey], *Examination of the pretensions of New England to commercial pre-eminence* (Philadelphia, 1814), 73.

91. Jacob Barker to George Campbell, April 30, 1814, in Jacob Barker Papers, HL; Oliver Wolcott to Rufus King, April 4, 1814, in Oliver Wolcott Papers, CHS.

92. Christopher Gore to Rufus King, July 28, 1814, in *LCRK*, 5: 403.

93. *NWR*, 7: 195–96; [Carey], *Examination of pretensions*, 83–84; Oliver Wolcott to Rufus King, April 4, 1814, in Oliver Wolcott Papers, CHS. See also *SS*, #32072.

94. Stagg, *Mr. Madison's War*, 427; Edwin J. Perkins, *American Public Finance and Financial Services 1700–1815* (Columbus; University of Ohio, 1994), 339–40.

95. *NWR*, 6: 94; Rufus King to Christopher Gore, July 11 and 15, 1814, in *LCRK*, 5: 398, 400–401.

96. State Bank had been chartered during Gerry's governorship, see *SS*, #20658, #23305.

97. [Carey], *Examination of pretensions*, 85–90, 95–97; Oliver Wolcott to Rufus King, March 8, 1814, in Oliver Wolcott Papers, CHS.

98. Stagg, *Mr. Madison's War*, 437; Perkins, *American Public Finance*, 335.

99. *SS*, #32038: *P*, September 28, 1814.

100. *BG*, October 3, 1814ff; *P*, November 5, 16, and 26, 1814; *LCRK*, 4: 403.

101. *IC*, November 24, 1814; see also November 7, 1814.

102. Cf. Stagg. *Mr. Madison's War*, 438–52, with Oliver Wolcott to Matthew Carey, December 16, 1814, and February 7, 1815, in Oliver Wolcott Papers, CHS.

103. See "The Prospect of Peace" and "Steadfast" in *IC*, September 29 and October 6, 1814.

104. *NEP*, October 7, 1814.

105. Detailed in *Collections of the Connecticut Historical Society*, Vols. 26–28 (1949–1954): passim. The rift between Brigadier General Thomas Cushing and state authorities developed during the last week in August and first two weeks of September. John C. Smith's subsequent account of Connecticut's contribution to the war effort, inserted in 26: 150–53, gives a misleading impression.

106. Ingersoll, *Sketch of the Second War*, Vol. 2: 120–121; H. A. S. Dearborn, *The Life of William Bainbridge, Esq. of the United States Navy* (Princeton, N.J.: Princeton University Press, 1931), 190–97; *BTR2*, 17–19, quotes from 18 and 19; *CC* and *Y*, September 9, 1814; *DWB*, 4: 280.

107. Caleb Strong to James Monroe, September 7, 1814, and Monroe to Strong, September 17 in *CC*, October 8, 1814; *NEP*, October 7 and 11, 1814; Henry Adams, *History of the United States of America during the Administrations of James Madison* (New York: The Library of America, 1986), 1105.

108. *CC*, October 1, and 12, 1814.
109. Ibid., October 19, 1814; *NWR*, 7: 70–76.
110. See 'The Prospect of Peace" in *IC*, September 29 and October 6, 1814.
111. Stagg, *Mr. Madison's War*, 485–88; Timothy Pickering to James Hillhouse, December 16, 1814, in *LLGC*, 553–54, 555; Timothy Pickering to Caleb Strong, January 10, 1815, in Caleb Strong Papers, MHS.
112. The anomalous nature of the call for a convention was not lost on the Republicans; see "The Soil in Danger," in *IC*, October 13, 1814.
113. *P*, October 8, 1814.
114. Text from *CC*, October 12, 1814.
115. *NI*, October 27, 1814.
116. *NI*, October 27, 1814; *Y*, October 28, 1814.
117. Text from *IC*, October 27, 1814.
118. Theodore Dwight, *History of the Hartford Convention: with a review of the policy of the United States Government, which led to the War of 1812* (Boston, 1833), 343.
119. *CSR*, 17: 153, quote 185–86.
120. See John Phillips and Timothy Bigelow to the governors of the New England states, October 17, 1814, in Dwight, *Hartford Convention*, 343.
121. *CSR*, 17: 182, 183; see also *NEP*, November 11, 1814.
122. *CSR*, 17: 194; *NI*, November 11, 1814; Samuel Willard to Dwight Foster, October 31, 1814, in Dwight Foster Papers, BPL.
123. *NWR*, 7: 181.
124. Ibid., 167; Simeon E. Baldwin, "The Hartford Convention," *New Haven Historical Society Papers* 9 (1915): 17.

Chapter 8

1. See *IC*, October 31, November 7, 24, and December 29, 1814.
2. James Madison to Wilson Cary Nicholas, November 26, 1814, in *WJM*, 8: 319; William Eustis to Matthew Carey, November 16, 1814, in William Eustis Papers, LC.
3. J. S. Martel, "A Side Light on Federalist Strategy," *American Historical Review* 43 (1937–38): 553–66, especially 561.
4. James Madison to David Humphreys, March 23, 1813, in *WJM*, 8: 241; John Randolph, *Letter from the Hon. John Randolph, to James Lloyd, esq. of Boston, late a member of the Senate of the United States, from the state of Massachusetts* (Georgetown, Md, 1814), 6–7; Matthew Carey, *A calm address to the eastern states, on the subject of the representation of slaves; the representation in the Senate; and the hostility to commerce ascribed to the southern states. By the author of The olive branch* (Boston, 1814), 16–17, 48; Robert A. East, "Economic Development and New England Federalism, 1803–1814," *New England Quarterly* 10 (1937): 430–46; J. C. A. Stagg, *Mr. Madison's War: Politics, Diplomacy, and Warfare in the Early American Republic, 1783–1830* (Princeton, N.J.: Princeton University Press, 1983), 480.

5. *IC*, November 21–December 2, 1814; James M. Banner Jr., *To the Hartford Convention: The Federalists and the Origins of Party Politics in Massachusetts, 1789–1815* (New York: Alfred A. Knopf, 1970), 329.

6. Harrison G. Otis, *Letters developing the Character and Views of the Hartford Convention* (Washington, D.C., 1820); Otis, *Letters in Defense of the Hartford Convention and the People of Massachusetts* (Boston, 1824); *Correspondence between the eastern Federalists and John Quincy Adams in relation to his charge against them of entertaining treasonable designs against the general government* (Poughkeepsie, N.Y., 1829); Theodore Dwight, *History of the Hartford Convention: with a review of the policy of the United States government, which led to the War of 1812* (New York, 1833); Simeon E. Baldwin, "The Hartford Convention," *Papers of the New Haven Colony Historical Society* 9 (1918): 1–28; Samuel E Morison, *The Life and Letters of Harrison Gray Otis: Federalist 1765–1848* 2 vols. (Boston: Houghton Mifflin Co., 1913) and *Harrison Gray Otis, 1765–1848: The Urbane Federalist* (Boston: Houghton Mifflin Co., 1969).

7. Stagg, *Mr. Madison's War*, 441–53; for the bank debacle see *AC*, 13th, 3rd, 561ff.; for the Federalist role in it, Elijah Brigham to Dwight Foster, February 8, 1815, in Dwight Foster Papers, BPL.

8. James Madison to Wilson Cary Nicholas, November 26, 1814, in *WJM*, 8: 319.

9. Stagg, *Mr. Madison's War*, 477–78; also Thomas Jesup to James Monroe, December 10, and 15, 1814, and Joseph L. Smith to Thomas Jesup, December 26, 1814, in Thomas Jesup Papers, LC.

10. See the series titled "Pandemonium" by "Aristides" in *AM*, November 21–December 20, 1814.

11. Matthew Carey, *The Olive Branch: or faults on both sides, Federal and Democratic. A serious appeal of the necessity of mutual forgiveness & harmony, to save our common country from ruin* (Philadelphia, 1814), 5ff. Edward C. Carter II, "Matthew Carey and 'The Olive Branch,' 1814–1818," *Pennsylvania Magazine of History and Biography* 89 (1965): 408 summarizes Carey's other complaints.

12. John Randolph, *Letter . . . to James Lloyd*, 6, acknowledged that separation might some day come about, but argued that this was the wrong moment.

13. William Eustis to Matthew Carey, November 16, 1814, in William Eustis Papers, LC.

14. James Monroe to Caleb Strong, December 1, 1814, in Caleb Strong Papers, MHS.

15. Stagg, *Mr. Madison's War*, 480.

16. Thomas Jesup to James Monroe, December 15, 1814, and Joseph L. Smith to Thomas Jesup, December 26, 1814, in Thomas Jesup Papers, LC.

17. *NEP*, October 21, 1814.

18. Ibid., October 25, 28, and November 1, 4, and 8, 1814.

19. Ibid., January 28, 1814; Timothy Pickering to James Hillhouse, December 16, 1814, in Timothy Pickering Papers, MHS.

20. *NI*, November 4, 18, and December 28, 1814.

21. James Lowell Jr. to Timothy Pickering, December 3, 1814, and Timothy Pickering to James Hillhouse, December 16, 1814, in *LLGC*, 549, 552.

22. James Madison to John Nicholas, April 2, 1813, in *WJM*, 8: 242; James Monroe to John Taylor, June 13, 1812, in James Monroe Papers, Series 1, LC.

23. *LLGC*, 551; quote from H. G. Otis to Noah Webster, May 6, 1840, in Morison, *Otis*, Vol. 2: 90; see also William Eustis to Matthew Carey, November 16, 1814, in William Eustis Papers, LC.

24. See Timothy Pickering to Samuel Putnam, February 7, 1814, to John Lowell Jr., November 7, 1814, and to James Hillhouse, December 16, 1814, in *LLGC*, 532, 539, 559.

25. Dwight, *History*, 312–36, 358–59.

26. *AC*, 13th, 3rd: 14.

27. Ibid., 482, 483, 485, 488–89; also 707–708.

28. Ibid., 710, 713, 724.

29. Ibid., 737, 728–29.

30. Ibid., 1837–38; see also *AC*, 12th, 2nd: 168–70; Timothy Pickering to Caleb Strong, January 9, 1815, in Caleb Strong Papers, MHS.

31. *NEP*, November 8, 1814.

32. John Lowell Jr. to Timothy Pickering, December 3, 1814, in *LLGC*, 546–47, 548.

33. *NEP*, November 18, 1814.

34. *NI*, November 18 and December 14, 1814.

35. *AC*, 13th, 3rd: 706; *IC*, December 5 and 8, 1814.

36. *IC*, October 12, 1814; also Thomas Jesup to James Monroe, December 10, 1814, in Thomas Jesup Papers, LC.

37. Excerpt from a piece by Washington Irving in the *Analectic Magazine* in *NI.*, October 27, 1814. The truth of the Republican caution had begun to dawn on some New England Federalists, but it did not reconcile them to their domestic adversaries; see *NEP*, October 28, 1814.

38. *NWR*, 7: 167.

39. Morison, *Otis*, Vol. 2: 157.

40. *The proceedings of a convention of delegates, from the states of Massachusetts, Connecticut, and Rhode Island; the counties of Cheshire and Grafton, in the state of New-Hampshire; and the county of Windham, in the state of Vermont; convened at Hartford, in the state of Connecticut, December 15th, 1814* (Hartford, 1815); for the legislative endorsements, see *CC*, January 25, 1815, and *CSR*, 17: 255–73.

41. *CC*, January 11, 1815.

42. *CSR*, 17: 175–76.

43. *AM*, February 7, 1815.

44. Thomas Jesup to James Monroe, January 21 and 23, 1815, with enclosures, in Letters Received by the Secretary of War (registered), RG 107, NA.

45. *CSR*, 17: 284–85.

46. Quote from Thomas Jesup to James Monroe, January 31, 1815, also February 1, 1815, in Letters Received by the Secretary of War (registered), RG 107, NA.

47. *NI*, October 20, 1814.

48. *NEP*, October 21 and 28, 1814; Timothy Pickering to George Cabot, December 31, 1814, in *LLGC*, 556; also Pickering to Samuel Putnam, February 4, 1814, in *LLGC*, 531.

49. *IC*, October 27, 1814; John Lowell Jr. to Timothy Pickering, December 3, 1814, in *LLGC*, 549; also Randolph, *Letter . . . to James Lloyd*, passim.

50. Morison, *Otis*, Vol. 2: 167, 171.

51. Charles J. Ingersoll, *Historical Sketch of the Second War between the United States and Great Britain, declared by Act of Congress, the 18th of June, 1812, and concluded by peace, the 15th of February, 1815* (Philadelphia, 1845–1849), Vol. 2: 24, 37, 56.

52. *NEP*, December 13, 1814.

53. Robert A. McCaughey, *Josiah Quincy, 1772–1864: The Last Federalist* (Cambridge, Mass.: Harvard University Press, 1974), 74.

54. Martel, "Side Light on Federalist Strategy," 553–66, especially 561.

55. Winfield Scott saw in their actions an intention to provide a fuse for igniting civil war, see his letter to James Monroe, February 15, 1815, in James Monroe Papers, NYPL. Cf. also William Freehling, *Prelude to Civil War: The Nullification Controversy in South Carolina 1816–1836* (New York: Harper & Row, 1965), 271ff.

56. Ben J. Wattenberg, *The Statistical History of the United States* (New York: Basic Books, 1976), 8, 25, 29, 34. The legislature of Rhode Island avoided explicitly sanctioning the convention's proceedings because it reassembled after news of the peace. See William Davis to Caleb Strong, February 15, 1815, in Caleb Strong Papers, MHS.

57. There were exceptions: see Winfield Scott to James Monroe, February 15, 1815, in James Monroe Papers, NYPL.

58. Henry Adams, *History of the United States of America during the Administrations of James Madison* (New York: The Library of America, 1986), 1249–52.

59. Morison, *Otis*, Vol. 2: 209–18.

60. *NI*, February 13 and 14, 1815.

61. Ibid., February 16, 1815; *NWR*, 9: 2–3.

62. Quote from Oliver Wolcott to George Gibbs, January 15, 1812, in Oliver Wolcott Papers, Box 29, Folder 10, CHS. Also Wolcot to Gibbs, March 27, 1813, and to Rufus King, April 4, 1814 in Oliver Wolcott Papers, CHS. Wolcott had served as secretary of a New York City meeting on August 10, 1814, which supported the war and the measures adopted by the state and federal governments for prosecuting it, *P*, August 17, 1814.

63. David M. Roth and Freeman Meyer, *From Revolution to Constitution: Connecticut 1763 to 1818* (Chester, Conn.: Pequot Press, 1975), 63–68.

64. Edmund Quincy, *Life of Josiah Quincy. By his son* (Boston: Little, Brown, and Co., 1891), 374, quoting an unidentified Federalist correspondent.

65. Eli Glasser, "Government and the Constitution (1820–1917)," in *Commonwealth History of Massachusetts, colony, province and state*, ed. Albert B. Hart (New York,: States History Co., 1927–1930), Vol. 4: 4–8.

66. For instance Pickering, born a year before Strong, lived to 1829. Most of the younger generation survived to midcentury, John Lowell Jr. dying in 1840, Otis in 1848, and

Quincy in 1864; only Gore suffered premature incapacity from rheumatoid arthritis. See Helen R. Pinkney, *Christopher Gore: Federalist of Massachusetts 1758–1827* (Waltham, Mass.: Gore Place Society, 1969), 139.

67. Quincy, *Life of Quincy*, 374–75.
68. See Matthew H. Crocker, *The Magic of the Many: Josiah Quincy and the Rise of Mass Politics in Boston, 1800–1830* (Amherst, Mass.: University of Massachusetts Press, 1999); McCaughey, *Quincy*, chaps. 6 and 7.
69. Morison, *Otis*, Vol. 2: 242.
70. Ibid., 245–46, 248.
71. Pinkney, *Gore*, 142; Herman V. Ames, *State Documents on Federal Relations* (Philadelphia: Department of History, University of Pennsylvania, 1906), 55; U.S. *House Reports*, 1408, no. 76. An additional payment was made in 1859, and the matter was not finally settled until the 1870s.
72. *The Identity of the Hartford Convention Federalists with the Modern Whig Party* (Boston, 1840).
73. The standard works are Marvin E. Gettleman, *The Dorr Rebellion: a Study in American Radicalism, 1833–1849* (New York: Random House, 1973); and George M. Dennison, *Republicanism on Trial, 1831–1861* (Lexington: University Press of Kentucky, 1976).
74. Joyce Appleby, *Inheriting the Revolution: The First Generation of Americans* (Cambridge, Mass.: Harvard University Press, 2000), 222; Richard R. John, *Spreading the News: The American Postal System from Franklin to Morse* (Cambridge, Mass.: Harvard University Press, 1998), 238–240.
75. *Pittsfield Sun*, January 17, 1833; *State Papers on Nullification: including the public acts of the Convention of the People of South Carolina, assembled at Columbia, November 19, 1832 and March 11, 1833: the Proclamation of the President of the United States, and the Proceedings of the several State Legislatures which have acted upon the subject. Collected and published by Order of the General Court of Massachusetts* (Boston, 1834).
76. The phrase is from John Winthrop's "A Model of Christian Charity" preached in 1630 on board the *Arabella* in mid-passage to Massachusetts.

Postscript

1. David H. Fischer, *The Revolution of American Conservatism: The Federalist Party in the Era of Jeffersonian Democracy* (New York: Harper & Row, 1965), 187–88; Ronald P. Formisano, *The Transformation of Political Culture: Massachusetts Parties, 1790s–1840s* (New York: Oxford University Press, 1983), 34.
2. Max M. Edling, *A Revolution in Favor of Government: Origins of the U.S. Constitution and the Making of the American State* (New York: Oxford University Press, 2003).
3. Richard Buel Jr., *Securing the Revolution: Ideology and Politics, 1789–1815* (Ithaca, N.Y.: Cornell University Press, 1972), 46–49.

4. James F. Simon, *What Kind of Nation: Thomas Jefferson, John Marshall, and the Epic Struggle to Create a United States* (New York: Simon & Schuster, 2002), 258.

5. Timothy Pickering to Rufus King, January 2, 9, 17, and 28, 1808, and Rufus King to Pickering, February 5, and to Christopher Gore, February ?, 1808, in *LCRK*, 5: 50, 51, 61, 69, 70, 71; *NEP*, January 25, July 7, and October 25, 1814.

6. See John Marshall to Charles C. Pinckney, October 19, 1808, in *PJM*, 7: 184.

7. See Jacob Mansfield, *An Oration, pronounced at Western, in commemoration of American independence, July 4th, 1812* (Worcester, Mass., 1812), 10–11; Matthew Carey, *The Olive Branch: or faults on both sides, Federal and Democratic. A serious appeal of the necessity of mutual forgiveness & harmony, to save our common country from ruin* (Philadelphia, 1814), 10.

8. *DWB*, Vols. 3 and 4, passim.

9. Louis M. Sears, *Jefferson and the Embargo* (Durham, N.C.: Duke University Press, 1927), 152–53 tabulated 5,581 separate signatures affixed to petitions against the embargo in Massachusetts during March and April 1808.

10. *NI*, February 9, 1814; *P*, September 24, 1814.

11. *NI*, September 14, 1814.

12. Most recently, Simon, *What Kind of Nation.*

13. Garry Wills, *"Negro President": Jefferson and the Slave Power* (New York: Houghton Mifflin Co., 2003), 191; also see "Negro President," in *New York Review of Books* 50, no. 17 (2003): 45–51.

14. For an example of one, see [John Lowell Jr.], *Thoughts in a series of letters, in Answer to questions respecting the division of the states by a Massachusetts Farmer* (Boston, 1813), 18.

15. Cf. Wills, *Negro President*, 105, 192 with Walter M. Merrill, ed., *The Letters of William Lloyd Garrison* (Cambridge, Mass.: Harvard University Press, 1971–1981), Vol. 1: 16–20, 21–23.

INDEX